MICHAEL SHAMIYEH (Ed.)

PRACTICES OF FUTURE CASTING

Ways of sharing imagined tomorrows

BIRKHÄUSER
BASEL

Michael Shamiyeh (Ed.)

Acquisitions Editor: David Marold, Birkhäuser Verlag, Vienna, Austria
Content and Production Editor: Bettina R. Algieri, Birkhäuser Verlag, Vienna, Austria
Proofreading: Rupert Hebblethwaite, Vienna, Austria
Layout, Cover Design: kest werbeagentur, Linz, Austria
Image Editing: Pixelstorm Litho & Digital Imaging, Vienna, Austria
Printing: Holzhausen, the book-printing brand of Gerin Druck GmbH, Wolkersdorf, Austria
Paper: Magno Natural, 120 g/m^2
Typeface: ABC Favorit, Helvetica Now

Printed with financial support from the University of Arts Linz.

Library of Congress Control Number: 2024937792

Bibliographic information published by the German National Library
The German National Library lists this publication in the Deutsche Nationalbibliografie; detailed bibliographic data are available on the Internet at http://dnb.dnb.de.

ISBN 978-3-0356-2919-4
e-ISBN (PDF) 978-3-0356-2920-0

Im Westfeld 8, 4055 Basel, Switzerland
Part of Walter de Gruyter GmbH, Berlin/Boston

9 8 7 6 5 4 3 2 1 www.birkhauser.com

FSC www.fsc.org MIX Paper | Supporting responsible forestry FSC® C108696

FOR STEVE

CONTENTS

Foreword 9

Introduction 12
Michael Shamiyeh

PRELIMINARY CONDITIONS

People, teams, and identity

Settling-in to the future: An organizational identity perspective 50
Trudi Lang and *Gail Carson*

Dos and don'ts of futurecasting 60
Alexander Mankowsky

Statement by *Marie Ringler,* Ashoka Europe 66

A transformative entrepreneurial journey: Addressing corporate future challenges with innovation and intrapreneurship 70
Guido Schwartz

Statement by *Susann Roth,* Asian Development Bank 78

Counterfactual thinking and imagination

Harnessing imagination to improve strategic decision-making 82
Martin Reeves

How we imagine the future 92
Ruth Byrne

Stories to imagine alternate futures 102
Julian Bleecker and *Tobias Revell*

Not-knowing as a heuristic of its own:
Certain uncertainties in futures research 112
Stefan Wolf

Ambitions, objectives, and sensemaking

Beyond the death sentence of striving for better futures: Can humanity hear the universe? 124
Riel Miller

Dealing with the future: Exploring ways to remain ambitious while putting a piece of yourself into the future you are looking for 130
Christin Pfeiffer

Statement by *Claudia Reinprecht,* Austrian Government 142

Enabling desired futures at Arup 144
Josef Hargrave

INTERVIEW with *Sohail Inayatullah,* Professor, Political Scientist, UNESCO Chair in Futures Studies 152

FUTURECASTING WITH DATA

Making probable futures discernible through facts

Learning and transforming with planetary futures 166
Nicolas Balcom Raleigh

Statement by *Chris Luebkeman,* Strategic Foresight Hub, ETH Zurich 180

Futures thinking: Anticipating society's embedding of new & emerging technologies 182
Eva Buchinger

Data dilemmas: The material and the imaginary 190
Dietmar Offenhuber

Donald, tell us how: Futurecasting principles for empowering human-centered design 200
Wei Liu, Xin Xin, Yancong Zhu, Di Zhu, Ruonan Huang

INTERVIEW with *Angela Wilkinson,* Secretary General and CEO of the World Energy Council 210

FUTURECASTING WITH FICTION

Making futures plausible through cognitive experience

Science fiction is a Luddite literature 222
Cory Doctorow

Except in science fiction? Why you can get there from here 224
Caroline Bassett

Future perfect? Telling better stories about AI and technology 232
Irini Papadimitriou

Teaching critical optimism: 242
Seven lessons from a decade of sci-fi prototyping
Sophia Brueckner

Statement by *Stefan Wally and Carmen Bayer,* 252
Robert Jungk Library for Future Studies

Using diegetic prototypes to create a future worth living in 256
David A. Kirby

Plausible futures: Cognitively balancing complexity, 270
corroboration, & conjecture in futurecasting
Mark T. Keane

The Iron Fist and The Velvet Glove: "The future simulator" 286
Ari Popper

INTERVIEW with *Alex McDowell,* 292
Creative Director, Production Designer, Professor, Worldbuilder

FUTURECASTING WITH MATTER

Making futures plausible with bodily experience

In praise of vacuums 308
Elliott P. Montgomery

Experiential insight: When we do, we understand 318
Time's Up

Statement by *Shahar Livne* 328
Atelier for Bespoke Conceptual Material Based Design

Embodying futures: The transformative power of embodied learning experiences 334
Nicklas Larsen

Statement by *Loes Damhof* 348
UNESCO Chair on Futures Literacy in Higher Education

Cultivating creativity and freeing the imagination: The case for participatory futuring 350
Cynthia Selin

Future making, futurecasting, and matter: The Berlin-Brandenburg International Airport case study 366
Alice Comi

The dilemmas & delights of corporate tomorrowing 380
Sarah DaVanzo

Using the power of gameworlds 394
Mary Flanagan

How to make futures plausible? Personal experiences from EU policymaking 408
Laurent Bontoux

Leaning into the unknown: Insights into an immersive method of co-creation 420
Stefanos Pavlakis

AFTERTHOUGHTS

What we can learn for practice

Beyond the obvious: Re-imagining corporate strategy 434
Karlheinz Schwuchow

What did I take away as a practitioner? 446
Bolko von Oetinger

Contributor biographies 457

Acknowledgement 470

FOREWORD

The subject of this book has accompanied me for more than two decades now. I still remember the early 2000s well. At the time, I was working on several projects with my company that repeatedly spurred us on to pursue fundamental questions about the future. The planning of a tourism project in the low three-digit million Euro range in Croatia presented us with a particular challenge. The architectural concept and, above all, our approach to a fundamentally new kind of tourism, was a major challenge for our clients. The in-depth examination of the topic, coupled with a radically new vision of what tourism could mean today, required them—as well as us—to leave familiar worldviews and thought patterns behind and embrace new ones. Still, as we quickly learned, changing internalized mental models is not an easy undertaking, especially as the worlds we came from could not have been more different.

Back then, my team and I were mainly operating from a design and cultural studies background—my expertise in strategic management only came later—and our client's decision-makers were all hard-nosed managers with an unwavering interest in financial performance. Our languages and perspectives of the future were as different as our worlds. We were challenged to shift a narrow, predominantly economic path into the future towards a perspective that takes a holistic view of our planet and recognizes the radical change in societal values. Without going into detail here, we addressed the issue of tourism as complementary to work and everyday life rather than as an opposing counter-world. In those days, my first insights into the subject in question crystallized vaguely:

First, the process of change, the reshaping and redesigning of our world towards an imagined future, is a collaborative process of articulation and negotiation that aims to achieve mutual understanding. It is not something that designers or other professionals do on their own and simply bring along in a suitcase for the purpose of presentation. Ideas about the new—the future—first arise in the mind of the individual, but if they are to be realized, they must be externalized, shared, and reconciled with those who are affected by them. Sense-making requires that the new be collectively understood, modified, and, thus, co-created. Established thought patterns and mental models about the world are to be abandoned and forgotten. This brings both the traditional relationship with the world and relationships between individuals into focus.

Second, construction of the new requires symbols; it takes place through narratives based on words, texts, images, physical experiences, and other means, depending on knowledge and background. Our visualizations and large-scale models of a different tourism, a tourism whose weak signals were already clearly visible at the time and which we were therefore convinced would shape the future, contributed immensely to mutual understanding. However, it was only through countless conversations and joint learning journeys that our entrenched mental models were challenged and clients and affected stakeholders (as well as we ourselves) were put in a position to question habitual worldviews. The experiences of the individual thus become part of the collective experience. A completely new consciousness emerges. Therefore, futuring processes are acts of permanent reconciliation and movement, events that cannot take place in isolation but only through social interaction.

With this wealth of experience, my further activities in St. Gallen, London, or Stanford, as well as in cooperation with international companies, emphasized learning from others. Recognizing that ideas about the future must leave the subjective and become part of the collective realm to be accepted as valid or meaningful, I wanted to know how others effectively cast the future and generatively reflect on it to develop unprecedented possibilities. For this very reason, I embarked on an odyssey and spent hundreds of hours in filmed conversations with remarkable people around the world.

I spoke with CEOs, technology pioneers, and social innovators who have spent (or still spend) a large part of their lives sharing and implementing ideas for a "different," "better," or "more desirable" future. What they all have in common is, firstly, the drive to effectively articulate their ideas to develop a mutual understanding, be it through stories, images, prototypes, or even theatrically staged performances, etc., and, secondly, the insight that the real challenge lies in developing a generative dialogue for collectively thinking about, creating, designing, and using the new. Many of the people to whom I spoke failed because they were unable to give new ideas room for reflection, for trial and error, or for joint modification. Their ideas about the future were therefore dismissed as implausible or meaningless during one-dimensional presentations.

This book makes the topic of "futurecasting," which I define as a reflective conversation with imaginations on what ought to be, accessible to a broad audience and gives thought-leaders from practice and theory a voice. I do not believe it is necessary to discuss the need for futurecasting here. Our society is characterized more than ever by disruptions and crises that require new ways of thinking and coping. Adapting to tomorrow by studying the future is only of limited use. What is needed is transformation guided by the ability to imagine the future and develop a shared understanding of it. With this in mind, we present a broad spectrum of futurecasting practices that contribute to the way forward by taking stock of the current state of the debate.

Michael Shamiyeh

Photo: Erich Goldmann

MICHAEL SHAMIYEH

UNESCO CHAIRHOLDER, PROFESSOR, AND ADVISORY BOARD MEMBER
LINZ, AUSTRIA

INTRODUCTION

Why talk about futurecasting?

Today's fascination with the future is twofold. On the one hand, we want to address how we can best explore and prepare for the new, the uncertain, the not-yet-existing. On the other hand, we wish to better understand the future and how it affects our daily perceptions and decisions. These two focal points define both ends of the spectrum, foresight at the one end and imagination at the other. With foresight, we go exploratively forward from the present into the future; with imagination, we go normatively backward from the future into the present.

The global challenges of our time make this highly relevant. Awareness that we need a more future-oriented and inclusive approach to shaping our world is growing. Solutions from the past can only help us to a limited extent, if at all, in dealing with the uncertainty of the future. We must rely upon imagination to proactively engage with the world. Both approaches help people prepare for uncertainty in the here and now and develop a sense of security and self-confidence to initiate change. Therefore, it is no surprise that academic, corporate, government-related institutions (see, e.g., ADB, 2020; Austrian Federal Ministry of Education, 2022), and global organizations such as UNESCO (2019) have taken up the issue with great zeal.

Research on this topic is extensive and now conducted from different disciplinary perspectives. An aspect that has received little attention in the current literature is how imaginations about the future, which first arise in an individual's mind, can be made explicit and shared with others in a form that facilitates mutual understanding. What forms of externalization are conceivable and how conducive are they for sensemaking and social agreement? In this book, we look at a wide range of forms of externalization, from the use of facts (data) to the telling and visualization of stories (fiction) to the possibility of making the future bodily experienceable (matter). To highlight the diverse forms of externalizing imaginations about the future, I speak of the practices of futurecasting.

How is the following introduction structured?

First, I will take a closer look at the term "futurecasting," especially its ambiguous use. Not entirely new, the term has a history dating back to at least the 1960s, and at times lacks a clear definition. The term has been used again and again, albeit sparingly, in various contexts that fail to differentiate it from other futuring methods. In a second step, I will define futurecasting in detail to create clarity. The focus of my definition will be on the following aspects. Bringing about change in our world—what one does when taking steps towards a different future in the here and now—is (or at least should be) a profoundly pluralistic act. An intervention in an existing social system, futurecasting requires the consent of the parties concerned. I will link futurecasting to the topic of reflective conversation. In addition, I will provide a thorough perspective on externalization, which I understand as the instantiation of imaginations in a verbal, visible, or tangible form for the purpose of sharing what is in the minds of the people involved in the process of futurecasting. Externalizing one's imaginations about the future is a prerequisite. In this context, I will discuss the role that artifacts (texts, images, objects, spaces, etc.) and their design characteristics play in the process of sense-making. After this definition, in the third major thematic block, I will continue with a differentiation of the term "futurecasting" from other terms and approaches in futures studies and related disciplines. Above all, I consider this step necessary to develop a better understanding of futurecasting itself and to avoid giving the impression of throwing yet another term into a field that is already characterized by Babylonian linguistic confusion. Just think of the many different definitions of scenario! I will conclude this introduction with an overview of the book's organization. Structured according to different futurecasting practices, I want to provide a multifaceted look at the topic from theory to practice.

Futurecasting and its ambiguous use

Researching for a thorough definition of the term "futurecasting" quickly reveals its limitations. The term has recently been used in a relatively inflationary way without specifying what is meant. In academic research, the term has received little attention to date. Hence, it makes sense to trace the roots of the term and then set out to provide a comprehensive definition.

The term "casting" is familiar to us today mainly through casting processes in the film industry or in the performing arts, where the aim is to select a certain type of actor or dancer for a certain role or part in a film or performance. The Merriam-Webster Dictionary defines the verb "cast" as, among other things, "to dispose or arrange into a suitable form or order" or "to assign a role or part to someone (e.g., an actor)." Taking a broader view of this term, futurecasting can simply be understood as a series of "auditions," in which visions of the future are presented and selected for further steps. In the earliest (found) mentions, which presumably date from the 1960s, the term is used in this sense. For instance, Maurice Woodruff (1969), an astronomer and clairvoyant who achieved dubious popularity in the British media, called himself a "futurecaster."

A more serious and elaborate discussion of the term can be found in the business book *Futurecasting: Charting a Way to Your Future,* published by Kurtzman (1984). Here we find the first concrete idea of the term "futurecasting," which, in his view, is an activity that focuses on planning and acting to attain identified outcomes and goals. The methodology he presents in his book differs considerably from forecasting, which he defines as the prediction of events based on the existing situation.

After years of apparent abstinence, the term has regained popularity since the 2010s, especially in the business world, although ideas of what the term stands for vary widely and are used in a highly unreflective manner. We are told, for example, that futurecasting is "more than just a prediction" and that it helps to "imagine the future of the company," is "a method for shaping the future without constraints," and can "help managers not only prepare for an uncertain future, but actually shape it." The output of futurecasting, we are also told, is "a vision that can serve as a basis for decision-making," consisting of "a series of trends, phenomena and predictions that provide a compelling argument or reason for change." *

---

* Further information on the quotations can be found under the following links: https://www.realspace3d.com/blog/futurecasting-architecture-predicting-and-adapting-to-future-trends-with-ai/; https://resources.businesstalentgroup.com/btg-insights-on-demand/futurecasting-through-disruption-uncertainty; https://www.cornerstoneondemand.com/de/resources/article/how-futurecasting-can-help-hr-leaders-prepare-workforce-changes/; https://www.stratalisgroup.com/futurecasting-the-power-of-foresight/; https://www.stratalisgroup.com/?s=futurecasting; https://trailhead.salesforce.com/de/content/learn/modules/innovation_customer_discovery/innovation_discov_future_now; http://fieldinnovationteam.org/futurecasting/. Viewed May 20, 2024.

In academia, where the term has also been found recently, albeit sparingly, futurecasting is largely used as a matter of course and without further definition, e.g., to reflect a picture of the future of ecological research (Allan et al., 2018), education (Leask & Younie, 2021), or business (Gardner, 2011; Parman, 2013), or in connection with the preparation for threats in the military sector (Lee, 2018), or as a useful tool in design practice (Manetti, Lara-Navarra, & Sánchez-Navarro, 2022).

A notable exception here is the work of Johnson (2011; 2021), who defines the term futurecasting in connection with his research on shaping the future by means of science fiction prototyping and in a methodologically modified way in his concept of "threatcasting," which followed years later. His definition of the term reads as follows:

"Future casting is not about predicting the future [...] Future casting is a process that we use to develop a vision for the future. We pull together trends, global projections and technology developments into this vision and then iterate it over time. The key to this process is to make things, develop prototypes and generally just create stuff that expresses the future as we currently see it. Then, we share these artifacts with people to start to continue the conversation about where we are headed" (Johnson, 2011: 4).

But even this definition of the term makes it difficult to demarcate the boundaries to forecasting and scenario planning, two approaches we will discuss in more detail later. In sum, all these alleged definitions are of little use in gaining a comprehensive understanding of the term.

Futurecasting as a reflective conversation

Futurecasting, as I define it here, is a reflective conversation with imaginations of what ought to be. This definition contains three central elements:

First, at the core of futurecasting is an inquiry about what the future could look like; that is to say, futurecasting is concerned with something that does not yet exist, but ought to be. Articulating and sharing something that does not yet exist requires more effort to develop a mutual understanding than communicating something that already exists. The aspect of externalization, i.e., how individuals can effectively articulate to others what they have in mind about the future, becomes particularly important.

Second, the inquiry into what ought to be takes place in a kind of "reflective conversation" in the broadest sense. On the one hand, at the level of the individual, where ideas about the future—which do not appear out of nowhere, but are formed, modified, and refined in the individual's mind—"talk back" and thus provide continuous feedback about other aspects that could or should be considered. On the other hand, the exchange at the level of social interaction also demands a reflective conversation, which leads us to the last central aspect.

Third, imagining a future is animated by the desire to bring about a difference from what already exists. This gap between vision and reality and the effort to bridge it represents an intervention in the existing social fabric and therefore requires a certain degree of acceptance on the part of those affected. The effort to achieve a mutual understanding of the future must lead to a kind of joint thinking and reflecting on what the future could look like or how those affected would like to see the future. It is not something one does alone (although that is of course possible, but not very effective, except under authoritarian power structures, which are not of interest to us here). It is something that people need to do together.

Let us now look at these three elements in detail:

Unconstrained imagination

In point one, I mentioned that futurecasting is a challenge for everyone involved, as it is essentially about what does not yet exist. We need to allow for the full spectrum of approaches in developing visions of the future, a spectrum that extends, at the one end, from the analysis and exponential extrapolation of current trends into the future, to an unconstrained imagination of the future at the other end. The real context of the present as a starting point for the development of future visions increases plausibility and, thus, understanding among those involved. Whereas entering completely new territories through an unconstrained act of total creativity in imagining possible futures can cause a consistent lack of understanding.

Peter Senge and Russell L. Ackoff have previously addressed this dichotomy in detail but have also pointed out its advantages and disadvantages. Senge (2003), for example, argues that the focus on the existing situation with the desire to improve it for the future can be an impediment, because people are then reacting to circumstances rather than directing their efforts towards creating what they truly value. "It can lead us to think of fixing something that is broken," Senge notes, and continues that "it can lead to imposing solutions from the past. And, it can lead to seeing reality as the adversary rather than the ally" (2003: 2).

Ackoff's research on "Redesigning the Future" by aiming to design an "idealized future" has reminded us over several decades how different the results are when one reacts to what already exists or, in contrast, creates something new from scratch. Approaching the future by imagining a desirable ideal removes all constraints, he argues (Ackoff, 1974). The process of designing an idealized future shifts the designer, who is de facto granted almost absolute freedom to conceive any future as long as it is still technically feasible, from a retrospective to a prospective posture (Ackoff, Magidson, & Addison, 2006). By retrospective, Ackoff means being preoccupied with recognizing and eliminating shortcomings in the past. "Retrospective planning," he argues, "moves from what one does not want rather than toward what one wants. It is like driving a train from its caboose. One who walks into the future facing the past has no control over where he [or she] is going" (1974: 30).

Opening up futurecasting to this broad spectrum of possible futures can help to overcome many critiques that have been raised in other futuring practices, as, for example, in scenario planning. Ramirez and Selin (2014) define scenarios as "a small set of stories of future contextual conditions linked with the present, made for someone and fulfilling an explicit purpose" (55). Imagining futures in a completely unconstrained manner and entering new and unexplored territories can challenge long-held internal beliefs, worldviews, or knowledge-based biases and open up minds to hitherto unimaginable possibilities as many researchers noted (Aldabbagh & Allawzi, 2019; Cordova-Pozo & Rouwette, 2023; Vervoort, Bendor, Kelliher, Strik, & Helfgott, 2015; Wilkinson, 2009). It helps to move beyond the often-criticized proximity to the known or the existing and to overcome narrow frames from which the future is viewed.

Charles Sanders Peirce's explanations in pragmatic philosophy as well as those of Ömar Akin in psychology underpin this view both theoretically and empirically. As I have discussed in detail elsewhere with reference to both authors (Shamiyeh, 2007, 2009, 2010), an examination of unconstrained imagination of what ought to be, in contrast to how things are, offers the benefit of an open-ended context within which a hypothesis about a future state is tested. Akin provides the apt example of the green grass, which, according to our scientific understanding, should naturally be green. "This context," as Akin (1986: 55) argues, "may be one we know of [...]; one we expect will be possible [...]; or one we desire the existence of." However, one could also claim with equal certainty that the grass should be red, and create the corresponding context in which the grass takes on these characteristics. In other words, the unconstrained imagination of the future opens "the door to the possibility of future contexts yet to be determined" (Shamiyeh, 2016: 207). Peirce (1965, CP 6.470) argues in this case that one cannot begin with the investigation of the phenomena, as is usual in the natural sciences, for example, but that one must begin with the investigation of the hypothesis and the testing of all possible tentative experimental implications that would arise out of its truth. He calls this form of reasoning "abduction," which, in his view, "is the only logical operation which introduces any new idea; [...]. Deduction proves that something must be; Induction shows that something actually is operative; Abduction merely suggests that something may be" (Peirce, 1965, CP 5.171).

This open-ended context, which is made possible by an unconstrained imagination of the future and which can bring about something truly novel, brings with it the following benefit: It can sharpen the level of curiosity of those involved in the futurecasting process in a way that leads them into areas they would not otherwise enter. An extrapolation of current trends into the future—as practiced by forecasters—would not be able to do this to the same extent, it would allow those involved in the futurecasting process to remain in the comfort zone and largely stick to what they know. Thus, the approach of unrestricted imagination, which I attribute to futurecasting, has the ability to push imaginations of the future to the edge of what is plausible.

Nonetheless, there is also a downside to this. Regardless of the fact that ideas that are diametrically opposed to the common worldview can lead to those involved in the process no longer identifying with them and turning away according to the motto "so what," as Wack (1985) describes in his Harvard notes. Communicating something novel is anything but trivial, as we know from cognitive linguistics and neuroscience. Lakoff and Johnson (1980 [2003]), who I will come back to later in more detail, have shown that interpersonal communication and mutual understanding is difficult—even without the aspect of novelty—because people who talk to each other do not necessarily share the same culture, values, or assumptions. Common understanding is possible through the negotiation of meaning, which presupposes that the conversation participants are aware that different worldviews exist and what they might be. Worldviews are what Johnson-Laird (1983) called "mental models," meaning the models of the world that people form to explain how they perceive reality, solve problems, and process information. These models simplify people's understanding of reality, and encompass how they think and believe and what they assume about the world. According to Lakoff and Johnson, meanings are not communicated in such a way that, despite a common language, all participants have all the relevant common knowledge, values, and assumptions. Rather, it is about finding out what the parties involved have in common and how they can pass on unshared experiences or develop a shared vision.

All of this becomes more complicated, of course, when something novel is conceived and subsequently articulated that offers new ways of structuring people's experience. Lakoff and Johnson (1980 [2003]), for example, ascribed this ability to create new coherences and thus new realities to the work of art. The problem here is that radical differences from the familiar cannot necessarily be explained directly by referring to the familiar.

Goodman (1978) reminds us in his *Ways of Worldmaking* that there are limits to bringing forth something novel. "Comprehension and creation go on together," meaning that the creative way of creating new realities, in his terms "worldmaking," is always linked to understanding (Goodman, 1978: 22). The process of bringing forth new realities (or worlds) that revise current ones is only successful when an understanding is reached between the parties involved. This requires linguistic background knowledge, a wealth of experience from previous creations, and acquired practices in dealing with the language that is to be brought into the situation (Goodman & Elgin, 1988). If problems can be solved, desired applications arise, anomalies are eliminated, significant distinctions are made, or informative connections are established. If a more consistent and comprehensive understanding has been achieved, then the conception of new realities has been successful on the cognitive level, understanding has set in. However, if discrepancies arise, this can lead to an active search and to trial and error, which can ultimately derail the entire process of establishing mutual understanding.

Cognitive science and the debate on counterfactual thinking also shed light on the challenge of understanding newly created coherences: There is widespread agreement in psychology that counterfactual thinking refers to mental models that explicitly contradict facts and assumptions (Byrne, 2007; Epstude & Roese, 2008). People are constantly developing counterfactual alternatives to reality, for example when they try to find answers to the mental questions of "if only" or "what if" (Roese & Olson, 2014). Counterfactual thinking does not always have to aim at imagining how the past would have turned out differently. A number of researchers have used the term with a view to describing future possibilities (Hoch, 1985; Johnson & Sherman, 1990). What interests us here is the role prior knowledge plays in the understanding of counterfactual thought. Plausibility is crucial to these cognitive phenomena of understanding.

Byrne (2016: 146) notes that "the meaning of a counterfactual depends on its truth in a possible world, one that is the same as this world except that the counterfactual is true in it," that is to say, "counterfactuals require a consideration of the possible world that is most similar to the actual world." To assess then the meaning of (counterfactual) futures is by no means easy. If we now assume that the mental representation of alternative possibilities is shared with others, for example in order to develop a mutual understanding of a future state with a possibly novel coherence, then the situation becomes even more complex. Not only is there a general language problem in terms of understanding each other during communication, but the counterpart must also be able to assess the meaning of a counterfactual imaginary situation.

With their research on plausibility, Connell and Keane (2003, 2004, 2006) have contributed extensively to our understanding of the cognitive processes involved in logical analyses of counterfactuals. They argue that people judge scenarios dependent on the perceived plausibility of the concept coherence as established by prior knowledge. For example, people consider the scenario of a bottle falling from a shelf and melting to be less plausible, as previous knowledge about the falling of objects has little to no correlation with the melting of objects. Rather, our experience would suggest that the bottle would break. In short, the scenario lacks conceptual coherence (Connell & Keane, 2003). Conversely, and following Byrne (2016), the goal for developing mutual understanding of future scenarios must be to establish plausibility, i.e., the existence of a familiar concept coherence. This is, naturally, particularly difficult in the course of developing new realities that call familiar concept coherences into question. As Connell and Keane (2006) explain, these new concept coherences would require the following attributes to be considered plausible: the use of "many different sources of corroboration," the sharing of the novel situation "without complex explanation," and the use of as "minimal conjecture" as possible (99).

What is inherent in all these considerations, whether from the philosophical or the social-psychological perspective, is that they are merely about understanding situations that make sense and serve as a springboard for action. Weick (1995) has explained this in detail and shown that plausibility plays a central role (see, e.g., Mills, 2003; Weick, Sutcliffe, & Obstfeld, 2005).

Let us move on to the second major topic inherent in futurecasting, the issue of reflective conversation, which, as I mentioned at the beginning, takes place both on an individual level and collectively, in the group.

Reflective conversation

Let us first take a look at the level of the individual. Ideas about the future do not arise out of nowhere, but, first and foremost, in people's minds. I would like to understand this process of imagining or "constructing" (e.g., Addis, Wong, & Schacter, 2007) and "evaluating" (e.g., Lee, Parthasarathi, & Kable, 2021) a future situation as a reflective conversation with oneself. Findings in social psychology and the neurosciences seem to support this view:

Human consciousness about the future—"to anticipate, predict, and imagine the future, to have hopes, dreams, and fears about the future, and to set goals and plans for the future" (Lombardo, 2007: 1)—is probably as old as human history (Lombardo, 2006). Above all, we know from research that humans can develop imaginations of the future for all kinds of reasons: for instance, to develop explanations for hypothetically possible future events and the consequences they may lead to (e.g., Kahneman & Tversky, 1973, 1982), to develop constructions of future "possible selves" (e.g., Markus & Nurius, 1986; Markus & Ruvolo, 1989), or to imagine how events could have unfolded differently (e.g., Byrne, 2007; Epstude, Scholl, & Roese, 2016; Roese & Hur, 1997). What all these studies seem to have in common is the aspect of "construction" and "evaluation" of mental representations of alternative realities. Following their arguments, this process seems to take place in a kind of inner conversation, in which what one imagines mentally about the future "talks back" and triggers further thought processes.

Kahneman and Tversky's early theory of "simulation heuristics" (1982), for example, already points to the difference between the mental operation of recalling events and scenarios from memory as opposed to "constructing" them. They outline a mental process in which imagined events are run through in a similar way to a simulation about a specific question. The parameters defined at the beginning can be changed. The simulation therefore does not always have to run the same way, which can lead to different results. What interests us here about the imagination of futures is the perspective that the path to constructing mental representations of alternative realities proceeds like a kind of simulation that is apparently subject to an internal feedback loop. We are familiar with this from conversations with others. The respective result leads to new insights that "talk back" to us and can thus trigger a modification of the original considerations, and so on.

The discussion on counterfactual thoughts, which is closely connected to Kahneman and Tversky's research, also seems to strengthen the view that the mental construction process happens in a kind of reflective conversation.

Counterfactual thoughts are generally considered mental simulations of alternative realities that contradict the facts (Byrne, 2007; Epstude & Roese, 2008; Roese & Morrison, 2009). Every day, people construct counterfactual scenarios when they imagine how a situation from the past may have gone differently. Starting from a perceived reality, the thought "if only..." or "what if..." forms the starting point for the construction of the counterfactual, which is then contrasted with the reality (Byrne, 2016; Kahneman & Miller, 1986). Counterfactual thoughts can take the following form, for example: "If only Bob had kept his eyes on the road [...] he would have avoided the accident" (Roese & Morrison, 2009: 16). Central to our discussion here is to emphasize that, as Johnson and Sherman (1990) point out, counterfactuals do not have to reside in the past. If a certain future appears probable and is practically accepted as truth, it can also be used as a springboard for constructing counterfactual scenarios.

Byrne (2016) and others (e.g., Markman & McMullen, 2003) point out that counterfactuals require not only the mental construction and simulation of a possible alternative reality in terms of whether it could be true, but also an assessment of the differences from the perceived reality. "People must resolve the conflict between the real world and the imagined counterfactual alternative," Byrne states (2016: 143). Therefore, it is a matter of, on the one hand, maintaining two states in parallel—the known or assumed state of affairs and the counterfactual—and, on the other hand, assessing whether the latter is plausible and reasonable. According to Byrne, if the plausibility of a counterfactual scenario is called into question, for example by gaining further insights, the counterfactual situation is supplemented or abandoned. This means that here, too, we are confronted with Kahneman and Tversky's parable of the simulation model, which, analogous to a reflective conversation, leads to feedback and thus to further modifications in the simulation. All of this holds true for a perceived possible true future reality.

Findings in the neurosciences seem to confirm the dual character of the imagination process, with construction and evaluation. The recording of brain activity using functional magnetic resonance imaging has shown that the mental activities involved in imagining the future consist of at least two different processes: the constructive process (Addis et al., 2007; Hassabis & Maguire, 2007; Schacter, Addis, & Buckner, 2007) and an evaluative process (D'Argembeau & Linden, 2004; Gilbert & Wilson, 2007). Recently, it has even been shown that the construction of new, imagined situations takes place in a different neural network than the evaluation of this construction (Lee et al., 2021).

It should also be mentioned here that the comparison of the process of imagining the future, by means of a construction and evaluation process, with a simulation that is modified step by step in a kind of feedback loop as knowledge is gained, is not dissimilar to views on the design process in architecture. Elsewhere, I have already dealt in detail with the relationship between design in the sense of a transformation process (as opposed to the gestalt of an object) and the imagination of the future (Shamiyeh, 2016). Here I would just like to briefly return to the perspective of the design process that was established in the cognitive sciences and behavioral psychology as early as the late 1960s and which is still widely regarded as valid today.

In the book *The Design of the Artificial*, Simon (1969) made a significant point regarding the difference between science and design (and thus also regarding the inherent differences in reasoning) when he argued that design "is concerned with how things ought to be," unlike science, which is about "how things are" (144). Both the open-ended context in which a design solution is to be generated and tested and the "ill-structured" or so-called "wicked" (Rittel & Webber, 1984) nature of the interlocking parameters require a kind of Kahneman and Tversky simulation—whose progression through feedback loops essentially determines the further steps. Simon (1986) gets specific when he says:

"An architect begins with some very general specifications of what is wanted by a client. The initial goals are modified and substantially elaborated as the architect proceeds with the task. Initial design ideas, recorded in drawings and diagrams, themselves suggest new criteria, new possibilities, and new requirements. Throughout the whole process of design, the emerging conception provides continual feedback that reminds the architect of additional considerations that need to be taken into account."

Due to the complexity with which a designer (or architect) is confronted, every further move produces new (sometimes unintended) ones that need to be considered. This "construction" process of the situation does not only lead to new understandings, but their "evaluation" triggers new moves. According to Schön (1983), who has taken a closer look at this process, the "situation 'talks back,' and he [the designer] responds to the situation's back-talk. In a good design-process, this conversation with the situation is reflective. In answer to the situation's back-talk, the designer reflects-in-action on the construction" (79). It is important to emphasize that Schön explicitly pointed out that the situation at hand is a fictitious one, that one is dealing with ideas of something that ought to be, but in no way exists. Designers or architects rarely create the actual artifact; rather, they create representations of possible futures, such as how a chair or house could look and be realized in reality (Evans, 1997).

Simon's (1969, 1986) and Schön's (1983) view of the construction and evaluation process of imagined futures that resembles a reflective conversation has subsequently been examined in detail by many design researchers and supported by empirical studies (Buchanan, 1992; Cross, 2006; Dorst & Cross, 2001; Rowe, 1991). From these insights and those found in social psychology and the neurosciences, a sense of futurecasting as a reflective conversation arises.

So far, I have looked at the reflective conversation on an individual level. It also takes place on a collective, group level. Since futurecasting aims to intervene in an existing social fabric, a certain degree of social agreement by the parties concerned is required if it wants to be successful. Futurecasting necessarily becomes a joint endeavor, an act of collective inquiry and reflection about what the future could look like or what the people concerned would like the future to be. It is not something one does alone or even in isolation (although that is of course possible but not very effective); it is something that people do together. I will now turn to this consideration.

Reconciling meaning

I have discussed the open-ended context for imagining futures in futurecasting and what we know from social psychology and neuroscience about the mental process involved. I have not mentioned anything about the purpose of futurecasting. But it is precisely this question of purpose that helps to explain why futurecasting must be understood as a reflective conversation on a collective level.

There are many reasons why people imagine the future as mentioned above, namely, to hope for or dream of a better future, to cope better with their fears, but also to set goals and plans for a desired future. How people deal with their imaginations of the future varies. In his widely cited book *Redesigning the Future*, Ackoff (1974) identified four attitudes. There are those, the "inactivists," who are content with the way things are, he asserts. They do nothing and believe that any effort to change something will not bring about any change. Then there are those who believe that things will only get worse. This group of people, the "reactivists," as he names them, retreats into the (better) past. Not only do they resist change, but they also return to where they were, to nostalgia. The third category of people, the "pre-activists," wants to prepare for the future. They measure the quality of the future according to their ability to predict it accurately or prepare well for it. Hence, this group is less concerned about doing nothing than doing the right thing. They want to proactively recognize challenges before they become serious. Last but not least, Ackoff (1974: 22f.) sees a type of people that he calls "interactivists." This group is not convinced about the present state of the world and wants to actively transform it according to its own ideas. They are the people who even invent ways to shape the future they envision.

The attitudes that lead to proactive steps towards being prepared for or even shaping the future are animated by the gap between imagined future and reality, simply because of the desire to close this gap between what is imagined and what is real. This, however, creates a tension between the people affected and the need for cooperation.

Our world is pluralistic, not only in terms of the worldviews of the people involved, but also in terms of their visions of the future. Imaginations of the future not only inhabit multiple social worlds (Goodman, 1978). Their implementation also demands working together to achieve a mutual understanding and social consensus that retains its integrity over time, space, and local contingencies (Searle, 1995). Those involved face the challenge of reconciling heterogeneous meanings if they want to cooperate. This requires entering into a dialogue to make sense of different meanings where appropriate, and negotiating and discussing the contributions in order to develop a mutual understanding. Reflective conversations must be able to create a framework in which each individual is valued and their voice is heard, and in which they can influence the steps needed to bring about the expected changes.

For Isaacs (1999), the term "conversation" means "turning around together" (37). In a conversation, the people involved "consciously and unconsciously [...] weigh out different views, finding some with which they agree, and others that they dislike" (Isaacs, 1993: 35). At the same time, we learn from Isaacs that a conversation can take two possible routes, either to discussion or dialogue. In discussion, as he defines it, people choose to defend their views and try to sustain their positions and thus "see themselves as separate from one another" (1999: 42). It is a route of conversation that is of little interest to us here. Instead, I would like to understand futurecasting as a form of conversation that leads to "reflective" and "generative dialogue," as Isaacs put it. Dialogue, for Isaacs (1999), means that people engaged in the conversation "become willing to think about the rules underlying what [they] do—the reasons for [their] thoughts and actions" (38).

People involved in this reflection aim to more clearly see "underlying causes, rules, and assumptions to get to the deeper questions and framing of problems" (Isaacs, 1999: 41). This route of conversation can then lead to a generative dialogue, in which people creatively begin to invent unprecedented possibilities and gain new insights (Jenlink & Banathy, 2008). It is precisely when people set aside their assumptions and listen deeply to each other that "new creative insights and new levels of wisdom emerge" (Banathy, 2000: 389).

Futurecasting defined as a reflective conversation is meant to encompass a reflective and generative dialogue. It aims to create alternative realities that go beyond the existing areas of human activity. I would like futurecasting to be understood as a vehicle that equips the individuals involved with the capability and capacity to participate in the conscious creation of a new situation. This includes changing existing thought patterns, but also creating a new consciousness (Banathy, 2000).

Bohm (1980 [2002]) is helpful in this context for understanding consciousness as an unfolding of thoughts, worldviews, and assumptions. A collective can also develop a social consciousness that, following Bohm, is reflected in its culture. When an individual's thoughts, assumptions, and worldviews are combined with those of others, patterns of values and beliefs become embedded in the cultural fabric. Dialogue is significant insofar as the meanings are made explicit in communication. A shared meaning is created through exchange with each other, a shift from individual to collective consciousness takes place. As Bohm and Peat (1987 [2011]) argue, "an inner relationship of people to each other and to society as a whole" (182) emerges.

In summary, if futurecasting is to be successful, it must develop into a reflective conversation and not a defense of points of view as in a discussion. And under no circumstances must it fall into demonstration mode, meaning that imaginations of the future are simply presented. In both cases, no collective consciousness of the new can emerge. The chance of creating a common understanding and a collective consciousness for the new will be lost. Conversation, especially in its reflective form, is therefore necessary to share ideas about the future, about how one imagines the new and what aspirations and hopes are associated with it, and to reconcile the meanings with one another.

The question we must now turn to is how imaginations of the future can be made explicit. As already mentioned at the outset, these do not arise out of nothing, but in our mind. For a reflective conversation to be successful, the ideas that arise in the mind must first leave the subjective realm of the individual to become part of the collective.

The various manifestations of futurecasting

For Berger and Luckmann (1966), a conversation and the use of a shared language are considered "the most important vehicle of reality-maintenance" (172). This reconciles different interpretations of experiences to create shared meanings. "The continuing use of the same language to objectify unfolding biographical experience" is thereby the fundamental reality-maintaining fact, they argue (173). But, as shown by Polanyi (1966), "we can know more than we can tell" (4).

What we know and can express in codified form with words and numbers does not encompass our entire knowledge. Polanyi (1958) therefore divided knowledge into "explicit," or codified, knowledge and "tacit" knowledge. While one can be articulated and transmitted through language, the other lies deep within us and is deeply connected to experiences, actions, and a particular context. It "indwells" the individual, as Polanyi noted, and is therefore difficult to formulate and communicate. Johnson-Laird (1983) felt that Polanyi's notion of tacit knowledge can encompass both cognitive and technical aspects. For him, cognitive aspects include mental models, i.e., the perspectives, assumptions, or schemas about the world we create in our mind. The technical aspect of tacit knowledge, according to his view, comprises skills or crafts that are applied in a specific situation. Decisive in our context of futurecasting is that the cognitive aspect refers to an "individual's images of reality and visions for the future, that is to say, what is and what ought to be," as Nonaka (1994: 16) argued. The articulation of these "visions" for the future, which are difficult to convey in formalized language, therefore plays a decisive role in futurecasting. If they are not brought forth from the realm of the individual, they cannot become part of a collective realm. Individuals involved in a conversation can only then decide which future they like and which they do not, what they see or would like to see differently, and whether they agree with the actions that need to be undertaken to realize this vision.

The issue at stake is that this is anything but easy, as Nyiri (1988) confirms when he notes that for individuals it is anything but easy "mining [information] out of [their] heads, painstakingly, one jewel at a time" as soon as they have absorbed it (21f.). As long as individual perspectives remain personal and are therefore not accessible to others, others cannot make sense of them to take further actions (Weick, 1995).

The question of interest here now is how tacit knowledge or, more specifically, imaginations of something that ought to be, can be shared with others. There certainly are different approaches to this. For this very reason I speak of futurecasting practices and not of a single approach to futurecasting. Let us start with Nonaka (1994) who, with his “Dynamic Theory of Organizational Knowledge Creation,” has provided essential insights into the question posed here. Regardless of the fact that his oft-cited theory has recently been subjected to critical examination (Bratianu, 2010; Gourlay, 2006; Hoe, 2006), there seems to be broad consensus on two forms of transformation of tacit knowledge: on the one hand, the transfer of tacit knowledge without language through social interaction, and, on the other, the conversion of tacit knowledge into explicit knowledge, which Nonaka (1994) calls “externalization” (19).

Sharing tacit knowledge without using language through social interaction is probably as old as human history. Apprenticeship training through observation and mimicking practice is typical of this form of acquiring knowledge without language. For example, for centuries the key to the successful acquisition of tacit knowledge in the training of architects was practical experience with the master craftsman (Cuff, 1992; Kostof, 1977 [2000]). More recent approaches in the design disciplines try to build on these findings and use experience, the key to acquiring tacit knowledge, to bring forth what people imagine in their heads about the future. “Experiential Futures” (Sterling, 2017) is one of many approaches in the field “of taking the invisible and making it meaningful” through experience and embodiment. As Nonaka (1994) put it, “without some form of shared experience, it is extremely difficult for people to share each other’s thought processes” (19). Using games or artistic or theatrically staged performances is one of many interactive ways of presenting and making sense of invisible aspects of imagined futures (e.g., Flanagan, 2013; Inayatullah, 2013).

The second approach to the exchange of tacit imaginations about the future is externalization. Of course, this cannot be viewed entirely without social interaction. Writing or text enables the mind to generate and share thoughts that would otherwise remain unarticulated (Havelock, 1986; Walter, 1982). However, they are not the only forms of externalization. It is also well known that art enables artists to externalize their personal feelings, internal states, and worldviews. One need only think here of Eduard Munch’s *The Scream*, Kurt Schwitters’s Dadaist collages that reflect the shattered state of the war-torn society of the time, or Alberto Giacometti’s meter-high and stick-thin figures, where we encounter the opposite of August Rodin’s *The Burghers of Calais*, an anecdotal, almost photographic view of people on the street. Instead, all these artworks reveal reality, not as it is, but as it feels to the artists.

Nevertheless, this (elitist) form of externalization is not accessible to everyone. What other forms are there and how effective are they at externalizing imaginations of the future?

Devising prototypes, early mock-ups, or other artifacts such as diagrams, visualizations, etc., may certainly also provide some sense of an imagined future. Schrage (2000), for instance, who has published extensively in the field of innovation, talks about artifacts or prototypes that open up a “shared space” for the common understanding of an idea. Arnheim (1993) has shown that the sketches that emerge in a design process can be understood as cognitive artifacts that reflect the current state of the design and can also be seen as directives for further steps precisely because of their vague and tentative quality. Schön (1983) also recognized this with his findings on reflective practice. Scholars in the field of scenario planning are also fundamentally aware of the issue: Seminal books such as van der Heijden's (2005) *Scenarios: The Art of Strategic Conversation* or Schwartz's (1996) *The Art of the Long View: Planning for the Future in an Uncertain World* view scenario work as a meditation vehicle by acknowledging that their "sensory perceptions can play a significant role in understanding plausible and challenging possible futures" (Ramírez & Selin, 2014: 62).

The question at stake: Are there some general principles or theoretical models that define which parameters or processes are helpful for effective externalization? Saying it right up front, I will not be able to answer this question—after all, this volume, with its wealth of contributions from so many authors, serves to provide a greater insight into the subject, which has until recently received little attention. However, I would like to focus here on two aspects that seem to be of central importance for the success of futurecasting (without attempting to form a theory about them here): On the one hand, the use of metaphors to effectively externalize tacit notions of what one imagines about the future and, on the other, the resolution or granularity with which these visions are shared.

The use of metaphors for effective externalization

Sterling (2017), as well as several authors in this volume (e.g., Celin, Flanagan, Kirby, Montgomery, Pavlakis, Popper), argue that, based on their practical experience, one way of making the invisible visible and senseable is to create alternative visions of future(s) that are then transformed into tangible, immersive, visual, or interactive experiences. This seems to be in line with what several scholars claim.

Nisbet (1969), for example, noted that "[m]uch of what Michael Polanyi has called 'tacit knowledge' is expressible—in so far as it is expressible at all—in metaphor" (5). According to Lakoff and Johnson (1980 [2003]), "the essence of metaphor is understanding and experiencing one kind of thing in terms of another" (5). But contrary to what most people think about metaphor, namely that it is merely a rhetorical device, Lakoff and Johnson (1980 [2003]) argue that "metaphor is pervasive in everyday life, not just in language but in thought and action [...] the way we think, what we experience, and what we do every day is very much a matter of metaphor" (3).

The intriguing aspect of Lakoff and Johnson's (1980 [2003]) work for our topic here is that metaphors not only create realities, especially social realities, but can also be a guide for further action. It is precisely from the experimentalist perspective that metaphors "allow us to understand one kind of experience in terms of another," they argue (235). In this way, the imaginative character of works of art can create opportunities to explore a common experiential space in relation to new forms of experience and, thus, new (future) contexts. Metaphors can help to "communicate the relevant parts of the unshared experiences or to emphasize the shared experiences and neglect the others" (Lakoff & Johnson, 1980 [2003]: 231). Metaphor is thus not only a first means of externalizing people's tacit ideas about what ought to be, but also an essential and effective method of gaining new insights into the not-yet-existing future through the use of existing knowledge and the creation of networks of conceptual contexts. Similar observations on metaphors can also be found in the work of Bateson (2000 [1972]) and Kövecses (2010).

The granularity of shared visions of the future

A second issue that comes up again and again in connection with our subject is the question of the granularity or resolution of imaginations about what ought to be—from low to high fidelity. Does a more precise articulation of ideas about the future promote social engagement and agreement or is it rather countorproductive? We get hints on this topic from authors in this volume, but also from architecture and sociology.

In architecture, the subject of detailing ideas about the future, in particular the as-yet-unbuilt construction, has always been an issue because, as Evans (1997) aptly put it, architects are "never working directly with the object of their thought, always working as if through some intervening medium, almost always the drawing" (156). It was therefore all the more surprising for Evans, as he self-critically remarked, how little drawings literally have to do with the later building and how this fact has not been made explicit before. "Recognition of the drawing's power as a medium turns out, unexpectedly," as he writes, "to be recognition of the drawing's distinctness from and unlikeness to the thing that is represented, rather than its likeness to it" (154). The reasons for this are certainly not only to be found in semiotics (e.g., Saussure) but, first and foremost, in the uncertain character of the drawing that leaves a lot of room for individual interpretation with regard to what is to be finally created. After all, a building can only become a reality in agreement with both the client and the specialists carrying out the work. Particularly in architectural competitions, drawings that are deliberately kept somewhat uncertain can be an effective lever for victory, as they invite the jury to experiment with the design and explore their own ideas in it. The architect and Pritzker Prize winner Rem Koolhaas (1991) once aptly summarized this as follows: "Where there is nothing, everything is possible. Where there is architecture, nothing (else) is possible" (156).

Montgomery (in this volume) argues in a similar vein when he is in favor of "voids" and "vessels" because of their indeterminacy and openness for projecting individual imaginations of the future into them. Voids are "stripped-down spaces that eliminate unwanted residue of our current moment, enabling participants to project a range of future contexts and situations," Montgomery argues, and continues, "vessels can be unrecognizable objects, placeholder items, or artifacts without strong social symbolism, allowing a participant to instantly envision the object serving any number of purposes that weren't predicted beforehand."

Issacs (1999) notes in this context that the success of conversations aiming for reflective and generative dialogue depends to a large extent on the presence of "suspension," the opposite of "certainty," among other important criteria. He derives the word "certainty" from "to determine," which generally carries the connotation of "rigidity," something non-negotiable (135f.). Only through suspension, the putting aside of certainties and, thus, the opening up of a space that allows other things to occur, is it possible for other participants in the conversation to think about shared or divergent values, paradigms, and worldviews within the context of the respective imagination of the future. It follows that the less one specifies what is to be shared with others, the more room there is for interpretation and other contributions. This subsequently stimulates participants' imaginations. Montgomery's strategy resonates well with Isaacs's remarks.

This demand for openness through uncertainty can also be found in related approaches from the broad field of futures studies, such as, for example, in scenario planning (whose difference from futurecasting will be discussed below). In prospective scenario planning, which follows qualitative, evidence-led, intuitive causal logics methods as opposed to probabilistic scenario planning, scholars argue that scenarios should be open to experimentation and exploration, rather than treated as self-contained, prefabricated stories that are then passed on for decision (Wilkinson, 2009). The aim of scenario planning is to create different narratives (scenarios) of the future with the impetus of generating discomfort and directing attention to current knowledge gaps (Ramírez & Selin, 2014; Ramirez & Wilkinson, 2016; Wilkinson & Eidinow, 2008). This can only succeed if the scenario planning process, which often remains within a single framework, opens up a space where one learns about other perspectives of the future, and deconstructs or recombines them with the views of others.

Futurecasting and its demarcation from other approaches

Due to the abundance of different terms and their sometimes inflationary use in the field of futures studies—just think of the ambiguous use of the term scenario (e.g., Cordova-Pozo & Rouwette, 2023; Kosow & Gaßner, 2008; Mietzner & Reger, 2005)—the following section discusses the differentiation between futurecasting and other approaches. The chronology of approaches is freely chosen and can also be regarded as a kind of glossary.

Futurecasting

As discussed in detail above, I define futurecasting as a reflective conversation with imaginations about what ought to be. Unconstrained imagination is the sine qua non of futurecasting. The aim is to creatively imagine visions of the future in an open-ended context, to articulate them as well as to evaluate them. Reflective conversation thereby means that futurecasting is not done alone; it is something people do together. Social interaction must therefore be shaped in such a way that the tacit imaginations of what ought to be can leave the realm of the individual and become part of a collective imagination to enable exploration of underlying assumptions, values, and worldviews and to generate future-oriented possibilities and insights. In this sense, futurecasting then acknowledges several actual social worlds and is inherently pluralistic.

Forecasting

Forecasts are generally understood to be predictions about what can be expected in the future in view of what is already known (e.g., Cuhls, 2003; Mietzner & Reger, 2005). The result is a single "most likely" future based on the assumptions made beforehand. The underlying causality is determined by the linear temporal sequence from past, to present, and then future (Wilkinson, 2009). The differences from futurecasting are as follows: (a) The purpose of futurecasting is not to predict a possible future based on what is known but to bring forth and jointly evaluate unconstrained imaginations of what ought to be. Futurecasting thus does not rely on probabilities, which can only succeed in stable environments anyway, as in forecasting. (b) The future is not determined by what is already known and extrapolated forwards in time, but is formed by open-ended social interaction in the form of a reflective conversation. The link to the present, i.e., how to get from the here and now to this future, is not an immediate priority task of futurecasting and must be established in a subsequent process (by means of backcasting).

Backcasting

Backcasting is concerned "not with what futures are likely to happen, but with how desirable futures can be attained" (Robinson, 1990). In other words, backcasting works its way back from a certain defined point in the future to the present and clarifies which measures are necessary to achieve this future. So, while the focus in forecasting is on discovering the underlying structural features of the world that would lead to the future coming about, backcasting, coming from the other direction, is about freely determining the steps necessary for reaching the future defined as the endpoint. Thus, backcasting can be downstream of the futurecasting process.

Foresight

Foresight, according to Martin's (1995) seminal definition, is "[...] the process involved in systematically attempting to look into the longer-term future of science, technology, the economy and society with the aim of identifying the areas of strategic research and the emerging of generic technologies likely to yield the greatest economic and social benefits" (140). Foresight is therefore a process that, by looking forward in time, provides a deeper understanding of how the future might evolve. Different means of gathering information can be applied, consisting of quantitative as well as qualitative ones. Foresight in general helps one to be better prepared for the future. It is therefore closely interwoven with planning and policymaking (e.g., Aldabbagh & Allawzi, 2019; Cuhls, 2003; Magruk, 2017, 2020; Mietzner & Reger, 2005). Forecasting and scenario planning, among other approaches in future studies, are therefore part of the overarching activity of foresight.

Scenario planning

Defining scenario planning is quite challenging because not only are there several schools within this field, but the term "scenario" is defined and used in extremely different ways. However, since there could quickly be superficial similarities between scenario planning and futurecasting, a more thorough discussion of the term is required here.

Certainly, one of the most prominent definitions of scenarios can be found in Glenn's (2009) *Millennium Project*: "A scenario is a story with plausible cause and effect links that connects a future condition with the present, while illustrating key decisions, events, and consequences throughout the narrative" (2). Since this definition is very universal, we turn to Cordova-Pozo and Rouwette (2023), who recently compiled a comprehensive overview of the current state of scenario planning research. On the basis of numerous publications, they define scenario more precisely: "scenarios are a set of narratives describing different alternative futures, constructed with an iterative approach based on the uncertainties of the context, with the aim to raise awareness of plausible futures and increase performance of the organization" (9). The focus on context, target group (organization), and purpose (awareness) distinguishes this definition from Glenn's definition. Their definition is echoed in the view of Ramirez and his colleagues, who gained international recognition for their Oxford Scenario Planning Approach. They consider scenarios "as a small set of stories of future contextual conditions linked with the present, made for someone and fulfilling an explicit purpose" (Ramírez & Selin, 2014: 55). Scenario planning is then understood as an "intervention: a set of social and intellectual processes that are designed for someone, or a group of people, and their specific needs" (Ramirez & Wilkinson, 2016: xiv).

The combination of scenario and planning, as it is often used by leading minds of this domain (e.g., Schwartz, 1996; Heijden, 2005), already reveals the first difference from futurecasting: the purpose and outcome of the method. The combination of scenario and planning suggests that the study of possible scenarios of the future in terms of what might happen determines the planning of actions necessary to prepare for all contingencies and to minimize surprise. Or, as Wilkinson (1995), Schwartz's colleague, puts it, "[scenario planning] can prepare us in the same way that it prepares corporate executives: It helps us understand the uncertainties that lie before us, and what they might mean. It helps us 'rehearse' our responses to those possible futures. And it helps us spot them as they begin to unfold." Thus, the purpose of scenario planning, as it is commonly understood, and in contrast to futurecasting, is to generate and explore (probable/possible/plausible) scenarios of the future from a user's perspective, given a specific context and with a dedicated purpose, in order to be prepared for the future (by adapting organizational strategies) (e.g., review by Cordova-Pozo & Rouwette, 2023). Typically, this view also implies that the future itself is not changeable and therefore one can only adapt to it, which is why the literature on scenario planning since the 1960s has repeatedly talked about turbulence and discontinuities affecting organizations, from Ansoff (1965) to Toffler (1984) to today's practitioners. The aim of futurecasting, on the other hand, is, to recall it here again, the unconstrained imagination of futures in an open-ended context (regardless of a specific user or purpose) and their articulation and joint evaluation. The difference between scenario planning and futurecasting thus somewhat echoes what Senge (2003) once aptly noted in reference to the difference between problem-solving and creating: "In problem-solving, we seek to make something we do not like go away. In creating, we seek to make what we truly care about exist" (4). Simply put, there are situations in which anticipation and adaptation is no longer a desirable goal or no longer leads to acceptable results. Think of the climate crisis, for example, whose solution can no longer consist of adaptive behavior that reacts with (only) more efficiency to CO_2 targets in the face of constant growth. Being "less bad," as Braungart (2007) and his colleagues put it, is no longer a viable option. Instead, we require a fundamental system change towards a closed-loop system, which cannot be understood or brought about through intensive foresight, but requires the transformative act of imagination. Scenario planning puts its focus on narratives about futures in order to examine and explore what could happen from the perspective of a particular context and clientele and for the purposes of preparedness and successful adaption (e.g., Wilkinson & Eidinow, 2008), whereas futurecasting assumes that investigating the future is insufficient. Futurecasting also uses narratives about the future, but these are based on unconstrained imagination with the aim of collectively generating unprecedented future possibilities.

This results in further differences between scenario planning and futurecasting: Futurecasting works in an unconstrained, open-ended space for creative imagination. The transformative repertoire is thus much larger. As Ackoff (2006) explained, in many cases the obstacles disappear when "we change our point of view and look backward at where we are from where we want to be" (12). If one starts from the future and goes back to the present, i.e., uses the backcasting method to determine the means needed to achieve it, then one is much freer, as Robinson (1990) showed. In addition, it solves many critical issues that are mentioned in connection with scenario planning. Futurecasting addresses the often-criticized lack of imagination in scenario planning (Cordova-Pozo & Rouwette, 2023); it emphasizes the importance of improvement through innovation to offset or overcome change, in contrast to the scenario approach, which tends to emphasize flexibility in dealing with change; it helps to break down the filters that often manifest themselves in the biased perceptions (Gilbert, 2005; Prahalad & Bettis, 1986; Tripsas, 2009; Tripsas & Gavetti, 2000) and beliefs (March & Simon, 1958; Tripsas, 2009) of organizational members; and, finally, futurecasting's immanent mode of reasoning, which is abductive, is the only form of reasoning that brings forth something truly novel, as opposed to the deductive or inductive approach that is often stated in relation to scenario planning (Heijden, 2005).

Wargaming

Wargaming uses analytic games to "simulate aspects of warfare at the tactical, operational, or strategic level. They are used to examine warfighting concepts, train and educate commanders and analysts, explore scenarios, and assess how force planning and posture choices affect campaign outcomes" (RAND, 2024). Used by both the military and private (hobbyists) sector, wargaming is part of foresight methods. Scenarios developed in the military sector are often played out in wargame exercises (Lee, 2018). It therefore differs from futurecasting in that scenarios, which might be developed in the course of scenario planning, are used in wargaming exercises for military training, sometimes with real replicas of urban situations. Futurecasting is primarily about articulating imaginations about futures (regardless of whether military, corporate, or civil society processes are subsequently played out). However, futurecasting can be particularly relevant for wargaming (or crisis management in general) with regard to imagining threats. The term "Threatcasting," i.e., futurecasting with a focus on threats, was coined for this purpose (Johnson et al., 2021; Vanatta & Johnson, 2019).

Worldmaking

Worldmaking is not to be confused with worldbuilding (see below), the constructing of an imaginary world, as in science fiction films, novels, etc. (see, for example, Bassett, Brueckner, and Kirby in this volume, 2024). The term was largely coined by the philosophical work of Goodman (1978), who showed in *Ways of Worldmaking* that the synthetic act of the social construction of the world (the reality; or German: *Wirklichkeit*) takes place with the help of symbols, whereby the concept of symbol is understood quite broadly: It "includes letters, words, texts, sounds, pictures, diagrams, maps, models" and much more (Goodman, 1978: 94). In other words, the world is inextricably linked to and constructed through the use of symbols. Through the use of symbols, individuals differentiate and delimit, compare and weigh, structure and organize. Goodman's insights are highly relevant to futurecasting:

By "ways" of worldmaking, Goodman means that there are different ways of making the world. The symbols for worldmaking can be assigned to different symbol systems (e.g., science, arts, etc.), none of which enjoy absolute epistemological priority over the others. For this very reason, there is no such thing as a single and true reality or world that results from these different ways of worldmaking but, rather, "multiple actual worlds" (2). Worldmaking, the transformation of reality, then only takes place when those involved manage to reconcile diverse meanings if they wish to come to an agreement. This is consistently challenging due to the heterogeneous nature of our many social worlds. In this sense, futurecasting, the articulation and collaborative evaluation and construction of what ought to be, is a way of (collective, future-oriented) worldmaking. The element that the participants in the futurecasting process share with each other in the dialogue—the symbols, whether in verbal, pictorial, or haptic form—has the same world-making status as the actual present world. The question that futurecasting poses in particular, in contrast to worldmaking, is how the symbols must be constituted—from low to high fidelity, etc.,—in order to contribute effectively to worldmaking. The central issue addressed in futurecasting—namely, how tacit imaginations of the future, i.e., that which does not yet exist, can be articulated and negotiated—remains on a meta-level in the philosophical discourse. Futurecasting seeks to find pragmatic answers here.

Worldbuilding

Worldbuilding is a human activity that often develops as early as childhood (Wolf, 2014). A decisive feature of imaginary worlds is that they are not based on a narrative and can become tremendous in size. Think of the Marvel or Star Wars Universe, for example, in which countless episodes, film spin-offs, and novels, etc., take place. In contrast to storytelling, where the details of the narrative contribute significantly to the success of the story's reception, the details in worldbuilding only provide a rich background and realism. Nowadays there is an almost inexhaustible fund of how-to books explaining how to build fictional worlds.

After an in-depth study of Wolf's (2014, 2017) seminal anthologies *Building Imaginary Worlds* and *Revisiting Imaginary Worlds*, the following difference between worldbuilding and futurecasting can be identified: Wolf (2014) notes that, although worldbuilding is an interdisciplinary process, there is always a kind of production director who, like a poet or novelist, brings about authorship. He notes, "authorship, then, can be conceptualized as a series of concentric circles extending out from the world's originator, with each circle of delegated authority being further removed from the world's origination and involving diminishing authorial contributions, from the originator and main author to estates, heirs, and torchbearers [...] A world's author or owner, however, can decide to what extent authorship will be delegated, or if it will be at all, determining whether a world will remain open or closed, as well as what material will be considered canonical" (269). This authorship, which is widely known in architecture and where, for good reason, the architect is seen at the top of the pyramid of all those involved in the project, strives for completeness and consistency. The process Wolf describes has little to do with the conversational model as proposed in the context of futurecasting, about convening all those affected to co-sense and generate visions of the future. Delegation, as it is apparently practiced in the context of worldbuilding, does not presuppose mutual understanding and does not necessarily lead to such understanding. The main difference between worldbuilding and futurecasting is one of modus operandi. Worldbuilding's understandable striving for completeness and consistency, which seems plausible and comprehensible from the perspective of films, games, or novels, stands in stark contrast to the pluralistic approach and striving for multiple worlds (which do not have to be brought into a consensus) of futurecasting.

Future-making

Future-making has recently attracted attention through at least three interwoven and yet differently oriented research interests in sociology, the humanities, and organizational studies. Consequently, there are also differences in what is understood by the term.

In sociology, interest in future-making has been evident since the early 2000s. Leading British sociologists have reflected in detail on the "future" and on how it is embedded in sociology (e.g., Adam & Groves, 2007; Levitas, 2013; Urry, 2016). This interest can be principally attributed to the discipline's desire to play an active role in making futures. Previously, research in sociology has usually been driven by the objective to "observe how others claim futures and that which makes claims to what futures will or should be" (Halford & Southerton, 2023, p. 266). Sociologists are now asking how the discipline's capacity can be used effectively for a future-making practice. They understand the process of "future-making" as an emergent process that takes place in everyday and institutional practices. In this sense, the futures are in the making in the present. By future-making practice they mean the "doings and sayings" of actors engaged in materializing their claims about futures (Schatzki, 2002, 73). Adam and Groves (2007), for example, now argue that sociology provides valuable resources, such as knowledge about temporality, complexity, inequality, power, and much more, which can help to overcome simplistic, predictive, and one-dimensional approaches to shaping the future. The debate on future-making in sociology is therefore driven by a redefinition of the discipline's repertoire from an original focus on research that observes and analyzes social situations and thus, also, the emergence of the future, to an active engagement in future-making that addresses what the future will or should be. In the humanities, especially in design, the concept of "future-making" gained significant attention in the course of the "maker turn," which recognizes artifacts, concrete objects, and their processes of "making" as an intellectual endeavor, thus breaking up the old dichotomy of doing versus thinking or creation versus critique. As Klein (2017) notes, "it brings the creative practice of design to the center of research, favoring process over product as well as versioning and extensibility over definitive editions and research silos" (25). This not only calls into question the historically higher status of interpretation and analysis as opposed to production and application, but also brings to the fore the fact that experience with objects can be a carrier of meaning. "The experience of things often involves pre-linguistic or pre-discursive forms of knowing," as Sayer (2017) aptly emphasizes, "where meaning is derived from thinking with objects" (32). Well, the design discipline has never shied away from pointing out its forward-looking influence on society and how it shapes and inhibits our lives (and therefore our future) (e.g., Appadurai, 2014). Regarding "Design as Future-Making" is thus comprehensible and "a testimony to the breadth and reach of the social character of design, or rather, to the social relationships embedded in and mediated by the spaces, places, messages and things one encounters daily" (Yelavich & Adams, 2014: 12).

Although both view the creation of physical objects (sketches, models, etc.) as an interpretative act from which meaning can be derived—a "way of worldmaking" in Goodman's (1978) sense—future-making and futurecasting have little in common. When design is not understood as a participative social practice (Manzini, 2015), but as a service-oriented activity, the framework for a reflective and generative dialogue on what ought to be is usually quite small, limited to the client, the designer, and some executing professionals. However, those who may be affected, such as customers (industrial design) or the public (architecture, urban design), are usually excluded, as design is still regarded and practiced in the sense of authorship.

The second strand of interest in future-making goes back to the process of "making" the future in the sense of concrete realizable actions. This line of interest has recently been debated by Alice Comi (in this volume) and her colleagues (Comi & Whyte, 2018; Whyte, Comi, & Mosca, 2022) in the field of organizational studies. Their focus is specifically on the performance of "visual artifacts," which, following their empirical observation, "do not merely provide the means to an end, but instead produce an end that prompts immediate action" (Comi & Whyte, 2018: 1059). "They do so," they continue, "by picturing a deliberately vague and maybe not even attainable future, which nevertheless will seduce audiences and mobilize commitment." With their observation and theorization of the respective phases in the design process, they have taken a path that has become known in the design discipline as "protocol studies." The work of Lloyd and Scott (1994), Gero and Mc Neill (1998), or Cross and Cross (1996) et al. are examples. This method has proven its worth when it comes to showing how design is capable of creating new knowledge, how ideas of what does not yet exist are gradually given form, and how the process subsequently leads to "testing, stabilizing and reifying" the design and, in the case of Comi (2018) and her colleague, the future. Futurecasting, however, differs from this consideration of future-making in purpose, means, and output.

Design work, which was the subject of the investigations for future-making, is essentially a service that is provided on the basis of a design briefing (e.g., Cross, 2006; Lawson, 1980). In his seminal book *Design for the Real World*, Papanek (1972) critiqued the design profession for committing itself to capital and not to society and the environment. Little has changed since then, as Dunne and Raby (2013) have made clear with their strategic move to "create a parallel [speculative] design channel free from market pressure" (12). What I want to stress here is that the design process is not as free as is assumed. It is usually subject to specific requirements and framework conditions and is therefore primarily dedicated to solving the task at hand, even if this can take a creative form.

In other words, future-making, which is derived from the analysis of the design process, is goal-oriented and therefore anything but unconstrained. The framework for the implementation measures cannot be freely conceived either. In few cases is it possible to respond to a given design task, for example the desire for a house for the homeless, with a social process as a solution. This is where future-making differs fundamentally from futurecasting.

The resources used in the respective processes also differ significantly. The "visual artifact," which is a central tool of mediation between the participants in future-making, is just one of many verbal and non-verbal means that can be used in futurecasting. Think of other forms of sensory perception, from sound to smell to embodiment. Selin's (in this volume) work with art, but also Hayashi's (2021) *Social Presencing Theater* are only mentioned here as examples.

Finally, there is also a difference in the output. In contrast to future-making, where the visual artifacts are intended to contribute to "the making sense of possible and probable futures" with the aim of turning them "into a realizable course of action" (Whyte et al., 2022), the output of futurecasting is a deep and mutual understanding of the collective vision about the future and of each other. The actions that need to be taken for implementation can be explored in a backcasting process that follows futurecasting, depending on the "user" or "purpose."

Outline of this volume

This volume is organized in five sections. Three central themes—data, fiction, and matter—form the core body of this volume. As I will explain in a moment, these three types are synonymous with three central forms with which tacit ideas about the future can be externalized and shared with others in a reflective conversation. They are thus representative of the practices of futurecasting. Each of these three core thematic blocks is also introduced by an interview that I conducted with a remarkable person from the subject area (Inayatullah, Wilkinson, and McDowell). The core body on the topic is preceded by a section on the basic prerequisites for futurecasting and followed by a section on what we can practically take away from futurecasting. There are four different types of contributions: papers, interviews, project presentations, and statements. Authors with a strong practical background choose short statements to provide readers with a view on the topic from the perspective of everyday operations.

The first section, "Preliminary Conditions," is divided into three parts. It explores the questions of what social or organizational settings are necessary for successful futurecasting ("People, Teams, and Identity"), how people construct and perceive the ideas about the future that are communicated to them ("Counterfactual Thinking and Imagination"), and what ambitions and objectives can drive futurecasting ("Ambitions, Objectives, and Sensemaking"). "People, teams, and identity" deals with the need to develop an awareness of one's own identity in order to carry out effective futurecasting (Lang & Carson) as well as what teams should consider at work to avoid falling into fantasy or science fiction (Mankowsky) and to ensure the organizational dissemination of ideas (Schwartz). The section on "Counterfactual Thinking and Imagination" addresses key skills of futurecasting and their value, which lies precisely in the fact that we do not have to rely solely on historical trends or current data—which are no longer meaningful for the future—but that futurecasting uses creativity and experimentation to not only predict the future, but also to shape it (Reeves). Related to this are contributions on the types of cognitive strategies we humans use when imagining the future (Byrne), how important these forms of imagination are for strategy, policy, and planning (Revell & Bleecker), and, last but not least, how knowledge about the unknowns in the course of dealing with the uncertainty of the future can help us to deal with questions of the future more wisely and with more foresight (Wolf). In the section "Ambitions, Objectives, and Sensemaking," we turn to the questions of how we should approach the future (Miller), why it is so important that we maintain our hopes and ambitions for a desirable future (Pfeiffer), and, last but not least, which future is desirable at all (Hargrave).

The first of the three sections on the forms of externalization of tacit imaginations of the future— "Futurecasting with Data"—is devoted to instantiation through data. In this section, we are concerned with how probable futures are discernible through scientific facts (forecasts, simulations, and models). How data can specifically contribute to developing a sense of the future can be seen, for example, in the creation of simulations of planetary futures (Raleigh) or data-enriched stories and briefs on how society or technology will develop in the future (Buchinger). At the same time, this section also reminds us about the predicament in which we find ourselves, namely, that data is insufficient to fully represent reality, not to speak of the future (Offenhuber). A holistic approach is needed when it comes to designing a more human-centered world (Liu et al.)

"Futurecasting with Fiction" is about making imagined futures perceptible through cognitive experiences (text, images, and film). How can fiction offer a space for imagination and provide clues to directions for innovation and change? This section deals with this question and opens the debate with the thought that science fiction helps us to understand less, for example, what the future of a technology looks like and more about the social relationships of that technology; it is taken and imagined for how it could be used—whom it could be used for and whom it could be used against (Doctorow; Bassett). According to the tenor of the subsequent contributions, art, as well as creative exchange and collaboration, could help to question or even rethink the prevailing narratives about for whom or for what a future is conceived (Papadimitriou). Science fiction in the context of art could thus become an experimental laboratory in which one learns to constructively imagine a range of possible futures and communicate them to others (Brueckner). In particular, the prototypical realization of the future—as we can experience all too often not only in art, but especially in movies—would even have the advantage that the presented fiction could convey the realism of future developments and thereby fuel dialogues about this future before any concrete realization (Kirby). In fiction however, as we learn from cognitive science, a balance must be achieved between conjecture and plausibility that manages to both involve speculations about unexpected people, objects, and events, and, at the same time, suggest something plausible that could actually happen (Keane). In all of this—if futurecasting is to be successful—the emotional factor must not be missing (Popper).

Making imagined futures tangible through direct experience with objects and space or role-playing games or performances is the subject of the subsequent section on "Futurecasting with Matter." This is therefore about embodiment, about experiencing the future through bodily experience. A physical experience of the future can unfold quite differently from the mere imagination. It is therefore advisable to try out and explore the future first before making a concrete realization (Montgomery). Experiences with artistic interventions in particular—whether through spatially tangible installations (Time's Up) or artifacts (Livne)—can help to gain insights into the lived possibilities of a future. Sensory experience through interaction can lead to a promising way of making the new tangible. Embodied learning frees individuals from their prejudices (Larsen; Damhof). This insight also leads us to the topic of participation. Performance and play, art, experiments, and design artifacts open up the possibility of involving individuals in a collective investigation to explore alternative futures and systemic change (Selin). Not involving individuals in the future and letting them experience it can even turn an imagined future into a dystopia (Comi). Bringing the future to life in different contexts and conveying it in a memorable way is therefore one of the most central tasks of futurists (DaVanzo). How the future can not only be made plausible for a large number of actors, but also be anchored in reality, is shown in concrete terms by the remarks on games (Flanagan), on role-playing in the policy-maker environment (Bontoux), and on staged transformative experiences through artistic-playful interventions in the field of organizational consulting (Pavlakis).

The book ends with practical learning points. There is a look at strategy work in organizations. We learn that a pure analysis and foresight process for adapting to the future hardly helps. A creative-analytical imagining process that proactively shapes the future is required (Schwuchow). The conventional approach to the future is being called into question (Oetinger). Futurecasting with its unconstrained imagination is then an important leap forward from conventional strategy.

References

Ackoff, R. L. 1974. ***Redesigning the future - A systems approach to societal problems***. New York: Wiley & Sons.

Ackoff, R. L., Magidson, J., & Addison, H. J. 2006. ***Idealized design: Creating an organization's future***. New Jersey: Wharton.

ADB. 2020. ***Futures thinking in Asia and the Pacific: Why foresight matters for policy makers.*** Manila, Philippines: ADB.

Adam, B., & Groves, C. 2007. ***Future matters: Action, knowledge, ethics.*** Leiden: Brill.

Addis, D. R., Wong, A. T., & Schacter, D. L. 2007. Remembering the past and imagining the future: common and distinct neural substrates during event construction and elaboration. ***Neuropsychologia***, 45(7): 1363-1377.

Akin, Ö. 1986. ***Psychology of architectural design***. London: Pion.

Aldabbagh, I., & Allawzi, S. 2019. Rethinking scenario planning potential role in strategy making and innovation: A conceptual framework based on examining trends towards scenarios and firms strategy. ***Academy of Strategic Management Journal***, 18(5): 1-14.

Allan, B. M., Nimmo, D. G., Ierodiaconou, D., VanDerWal, J., Koh, L. P., & Ritchie, E. G. 2018. Futurecasting ecological research: the rise of technoecology. ***Ecosphere***, 9(5): e02163.

Ansoff, I. 1965. ***Corporate strategy***. New York: McGraw Hill.

Appadurai, A. 2014. Foreword. In S. Yelavich, & B. Adams (eds.), ***Design as future-making***: 9-11. London: Bloomsbury Publishing.

Arnheim, R. 1993. Sketching and the psychology of design. ***Design Issues***, 9(2): 15-19.

Austrian Federal Ministry of Education, Science and Research. 2022. ***Austrian University Development Plan [Gesamtösterreichischer Universitätsentwicklungsplan] 2025-2030,*** Oct 2023 ed.

Banathy, B. H. 2000. ***Guided evolution of society: A systems view***. New York: Kluwer Academic/Plenum Publishers.

Bateson, G. 2000 [1972]. ***Steps to an ecology of mind: Collected essays in anthropology, psychiatry, evolution, and epistemology***. Chicago: University of Chicago Press.

Berger, P. L., & Luckmann, T. 1966. ***The social construction of reality: A treatise in the sociology of knowledge***. New York: Anchor Books.

Bohm, D. 1980 [2002]. ***Wholeness and the implicate order***. Oxford: Routledge.

Bohm, D., & Peat, F. D. 1987 [2011]. ***Science, order and creativity***. Oxford: Routledge.

Bratianu, C. 2010. ***A critical analysis of Nonaka's model of knowledge dynamics***. Paper presented at the Proceedings of the 2nd European Conference on Intellectual Capital, ISCTE Lisbon University Institute, Lisbon, Portugal.

Braungart, M., McDonough, W., & Bollinger, A. 2007. Cradle-to-cradle design: creating healthy emissions–a strategy for eco-effective product and system design. ***Journal of cleaner production***, 15(13-14): 1337-1348.

Buchanan, R. 1992. Wicked problems in design thinking. ***Design issues***, 8(2): 5-21.

Byrne, R. M. 2007. ***The rational imagination: How people create alternatives to reality***. Cambridge, MA: MIT Press.

Byrne, R. M. 2016. Counterfactual thought. ***Annual review of psychology***, 67: 135-157.

Comi, A., & Whyte, J. 2018. Future making and visual artefacts: An ethnographic study of a design project. ***Organization studies***, 39(8): 1055-1083.

Connell, L., & Keane, M. T. 2003. ***PAM: A cognitive model of plausibility***. Paper presented at the Proceedings of the Twenty-Fifth Annual Conference of the Cognitive Science Society, Hillsdale, NJ.

Connell, L., & Keane, M. T. 2004. What plausibly affects plausibility? Concept coherence and distributional word coherence as factors influencing plausibility judgments. ***Memory & Cognition***, 32(2): 185-197.

Connell, L., & Keane, M. T. 2006. A model of plausibility. ***Cognitive Science***, 30(1): 95-120.

Cordova-Pozo, K., & Rouwette, E. A. 2023. Types of scenario planning and their effectiveness: A review of reviews. ***Futures***: 103153.

Cross, N. 2006. ***Designerly ways of knowing***. London: Springer.

Cross, N., & Cross, A. C. 1996. Winning by design: the methods of Gordon Murray, racing car designer. ***Design studies***, 17(1): 91-107.

Cuff, D. 1992. ***Architecture: The story of practice***. Cambridge, MA: MIT Press.

Cuhls, K. 2003. From forecasting to foresight processes—new participative foresight activities in Germany. ***Journal of forecasting***, 22(2-3): 93-111.

D'Argembeau, A., & Linden, M. van der. 2004. Phenomenal characteristics associated with projecting oneself back into the past and forward into the future: Influence of valence and temporal distance. ***Consciousness and cognition***, 13(4): 844-858.

Dorst, K., & Cross, N. 2001. Creativity in the design process: co-evolution of problem–solution. ***Design studies***, 22(5): 425-437.

Dunne, A., & Raby, F. 2013. ***Speculative everything: design, fiction, and social dreaming***. Cambridge, MA: MIT Press.

Epstude, K., & Roese, N. J. 2008. The functional theory of counterfactual thinking. ***Personality and social psychology review***, 12(2): 168-192.

Epstude, K., Scholl, A., & Roese, N. J. 2016. Prefactual thoughts: Mental simulations about what might happen. ***Review of General Psychology***, 20(1): 48-56.

Evans, R. 1997. ***Translations from drawing to building***. London: Architectural Association.

Flanagan, M. 2013. ***Critical play: Radical game design***. Cambridge, MA: MIT Press.

Gardner, J. A. 2011. ***Innovation and the future proof bank: A practical guide to doing different business-as-usual***. Chichester: John Wiley & Sons.

Gero, J. S., & Mc Neill, T. 1998. An approach to the analysis of design protocols. ***Design studies***, 19(1): 21-61.

Gilbert, C. G. 2005. Unbundling the structure of inertia: Resource versus routine rigidity. ***Academy of Management Journal***, 48(5): 741-763.

Gilbert, D. T., & Wilson, T. D. 2007. Prospection: Experiencing the future. ***Science***, 317(5843): 1351-1354.

Glenn, J. C., & International, T. F. G. 2009. Scenarios. In J. C. Glenn (ed.), ***The Millennium Project: Futures Research Methodology—V3.0***.

Goodman, N. 1978. ***Ways of worldmaking***. Indianapolis: Hackett Publishing.

Gourlay, S. 2006. Conceptualizing knowledge creation: A critique of Nonaka's theory. ***Journal of management studies***, 43(7): 1415-1436.

Halford, S., & Southerton, D. 2023. What future for the sociology of futures? Visions, concepts and methods. ***Sociology,*** 57(2): 263-278.

Hassabis, D., & Maguire, E. A. 2007. Deconstructing episodic memory with construction. ***Trends in cognitive sciences***, 11(7): 299-306.

Havelock, E. A. 1986. ***The muse learns to write: Reflections on orality and literacy from antiquity to the present***. New Haven: Yale University Press.

Hayashi, A. 2021. ***Social presencing theater: The art of making a true move.*** Cambridge, MA: PI Press.

Heijden, K. van der. 2005. ***Scenarios: The art of strategic conversation*** (2nd ed.). Chichester: John Wiley & Sons.

Hoch, S. J. 1985. Counterfactual reasoning and accuracy in predicting personal events. ***Journal of Experimental Psychology: Learning, Memory, and Cognition***, 11(4): 719.

Hoe, S. L. 2006. Tacit knowledge, Nonaka and Takeuchi SECI model and informal knowledge processes. ***International Journal of Organization Theory & Behavior***, 9(4): 490-502.

Inayatullah, S. 2013. Using gaming to understand the patterns of the future-the sarkar game in action. ***Journal of Futures Studies***, 18(1): 1-12.

Isaacs, W. 1999. ***Dialogue: The art of thinking together***. Surry Hills, NSW: Currency.

Isaacs, W. N. 1993. Taking flight: Dialogue, collective thinking, and organizational learning. ***Organizational dynamics***, 22(2): 24-39.

Jenlink, P. M., & Banathy, B. H. 2008. Dialogue and designing our future: Conversation as culture creating and consciousness evolving. In P. M. Jenlink, & B. H. Banathy, ***Dialogue as a collective means of design conversation***: 159-168. Boston: Springer.

Johnson-Laird, P. N. 1983. ***Mental models: Towards a cognitive science of language, inference, and consciousness***. Cambridge, MA: Harvard University Press.

Johnson, B. D. 2011. ***Science fiction prototyping: Designing the future with science fiction***. San Rafael, CA: Morgan & Claypool Publishers.

Johnson, B. D., Vanatta, N., & Coon, C. 2021. ***Threatcasting***. Cham: Springer.

Johnson, M. K., & Sherman, S. J. 1990. Constructing and reconstructing the past and the future in the present. In E. T. Higgins, & R. M. Sorrentino (eds.), ***Handbook of motivation and cognition: Foundations of social behavior***, Vol. 2: 482–526. New York: The Guilford Press.

Kahneman, D., & Miller, D. T. 1986. Norm theory: Comparing reality to its alternatives. ***Psychological review***, 93(2): 136.

Kahneman, D., & Tversky, A. 1973. On the psychology of prediction. ***Psychological review***, 80(4): 237.

Kahneman, D., & Tversky, A. 1982. The simulation heuristic. In D. Kahneman, P. Slovic, & A. Tversky (eds.), ***Judgment under Uncertainty: Heuristics and Biases***: 201-208. Cambridge, UK: Cambridge University Press.

Klein, J. T. 2017. The Boundary Work of Making in Digital Humanities. In J. Sayers (ed.), ***Making things and drawing boundaries: Experiments in the digital humanities***: 21-31. Minneapolis: University of Minnesota Press.

Koolhaas, R. 1991. Imagining the Nothingness (1985). In J. Lucan (ed.), ***OMA - Koolhaas, Rem: Architecture 1970-1990***: 156-157. New York: Princeton Architectural Press.

Kosow, H., & Gaßner, R. 2008. ***Methods of future and scenario analysis: overview, assessment, and selection criteria***. Bonn: Deutsches Institut für Entwicklungspolitik gGmbH.

Kostof, S. 1977 [2000]. ***The architect: Chapters in the history of the profession***. Berkeley - Los Angeles: Univ of California Press.

Kövecses, Z. 2010. ***Metaphor: A practical introduction***. Oxford: Oxford University Press.

Kurtzman, J. 1984. ***Futurecasting: Charting a Way to Your Future***. Palm Springs: ETC Publications.

Lakoff, G., & Johnson, M. 1980 [2003]. ***Metaphors we live by*** (2003 ed.). Chicago: University of Chicago Press.

Lawson, B. 1980. ***How designers think: The design process demystified,*** 4th 2007 ed. Amsterdam: Elsevier.

Leask, M., & Younie, S. 2021. ***Education for all in times of crisis: Lessons from Covid-19***. Oxford: Routledge.

Lee, R. J. 2018. Strategic foresight methods in the public and private sectors. ***Air & Space Power Journal***, 32(2): 60-73.

Lee, S., Parthasarathi, T., & Kable, J. W. 2021. The ventral and dorsal default mode networks are dissociably modulated by the vividness and valence of imagined events. ***Journal of Neuroscience***, 41(24): 5243-5250.

Levitas, R. 2013. ***Utopia as method: The imaginary reconstitution of society.*** London: Palgrave Macmillan.

Lloyd, P., & Scott, P. 1994. Discovering the design problem. ***Design studies***, 15(2): 125-140.

Lombardo, T. 2006. ***The evolution of future consciousness: The nature and historical development of the human capacity to think about the future***. Bloomington, IN: AuthorHouse.

Lombardo, T. 2007. The evolution and psychology of future consciousness. ***Journal of Futures Studies***, 12(1): 1-24.

Magruk, A. 2017. Concept of uncertainty in relation to the foresight research. ***Engineering Management in Production and Services***, 9(1): 46-55.

Magruk, A. 2020. Uncertainties, knowledge, and futures in foresight studies—a case of the industry 4.0. Форсайт, 14(4 (eng)): 20-33.

Manetti, A., Lara-Navarra, P., & Sánchez-Navarro, J. 2022. Possibilities for futurecasting: Designing a digital map of trends. ***Artnodes,*** (30): 1-10.

Manzini, E. 2015. ***Design, when everybody designs: An introduction to design for social innovation***. Cambridge, MA: MIT press.

March, J. G., & Simon, H. A. 1958. ***Organizations***. New York: Wiley.

Markman, K. D., & McMullen, M. N. 2003. A reflection and evaluation model of comparative thinking. ***Personality and Social Psychology Review***, 7(3): 244-267.

Markus, H., & Nurius, P. 1986. Possible selves. ***American psychologist***, 41(9): 954.

Markus, H., & Ruvolo, A. 1989. Possible selves: Personalized representations of goals. In L. A. Pervin (ed.), ***Goal concepts in personality and social psychology***: 211–241. London: Lawrence Erlbaum Associates, Inc.

Martin, B. R. 1995. Foresight in science and technology. ***Technology analysis & strategic management***, 7(2): 139-168.

Mietzner, D., & Reger, G. 2005. Advantages and disadvantages of scenario approaches for strategic foresight. ***International Journal of Technology Intelligence and Planning***, 1(2): 220-239.

Mills, J. H. 2003. ***Making sense of organizational change***. London: Routledge.

Nisbet, R. A. 1969. ***Social change and history: Aspects of the western theory of development***. New York: Oxford University Press.

Nonaka, I. 1994. A dynamic theory of organizational knowledge creation. ***Organization Science***, 5(1): 14-37.

Nyiri, J. C. 1988. Tradition and practical knowledge. In J. C. Nyiri, & B. Smith (eds.), ***Practical knowledge: Outlines of a theory of traditions and skills***: 17-52. London: Croom Helm.

Papanek, V., & Fuller, R. B. 1972. ***Design for the real world: Human ecology and social change.*** Toronto/New York/London: Bantam Books.

Parman, L. 2013. ***Above the fray: Leading yourself, your business and others during turbulent times***. New York: Morgan James Publishing.

Peirce, C. S. 1965. ***Collected papers of Charles Sanders Peirce***. Cambridge, MA: Harvard University Press.

Polanyi, M. 1958. ***Personal knowledge: Towards a post-critical philosophy*** (Paperback 1958 ed.). Chicago: The University of Chicago Press.

Polanyi, M. 1966. ***The tacit dimension***. London: Routledge&Kegan Paul.

Prahalad, C. K., & Bettis, R. A. 1986. The dominant logic: A new linkage between diversity and performance. ***Strategic Management Journal***, 7(6): 485-501.

Ramírez, R., & Selin, C. 2014. Plausibility and probability in scenario planning. ***Foresight***, 16(1): 54-74.

Ramirez, R., & Wilkinson, A. 2016. ***Strategic reframing: The Oxford Scenario Planning Approach***. Oxford: Oxford University Press.

RAND. 2024. ***Wargaming,*** Vol. 2024: RAND Corporation.

Rittel, H. W., & Webber, M. M. 1984. Planning problems are wicked problems. ***Developments in design methodology***: 135-144.

Robinson, J. B. 1990. Futures under glass: A recipe for people who hate to predict. ***Futures***, 22(8): 820-842.

Roese, N. J., & Hur, T. 1997. Affective determinants of counterfactual thinking. ***Social cognition***, 15(4): 274-290.

Roese, N. J., & Morrison, M. 2009. The psychology of counterfactual thinking. ***Historical Social Research/Historische Sozialforschung***. 10-20.

Roese, N. J., & Olson, J. M. 2014. ***What might have been: The social psychology of counterfactual thinking***. New York: Psychology Press.

Rowe, P. G. 1991. ***Design thinking.*** Cambridge, MA: MIT Press.

Sayers, J. 2017. On the "Maker Turn" in the Humanities. In J. Sayers (ed.), ***Making things and drawing boundaries: Experiments in the digital humanities***: 32-41. Minneapolis: University of Minnesota Press.

Schacter, D. L., Addis, D. R., & Buckner, R. L. 2007. Remembering the past to imagine the future: the prospective brain. ***Nature reviews neuroscience***, 8(9): 657-661.

Schatzki, T. R. 2002. ***The site of the social: A philosophical account of the constitution of social life and change.*** Pennsylvania: Penn State University Press.

Schön, D. A. 1983. ***The reflective practitioner: How professionals think in action***. New York: Basic Books.

Schrage, M. 2000. ***Serious play: How the world's best companies simulate to innovate***. Boston: Harvard Business School Press.

Schwartz, P. 1996. ***The art of the long view: Planning for the future in an uncertain world***. New York: Crown Currency.

Searle, J. R. 1995. ***The construction of social reality***. New York: Penguin Books.

Senge, P. M. 2003. Creating desired futures in a global economy. ***Reflections: The SoL Journal***, 5(1): 1-12.

Shamiyeh, M. 2007. Design new futures! ***Archis Volume Magazine,*** 14(4): 14-19.

Shamiyeh, M. 2009. ***The relevance of abduction for theory building and testing*** [Seminar paper]. St. Gallen: University of St. Gallen.

Shamiyeh, M. (ed.). 2010. ***Creating desired futures: How design innovates business***. Basel: Birkhäuser.

Shamiyeh, M. 2016. Designing from the future. In W. Brenner, & F. Uebernickel (eds.), ***Design thinking for innovation: Research and practice***: 193-219. Cham: Springer.

Simon, H. A. 1969. ***The science of the artificial*** (3rd 1996 ed.). Cambridge, MA: MIT Press.

Simon, H. A. 1986. ***Decision making and problem solving.*** Washington, DC: National Academy of Sciences.

Sterling, B. 2017. Design fiction: A field guide to ethnographic experiential futures. ***Wired,*** June 28. Accessed online https://www.wired.com/beyond-the-beyond/2017/06/design-fiction-field-guide-ethnographic-experiential-futures/. Viewed May 20, 2024.

Toffler, A. 1984. ***Future Shock***. New York: Bantam.

Tripsas, M. 2009. Technology, identity, and inertia through the lens of 'the digital photography company'. ***Organization science***, 20(2): 441-460.

Tripsas, M., & Gavetti, G. 2000. Capabilities, cognition, and inertia: Evidence from digital imaging. ***Strategic Management Journal***, 21(10/11): 1147-1161.

UNESCO. 2019. ***Futures literacy: Anticipation in the 21st century*** (SHS/2019/PI/H/10). Accessed online https://unesdoc.unesco.org/ark:/48223/pf0000372349. Viewed May 20, 2024.

Urry, J. 2016. ***What is the Future?*** Cambridge, UK: Polity Press.

Vanatta, N., & Johnson, B. D. 2019. Threatcasting: A framework and process to model future operating environments. ***The Journal of Defense Modeling and Simulation***, 16(1): 79-88.

Vervoort, J. M., Bendor, R., Kelliher, A., Strik, O., & Helfgott, A. E. 2015. Scenarios and the art of worldmaking. ***Futures***, 74: 62-70.

Wack, P. 1985. Scenarios: Uncharted waters ahead. ***Harvard Business Review***, 63(5): 72-89.

Walter, O. 1982. ***Orality and literacy: the technologizing of the word.*** London and New York: Taylor and Francis Group.

Weick, K. E. 1995. ***Sensmaking in organizations***. Thousands Oaks:
Sage Publications.

Weick, K. E., Sutcliffe, K. M., & Obstfeld, D. 2005. Organizing and the process of sensemaking. ***Organization Science***, 16(4): 409-421.

Whyte, J., Comi, A., & Mosca, L. 2022. Making futures that matter: Future making, online working and organizing remotely. ***Organization Theory***, 3(1): 26317877211069138.

Wilkinson, A. 2009. Scenarios practices: In search of theory. ***Journal of futures studies***, 13(3): 107-114.

Wilkinson, A., & Eidinow, E. 2008. Evolving practices in environmental scenarios:
A new scenario typology. ***Environmental Research Letters***, 3(4): 045017.

Wilkinson, L. 1995. How to build scenarios. ***Wired,*** (11): 74-81.

Wolf, M. J. 2014. ***Building imaginary worlds: The theory and history of subcreation***.
New York, London: Routledge.

Wolf, M. J. 2017. ***Revisiting imaginary worlds***. New York, London: Routledge.

Woodruff, M. 1969. ***The secrets of foretelling your own future***. New York: The World Publishing Co.

Yelavich, S., & Adams, B. 2014. ***Design as future-making***. London: Bloomsbury Publishing.

PRELIMINARY CONDITIONS

Photo: Erich Goldmann

TRUDI LANG

CO-DIRECTOR, OXFORD-HYUNDAI
MOTOR GROUP FORESIGHT CENTRE
OXFORD, UNITED KINGDOM

SETTLING-IN TO THE FUTURE: AN ORGANIZATIONAL IDENTITY PERSPECTIVE

TRUDI LANG AND GAIL CARSON

To realize and settle-in to plausible and desirable futures in the context of turbulence and unpredictable uncertainty, we propose that executives need to pay as much attention to explicit questions about their organization's identity as they do to questions about strategic choices. In futures and strategy engagements such as scenario planning, forecasting, search conferences, etc., there invariably comes a point where the consideration of new strategic options emanating from this work about "what we should do" comes up against current understandings of an organization's identity—"who we are." Unless the question of the organization's future identity is handled well, executives can experience inertia—"this option may make sense given the changes we are seeing in the world, but it is not aligned with who we are." As a result, they scale back ambitions to avoid imperiling the current identity but in so doing compromise the achievement of the strategic objectives they hold dear.

Organizational identity reflects executives' deep sense of a "collective self" (Ashforth, Schinoff, & Brickson, 2020: 30), which guides their judgment and action as to what is relevant, inspiring, and the right thing for their organization to do and not to do (March & Olsen, 2011). It can be formally defined as how "senior executives define the central and temporally coherent attributes of their organization that make it distinct from others (Albert & Whetten, 1985; Whetten, 2006)" (Lang, forthcoming: 3). Identity is defined through cycles of "sensemaking and sensegiving," where executives "periodically reconstruct shared understandings and revise formal claims of what their organization is and stands for" (Ravasi & Schultz, 2006: 436).

Organizational identity is core to questions of strategy ("what we as an organization choose to do"), with which it forms an interdependent relationship: "identity frames and shapes strategy while strategy enacts and informs identity (Ashforth & Mael, 1996; Schultz & Hernes, 2020; Sheard, 2009)" (Lang, forthcoming: 1). This interdependency means that, when considering different futures, organizational identity is inevitably a key consideration for executives.

Identity not only lends significant power of justification and meaning to what executives choose to do on behalf of their organizations (Normann, 2001). It also acts as a "perceptual screen" for what is observed in the external environment and how this is interpreted and acted on (Gioia & Thomas, 1996: 372; Tripsas, 2009). Consider the experience of the UK-based firm Rolls Royce, which produces power systems for civil and defense aerospace, marine, and nuclear applications (as discussed in Lang, forthcoming). Lang describes how, in 2014 and 2015, the firm issued five profit warnings indicating that the futures they were expecting had not arrived. The firm subsequently introduced a leadership program including scenario planning with the explicit intention of "creating a new set of filters" by which 150 executives could "think and talk differently" about their future context. Three scenarios were developed that enabled executives to take a fresh look at their changing environment and to explore questions of strategy and identity. A core outcome of this process was that it contributed to a shift in the organization's identity from an engineering to an industrial technology company with subsequent implications for the strategic options the firm chose to pursue.

Turbulence brings organizational identity front and center

In stable conditions, identity very often remains implicit because taken-for-granted assumptions about the context mean "what we choose to do" remains aligned with settled understandings of "who we are." However, in turbulent and unpredictably uncertain times, identity comes explicitly to the fore (Whetten, 2006), as Rolls Royce experienced. This is because, for executives, turbulence is not just about objective changes in the external environment but is subjectively experienced as a sense that "the 'ground' is in motion" (Emery & Trist, 1965:26) due to the interplay of those external changes and the organization's sense of who it is and, subsequently, what it does (McCann & Selsky, 1984). It is this interplay that raises questions for executives about whether their organization's identity and unique set of activities will remain relevant and successful. The consequence is that, when executives are considering very different future contexts for their organizations, discussions about identity will be evoked.

However, engaging explicitly with questions of identity is not always easy. Such conversations can be uncomfortable as they are less familiar for executives who are more oriented to "doing" than "being" and can feel threatening, even existential, for their organization, as well as having potential implications for their own professional and personal identities and roles. These conversations are even more complex when organizations work together, which many now increas-

Photo: WHO

GAIL CARSON

DIRECTOR OF NETWORK
DEVELOPMENT AT
ISARIC & CHAIR OF GOARN
OXFORD, UNITED KINGDOM

ingly do in order to have more influence over their context, capture big opportunities, and address complex, systemic problems (Ramirez, Lang, Finch, Carson, & Fisher, 2023). To enable their effective collaboration, executives from a diverse set of organizations must develop a joint identity that co-exists in relation to their own organizations' individual identities (Berkowitz, Brunsson, Grothe-Hammer, Sundberg, & Valiorgue, 2022).

Providing a safe and creative space for executives to imagine possible identity options and strategy implications ahead of time is key to settling-in to different futures effectively. Using scenarios for the organization's future context can be of help here (Lang, forthcoming). Acting as transitional objects (Winnicott, 1971), scenarios enable leaders to explore changes that will be needed between the present and the future without any immediate need for action (Burt, 2003; Ramirez & Drevon, 2005). Scenario-based strategic conversations can thus provide a learning experience for executives to explore questions of both identity and strategy evolution (Brown & Starkey, 2000).

To understand how this can work, we present the recent strategy development work of the Global Outbreak and Alert Response Network (GOARN) that was undertaken in the context of the turbulence of the COVID-19 pandemic.

GOARN engages with its identity as it sets its strategy

GOARN is a network of technical experts and institutions that prepare for and respond to disease outbreaks around the world. The network was created in 2000 to ensure more coordination of partners (members) during responses at the country level, and to facilitate working together outside emergencies. Over the subsequent decades it has grown to over 300 institutional partners and is hosted by the World Health Organization (WHO).

In 2021, GOARN decided to revise its strategy to ensure it remained strategically focused during the upcoming four-year period 2022-2026, given the turbulence caused by the pandemic. Health outbreaks tend to expose weaknesses in systems and this is exactly what happened with COVID-19 as it disrupted economies, supply chains, and health services, and laid bare social and income inequalities. The magnitude of the pandemic represented a significant change in GOARN's context, with ramifications for the group's strategy as one of the world's major preparedness and response organizations.

To ensure a sufficiently rich strategic conversation (Heijden, 2005) given the complexity of the changing context and the network itself, GOARN not only surveyed member-partners and interviewed key stakeholders, but also partnered with the Saïd Business School, University of Oxford to run a strategy lab. The lab involved four phases; surveying the strategic environment (contextual factors, key actors, and the way GOARN is currently organized to create value); developing a set of scenarios about how the network's future context might evolve; mapping future actors and their roles and relationships—"value-creating systems" (Ramirez & Mannervik, 2016: 31)—in each scenario; and generating strategic options. In all, around 100 people were involved.*

The scenarios and their related value-creating systems provided GOARN member-partners with the space to explore identity and strategy implications related to potential changes in their future context. One scenario, for example, explored the negative impact on global collaboration caused by rising geo-political tensions. In this world, GOARN's identity as a neutral network of technical experts comes to the fore, providing one way for countries to access needed assistance. During the scenario exercise, the strength and value of GOARN's neutrality surprised some within the network but it has led to a sense of confidence and clarity.

Another scenario explored the consequence of a demand for more national capacity-building to address disease outbreaks, building off the experience of nations in dealing with COVID-19. Taking a more in-country approach to preparedness and response contrasts with the historical deployment of global experts to help with a health emergency. For GOARN, it brought to the fore that they are a network of regional and national partners as much as a global grouping and can catalyze important in-country conversations. This puts more emphasis on GOARN's strategy being shaped and implemented by the member-partners in their specific parts of the world rather than only by the global steering committee or Geneva-based staff.

Yet another scenario explored the increasing involvement of the private sector in disease outbreak preparedness and response. The private sector played a significant role in the pandemic, and it was assumed in one scenario that this would continue. For GOARN, this led to an invaluable conversation about who the network was and may need to become vis-à-vis the private and public sectors. Language is important and "private sector" meant different things to different people. In particular, the scenario prompted a detailed consideration of governance models for GOARN as well as funding mechanisms. The outcome was clarity among the member-partners that GOARN was a public community group whose hosting by the WHO was a big part of who it was and that this should continue. To do well in this scenario would require strategies that complement (rather than compete with) the private sector.

A final scenario explored a world in which the number and nature of health emergencies, including due to climate change, overwhelms the effectiveness of the multilateral system. In its place, bilateral government relations emerge, along with collaborations with the private sector and professional health associations. For GOARN, this scenario was perhaps the most challenging as it would suggest that it could

---

* For a more detailed description of the scenarios and the strategy development process including the lab, see the Global Outbreak Alert and Response Network 2022-2026 strategy document: https://iris.who.int/bitstream/handle/10665/366066/9789240067028-eng.pdf?sequence=1 (Viewed April 23, 2024).

become more a grouping of individual health professionals supporting each other in their work, rather than a network of institutions coordinating their activities globally. The outcome of this conversation at the time was a clarity that this is not what member-partners think GOARN is or would want it to become. To do well in this scenario, the emphasis would be on the value of GOARN as a network rather than as an organization and, thus, on its ability to morph to meet the needs of the people, institutions, and governments it is supporting. One senior GOARN member, for example, could provide sufficient support in an outbreak as opposed to a large team or teams.

These insights from the scenarios were combined with survey outputs, stakeholder interviews, regional consultations, and the work of three groups who investigated certain strategic options in more detail, to draft the strategy. Reflecting the understanding that organizational identity frames and shapes strategy and strategy in turn enacts and informs identity, the strategy document (GOARN, 2023) outlined a set of identity claims (Albert & Whetten, 1985; Whetten, 2006) that were then followed by related strategic actions.

These claims were represented by statements of "is": GOARN is community centered; is committed to the global public health emergency; is about creating solutions for a better disease outbreak response; and is a collaborative network of institutions. Strategic actions were then listed below each of these claims as statements of "will." Listed, for example, under the heading "GOARN is community centered," is the action that the network will help build the capacity of local communities to support public health and outbreak responses.

The explicit engagement with questions of identity, and the rendering of identity claims, had three key benefits for GOARN as it settled-in to its future.

The first benefit came from directly engaging with the question that repeatedly came up throughout the process: "as part of the WHO family, who is GOARN, what makes us distinctive?" If this question had not been acknowledged and taken seriously this would have limited the quality of the strategic conversation and the resulting strategic actions, while also missing the opportunity to communicate, to all stakeholders, who the network understood itself to be (and not to be) as it positioned for the future.

A second benefit was providing essential clarity about something that, in effect, limited the range of acceptable strategic choices—what GOARN would do and not do. For example, it was decided that the network was an implementation organization rather than a standards-setting organization and that, therefore, setting standards was not an option for the strategy, and that that role should be left to others such as the WHO.

The third related benefit was that clarity about identity helped the network define what made it distinctive vis-à-vis others and what it could uniquely contribute that others could not, as well as what collaborations to pursue. A clear sense of identity has lent a sense of confidence and meaning to what GOARN does, and with whom.

Helpful principles to engage your organization's identity to settle-in to the future

Based on our experience working with GOARN and with many other public, private, and non-governmental organizations, we have found that the following suggestions are of help for executives wanting to engage with their organization's identity as a means of settling-in to new plausible and desirable futures.

Don't take identity for granted or as a static, implicitly unchallenged assumption. Keep in mind that the sense of turbulence is not only located in external changes in the environment, but also plays within, affecting subjective views of the identity and strategy of the organization. Acknowledging and engaging with the question of an organization's identity can create strategic value by providing insight and clarity for executives and other stakeholders, not least by making changes easier and cheaper to implement.

Use scenarios to create alternative frames of reference. Perceptions of and claims about a given view of an organization's identity are at the heart of the way executives frame their strategy and its future context. When changes start to emerge in the context, existing frames can limit what executives notice or how they interpret and act on those changes. Scenarios provide alternative frames of reference that enable executives to see differently and explore more possible implications than would be the case if only one frame was used (Ramirez & Wilkinson, 2016).

Invest sufficient time and resources. In the context of relatively stable conditions it is possible that strategy development processes are undertaken quickly with fewer resources and consultation. But engaging with the implications of potentially very different futures, especially when the organization itself is complex, means involving all relevant stakeholders and giving them time to converse, challenge pre-conceived understandings, and create new strategic options. It takes time for questions of identity to move from the implicit to the explicit and to be productively engaged with. Designing processes that enable this to happen will counter-intuitively save subsequent time and resources.

In our experience, the question of organizational identity is underestimated and inadequately attended to when executives develop strategy in turbulent conditions. As identity is usually implicit and executives are more comfortable with doing rather than being, the explicit question of "who the organization may need to become" is far less familiar. Developing the capacity to expertly engage with questions of identity will help executives and their organizations to more effectively (and at less cost) create and settle-in to truly new and desirable future courses of action.

Acknowledgments

The authors wish to acknowledge the support of the Saïd Business School, University of Oxford and the Wellcome Trust and to thank all those involved in the GOARN strategy development work for their contribution to the ideas discussed in this article.

References

Albert, S., & Whetten, D. A. 1985. Organizational identity. ***Research in Organizational Behavior***, 7: 263-295.

Ashforth, B. E., & Mael, F. A. 1996. Organizational identity and strategy as a context for the individual. ***Advances in Strategic Management***, 13: 19-64.

Ashforth, B., Schinoff, B., & Brickson, S. 2020. "My company is friendly," "mine's a rebel": Anthropomorphism and shifting organizational identity from "what" to "who". ***Academy of Management Review,*** 45(1): 29-57.

Berkowitz, H., Brunsson, N., Grothe-Hammer, M., Sundberg, M., & Valiorgue, B. 2022. Meta-Organizations: A clarification and a way forward. ***M@n@gement,*** 25(2): 1-9.

Brown, A., & Starkey, K. 2000. Organizational identity and learning: A psychodynamic perspective. ***The Academy of Management Review***, 25(1): 102-120.

Burt, G. 2003. Epigenetic change: New from the seeds of the old. ***Strategic Change,*** 12(7): 381-393.

Emery. F., & Trist, E. 1965. The causal texture of organisational environments. ***Human Relations,*** 18(1): 21-32.

Gioia, D., & Thomas, J. 1996. Identity, image and issue interpretation: Sensemaking during strategic change in academia. ***Administrative Science Quarterly,*** 41(3): 370-403.

Heijden, K. van der. 2005. ***Scenarios: The art of strategic conversation,*** *2nd edition*. Chichester: John Wiley & Sons.

Lang, T. forthcoming. Being and becoming: Reconciling the temporal mismatch between organizational identity and strategy by providing identity with a future. ***Strategic Management Review.***

March, J., & Olsen, J. 2011. The logic of appropriateness. In R. Goodin (ed.), ***The Oxford Handbook of Political Science***: 1-22. Oxford: Oxford University Press.

McCann, J., & Selsky, J. 1984. Hyperturblence and the emergence of type 5 environments. ***Academy of Management Review,*** 9(4): 460-470.

Normann, R., 2001. ***Reframing Business: When the map changes the landscape.*** Chichester: John Wiley & Sons.

Ramirez, R., & Drevon, C. 2005. The role and limits of methods in transitional change processes. In G. Amado, & L. Vansina (eds.), ***The Transitional Approach in Action***: 192-226. London: Karnak Books.

Ramirez, R., & Mannervik, U. 2016. ***Strategy for a Networked World.*** London: Imperial College Press.

Ramirez, R., & Wilkinson, A. 2016***. Strategic Reframing: The Oxford scenario planning approach.*** Oxford: Oxford University Press.

Ramirez, R., Lang, T., Finch, M., Carson, G., & Fisher, D. 2023. Strategizing across organizations. ***MIT Sloan Management Review,*** Spring.

Ravasi, D., & Schultz, M. 2006. Responding to organizational identity threats: Exploring the role of organizational culture. ***Academy of Management Journal,*** 49(3): 433-458.

Schultz, M., & Hernes, T. 2020. Temporal interplay between strategy and identity: Punctuated, subsumed, and sustained modes. ***Strategic Organization***, 18(1): 106-135.

Sheard, G. 2009. Strategy as a feature of reflective action: Edmund Husserl's theories as a temporal model of organisational identity. ***Philosophy of Management***, 7(2): 25-40.

Tripsas, M. 2009. Technology, identity, and inertia through the lens of 'The Digital Photography Company'. ***Organization Science***, 20(2): 441-460.

Whetten, D. A. 2006. Albert and Whetten revisited—Strengthening the concept of organizational identity. ***Journal of Management Inquiry,*** 15(3): 219–234.

Winnicott, D. 1971. ***Playing and Reality.*** London: Routledge.

World Health Organization. 2023. ***Global Outbreak Alert and Response Network (GOARN): strategy 2022-2026.*** World Health Organization. Available online https://iris.who.int/handle/10665/366066. Viewed February 5, 2024.

Photo: Erich Goldmann
ALEXANDER MANKOWSKY
FUTURES STUDIES AND IDEATION,
FORMERLY AT MERCEDES-BENZ
BERLIN, GERMANY

DOS AND DON'TS OF FUTURECASTING

Introduction

As a working definition for "futurecasting," I suggest "the activity of opening the views of an audience into a related reality, which is guided by predicted, relevant developments."

The intended realities should be related to the experienced reality, to avoid sci-fi or fantasy style imaginations. There are several hurdles to overcome, spanning from group think to individual anxieties. The goal of futurecasting should be the initiation of activities.

Since I have been working in this area for more than a decade now in the automotive industry, I want to share some of my experiences.

Let us start with what is better avoided: What NOT to do.

1. Don't sell change as progress

Progress is a metaphor for a development which is unavoidable, enriched with the notion that the future will become "better" through technology. In reality, "progress" has most often backfired in different ways. These effects are euphemistically called side-effects, which translates into unintended effects because of a lack of knowledge and imagination.

Cars, for example, have convenient features, with the unintended effect that they could lose all their electrical power when parked a while, waiting for "input." In effect, they could be rendered totally useless through progress. Progress in aerodynamics made getting into the front door so inconvenient that people chose SUVs over limousines, only in order to avoid bumping their heads on the A-pillar.

2. Avoid being too emotionally attached

The automotive industry operates as an organized interplay between very different professions. The overlap between these professions is—in the case of Mercedes-Benz—a strong brand, which serves as a beacon for everyone. Therefore, the futurist cannot expect to function as a leader or guide. A strong attachment to a desired outcome will be sensed by the other actors in the process, and lead to resistance.

Personally, I was too attached to "direct air capturing" as an industrial method of removing CO_2 from the atmosphere, where the auto industry could contribute through its competence in industrialization. Consequently, I failed.

3. Do not teach

Some colleagues tend to hold speeches full of data and expert jargon. The assumption is that, when lectured well enough, people will automatically come to the proposed conclusions themselves. If it fails, gather more data, extend the "back-up" files. More proof! Try the same approach, only harder. After consuming all their mental energy, these colleagues end up as cynics or worse. Nobody listened!

I would call this the Watzlawick-Fallacy, after Paul Watzlawick's famous booklet "How to Fail Most Successfully," a must-read for practical working futurists.

But WHAT to do?

Preparation

To ground the futurist mindset, it is useful to select theoretical models which are open to different, not competing, interpretations of "reality." I have found constructivism very helpful, since the concept allows for tweaking "realities" freely, which helps with the process of imagining different futures. Radical constructivism was presented by Humberto Maturana and Francisco Varela in *The Tree of Knowledge: The Biological Roots of Human Understanding* in 1992.

Practical applications can be found in therapeutics as set out by Paul Watzlawick. In organizational development, this is called "systemic counseling." Nowadays, neuroscience has done a great deal to underscore and limit the scope of constructivism.

If the transformational process deals with existential threats, like the reaction to global warming, therapeutic advice should be included in the preparation.

Further preparation should be done in developing one or more conceptual actor models, as used in the social sciences. We want to open the room for activities with futurecasting; therefore, actor models are useful. Contemplating possible futures would be insufficient.

Remember: It is unlikely that today's challenge has never happened before in a similar way. People were not stupid in the past. Studies on the topic in question that address previous best and worst practices are extraordinarily helpful.

Be critical with promised technical solutions for real-world challenges. The tech industry is magnificent in marketing its products, like AI or whatever it has invested in. Try to understand what the true opportunities and limits are. The promises of AI are the worst in the field—people are prone to interpret AI as anthropomorphic, following the guiding marketing metaphors of the industry. They have difficulties understanding machine learning as applied statistics. It is the job of the futurist to push them to understand—not to ride the wave. The same, or similar, applies to robotics, block chain, NFT, cyber whatsoever, or metaverse. These are known, path-dependent technologies, disguised by fresh marketing.

Train your sense of time: Technological development is—compared with our personal perception of time—slow, very slow. Developments typically run over decades. You can realize these time spans if you follow basic scientific research, then the first application in the military industry, until the technology reaches the first commercial applications. The Internet, with its already existing distribution networks, can give the impression of speed, but only the distribution is speedy, not the distributed technology itself.

What really can happen fast is cultural, social, and political change. Long simmering conflicts can dissipate in weeks—think of the fall of the Berlin Wall. Only this kind of disruption can emerge overnight.

Once we are prepared with a fitting theoretical background, certainty about the means available in the future, and a pragmatic actor model, it is time to create mind-opening stories and visualizations. This task will test your talent, nobody can help you out.

Dos in applied futurism

1. Be responsible

What I learned about responsibility: If an impulse bears fruit, and people start to work on it, then it will become very expensive. Nothing can be got on the cheap in industry. As an example, I was involved in the initiation of a device that was tiny—compared to the whole car—for bringing pleasant perfume into the interior of cars. Today's ubiquitous fragrance device in the Mercedes cars took ages to develop, since it was unknown before. The marker lamps for self-driving cars, which are now going to be introduced in China, are similar. So be careful and double-check your sources, the dynamism of your framework, and your own enthusiasm.

2. Look for diversity

Typically, I am invited to internal talks and workshops, sometimes over longer time spans in development processes. In the company, I rely on a network of open-minded people from different departments with different perspectives on topics. The importance of intellectual, emotional, and practical diversity cannot be overstated.

3. Listen and learn

Follow any invitation on your topic, as long it is a relevant one for the audience. People may not be labeled as "executives," "thought leaders," or "leaders" at all, but they may contribute with surprising perspectives. Once, when talking about the rush to follow the "inventions" of Big Tech (in this case Microsoft's ChatGPT), one man came up with a perfect metaphor: We tell our children "not to take chocolate offered by strangers." It is the same with Big Tech. Everybody understood immediately.

Moreover, you will be able to refine and test your impulse on real everyday cases, with professions you may never have heard of.

4. Humor

Ten thousand troubles waving from the shore. Light and easy. (Amanda Jenssen, Hymns for the Haunted, 2012).

Not everybody is open for change, like the girl about whom Amanda Jenssen sang to us. Some people may be scared. Therefore, a lightweight approach is best suited to give your audience room for imagination. Tension can be released by laughter, discussing afterwards is much easier.

Most important: Initiate creation

The auto industry has the advantage of creating tangible visions of the future in the form of research, or show cars. Therefore, my impulses have often targeted the creation of these artifacts. Once people can work together on a relevant object, the discourse tends to become constructive. The resistance of material is needed to order the thoughts.

At last: Creating something is rewarding: Showing it to the public on a given date provides thrust and energy.

STATEMENT

MARIE RINGLER

MEMBER OF THE GLOBAL
LEADERSHIP GROUP ASHOKA
VIENNA, AUSTRIA

Skills for our uncertain future: Let's ask kids which problem they'll solve, not which career they'll choose.

We live in an era of rapid change across various domains, from technology to human rights to climate. We often forget the importance of intergenerational exchange in shaping that future in ways that will benefit all: Putting children and young people's wisdom and agency at the center is essential to drive meaningful solutions.

We're all familiar with the classic question asked of youngsters, "What do you want to be when you grow up?" It's a staple inquiry, especially during family gatherings.

Yet, it's time to retire this question, not because we lack interest in our children's futures but because their paths won't necessarily adhere to conventional career trajectories. They're growing up in a world that demands adaptability and innovation for success.

Instead of asking about future professions, why not inquire, "What problem do you want to solve?"

The spark for making change often ignites early in life—and the earlier it starts, the grander the aspirations become. This underscores the vital role of adults as supportive guides rather than as controllers for future innovators.

The earlier young people adopt a mindset focused on making a difference and problem-solving, the more likely they will seek profound societal transformations later in life. This was evident in our recent Global Fellows Impact Report at Ashoka (Post Reporters, 2022), where we discovered that 43% of Ashoka Fellows (Ashoka, n.d.) initiated their own projects to create change in their communities before the age of 20. Ashoka Fellows are recognized leaders in the field of social entrepreneurship who have demonstrated innovative systems-changing solutions to pressing social and environmental challenges. These individuals are selected based on the impact and sustainability of their initiatives, and they become part of a global network of changemakers supported by Ashoka. Through their work, Ashoka Fellows inspire and empower others to create positive change in their communities and beyond. Through their systems-changing work, Ashoka Fellows report changing, on average, the lives of 800,000 people annually.

Further exploration revealed an interesting correlation: Those Ashoka Fellows who took leadership roles at a young age were more inclined to collaborate with various partners later in life, such as NGOs, universities, media outlets, and companies. They also demonstrated a penchant for effecting profound change by influencing social norms and cultural mindsets, envisioning a world where everyone contributes to positive transformation.

In a rapidly evolving world, the skills of a changemaker are paramount. How can we move away from traditional notions of education and growing up and instead foster the development of changemaker abilities that are essential in an uncertain future?

Skills like empathy, collaborative leadership, teamwork, and creative problem-solving will always be in demand as our world continues to evolve.

Reflecting on my own journey, I'm grateful for the early opportunities I had to engage in changemaking. Inspired by the legacy of my grandparents, who fought against injustice during the Second World

War, I resisted gender stereotypes even as a 10-year-old. Whether as an activist during the early days of the Internet, a young politician advocating for government transparency, or an entrepreneur contributing to the launch of Ashoka in Austria, I drew upon those early experiences and the examples set by changemakers who inspired me.

Today, I'm continually inspired by the changemakers I encounter, many of whom are young people like Alejandra Acosta, who tackled the issue of sexual violence against women in Spain. Alejandra and her team of ambitious young women collaborated with local policymakers, reaching tens of thousands of teenagers with workshops aimed at combating gender-based violence and human trafficking in their communities.

Stories like Alejandra's highlight how young people make their voices heard and mobilize for change. As adults, our role is to create an environment where everyone feels supported and empowered to address the issues they're passionate about.

To build this environment, we need adults—specifically, non-controlling adult allies who create space for children and young people to grow as changemakers without taking over. Ashoka Fellows are already doing this; the vast majority who work with young people are putting them in charge (89%). In Ashoka's Global Fellows Impact Report, we found that of the social entrepreneurs (43%) who started out as children or teenagers, 66% said that their parents played an important role in their development as a changemaker, compared with just 45% of those who didn't lead from a young age. They were also more likely to credit teachers (38%, compared with 24%). As Vinnicius, an Ashoka Young Changemaker from Brazil (Ashoka, n.d.b), pointed out at a recent Ashoka Changemaker Summit (Ashoka, n.d.c), we currently have students from the 21st century, educators from the 20th century, and systems from the 19th century. He offers us a challenge: Reimagine education to prepare young people to follow their passions and drive decisions.

We live in a world of exponential change—regarding not just technology but also human rights, health care, the climate, and countless other issues. Uniting across generations, we can build forward for the welfare of future generations. Anyone, at any age, can contribute. We must trust that young people have the wisdom and agency to drive solutions.

So, what problem will you contribute to solving?

References

Ashoka. n.d. ***Ashoka fellows.*** Accessed online https://www.ashoka.org/en-gb/ashoka-fellows. Viewed March 14, 2024.

Ashoka. n.d.b. ***Vinnicius - Ashoka young changemaker.*** Accessed online https://www.ashoka.org/en-gb/changemaker/vinnicius. Viewed March 14, 2024.

Ashoka. n.d.c. ***The Ashoka Changemaker Summit.*** *Accessed online https://community.ashoka.org/en/ashoka-changemaker-summit. Viewed March 14, 2024.*

Break the Silence. 2018. ***Quiénes somos.*** Accessed online https://www.proyectobts.org/who-we-are. Viewed March 14, 2024.

Post Reporters. 2022. Ashoka global survey: Changemaker identity helps sustain lifelong work. ***Pioneers Post,*** February 25. https://www.pioneerspost.com/news-views/20220225/ashoka-global-survey-changemaker-identity-helps-sustain-lifelong-work. Viewed March 14, 2024.

GUIDO SCHWARTZ

STRATEGY & INNOVATION
LEAD, AIRBUS
LEIDEN, NETHERLANDS

Photo: Erich Goldmann

A TRANSFORMATIVE ENTREPRENEURIAL JOURNEY: ADDRESSING CORPORATE FUTURE CHALLENGES WITH INNOVATION AND INTRAPRENEURSHIP

Today, being competitive in the aerospace sector means staying ahead of the game and ensuring a mostly technology-driven advantage. With evolving consumer demands and a constantly changing environment, the aerospace industry has to adapt and innovate continuously. Ten years ago, back in 2013, the aerospace giant EADS anticipated that market dynamics would increase and that entrepreneurs in all industrial segments would start to disrupt existing and established business models, also in aerospace. EADS took the strongest and best-known brand within the portfolio and rebranded the company as Airbus—the European aerospace company. This was the first step under the leadership of the then CEO Tom Anders to embark the world's foremost aerospace manufacturer on a transformational journey, implementing entrepreneurship as a key initiative and a driver within the company. The motivation was to transform the aviation-driven company with a stable portfolio in single-aisle and wide-body aircraft into an innovative mobility provider through cross-divisional and international innovation initiatives. The company's motivation and strategy for tackling future challenges involved an array of innovative projects, ranging from Airbus BizLab or BlueBox to the Varhana project as part of the newly established Silicon Valley Innovation Center. Preparing for a challenging future with disruptive technological and business models, it saw the need to recruit global talent with the skills and mindsets to entrepreneurially transform the company.

The aerospace industry has always concentrated on incremental developments that take place over the years and, thus, keep the status quo, and on mainly providing customized solutions for existing global demand. Nowadays, rising environmental concerns and shifting customer expectations show that the sector faces new challenges. In particular, by 2014, the rise of entrepreneurship on a global scale was very present, with startups challenging the status quo with cheap and efficient space rockets, drone companies who focused on easy and efficient 3D prints, or electrical vehicles that displayed the end of the dominance of fossil fuel-burning cars. The shared economy started to grow and startups in all industries mushroomed and challenged established corporations. The future suddenly seemed to start looking different and Airbus realized that, in such a scenario, business as usual was no longer an option. The company did not want to get disrupted but, rather, wanted to disrupt itself and be prepared for this potential new future. The idea was to shift, with new talents, a different mindset, disruptive projects, dedicated budgets, adjacent business models, and top-management support, from being solely an aircraft manufacturer to being a holistic mobility company that offers innovative solutions beyond traditional aircraft. Driven by entrepreneurial mindsets, the company wanted to develop new technologies that shape markets before they exist. It wanted to have the first-mover advantage and drive developments from the beginning to create new, promising business models and products.

Various initiatives were launched to get insights into and opportunities to participate in this startup-driven world. One of the first was the creation of its own venture fund. Airbus recognized that the most groundbreaking ideas often emerged outside its traditional boundaries. "Airbus Ventures" provided the company with access to emerging technologies and startups while fostering external innovation and collaboration. It gave a glance to new ideas that might disrupt the market in some years and also showed opportunities for potential new technologies. The broad portfolio ranged from space technology to digitalization projects and beyond. For closer access and direct interaction with startups, the Airbus BizLab—Airbus's flagship accelerator program aimed at nurturing innovative ideas and startups within the aerospace and aviation industry—was established in 2015. The accelerator focused from the very start on aviation-relevant startups. With offices in Bangalore, Hamburg, Madrid, and Toulouse, a wide diversity of global startups could be attracted. Over time, the portfolio grew beyond aviation towards drones, remote sensing, and environmental and digitalization topics. The BizLab could leverage external talents and ideas while simultaneously fostering internal entrepreneurship for anticipated future scenarios. It was Airbus's response to the need for agility and innovation in a highly competitive environment. In a rapidly changing technological landscape, the company sought fresh and disruptive ideas to complement and match its internal research and development efforts. Airbus BizLab served as a bridge between the company and those innovative entrepreneurs, the startups, and its own intrapreneurs. Airbus BizLab provided selected startups with financial support, mentoring, office space, and access to Airbus's vast resources, networks, and expertise. By pushing these startups, Airbus could potentially accelerate the development of breakthrough technologies and solutions that aligned with the company's future expectations. Additionally, it helped to create a wider entrepreneurial mindset within Airbus itself, inspiring employees to think and act like entrepreneurs.

New initiatives emerged at the BizLab, such as #Africa4Future, which wanted to tap into the aerospace potential of the African continent's increasingly entrepreneurially driven and young population. Airbus's Africa for Future demonstrated the company's commitment to exploring opportunities in emerging markets. Created by a handful of motivated employees with African insights and innovation backgrounds, the initiative tapped into Africa's growth potential and entrepreneurial ideas. The initiative collaborated across the continent with local partners like Novato Africa, Silicon Cape, Innocircle, LaunchLab, MEST, or CCHub and was supported internally by the CTO of Airbus and the CEO of Airbus DS. This created momentum for looking with local partners into the future potential of the continent and identifying relevant opportunities—powered by the support of key executives within the company. This forward-looking, bottom-up approach with top-down support acknowledged the importance of this region, its future relevance, and specific innovations. It also took into account the future scenario of the growing, young African population and its needs for solutions in an African context, the soon-to-be-most populated continent on the planet with the youngest inhabitants. Communication motivated many employees internally to support this African initiative with their network and expertise in order to make it a success.

With the inauguration of the new division, Airbus DS, the divisional CEO decided that, from the beginning, an innovation department would be key to the creation of an internal innovative and entrepreneurial mindset and of structures that would increase the level of readiness vis-à-vis potential disruptions from the outside by new market entries—those young, hungry, fresh startups. Supported by the divisional CFO and CTO, an innovation charter was launched that provided the authorization for making innovation a driving force for intrapreneurship, new business models, and technological advancements, and also initiated external collaborations with the likes of StartupBootcamp, AZO, Starburst, ESA Business Incubation Center, Cyber Innovation HUB, and various others. The department was staffed with diverse people from different European countries, with different technical and non-technical backgrounds, from military departments and space sites, and also by new talents that joined from outside. Startups were mixed with internal intrapreneurs, executives took startup classes, budgets were provided, and transparent marketing was launched to promote innovation initiatives that informed all employees about the progress of the internal startups and all ongoing collaborations.

External startups were given access to internal Airbus departments to pitch their ideas. Internally, an innovation system was implemented in the shape of the #BlueBox, which gave intrapreneurs the chance to come forward with their ideas. They got support to develop business models and technical ideas that could make a relevant contribution to the Airbus DS portfolio. Cross-divisional collaborations started with the likes of BizLab, Airbus's makerspace ProtoSpace, or other initiatives in order to live the "We are one" credo, in particular when it comes to innovations. New divisional initiatives emerged, such as the Innovation Factory, an internal physical hub for creative thinking and innovation. This was motivated by the desire to provide employees with a dedicated space to brainstorm, experiment, and collaborate. The Innovation Factory encouraged cross-functional and cross-divisional collaboration, supporting Airbus's transformational journey. Externally, the "Airbus Café" was introduced, an open-innovation initiative in collaboration with universities in Europe and the US, where students from interdisciplinary backgrounds worked together on topics provided by Airbus DS that were relevant to the future of aerospace.

In parallel, a global campaign was launched to recruit talent for a sustainable, companywide mindset transformation. Airbus recognizes that, to remain competitive, it must attract top talent from around the world and cultivate a collective mindset shift. The company understood that diverse talents from different cultural backgrounds can bring fresh perspectives and innovative ideas. By recruiting globally, Airbus could access a broader talent pool that would enrich the company's innovation efforts. Additionally, the company tried to foster an environment where employees are encouraged to challenge the status quo, experiment, and embrace an entrepreneurial spirit. The goal was to create a consistent workforce that is innovative, agile, and driven to tackle the future challenges of the aerospace industry.

Cultivating a stronger entrepreneurial mindset was in focus, companywide. Hence, new formats with external partners were also needed. With the Airbus-wide initiative "DreamBig," employees across all divisions were asked to come forward with their disruptive ideas for the future of Airbus. The interest was big and many pitchdecks were received. It became obvious that the entrepreneurial spirit had spread throughout the company. The initiative unlocked the intrapreneurial mindset, creative talents, and the desire to collectively transform Airbus and shape the future of the business. Top management became heavily involved and was motivational and supportive of each employee in a very inclusive manner. From 150,000 employees, the best ideas were chosen and people were invited to the DreamBIG summit, where this concentrated intrapreneurial power was channeled and evaluated to develop new business models. Airbus acknowledged that creating innovation and entrepreneurship requires a shift in the organizational culture. The motivation behind #DreamBig was to inspire and empower employees to think beyond the traditional boundaries of their roles, encouraging them to generate and champion innovative ideas. The initiative promoted an entrepreneurial mindset, and a culture that celebrated calculated risk-taking and a willingness to explore new frontiers. By providing employees with the tools, knowledge, and support to dream big, Airbus aimed at innovation from within. All initiatives were empowered by dedicated departments of innovators, digitalizers, venture builders, and technical experts that helped employees to build and mature their ideas. They strongly encouraged thinking about the next steps in developing business models, and coached those idea-givers to present their venture to top management, who then decided in pitch sessions on the way forward and the necessary budgets. This strongly boosted empowerment and inclusivity, since employees became directly involved in the future developments of the company and could interact with decision-makers personally to promote the relevance of their ideas.

Various new physical innovative locations were inaugurated to further tap into the global pool of innovation opportunities. With the launch of the Acubed Innovation Office in the heart of Silicon Valley, Airbus set up a site in direct proximity to Big Tech, from Facebook to Google and from SpaceX to Apple. The idea was to harness the region's expertise in technology and innovation, find talent and new business models, and gain access to probably the most dynamic entrepreneurial ecosystem of that time. The strategy was to connect with startups, research institutions, and tech giants to access cutting-edge solutions. These initiatives served as a key pillar of Airbus's global outlook for the future, a scenario driven by startups and new technologies such as big data or quantum. Talents from Europe were nominated to work on special projects in their field of expertise together with regional tech companies and other partners. Talents from the region were hired and joined those projects that were enjoying top management attention and support. Regular tech classes were organized to help visitors and employees from Europe to get familiar with the way of working, thinking, and innovating in the valley.

This environment created disruptive new projects such as Vahana, Airbus's tech investigation of the concept of flying taxis. Airbus stated back then: "Rush-hour traffic is unbearable for many commuters today—and the problem is growing. By 2030, 60% of the world's population will live in cities, which is 10% more than today. To address this rising concern, Airbus harnessed its aviation experience to make the dream of all commuters and travelers come true one day: to fly over traffic jams at the push of a button." The Silicon Valley office was playing a key role in this development.

The Vahana project was a testament to Airbus's commitment to electric vertical take-off and landing (eVTOL) technology. The motivation was to revolutionize urban air mobility by developing an autonomous, eVTOL aircraft. The project recognized the importance of sustainable, efficient, and innovative transportation solutions. The project team worked towards a solution that wanted to set standards for future mobility. The design and certifications were driven towards application in real life. Besides hardware, software solutions were also developed, such as VOOM—for UBER-like on-demand helicopter booking in global mega-cities.

In Europe, flying taxi concepts were also pushed, with various projects in the making. Existing expertise and skills for this relevant future market for urban air mobility were provided by the internal expertise pool. Projects for a #Pop-Up Concept for modular and adaptable mobility were created with partners like Audi and Italo Design. The #Pop-Up concept was introduced as a novel approach to urban mobility. Airbus recognized the need for modular, adaptable solutions to address the growing demands of urban transportation. The concept leveraged eVTOL technology to create a flexible and efficient mode of transportation. In particular, it was relevant for seamless mobility connections in urban areas.

This very ambitious concept was supported by Audi and, thus, even displayed at the Geneva Motor Show in 2018. Besides this, the

#CityAirbus initiative also looked at reimagining mobility in urban spaces. According to Airbus, this was needed "since by 2030, 60% of the world's population will be urban. This significant population growth is expected to create a real need for innovative mobility options as ground infrastructure becomes increasingly congested. Providing people with a safe, low-carbon and convenient solution that leverages the airspace above cities could be a solution" (Airbus, n.d.). City Airbus aimed to create a future where mobility was seamlessly integrated into city life.

Beyond urban air mobility, Airbus was also anticipating that a stronger need for logistic solutions would emerge and different ways of working together on relevant solutions be needed. The concept of co-development and design thinking became very relevant. The collaborations with Auto Desk or Local Motors provided evidence of this kind of belief that the production of aerospace solutions can also be more decentralized in future, in not just the production of parts but also the integration of complete flying vehicles. The collaboration with Local Motors, which emerged as part of the 2016 Airbus Drone challenge, focused on this kind of approach and a better understanding of the development of flying solutions and its decentralized production. The core of this collaboration was the quadcopter concept and its revolutionary potential for the aviation of tomorrow. Airbus's collaboration with Local Motors underscored the importance of engaging with external partners to drive innovation. The project aimed to develop a quadcopter, a compact and versatile aircraft, designed for urban mobility. The motivation was to leverage the expertise of Local Motors and combine it with Airbus's aviation experience to push the boundaries of aerial transportation.

Strongly driven by the further development of innovation, the company also engaged in other emerging global markets. In 2016, the Airbus China Innovation Center was opened, which took into account the great innovative power of the country and also the strong interest in concepts of urban mobility. Going to Shenzhen underlined Airbus's ambition to tap into the vibrant innovation ecosystem of the Asia-Pacific region. The company was motivated by the vast talent pool and dynamic of this future-oriented innovation landscape. The Innovation Center served as a hub for fostering open collaboration between Airbus and the local innovation community. The company gained access to cutting-edge technologies and disruptive solutions. This cross-border collaboration is a strategic move to stay at the forefront of innovation. Airbus aims to facilitate the exchange of ideas and technologies.

The aerospace industry is a dynamic and ever-evolving sector that demands continuous innovation and adaptability. In 2013, Airbus, as a leading aerospace manufacturer, embarked on a transformative journey by implementing entrepreneurship as a key driver within the company. The goal was to shift from being solely an aircraft manufacturer to being an innovative mobility provider, offering solutions beyond traditional aircraft production. Airbus recognized the rise of entrepreneurship globally, with startups challenging established business models, and the company sought to disrupt itself rather than being disrupted. Various initiatives were launched to foster an entrepreneurial mindset and leverage external talents and ideas by empowering its own human resources and mindsets. Initiatives like #Africa4Future or #DreamBig aimed to tap into emerging markets and address potential disruptions. The company also engaged in collaborations with external partners like Local Motors or Audi to drive innovation in aerial transportation. Through various initiatives, Airbus positioned itself as a visionary leader in mobility solutions, driving progress from within.

Airbus's transformative entrepreneurial journey has been a testament to its commitment to innovation and intrapreneurship. The company recognized the need to adapt rapidly to a culture of entrepreneurship as a key driver for future success. The company's initiatives, such as Airbus BizLab and Airbus Ventures, have been instrumental in nurturing innovative ideas and startups within the aerospace industry. Projects like Vahana and the #Pop-Up Concept for modular and adaptable mobility have showcased Airbus's commitment to revolutionizing urban air mobility and addressing future mobility challenges. Through these initiatives, it has demonstrated its agility and commitment to shaping a sustainable and innovative future of global mobility. While global air transport almost came to a standstill during COVID-19, priorities shifted and a new future scenario materialized. Driven by the fact that the number of passengers will drastically increase and the number of planes will double by 2040, it became necessary to find suitable industrial and environmental solutions. The learnings from the innovative path that Airbus started back in 2013 support this new approach. As the aerospace industry continues to evolve, Airbus's transformative journey positions the company for future success driven by innovation and a culture of intrapreneurship.

References

Airbus. n.d. ***Urban Air Mobility – Taking urban transport to the sky*** [Website Entry]. Accessed online https://www.airbus.com/en/innovation/low-carbon-aviation/urban-air-mobility. Viewed May 20, 2024.

Airbus. 2014. ***Airbus – Creating better ways to fly.*** Corporate presentation. Accessed online https://slideplayer.com/slide/8714860/. Viewed May 20, 2024.

Airbus. 2016. Future of urban mobility. ***Airbus,*** December 6. Accessed online https://www.airbus.com/en/newsroom/news/2016-12-future-of-urban-mobility. Viewed May 20, 2024.

Aviation Week Intelligence Network. 2016. Local Motors, Airbus Move To Enable Cargo Drone Services. ***Aviation Week Intelligence Network,*** September 8. Accessed online https://aviationweek.com/business-aviation/local-motors-airbus-move-enable-cargo-drone-services. Viewed May 20, 2024.

Gabriel. 2016. Découvrez les taxis volants du futur d'Airbus qui arrivent dès 2017. ***Paper Geek,*** August 22. Accessed online https://www.papergeek.fr/decouvrez-taxis-volants-futur-airbus-qui-arrivent-des-2017-6953. Viewed May 20, 2024.

Ostrower, J. 2018. Airbus' 'flying car' takes to the skies for the first time. ***CNN Business,*** February 1. Accessed online https://money.cnn.com/2018/02/01/technology/airbus-vahana-first-flights/index.html. Viewed May 20, 2024.

Pallini, T. 2020. Airbus' new eVTOL that aims to usher in an era of flying taxis just took its first public flight – take a look at CityAirbus. ***Business Insider,*** July 28. Accessed online https://www.businessinsider.com/cityairbus-makes-first-public-flight-airbus-flying-taxi-evtol-2020-7. Viewed May 20, 2024.

STATEMENT

SUSANN ROTH

ADVISOR, DEPARTMENT OF COMMUNICATION AND KNOWLEDGE MANAGEMENT, ASIAN DEVELOPMENT BANK (ADB)
MANILA, PHILIPPINES

Photo: private

Summary of the presentation held at the conference "Practices of Futurecasting", 10–12 May 2023*

Since its establishment in 1966, the Asian Development Bank (ADB) has had inherently a futures-oriented approach. As a regional development bank, ADB envisions an Asia and Pacific region free of poverty and characterized by sustainable and inclusive development (Asian Development Bank, 2019). Recognizing the importance of explicit foresight work, ADB has played three key roles in promoting futures thinking and foresight: (i) provider of capacity development for developing member countries (DMCs); (ii) instigator for internal reforms; (iii) documenter and sharer of practices and knowledge.

As capacity development provider, ADB has financed a technical assistance project for 10 DMCs, including Armenia, Cambodia, the People's Republic of China, Indonesia, Kazakhstan, Mongolia, the Philippines, Timor-Leste, Uzbekistan, and Viet Nam, to apply futures thinking and foresight in long-term planning, strategy development of agencies, and to enhance multi-stakeholder dialogues to inform future oriented visions for sectors (Asian Development Bank, 2020).

Internally, ADB is applying futures thinking and foresight to inform reforms. This includes training of over 400 ADB staff in theory, methods, and practices since 2016. Topics have included gender equality futures, knowledge management futures, and innovation futures. Since 2021, futures thinking and foresight have been integrated into ADB's Innovation Hub service lines. The hub itself was conceptualized using futures thinking and foresight. These efforts have played a pivotal role in ADB's reforms toward a new operating model, shifting from an infrastructure bank to a climate bank, in alignment with emerging global priorities.

---

* The views expressed in this publication are those of the authors and do not necessarily reflect the views and policies of the Asian Development Bank (ADB) or its Board of Governors or the governments they represent.
ADB does not guarantee the accuracy of the data included in this publication and accepts no responsibility for any consequence of their use. The mention of specific companies or products of manufacturers does not imply that they are endorsed or recommended by ADB in preference to others of a similar nature that are not mentioned.
By making any designation of or reference to a particular territory or geographic area in this document, ADB does not intend to make any judgments as to the legal or other status of any territory or area.

ADB has shared application of futures thinking and foresight in the development practice at conference and workshops and by publishing manuals, briefs, and reports, such as the *Futures Thinking in Asia and the Pacific: Why Foresight Matters for Policymakers* (Asian Development Bank, 2020), *How ADB Uses Futures and Foresight Tools to Help Countries Prepare for an Uncertain Future* (Roth & Parry, 2023), and *Asian Development Bank Foresight in Action: Prospective Policy Making in Asia and the Pacific* (Milojević & Roth, 2024).

By engaging a diverse spectrum of stakeholders, including governments, civil society, academia, and the private sector, ADB fosters a collective understanding of future challenges and opportunities, fostering dialogue and co-creation of solutions without focusing only on the most desired future.

Lessons learned from external engagements and internal adaptations in ADB's own reforms collectively contribute to a more robust and informed application of futures thinking and foresight across ADB's operations. ADB appreciates the critical role of multilateral organizations in creating and legitimizing architectures and processes that foster foresight and participation, as well as holding the space for alternative futures and facilitating cross-sectoral and cross-regional dialogues.

References

Asian Development Bank. 2019. ***Strategy 2030 operational plans: Overview.*** Metro Manila: Asian Development Bank. Accessed online https://www.adb.org/sites/default/files/institutional-document/495946/strategy-2030-operational-plans-overview.pdf. Viewed February 20, 2024.

Asian Development Bank. 2020. ***Futures thinking in Asia and the Pacific: Why foresight matters for policymakers.*** Metro Manila: Asian Development Bank. Accessed online https://www.adb.org/publications/futures-thinking-asia-pacific-policy-makers. Viewed February 20, 2024.

Milojević, I., & Roth, S. 2024. ***ADB foresight in action: Prospective policy making in Asia and the Pacific.*** Metro Manila: Asian Development Bank.

Roth, S., & Parry, J. 2023. ***How ADB uses futures and foresight tools to help countries prepare for an uncertain future.*** ADB Briefs No.271. Metro Manila: Asian Development Bank. Accessed online https://www.adb.org/sites/default/files/publication/922696/adb-brief-271-adb-uses-futures-foresight-tools.pdf. Viewed February 20, 2024.

MARTIN REEVES

CHAIR, BCG HENDERSON INSTITUTE
SAN FRANCISCO, UNITED STATES

Photo: Erich Goldmann

HARNESSING IMAGINATION TO IMPROVE STRATEGIC DECISION-MAKING

The future has never seemed more unpredictable. Driven by multidimensional uncertainty—an ever-accelerating pace of technological change, a shifting geopolitical landscape, encroaching resource constraints, and existential environmental threats—organizations are no longer facing a handful of potential global scenarios, on the basis of which they must plot their course. Instead, they are confronted by a virtually limitless spectrum of possible futures. This calls for new principles and tools to guide strategic decision-making.

One potential solution is "futurecasting," which sits at the intersection of analysis and imagination: Rather than solely relying on historical trends or current data—which are no longer strong predictors of the future—futurecasting leverages creativity and experimentation to not just predict but also shape the future. This approach empowers leaders to render the future more graspable, and guides them to fine-tune their strategic approaches.

While many companies already possess strong analytical capabilities—which are increasingly bolstered by powerful artificial intelligence tools, imagination remains an underdeveloped skill. What is this mysterious capacity, and how can organizations harness it systematically?

As we describe in *The Imagination Machine* (Reeves & Fuller, 2021), imagination is our distinct ability to think counterfactually—to envision "what is not, but could be." It underpins all advances in science, art, and business. Imagination grants us agency and optionality, acting as the lens through which we can not only glimpse into the future, but also actively mold it. As Einstein once observed, "Imagination is more important than knowledge. Knowledge is limited. Imagination encircles the world."

Despite its importance, data shows that corporate imagination remains lacking: Over 90% of leaders recognize its importance, yet only 40% believe that their organizations are effectively leveraging imagination (see Figure 1).

While roughly 90% of leaders believe imagination is important …

… only about 40% are confident their organizations are harnessing it

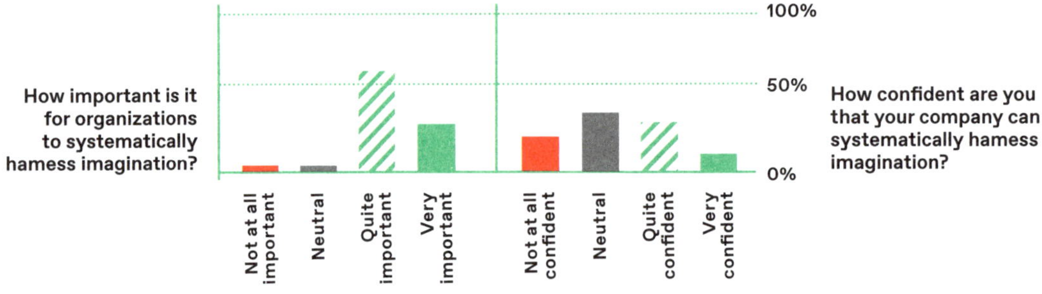

Figure 1: Organizations that do not systematically harness imagination. Respondents from 37 senior business leaders at BCG hosted events.
© Reeves & Fuller, 2021

In today's uncertain and dynamic context, imagination is more crucial than ever. Data shows that competitive advantage is eroding faster than ever (see Figure 2): While, at the start of the 1990s, the companies that best outperformed their average competitor held this edge for eight to ten years, the same cohort of firms now regresses to mean performance in just one year.

Outperformance is fading faster than ever before

Figure 2: Now every company needs to be an imagination machine
© Reeves & Fuller, 2021

Represents exponential decay of aggregate industry outperformance for companies that had been outperformers; Source: "Defying the Gravity of Average" (BHI/SMR, 2020)
© 2021 by Boston Consulting Group

Imagination is often misconstrued as an unmanageable phenomenon, a solitary pursuit, with inspiration striking randomly and unpredictably. But this perspective is limited: Our research shows that imagination can be harnessed systematically and collectively. In this article, we outline how businesses and institutions can become "imagination machines"—entities that inherently support and enhance the collective imaginations of collaborating individuals, with intent, and by design.

Barriers to imagination

Why is imagination in a corporate context such a daunting task? As firms grow, they frequently encounter several hurdles that limit the organization's imaginative potential:

Entrenched mental models. Organizations often get into a rut in which mental models become uniform and deeply entrenched (a by-product of "organization alignment")—and get mistaken for common sense or objective reality. This situation may be compounded by a lack of diversity in cognition or perspectives.

Organizational insularity. Large companies can become isolated from external perspectives and ideas—fewer of the employees ever interact with a customer—which limits their sources of inspiration or surprise, and thereby restricts their imaginative capacity.

Over-specialized roles. Excessively specialized teams run the risk of forming isolated subcultures and developing jargon that can impede cross-group collaboration and impair communication between the imaginers and the executors.

Complacency. Leaders may fall into the trap of believing that the strategy and tactics that led their organization to success will always remain optimal, irrespective of changing circumstances. This belief can create an over-reliance on past recipes for success and stifle imagination.

The tyranny of metrics. Firms commonly focus on the efficient execution of their established business strategies, using related metrics as the main indicators of success. However, the supremacy of these efficiency metrics can hinder the exploration of opportunities and experimentation with new models.

How to become an imagination machine

To overcome these barriers and harness imagination systematically and collectively, organizations can follow a six-step approach (see Figure 3).

Figure 3: Imagination can be harnessed "systematically" and "collectively"
© *Reeves & Fuller, 2021*

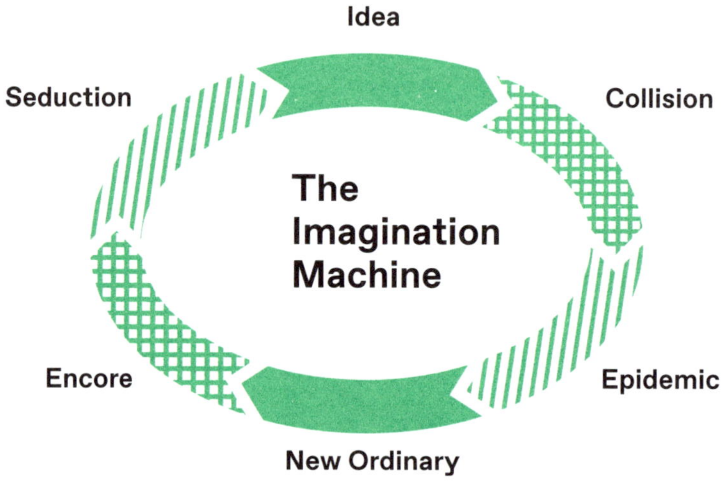

Seduction. For imagination to be harnessed in business, it first needs to be triggered or inspired. Something needs to "seduce" us away from our routine way of looking at things, into the realm of counterfactual thinking. Systematizing this requires the normalization of seeking surprise—i.e., actively being on the lookout for new information that will inspire new thoughts: Anomalies rather than averages, and external rather than internal data. For example, Brooks Automation, a semiconductor machine parts manufacturer, reinvigorated its stagnant growth by actively pursuing the unexpected: Studying all the patents that cited their own patents, as well as the patents that cited these patents, Brooks realized that its equipment for manipulating semiconductors at cold temperatures could also be used for better tissue storage—thus unearthing new business opportunities in the life sciences industry. Brooks pivoted its business completely and became a leader in "bio-banking."

Idea. We might encounter inspiring accidents, anomalies, or analogies, but these will not amount to much if we put no effort into developing an "idea." To harness imagination, we need to turn passive thoughts into starting points for rethinking mental models, to develop new, counterfactual models. Systematizing this requires time for thinking and reflection, and the patience to work and rework ideas in your mind. Alexander Graham Bell, for example, was inspired by the accidental pluck of a transmitting reed while working on a multiple telegraph system. This led to his development of the telephone.

Collision. A new mental model remains a mere individual indulgence until we act on it to collide the idea with reality to further its evolution. This step entails probing for validation and surprise and generating feedback—not only to know whether an idea is good or not, but also to produce new ideas that will provoke further thinking. LEGO exemplifies this step, evolving its business over the years through continuous iteration and interaction with the world. Starting as a woodworking and carpentry shop in 1916, LEGO transitioned into wooden toys in 1932, then wooden blocks in 1946. In 1958, about 40 years after its founding, LEGO developed the unique system of interlocking pieces that we now know. Today, LEGO continues its tradition of iteration by gathering real-time customer feedback through forums like LEGO Ideas.

Epidemic. For an idea to make an impact, it needs to be amplified so it can inspire others. We can share ideas socially by creating a prototype, by sharing the experience of developing an idea together, or by creating a narrative that underlines the significance of the idea. Recruit Holdings does this well, successfully identifying imaginative ideas from its employees and spreading those ideas to others. The company holds two annual events, where it hosts short presentations on new business ideas and improvements in ways of working. They encourage the originator of new ideas to see themselves as an entrepreneurial hero by letting them build their own team and champion their own idea. And they provide funding for new teams to try their new ideas out. As a result, ideas that have come from their employees have generated almost $800 million in revenue.

New Ordinary. For a new model to be successful, it must lead to a new reality: by changing the actions of people far removed from the idea's originators. Ubiquity and un-remarkableness are hallmarks of success. To make this happen, organizations need to codify the idea through evolvable "scripts." We might see procedures as the antithesis of imagination but, in fact, institutionalizing an idea—in order to allow it to be replicated by others—is a necessary step if we are to broadly shape reality. Apple, for instance, realized that the consumer experience in its stores was key to its success, and thus codified the script through clear action-oriented guidelines for store employees.

Encore. The last step in the lifecycle of imagination is the need to "sustain it over time." As companies grow and become successful, the procedures and mental models around the original idea become entrenched, which naturally dampens the capacity for re-imagination. Companies need to be ambidextrous: to continue to harness imagination to discover new paths to growth while running the current business at the same time. Amazon exemplifies the ability to combine exploitation and exploration in the way in which it is consistently imagining and creating new businesses. In 1994, it was the world's biggest bookstore, before using third-party sellers in 2000, moving to cloud computing in 2006, becoming a film and TV studio in 2010, and so on.

A leadership agenda for igniting imagination

A set of high-impact tactics can help leaders to ignite imagination in their organization.

See constraints as opportunities. Often, constraints are seen as impediments or risks. However, when approached differently, they can be springboards for innovation—and, if tackled first, can even provide a competitive edge. Executives should encourage the sharing of intriguing, perplexing findings (alongside averages and expected results) in order to ensure that such information is not dismissed but sparks imaginative thinking.

Engage with the unknown. Leaders should ensure that teams are regularly exposed to the unfamiliar and the unknown, and trained to treasure it. This could involve short-term job rotations to diverse work settings, exposure to markets where the organization's product is more (or less) successful, or even the tailoring of daily information flows to ensure that people are not simply reading from their habitual websites.

Self-disrupt. Sometimes leaders need to instigate a crisis to shake complacency. A crisis can bring to light the inadequacies of current strategies, pushing the organization towards reinvention. A.G. Lafley's transformative approach at P&G in 2000 serves as a prime example of this: When he took over, the company was already struggling, but he deepened the internal crisis further by doing extensive customer research to identify where the company's brands were not meeting customer needs. This ultimately led to a revamp of the portfolio and accelerating sales.

Establish heroic goals. Rather than maintaining the status quo, bold and audacious goals can help galvanize the organization, stretch minds, and spark imaginations. For instance, when Hindustan Unilever's CEO set an ambitious target for store expansion—from 2-3% year-on-year growth to the "ridiculous-sounding" goal of 50%, it led to a burst of creativity in the organization and the identification of new solutions.

Evolving routines and models. Over time, the patterns of collective action in a company shape the dominant set of mental habits, roles, and expectations, which can become a self-sustaining system. The imagination machine avoids stagnation by allowing practices to evolve continuously. Rather than being "self-protecting," it becomes "self-tuning," evolving and refining practices based on data and imagination. This may involve giving up on the vision that processes can or should be completely optimized for efficiency, or perfectly uniform. For example, Alibaba has evolved its vision over time from "serving China's small exporters" to "developing an e-commerce ecosystem" to "building the future infrastructure of commerce."

Foster playfulness and experimentation. Companies should encourage a sense of play and experimentation: improvised, imaginative exploration. Play involves testing out things that one can do easily but might not yet have thought of trying, without much premeditation. Play can be mental (throwing around ideas) and physical (trying things out). A company fostering playfulness would appreciate randomness and messiness as much as order, allowing people to tinker and customize, suggest idiosyncratic ideas in meetings, try out modifications to processes, and be forgiven for trying new things without permission. Allowing low-cost action and feedback is key for a company that wants to support the cycle of imagination.

As we continue to grapple with escalating uncertainty, the value of imagination will only increase: As the ability that is central to futurecasting, imagination empowers leaders to shape the future of their organization and industry, rather than merely predict or react to it.

References

Reeves, M., & Fuller, J. 2019. ***Competing on imagination.*** BCG Henderson Institute. Accessed online https://bcghendersoninstitute.com/competing-on-imagination/. Viewed January 23, 2024.

Reeves, M., Whitaker, K., & Deegan, T. 2020. ***Fighting the gravity of average performance.*** MIT Sloan Management Review, 61305.

Reeves, M., & Fuller, J. 2020. ***We need imagination now more than ever.*** Harvard Business Review. Accessed online https://hbr.org/2020/04/we-need-imagination-now-more-than-ever. Viewed January 23, 2024.

Reeves, M., & Fuller, J. 2021. ***The imagination machine: How to spark new ideas and create your company's future.*** Brighton: Harvard Business Review Press.

Photo: Erich Goldmann

RUTH BYRNE

PROFESSOR OF COGNITIVE SCIENCE AT TRINITY COLLEGE DUBLIN, UNIVERSITY OF DUBLIN
DUBLIN, IRELAND

HOW WE IMAGINE THE FUTURE

To futurecast desired futures we deploy many cognitive strategies, chief among them causal strategies, which are based closely on our knowledge and beliefs about current reality and constrained by our understanding of what is possible, or counterfactual strategies, which are based instead on our ability to create imagined alternatives to reality that can even include conjectures about impossibilities. We may ask which of these strategies provides better futurecasting: our causal understanding of the world as it is or our counterfactual imagination of alternatives? Experimental evidence from cognitive science research into how we intuitively use such strategies in our daily lives is useful if we are to address this question. Firstly, I will consider whether, in our daily lives, we tend to think about the same sorts of things when we engage our causal knowledge or our counterfactual imagination. Next, I will discuss whether we naturally tend to think about the same number of possibilities when we engage our causal knowledge or our counterfactual imagination. And thirdly, I will sketch out a test case for comparing the usefulness of our counterfactual imagination or our causal knowledge for thinking about the future: the test case of how we naturally understand explanations for decisions offered by artificial intelligence decision support systems.

Counterfactual imagination

We can explain events such as how an outcome came to be, or why another person acted as they did, by relying on our causal knowledge and beliefs about them (e.g., Keil, 2006). Our causal models of the world contain rich information about many different aspects of matters of fact, and of their relationships (e.g., Johnson-Laird & Khemlani, 2017). But we can also explain events by relying on our imagination and, especially, on our ability to create counterfactual alternatives to reality. In everyday life, we frequently tend to imagine how things could have turned out differently, "if only..." (e.g., Byrne, 2005; Kahneman &

Tversky, 1982). We usually engage in "if only..." thoughts after bad outcomes (e.g., Roese & Epstude, 2017). For example, suppose that you fall off your bike on your way home; you may be irresistibly drawn to thoughts about how the fall could have been avoided. You may dwell on various things that occurred before the bad outcome. For example, the bike's tires skidded on oil on the road, or its brakes jammed, or its lights were too dim to pick out stones lying in your path. You may zoom in on one of these things, guided by factors such as whether it was unusual to find oil on that stretch of road, or whether your decision to brake particularly hard was within your control (e.g., Dixon & Byrne, 2011; Pighin, Byrne, & Tentori, 2022). You may eventually conclude, "if only I had had better lights, I wouldn't have fallen." There are remarkable regularities in the counterfactual alternatives that we all naturally tend to create (see Byrne 2016 for a review).

Such counterfactual alternatives to reality help us to explain an outcome, in part because they help us to work out the causal relations between events—such as the fact that your poor lights caused you to fall off your bike (e.g., Frosch & Byrne, 2012; Gerstenberg, Goodman, Lagnado, & Tenenbaum, 2021). We construct conjectures about how an event could have turned out differently, or how a person could have acted differently, in order to probe how things came to be as they are. The idea that the counterfactual imagination can help us to figure out the causal relations between events has a long history in philosophy (Hume, 1739; Mill, 1861). Counterfactual and causal explanations have been considered to be two sides of the same coin; i.e., when you have understood, "If A hadn't happened, B wouldn't have happened," you have understood "A caused B." We often use such "if only..." thoughts to justify or defend past actions, as is commonly seen in political social discourse, media commentary, and accident reports; e.g., "if only I had known then what I know now..." (e.g., Catellani & Covelli, 2013; Markman, Mizoguchi, & McMullen, 2008). We even use them to abrogate moral responsibility and legal accountability, and to excuse our own poor performance (e.g., Malle, Guglielmo, & Monroe, 2014; McCrea, 2008).

More strikingly, however, we can use our imagined alternatives to reality to help us to avoid similar bad outcomes from occurring again, by helping us to prepare for the future. A rich seam in human cognition is our ability to rely on our imaginations not only to understand the world around us, but also to anticipate, form intentions, and plan for the future. We can learn from a past mistake by forming an intention for the future; for example, you may decide to buy new lights for your bike to ensure that you prevent a similar fall in the future (e.g., Brigard, Addis, Ford, Schacter, & Giovanello, 2013; Roese & Epstude, 2017). We rely on these imagined alternatives to the past to make better decisions in the future, to guide our plans, intentions, and predictions. We use our "if only..." thoughts about the past to guide our "what if..." thoughts about the future.

An important question when we try to understand an outcome or a decision is: To what extent do the alternatives to reality, which we naturally create, equip us with the machinery for accurate futurecasts? In particular, one key question is whether our causal understanding of existing reality or our counterfactual imagination of alternatives to that reality serves us better in our everyday forecasting. I will consider recent experimental evidence from cognitive science on three aspects of such causal and counterfactual strategies that contribute to an answer to this question.

What sorts of possibilities do we think about?

We tend to focus on very different aspects of the world when we imagine how things could have been different in the past or could be different in the future, compared with when we think about how one thing led to another. For example, when participants in experiments created an imagined alternative, they tended to regard an exceptional event as normal. They first read stories such as one about an individual, Paul, who had a car accident when a driver under the influence of drugs charged through an intersection and crashed into him. Paul left the office at his usual time but he drove an unusual route home. They were asked to consider how things could have turned out differently. Most of them imagined that things could have turned out differently if he had taken his usual route (e.g., Kahneman & Tversky, 1982). But participants do something quite different when they think about how one thing led to another. When they were asked instead what caused the accident, they said that the other driver caused it (e.g., Mandel & Lehman, 1996; N'gbala & Branscombe, 1995). They did not tend to focus on the exceptional event in their causal explanations. The results suggest that our imagination of alternatives to reality is not constrained by causal relationships of how one thing led to another in the same way that our causal thinking is.

Another example is the way in which, when participants imagined an alternative to reality, they tended to focus on events within a person's control. They first read stories, such as one about Anna, who had to do a multiplication sum in her head in 30 seconds, in order to win some chocolates. The two sums were in two sealed envelopes, marked A and B, which contained either two one-digit numbers (e.g., 7 x 3) or two two-digit numbers (e.g., 67 x 83). Anna chose envelope A, which she then discovered contained the two-digit multiplication problem. She tried to solve it but failed. When participants imagined how the outcome could have been different, they tended to say "if only she had chosen the other envelope," that is to say, they focused on the decision choice within her control (e.g., Girotto, Ferrante, Pighin, & Gonzalez, 2007). But when they thought about the causes of the outcome, they tended to focus on internal factors, such as her concentration, or the external situation, such as the time limit, i.e., factors outside her control (Byrne & Deighan, 2023). The results suggest that our imagination of alternatives to reality liberates us from focusing on merely how one thing led to another in the real world and, instead, allows us to imagine a wide variety of ways in which things could be different.

How many possibilities do we think about?

We tend to find it more arduous to imagine how things could be different, compared with thinking about how one thing led to another. For example, when participants in experiments were asked to write a diary entry based on a fictional character's experience of events in the past few weeks, they spontaneously tended to write causal explanations of why the past events had turned out as they had, more often than they tended to imagine how the events could have turned out differently (McEleney & Byrne, 2006). Imagining how things could be different seems to be more difficult than explaining why things have come to be as they are. Imagining alternatives requires more cognitive resources than understanding causes, because this requires the construction and consideration of more possibilities.

In a simple test of this idea, participants in experiments listened to lots of very short stories about various different sorts of everyday events. Some of the stories included an imagined alternative to what had actually occurred. For example, in the course of a short story about two people having a conversation in a grocery shop, participants heard that one person said, "if there had been oranges, there would have been pears." As they listened to each recorded story, they saw a visual display of images on a computer screen in front of them, such as an image of an orange and a pear, an image of an apple and a strawberry, an image of an orange and a pear with a line through it, and an image of an apple and a strawberry with a line through it. Small cameras on a headset recorded exactly—at precise 50-millisecond intervals—where their eyes moved to as they looked at the screen (Orenes, García-Madruga, Gómez-Veiga, Espino, & Byrne, 2019). The rationale for such eye-tracking studies is the fact that, at any given time during an experiment, what people look at gives us an important clue about what they are thinking about.

As soon as participants heard a word like "oranges" in a sentence such as "if there had been oranges...," their eyes began to move very rapidly (within a few hundred milliseconds) to look at the image corresponding to it, the image of an orange and a pear. But their eyes also began to move very rapidly to look at the image corresponding to its opposite, the image of an orange and a pear with a line through it. By the end of the short measurement period of a few seconds, participants' eyes were alternating between the two images, looking equally at each of them (Orenes et al., 2019). The results support the idea that when participants thought about a conjecture about an imagined alternative to reality, they immediately mentally simulated dual possibilities, one corresponding to the conjecture, e.g., "there were apples and pears," and one corresponding to the presupposed facts, e.g., "there were no apples and no pears." And they did so within a remarkably short period of time.

Conversely, other experimental results indicated that participants do something quite different when they hear a causal assertion, such as when they hear in the course of the conversation in the grocery shop, "because there were oranges, there were pears" (Orenes, Espino, & Byrne, 2022). In this case, their eyes began to move rapidly (within a few hundred milliseconds) to look at the depiction of the orange and the pear, but at the end of the measurement period of a few seconds they were still looking only at this depiction. Their eyes did not move to look at the opposite image. The results support the idea that when participants thought about how one thing led to another, they simulated a single possibility at the outset that corresponded to the facts, "there were apples and pears." The evidence points to a very important difference between how we imagine how things could have been different and how we think about how one thing led to another: When we imagine how things could have been different, we tend to think about more possibilities at the outset. These differences emerge even in the first few seconds. This supports the idea that imagining alternatives to what happened may provide richer information than thinking about what happened, because imagining alternatives requires the construction and consideration of more possibilities.

When we think about the world of the future and its many alternatives, our minds construct iconic mental simulations of possibilities that correspond to how the world is or could be (e.g., Khemlani, Byrne, & Johnson-Laird, 2018). The constraints of our limited working memories lead us to mentally represent few possibilities whenever we can, such as when we think about what actually happened and how one thing led to another. But when we imagine alternatives to reality, we must imagine not only the possibilities consistent with a conjecture. We also need to keep in mind what we know about what really happened, so that we can compare reality to its alternatives (e.g., Espino & Byrne, 2021). We keep track of the epistemic status of the possibilities we consider, of how they correspond to reality or to an imagined alternative to it. The simulation of dual possibilities when we imagine alternatives to reality occurs very rapidly but it also appears to have lasting consequences for the inferences that we subsequently make about reality and its alternatives (see Byrne, 2016).

Is imagining alternatives more helpful than thinking about causal facts?

There are few prescriptive analyses against which we can measure the accuracy of our imagined "what if…" thoughts about the future, other than waiting for the future to unfold. Nonetheless, participants in experiments tend to judge that some imagined alternatives to reality seem true and others seem false (Byrne & Johnson-Laird, 2020), some seem probable and others seem improbable (Petrocelli, Percy, Sherman, & Tormala, 2011), and they even appear willing to consider that some imagined "impossibilities" could be true, whereas others seem false (Byrne, 2023).

A fruitful domain in which to test whether imagined alternatives to reality are helpful for everyday futurecasting is the domain of artificial intelligence (AI) decision support systems. AI decisions prevail in many areas of daily life, such as finance: as a tool, for example, that helps a bank clerk to determine whether a customer's loan application should be approved. We are entitled to an explanation for decisions made about us, and there has been intense interest in eXplainable AI (XAI) and in the development of algorithms that provide explanations based on imagined counterfactual alternatives, such as "if you had asked for a lower amount, your loan application would have been approved" (Byrne, 2023; Keane, Kenny, Delaney, & Smyth, 2021; see also Miller, 2019). But little is known about how we as users of AI apps may understand such automated counterfactual explanations (e.g., Lage et al., 2019; Lucic, Haned, & Rijke, 2020).

To illustrate: Suppose you have had a few drinks at a family party and need to know whether you can legally drive home. You have an application (app) on your smartphone that helps: You enter the number of units you have drunk, the duration over which you drank, and whether you have eaten, as well as details such as your weight and gender, and it tells you if "you are over the limit." It also explains its decision: "You would have been under the limit if you had drunk on a full stomach." Your Aunt Violet wants to know whether she is over the limit and so you enter her details and tell her the app's decision: She is over the limit. Your Uncle Jared asks you to try it for him, so you enter his details and tell him the result: He is not. Later, when you no longer have your phone with you, your Cousin Betty asks what it would say about her; you have used the app a few times by now so you ask for her details and tell her your prediction of the app's decision: You believe that it would have said that she is under the limit (Celar & Byrne, 2023). The example illustrates the sort of information that participants in experiments received about the decisions made by an app in similar cases. Some participants also received counterfactual explanations for the AI's decisions, e.g., "Violet would have been under the limit if she had drunk on a full stomach." On the other hand, others received matched causal explanations with the same content, e.g., "Jared was over the limit because he drank on an empty stomach." They tended to judge the counterfactual explanations to be more helpful than causal ones (Celar & Byrne, 2023; Warren, Byrne, & Keane, 2023).

Subsequently, participants had to attempt to predict the future decisions of the AI system. Their predictions were reasonably accurate, but they were accurate regardless of whether or not they had earlier received counterfactual or causal explanations for the AI's decisions. The dissociation between subjective self-reporting preferences for counterfactual explanations and objective measures of their helpfulness in improving accuracy may be ethically troubling because they potentially lead people to trust AI decisions without accurately understanding them (Warren et al., 2023). Conversely, however, when participants had to decide whether they themselves were over the limit and whether they would be prepared to drive or not, their decisions were more accurate if they had earlier received counterfactual explanations rather than causal ones (Celar & Byrne, 2023). The results suggest that counterfactual explanations may be particularly suited to helping us prepare for the future and, hence, that they may be especially helpful when we have to make our own decisions about the future rather than just attempt to forecast the decisions of others.

The evidence from experiments examining how people understand and predict decisions made by artificial intelligence support systems indicates that the enriched mental representation of two possibilities that people naturally construct for imagined counterfactuals outweighs the cognitive costs of having to keep in mind multiple models. The additional information in the dual representation of counterfactuals compared to causal explanations is of greater use to us, at least when we consider our own decisions.

Conclusions

Experimental evidence from cognitive science suggests that the imagination of alternatives to reality may be not only very useful for futurecasting but also as useful as (if not more useful than) thinking causally about how one thing led to another in reality. First, when we imagine counterfactual alternatives compared to when we think causally we tend to focus on different content. This difference indicates that human imagination can provide more nuanced possibilities than causal understanding alone. Second, when we imagine alternatives to reality, we think about more possibilities than when we think causally. This difference illustrates that imagining alternatives provides richer information than causal thoughts, even if this is more cognitively arduous, and that this enables richer futurecasting than causal understanding alone. Third, in forecasting the decisions of artificial intelligence support systems, we tend to find explanations based on how things could have been different more helpful than explanations based solely on how things came to be as they are. The accuracy of our own decisions in terms of how well they align with the decisions of an AI is improved more by such counterfactual explanations than by causal ones. These differences show that the human imagination can do more to improve future decisions than causal understanding alone.

Our imagination-based conjectures about the future thus complement the extrapolations that we base solely on our knowledge and beliefs about the world as it is. Our imagination of counterfactual alternatives to reality supports our natural everyday futurecasting. And it does so as much as, if not even more than, our construction of causal explanations.

References

Brigard, F. de, Addis, D. R., Ford, J. H., Schacter, D. L., & Giovanello, K. S. 2013. Remembering what could have happened: Neural correlates of episodic counterfactual thinking. ***Neuropsychologia***, 51(12): 2401-2414.

Byrne, R. M. J. 2005. ***The rational imagination: How people create alternatives to reality.*** Cambridge, MA: MIT Press.

Byrne, R. M. J. 2016. Counterfactual thought. ***Annual Review of Psychology,*** 67: 135-157.

Byrne, R. M. J. 2023. Good explanations in explainable artificial intelligence (XAI): Evidence from human explanatory reasoning. ***Proceedings of the Thirty-Second International Joint Conference on Artificial Intelligence (IJCAI-23):*** 6536-6544.

Byrne, R. M. J. 2023. How people think about hypothetical impossibilities. ***Memory & Cognition***, 52: 182-196.

Byrne, R. M., & Johnson-Laird, P. N. 2020. If and or: Real and counterfactual possibilities in their truth and probability. ***Journal of Experimental Psychology: Learning, Memory, and Cognition***, 46(4): 760.

Byrne, R. M. J., & Deighan, L. 2023. ***Counterfactuals as explanations.*** Manuscript in preparation.

Catellani, P., & Covelli, V. 2013. The strategic use of counterfactual communication in politics. ***Journal of Language and Social Psychology***, 32(4): 480-489.

Celar, L., & Byrne, R. M. 2023. How people reason with counterfactual and causal explanations for Artificial Intelligence decisions in familiar and unfamiliar domains. ***Memory & Cognition***, 51: 1481-1496.

Dixon, J. E., & Byrne, R. M. 2011. "If only" counterfactual thoughts about exceptional actions. ***Memory & Cognition***, 39: 1317-1331.

Espino, O., & Byrne, R. M. 2021. How people keep track of what is real and what is imagined: The epistemic status of counterfactual alternatives to reality. ***Journal of Experimental Psychology: Learning, Memory, and Cognition***, 47(4): 547.

Ferrante, D., Girotto, V., Straga., M., & Walsh, C. 2013. Improving the past and the future: A temporal asymmetry in hypothetical thinking. ***Journal of Experimental Psychology: General,*** 142(1): 23-27.

Frosch, C., & Byrne, R. M. J. 2012. Causal conditionals and counterfactuals. ***Acta Psychologica,*** 14: 54-66.

Gerstenberg, T., Goodman, N. D., Lagnado, D. A., & Tenenbaum, J. B. 2021. A counterfactual simulation model of causal judgments for physical events. ***Psychological Review,*** 128(5): 936-975.

Girotto, V., Ferrante, D., Pighin, S., & Gonzalez, M. 2007. Postdecisional counterfactual thinking by actors and readers. ***Psychological Science,*** 18(6): 510-515.
Hume, D. 1739/2004. ***A treatise of human nature.*** Mineola, NY: Dover.

Johnson-Laird, P. N., & Khemlani, S. 2017. Mental models and causation. In M. Waldman (ed.), ***Oxford handbook of causal reasoning***: 169-188. Oxford: Oxford University Press.

Kahneman, D., & Tversky, A. 1982. The simulation heuristic. In D. Kahneman, P. Slovic, & A. Tversky (eds.), ***Judgment under uncertainty: Heuristics and biases:*** 201-208. New York: Cambridge University Press.

Keane, M. T., Kenny, E. M., Delaney, E., & Smyth, B. 2021. If only we had better counterfactual explanations: Five key deficits to rectify in the evaluation of counterfactual XAI techniques. ***Proceedings of the Thirtieth International Joint Conference on Artificial Intelligence (IJCAI-21):*** 4466-4474.

Keil, F. C. 2006. Explanation and understanding. ***Annual review of psychology,*** 57: 227.

Khemlani, S. S., Byrne, R. M., & Johnson-Laird, P. N. 2018. Facts and possibilities: A model-based theory of sentential reasoning. ***Cognitive science,*** 42(6): 1887-1924.

Lage, I., Chen, E., He, J., Narayanan, M., Kim, B., Gershman, S. J. & Doshi-Velez, F. 2019. Human evaluation of models built for interpretability. ***Proceedings of the AAAI conference on Human Computation and Crowdsourcing,*** 7: 59-67.

Lucic, A., Haned, H., & Rijke, M. de. 2020. Why does my model fail? Contrastive local explanations for retail forecasting. ***Proceedings of the 2020 Conference on Fairness, Accountability, and Transparency:*** 90-98.

Malle, B. F., Guglielmo, S., & Monroe, A. E. 2014. A Theory of Blame. ***Psychological Inquiry,*** 25(2): 147-186.

Mandel, D. R., & Lehman, D. R. 1996. Counterfactual thinking and ascriptions of cause and preventability. ***Journal of Personality and Social Psychology,*** 71(3): 450-463.

Markman, K. D., Mizoguchi, N., & McMullen, M. N. 2008. "It would have been worse under Saddam:" Implications of counterfactual thinking for beliefs regarding the ethical treatment of prisoners of war. ***Journal of Experimental Social Psychology,*** 44(3): 650-654.

McCrea, S. M. 2008. Self-handicapping, excuse-making, and counterfactual thinking: Consequences for self-esteem and future motivation. ***Journal of Personality and Social Psychology,*** 95: 274-292.

McEleney, A., & Byrne, R. M. J. 2006. Spontaneous causal and counterfactual thoughts. ***Thinking and Reasoning,*** 12: 235-255.

Mill, J.S. 1861/1998. ***Utilitarianism*** (ed. by R. Crisp). Oxford: Oxford University Press.

Miller, T. 2019. Explanation in artificial intelligence: Insights from the social sciences. ***Artificial intelligence,*** 267: 1-38.

N'gbala, A., & Branscombe, N. R. 1995. Mental Simulation and Causal Attribution: When Simulating an Event Does Not Affect Fault Assignment. ***Journal of Experimental Social Psychology,*** 31: 139-162.

Orenes, I., Espino, O., & Byrne, R. M. 2022. Similarities and differences in understanding negative and affirmative counterfactuals and causal assertions: Evidence from eye-tracking. ***Quarterly Journal of Experimental Psychology,*** 75(4): 633-651.

Orenes, I., García-Madruga, J. A., Gómez-Veiga, I., Espino, O., & Byrne, R. M. 2019. The comprehension of counterfactual conditionals: Evidence from eye-tracking in the visual world paradigm. ***Frontiers in psychology,*** 10: 1172.

Petrocelli, J. V., Percy, E. J., Sherman, S. J., & Tormala, Z. L. 2011. Counterfactual potency. ***Journal of personality and social psychology,*** 100(1): 30.

Pighin, S., Byrne, R. M., & Tentori, K. 2022. "If only" counterfactual thoughts about cooperative and uncooperative decisions in social dilemmas. ***Thinking & Reasoning,*** 28(2): 193-225.

Roese, N. J., & Epstude, K. 2017. The functional theory of counterfactual thinking: New evidence, new challenges, new insights. In J. M. Olson (ed.), ***Advances in experimental social psychology,*** 56: 1-79. Academic Press.

Warren, G., Byrne, R. M. J. & Keane, M. T. 2023. Categorical and continuous features in counterfactual explanations of AI systems. ***Proceedings of the 28th International Conference on Intelligent User Interfaces:*** 171-187.

Photo: Marc Royce
JULIAN BLEECKER
DESIGNER, ENTREPRENEUR,
AND RESEARCHER
LOS ANGELES, UNITED STATES

STORIES TO IMAGINE ALTERNATE FUTURES

JULIAN BLEECKER AND TOBIAS REVELL

Introduction

The faculty of imagination is easily dismissed when compared with the professional services of foresight, forecasting, strategy, and planning. Design fiction and speculative design can be the interface between them. Often not treated as a driving factor in the ways we approach, work upon, and materialize the kinds of futures that we desire to inhabit, imagination is a vital and existentially advantageous human capability. Integral to any meaningful work, imagination can enable us to anticipate possibilities through design fiction, speculative design, futures design, and other emerging methodologies and approaches.

In this essay, we highlight how a lack of imagination stymies futures work and argue that it should therefore play a more crucial and central role in the activities of foresight, strategy, policy, and planning. For organizations, institutions, and individuals that have to take decisions based on possible futures, with their planetary and species-scale implications, our paper aims to expand their imaginative potential. These futures practices, in dealing with complexity at a massive scale, can benefit enormously by drawing on the common and empowering potential of imagination. Design is a tool for materializing abstract notions and challenging the status quo. Taking imagination seriously drives better futures work.

Serious imagination

In the serious world of foresight, strategy, policy, and planning, one rarely hears the word "imagination." It is dismissed as hard to either measure or verify, making it inappropriate for the sciences of business and policy. Or it is a luxury; superfluous to the needs of the organization or project. However, we suggest that it is arguably the most critical and consistent component of futures work because—even in the most mundane of foresight projects—we constantly use imagination. For instance, in the interpretation of a prediction, the mind cannot help but imagine future interactions, opportunities, or threats. The sense of unease that accompanies uncertainty and risk and the relief that goes with a confident projection are both products of imagination that connect cause with effect and pattern with meaning. *All* work in the future necessarily requires imagination insofar as *the future has not happened yet.* No other animal we know of (other than corvids, the crow family et al.) can use its imagination to simulate a scenario outside the present (Burgess, 2017) and some people even attribute the uniquely prevalent high stress levels of humans to an overabundance of imagination; imagining the worst, how others might be thinking of us, or all the ways in which we might suffer from speculative maladies or misfortunes (Sapolsky, 2004).

Engaging in futures engages us in imagination. Serious engagement with imagination and imaginative potential is fertile soil for critical and meaningful futures work. Further, imagination introduces the constraints by which "serious" futures work can operate: We are only able to respond to the futures that we can contemplate through our imaginings. What we are able to imagine, and who is *permitted* to imagine, predefines the futures that we can build and anticipate.

Predetermined imaginaries

We are notoriously poor at imagining beyond the predetermined imaginary futures space laid out before us. For instance, coverage of technological advances in labor for the past 150 years has largely focused on how they will lead to mass unemployment even as general employment continues and, in fact, increases with a growing population and more people entering the workforce over the 20th century (Autor, 2015).

Why is an imaginary future of mass joblessness so prevalent and easy to contemplate while the opposite—a world in which we no longer have to work at all—is generally dismissed as fantasy? We might infer that the challenge of contemplating a world without work, or even imagining what "work" itself might mean in such a toil-less world, is not because such a concept is impossible, but because this has not been imagined to such a degree that it is considered credible enough to be sensible, to be described, represented, and discussed reasonably. This is evidence of how we find it so easy to update our technological settings and context but difficult to challenge social norms. In modern capitalism, the conflation of life with work has made it impossible to extricate the two.

In another example, why can we so easily imagine green cars, robot cars, smart cars, shared cars, hydrogen cars, or cars that are 3D printed from mushrooms, whereas imagining that we might find a design solution that abolishes the car from our cities, saving the lives of up to 1.35 million people a year (CDC, 2023), is deemed ludicrous or unachievable? Again, the car is so thoroughly embedded in our society, infrastructure, cities, and, indeed, our imaginaries, that after

TOBIAS REVELL

DESIGN FUTURES LEAD,
ARUP
LONDON, UNITED KINGDOM

only three or four generations and without concerted effort, we cannot fathom a world without it, even though the historical record of human civilization is dominated by thriving carless societies.

Critical futures scholars suggest that a paucity of imagination applied to futures work simply reinforces an "extended present" (Sardar & Sweeney, 2016) or our tendency "to read the future as a fancier version of the present" (Borup, Brown, Konrad, & Lente, 2006: 288). Put simply, we are like the fish in the David Foster Wallace parable who, when asked how the water is, wonder "what the hell is water?" Without imagination, we are unable to consider how we may be within an ontological volume that seems so fixed that it is impossible to imagine another existence.

Figure 1: *Star Trek III*
© Paramount Pictures, 1984

In a historic example, the designers of *Star Trek III* (1984) could imagine a future two hundred years away in which a technology exists that could disassemble someone into atoms, send them across space, and reassemble them again at the other side, but they could not imagine a society in which smoking was eradicated. Again; we have a predilection towards easily imagining radical technological advance while we find it difficult to challenge social norms.*

Scholars of social constructionism call this "stabilization" (Pinch & Bijker, 1984); the point at which a new or emerging technology, policy, or trend achieves such general acceptance that it is assumed there are no viable alternatives, and no need (or credible faculty) to imagine the world otherwise. Returning to AI and automation, a recent review of ethics guidelines found that technology is imagined as the result of "world-historical forces of change—inevitable seismic shifts to which humans can only react...It is taken for given that AI/ML technologies are a) coming and b) they will replace a broad swathe of human jobs and decisions... Consequently, ethical debate is largely limited to appropriate design and implementation—not whether these systems should be built in the first place" (Greene, Hoffmann, & Stark, 2019: 6). In other words, the imaginary of a future of AI is so stabilized that public debate mostly centers on reducing the potential and real harms it inflicts rather than questioning or imagining alternatives to the fundamental assumptions about what kind of AI we have, for whom, what, and why?

This gets us to the "who" of imagining. "[I]maginaries are at once products of and instruments of the coproduction of science, technology, and society" (Jasanoff, 2015: 19). For science, technology, and society, those with wealth and access to labs, demo stages, press coverage, policy research, users' eyeballs, advertising, legislative forums, and the right conferences are the producers; they are given the privilege to contest their imaginary futures in public and to fight to build and stabilize consensus around their own version of the future (Pinch & Bijker, 1984).

It is often the role of good foresight to try and challenge this stabilization and reflect real uncertainty; to broaden perceptions of the future; to consider the possible beyond the probable or prescribed; and to use this breadth of understanding to make strategy resilient and to write adaptable policy or rigorous business plans. However, most people do not encounter the future through these prioritization exercises of policy, strategy, foresight, and business planning (Kerr, Barry, & Kelleher, 2020). The common experience of the future is not found in spreadsheets, white papers, flow charts, and diagrams but in the stuff and stories of the world. Many studies have shown the influence of science fiction movies, video games, and TV on real-world innovation, how it shapes public demand for future products

* The world of Star Trek also has an interesting relationship with work: The Star Trek universe is situated in a post-scarcity age, when people can travel and settle freely and anything can be materialized at will. Yet, in order to drive the drama, various tropes of capitalism are leveraged to introduce conflict over space, resources, or power. In theory, no one in the Federation needs to work but they do so and, despite this, there is almost no political discourse between characters within the Federation.

and services (e.g. Bassett, Steinmueller, & Voss, 2013; Goode, 2018; Romic, 2022), and then how these demands reshape policy and strategy in a mutual feedback loop.

So, how can we draw on this common understanding of stories and fictions about change in order to re-imagine the taken-for-granted? How do we imagine alternatives to the worlds we inhabit, even if we only do this for the sake of invigorating the capacity that we all have to imagine that the worlds we inhabit can be otherwise?

Design fictions

The question for practitioners is how to tell alternative stories that dislodge status quo futures and challenge the commonly held beliefs that underpin them. In a world hungry for stories, how can we liberate the future and empower more people to have a voice in shaping it? How might storytelling through design be used to create new spaces for imagination?

In the quest to expand the scope of imagination in futures work, various methodologies have emerged for challenging the status quo and thinking creatively about the task of exploring and representing possible futures. Two of these methodologies, design fiction and speculative design, have gained prominence for their ability to help us to anticipate multiple and varied possible futures with rich, acute, and vivid tangibility. These approaches go beyond traditional forecasting and report-generation to problematize dominant future imaginaries,

Figure 2:
Abundance
© *Arup, 2022*

providing space for creative innovation and the discovery of future unknown unknowns and allowing immersion in and exploration of unexpected and unconventional ideas.

The increasingly popular practices of design fiction and speculative design indicate a wider acceptance that problematizing, questioning, and challenging our assumptions about the future are just as important as finding rich data to back up our projections. Design projects like *Abundance*, produced by Arup Foresight for the London Design Festival 2022, challenge the accepted norms of the future of our cities through visual storytelling and the careful consideration of the design and material experience of the future (Arup, 2022).

Abundance is set in a future London in which the city has transitioned to a regenerative urban culture. Regenerative design imagines humans as *part* of nature rather than above it: The way we live, interact, and consume contributes to the health and resilience of the natural ecosystem around us. The premise is that this would result in a cleaner, healthier, and more resilient way of life and experience for everyone and everything, but that there are trade-offs. For instance, you might only be able to buy food grown locally to reduce the carbon cost of importing it and might have to eat as a larger group to reduce the fuel costs of cooking. You might not be able to travel wherever you want, whenever you want, or use as much energy as you like. The shift to a regenerative world is also a shift in values, from consumption, individualism, and extraction to contribution, restoration, and community.

On the surface, however, these ideas can be quite abstract or intimidating. Regenerative design is a growing field with some strong principles and few case studies. So, importantly, *Abundance* takes the abstract and complex notions of life in a regenerative future and materializes them. The design scholar Carl DiSalvo has shown how people assemble around "issues" that are often material: the closure of a factory, the building of a new block of flats, the moving of a school, the termination of a service (DiSalvo, 2009). When dealing with somewhat "immaterial" issues like alternative futures, the future of AI, or how we might live differently, he shows how design can materialize these abstract notions into issues that people can assemble around, discuss, and deliberate over. By examining the lived experience of an average person and eschewing a heroic narrative that might be seen in mainstream TV or film, *Abundance* invites the audience to compare the life of this future fiction with their own and engage with the way a humble corner of the future really plays out; in the domestic, social, political, and community spheres, not with big heroes; human or technological.

But designs and stories alone are not enough. We must also address the "who" of imagining. For a healthy society, we *must* empower more people to create and imagine. Work from organizations like Camden Council and the Joseph Rowntree Foundation in the UK (Imagination Infrastructuring, n.d.) point towards the more general legitimization of "imagination" as a tool of collective decision-making and civic participation in futures by providing the space, time, and support for more people to contribute to imagining solutions to social issues.

Those shaping possible futures challenge "transhistorical continuity; The sense that we are on an inevitable future path with one particular version of 'progress'" (Romic, 2022). As Frederic Jameson observed: Most futures work "does not seriously attempt to imagine the 'real' future of our social system. Rather, its multiple mock futures serve the quite different function of transforming our own present into the determinate past of something yet to come" (Jameson, 1982: 152). For many, the future feels inevitable; the coming of AI, the release of the next car or smartphone, worsening weather and climate—a long line of incremental "improvements" on an extended present stretching infinitely into the status quo future.

The promises and inevitability of status quo futures *have*, however, been reversed at times: nuclear proliferation happily stopped; human cloning *could* have been a part of our world but was swiftly and universally prevented. Even further back, the abolition of slavery, women's suffrage, modern democracy, and then, thinking forward; the green transition. All seem impossible until the right story inspires leaders and decision-makers to believe that other worlds are possible. As science fiction writer Ursula Le Guin reminded us: "We live in capitalism, its power seems inescapable—but then, so did the divine right of kings" (Le Guin, 2014).

References

Arup. 2022. ***Abundance*** [Short film]. Directed by Luke & Josh Exell (Exell Film).

Autor, D.H. 2015. Why are there still so many jobs? The history and future of workplace automation. ***Journal of Economic Perspectives,*** 29(3): 3-30.

Bassett, C., Steinmueller, E., & Voss, G. 2013. ***Better made up: The mutual influence of science fiction and innovation.*** Nesta Working Paper 13/07. London: Nesta. Accessed online https://www.nesta.org.uk/report/better-made-up-the-mutual-influence-of-science-fiction-and-innovation/. Viewed February 26, 2024.

Borup, M., Brown, N., Konrad, K., & Lente, H. van. 2006. The sociology of expectations in science and technology. ***Technology Analysis & Strategic Management,*** 18(3-4): 285-298.

Burgess, M. 2017. Calculating, plotting ravens make plans for their future. ***WIRED,*** July 14. Accessed online https://www.wired.co.uk/article/ravens-plan-future. Viewed February 26, 2024.

CDC. 2023. ***Road traffic injuries and deaths—A Global problem, centers for disease control and prevention.*** Accessed online https://www.cdc.gov/injury/features/global-road-safety/index.html. Viewed October 18, 2023.

Cyran, R. 2023. AI offers leisure, if not happiness. ***Reuters,*** May 12. Accessed online https://www.reuters.com/breakingviews/ai-offers-leisure-if-not-happiness-2023-05-12/. Viewed October 18, 2023.

DiSalvo, C. 2009. Design and the construction of publics. ***Design Issues,*** 25(1): 52.

Elish, M.C., & Boyd, D. 2018. Situating methods in the magic of Big Data and AI. ***Communication Monographs,*** 85(1): 57-80.

Goode, L. 2018. Life, but not as we know it: A.I. and the popular imagination. ***The Journal of Current Cultural Research,*** 10(2): 185-207.

Greene, D., Hoffmann, A. L., & Stark, L. 2019. Better, nicer, clearer, fairer: A critical assessment of the movement for ethical artificial intelligence and machine learning. ***Proceedings of the 52nd Hawaii International Conference on System***: 2122-2131.

Imagination Infrastructuring. (n.d.). ***Imagination infrastructures*** [Website]. Accessed online https://www.imaginationinfrastructuring.com/. Viewed October 18, 2023.

Jameson, F. 1982. Progress versus utopia: Or, can we imagine the future? ***Science Fiction Studies,*** 9(2): 147-158. DOI: 10.5040/9781474248655.

Jasanoff, S. 2015. Future imperfect: Science, technology and the imaginations of modernity. In S. Jasanoff, & S.-H. Kim (eds.), ***Dreamscapes of modernity: sociotechnical imaginaries and the fabrication of power:*** 1-33. Chicago/ London: The University of Chicago Press.

Kerr, A., Barry, M., & Kelleher, J. D. 2020. Expectations of artificial intelligence and the performativity of ethics: Implications for communication governance. ***Big Data & Society,*** 7(1): 1-12.

Le Guin, U. K. 2014. ***Speech in acceptance of the National Book Foundation Medal for Distinguished Contribution to American Letters.*** Accessed online https://www.ursulakleguin.com/nbf-medal. Viewed May 8, 2023.

McKinsey & Company. 2022. ***Value creation in the metaverse: The real business of the virtual world.*** Report. Accessed online https://www.mckinsey.com/capabilities/growth-marketing-and-sales/our-insights/value-creation-in-the-metaverse. Viewed October 18, 2023.

Paramount Pictures. 1984. ***Star Trek III: The Search for Spock*** [Movie].

Pinch, T. J., & Bijker, W. E. 1984. The social construction of facts and artefacts: Or how the sociology of science and the sociology of technology might benefit each other. ***Social Studies of Science,*** 14(3): 399-441.

Romic, B. 2022. Negotiating anthropomorphism in the Ai-Da robot. ***International Journal of Social Robotics,*** 14(10): 2083-2093.

Sapolsky, R. 2004. ***Why zebras don't get ulcers.*** New York: St. Martin's Press.

Sardar, Z., & Sweeney, J. A. 2016. The three tomorrows of postnormal times. ***Futures,*** 75: 1-13.

Suchman, L., & Weber, J. 2016. Human-machine autonomies. In N. Bhuta, S. Beck, R. Geiß, H.-Y. Liu, & C. Kreß (eds.), ***Autonomous weapons systems - Law, Ethics, Policy:*** 75-102. Florence: European University Institute.

STEFAN WOLF

CORPORATE FORESIGHT AND FUTURE RESEARCH, VOLKSWAGEN
HANNOVER, GERMANY

Photo: Erich Goldmann

NOT-KNOWING AS A HEURISTIC OF ITS OWN: CERTAIN UNCERTAINTIES IN FUTURES RESEARCH

Strangely
we do not have to believe
what we know. (Christa Wolf)

Introduction

The future: What kind of future will it be and who is responsible for it? In the late 1980s, this question was already being raised by Zimmerli (1988). The future is generally open and a so-called *black box* (Popper). What we call "the future" is a mixture of wishes and anxiety, of hopes and fears. In these four basic elements of foresight thinking, *not-knowing* plays a major role. What makes futures plausible? *Not-knowing* is essential for the understanding of scenarios. Both a creative and a cognitive (re)source, the more that we have *not-knowing* in mind when thinking about future(s), the more convincing and impactful our analysis and perspectives will be. Managing *non-knowledge* in such a manner means practicing a reflexive methodology of futures research. *Not-knowing* has its own heuristic quality; it is an independent form of knowing and emphasizes the diversity of views: As critical thinking, *not-knowing* makes path dependencies and certain uncertainties about the future obvious and transparent. When we know better what we do not know, we are more aware, open-minded, and thoughtful. We differentiate various possible futures and take more responsibility for our *non-knowledge*. This is, to my mind, the *Art of the Long View* (Schwartz). Finally, *unlearning* is a creative form of *not-knowing*. It is a strong tool for training future thinking. In a nutshell: Managing *not-knowing* is a heuristic of its own in thinking about *tomorrow*.

Outdated prejudices about *novelty*

There is a visionary idea through the last centuries, that knowledge societies are enlightened, educated and after all learning societies. (Prisching, 2004: 11)

While the knowledge society as a sociological item is fading out, *non-knowledge* seems to be back on the daily agenda of futures research. However, *not-knowing*, due to its nature, seems to be uncomfortable, as it reveals a knowledge gap. Publicly, the notion of *non-knowledge* is quite unfair, since closing this gap is only a matter of time and the right methodology.

Of course, in the Anthropocene we all learn that new scientific knowledge produces more questions than answers. Mittelstraß (1996) painted the picture of a ball, whose surface becomes bigger when you add more knowledge to it. So, the space of *not-knowing* is also increasing. However, *non-knowledge* keeps its bad image, especially in futures research: It impairs further development and emphasizes threats rather than opportunities. But transdisciplinary futures research is turning these disadvantages into advantages: *Not-knowing* makes futures plausible, by being a cognitive resource, a creative power, and an epistemic category for thinking about possible future scenarios in a holistic way. *Not-knowing* leads to a specific understanding of futures, as I would like to point out:

If we better know what we do not know, our steps referring to different futures are wiser and more far-seeing. We have various impacts in mind, analyze relevant matters, and take unintended consequences into account. More ideas are created, which are better related to each other (holistic approach). The sustainable way to treat not-knowing—as the art of the long view—shapes more perspectives and opportunities for building plausible, robust, and responsible solutions.

A short notion about *not-knowing*

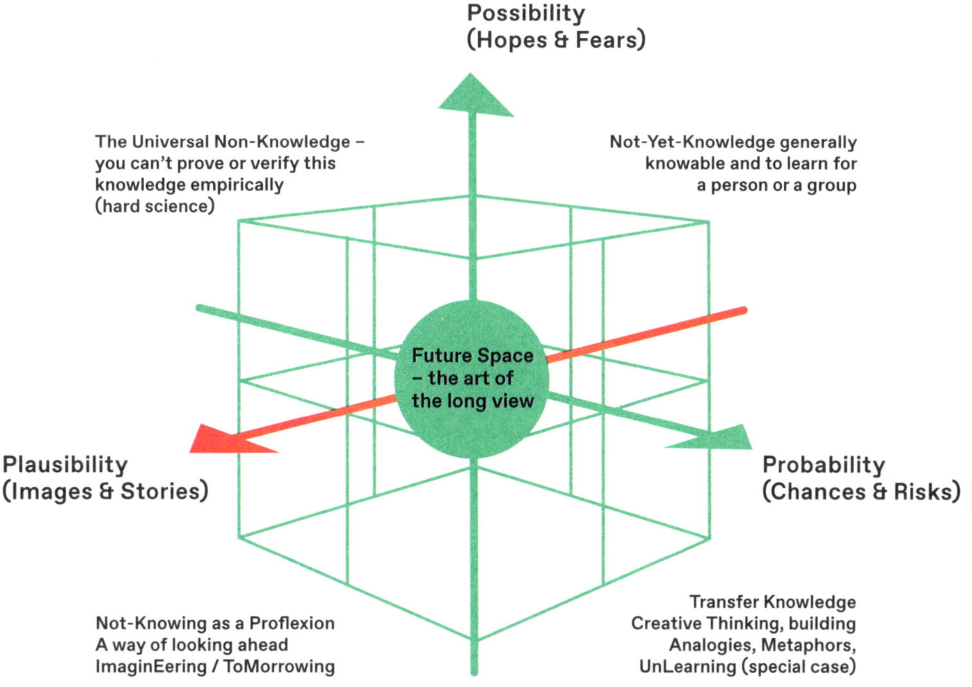

Figure 1:
FuturesSpace—Managing non-knowledge
© *Stefan Wolf*

Any thinking about *not-knowing* must start with Socrates's: *scio, nescio.* We do not really know if the Greek philosopher said these words (we must believe it—another way of *not-knowing*), but he revealed the consciousness of *not-knowing*: *I know that I do not know.* Other forms of *not-knowing* refer to learning (I do not know it now, but I will and can learn it later). Not-yet-knowledge is the most common definition of *not-knowing.* According to the art of the long view (see image above), this way of learning occurs between *possibility* and *probability*. Transfer-knowledge is based on *probability* and *plausibility*. Knowledge that already exists in one discipline is transferred to another discipline to create new knowledge (e.g. biology to sociology in the idea of autopoiesis). The universal *non-knowledge* can be seen as the axis between *possibility* and *plausibility*. Some basic human questions, like the existence of God or where do we come from (and why), etc., are not yet empirically or objectively answered. The fourth and last axis demonstrates *not-knowing* as a *proflexion*. This word does not exist as such but is a creative metaphor for forward-looking reflection. Similar expressions such as *ImaginEering* (© by Walt Disney) or *ToMorrowing*

(Sarah DaVanzo) are used to illustrate a difference in thinking about futures—between *forecast* and *futurism*.

Each element of *not-knowing* is of a different quality. Learning is the easiest and fastest way to close the gap. However, most of the open points in futures questions are not to be learned but to be estimated and evaluated. For instance, *probability* presents questions of uncertainties and demands making decisions between risks and chances. *Possibility*, on the other hand, initiates questions of hopes and fears since it is less calculating and more imaginative than *probability*. In this case, *not-knowing* is more visible due to the way in which the cultural background sounds through the possible future descriptions. At least there is *plausibility*. *Non-knowledge* is an essential part of the narratives, as future stories cannot be understood without discussing questions of the unknown. Plausible futures must reflect the values and settings of the unknown and its need to be transparent to everybody concerned. Even in this short notion of *not-knowing* it becomes apparent how crucial it is to consider the unknown when we talk about future(s).

Knowledge, being a personal competence, is unique. This is why we call it a human *inner capacity*. However, there is a difference between certainty and inner knowledge. Knowledge can be shared in several forms with other people. A certainty is more of an individual conviction or a personal belief. You can also share it by giving examples but not reasons. To discuss *not-knowing*, I will focus on these various forms of knowledge which can be shared with others. Access to explicit knowledge—I assume—will not be an issue for much longer. When we see the progress of OpenAI (Chat GPT, generative artificial intelligence) we get an idea of the possibilities for managing information. *Not-knowing* of that kind will soon disappear (it mostly already has). Searching for facts, figures—any kind of data—will become as easy as a mouse click. We will be *always on* in our *OnLife*, so information is directly at hand. Finally, there is *not-knowing* as cultural bias. When we look at our postcolonial discussion, many of these misunderstandings are obvious.

The philosopher Hans Jonas wanted to follow a *heuristic of fears* in order to cope with possible risks by managing future(s). He made his highly regarded statements about *future ethics* in the 1980s and focused on the unknown threats raised by technological innovations like nuclear power. We knew much less at the time about nuclear waste and we still do not have an adequate solution to this day. His approach was to consider and prioritize *worst-case scenarios* as a means of acting more responsibly. To Jonas, the quality of *non-knowledge* came from thinking future(s) not out of possible technologies or other innovations, but out of these unidentified circumstances. For him, it was a question of the reversibility of decisions and possible consequences. This kind of *future ethics* was also in the mind of Ulrich Beck (1986) and in his idea of *reflective modernity*. Reframing *non-knowledge* in a risk society means managing the progress and welfare of a nation or state in a different way. Beck identified an *organized irresponsibility* of governments and administrations in the way that they did not consider the *non-knowledge* aspects of new technologies like nuclear power or genetic engineering.

Beck's assertion reached the attention of a wide public since the book was published around the time of the catastrophe at Chernobyl. And scandals like Seveso or Bhopal or issues with unhealthy ingredients in food in the 1970s and 1980s came back into the (public) mind.

All these disasters revealed an ineffective approach to managing *non-knowledge* and handling societal anxieties. The ultimate worst case of *not-knowing* was the use of CFCs (chlorofluorocarbons). In the 1960s, none of the scientists would have thought about the possibility that CFCs would cause ozone layer depletion. This was the first time the public took notice of unintended consequences. It was clearly nobody's intention to destroy the atmospheric ozone needed to protect us from sunrays. However, now we realize how important it is to think about unintended consequences in advance in order to avoid, as effectively as possible, undesired futures. Technology assessments are one of the outcomes of managing *not-knowing*, but there is currently not much emphasis on this.

Finally, I would like to discuss systems theory. *Non-knowledge* plays a major role in the concept of *observation* and *distinction* (Maturana & Varela, 1986), meaning that what we observe is merely the result of distinctions made by the observer and not the world *as such*. And, following this approach, *not-knowing* has its own heuristic quality regarding *blind spots* or *unmarked spaces*. Talking about an issue that is a subject of public dispute opens up the field of what is not mentioned. The discussion is focused on opinions, but much is unsaid or unseen and this needs to be relevant to be brought into the debate. And relevance is a matter to be discussed on the second, not the first, level of *observing*. This, in my opinion, is the problem of systems theory as such. It is useful for understanding conflicts in society due to the different levels of *observing* and of openly discussing the findings, but it is not at all solution-oriented and, therefore, not appropriate for handling political problems regarding futures. *Non-knowledge* can be described in systemic thinking as a *risk* (with opportunities) or a *threat* (unspecific fears). So far so good, but systems theory is unsuitable for solving different kinds of understanding in order to orient or evaluate public debates. Systems theory has its limits, but it is useful for understanding different points of view and clarifying arguments about future issues. So, Luhmann stated that societies must manage the paradoxes facing *non-knowledge*, because increasing knowledge does not lead to more certainty and accountability but, rather, to more openness, contingency, and insecurity.

Different forms of knowledge in futures research

As we know, there are known knowns; there are things we know we know. We also know there are known unknowns; that is to say we know there are some things we do not know. But there are also unknown unknowns — the ones we don't know we don't know.

Donald Rumsfeld, the former US Secretary of Defense, made this statement, which seems redundant when talking about the war in Iraq. I stress his statement because it shows how strong uncertainty can become. And yet action is still taken. I will now expand on the idea of *not-knowing* as an equivalent category for futures research: like responsibility, sustainability, the capacity to manage errors, or even risk management. Regarding computer simulations for coping with complex processes like climate change and global warming, *not-knowing* is of high importance. Linear algorithms advance over time, developing patterns to deepen information. What is not in the code is not in the pattern recognition and can lead to unintended discrimination or errors in the system. We describe knowing as a willingness to learn and as an individual capacity to act. What then could be the equivalent in the case of *not-knowing*? Considering fears and hopes, risks and chances as being an essential part, what else could we add?

Not-knowing and *non-knowledge*: Both could have the power to lead to heuristics and new knowledge. The continued existence of knowledge societies is directly related to their capacities to transform *not-knowing* into challenges that can be described and solved in a feasible way, i.e., looking for reversible steps and having unintended consequences in mind, which are evaluated and reframed constantly (Krohn, 1997: 70). However, this is not the only way to look at knowledge and *non-knowledge*. Furthermore, in an economic context it is a question of using knowledge as a market asset. If you cannot make use of it, leave it. My idea of *not-knowing* goes far beyond exploiting knowledge. It is a question of accepting *non-knowledge* as an independent source.

Future ethics as a culture of *not-knowing*

Here, I would like to introduce and add the concept of *Mode-2-knowledge* to futures research. The problem of uncertainties and weaknesses defined by a too narrow-minded understanding of *not-knowing* can be transformed into a capacity for prudent error management. We are living in a diverse and pluralistic society (diversity as an asset and value) with a higher level of contingency (managing uncertainty). And in science, the increasing awareness of the inability to obtain and deliver objective knowledge verified by scientific facts is a step in the right direction. This new understanding is crucial for futures research since futures cannot be assessed by using and proving any experimental hypothesis—this is future thinking rather than an analysis of the present. Therefore, other academic virtues like honesty, transparency, and criticism are indispensable. Futures research must name its stakeholder interests, the point of view, and the figures used (presumptions selected) and must be aware of blind spots in its own future world making. Nowotny et. al. (2004: 7) describe four pillars for defining this new way of *knowledge production*:

Mode-2-knowledge is characterized by

(a) *the structure of a mode-2-society itself (pluralism, diversity),*
(b) *a contextualization of knowledge in the public sphere (agora),*
(c) *a certain robustness of knowledge shown in public discussion and criticism (stand the test of time),*
(d) *a higher expertise in the whole society (higher level of education and information).*

Futures discourses are based on values and should be organized by an *institutional scepticism* (Merton) in order to acknowledge *not-knowing* as an entity in itself (Mayntz). So why not start by asking the question: *What is most important about the future that we do not know?* This would open horizons of unknown ideas and possible futures. The interaction and intellectual exchange of plural and diverse cultures of *not-knowing* (Mayntz et al., 2008: 29) is vital if we want to describe possible and desired futures. The participation of the public would create more of a learning culture and less of a teaching culture. This could be a tipping point for futures research:

"In democratic societies the role of science is not to explain in what kind of future we should live. Academia and science can offer opportunities, ideas and maybe visions and deliver some good reasons to make them true. And science can describe conditions which are indispensable to realize these possible and desired futures." (Economists4Future, 2020, 8)

All four pillars of *Mode-2 knowledge* production are essential for defining the new culture of *not-knowing*. **(a)** In the era of adaptation (Staab, 2022), society discusses not only technological innovations but also socio-cultural ones. In the process of innovation, technology assessment must start as early as possible and bear multiple aspects in mind. *Not-knowing* is a basic element of public opinion regarding futures. To make this happen, plausible scenarios are needed. Plausibility means not only being transparent in the presumptions you make, but also naming the unknown and offering ways to handle this kind of uncertainty. **(b)** In public space (Agora), the difficulty is to differentiate the forms of knowledge and *non-knowledge*. The contextualization of knowledge, proven by time and different stakeholders in society (scientific communities, the public mind, media), is an iterative process. The use of the Delphi method—like Delphi of old Athens giving advice for the future—might be useful. Today, scientists and experts would describe possible futures by bringing in rationality and reasons. Of course, this process works best with technological innovations since there is a roadmap. However, the attention to *not-knowing* is essential here, as it opens the mind to what cannot be seen at first sight because, although important, it is not intended. **(c)** Robust knowledge is generally restricted spatially and temporally. In this case, *not-knowing* helps to reduce the risk of oversimplification, when stakeholders stick too close to the context and lose sight of the bigger picture and its overall questions.

Being responsible can only be realized in an intermediate period and a limited range (Dahrendorf, 2006: 17ff). When planning an action, taking responsibility is more successful in acknowledging what is not known. The COVID-19 pandemic demonstrated the power of private research institutions to invent and innovate vaccines. This is *Mode-2-knowledge* that combines public research done by universities and research centers with privately funded institutions. *Not-knowing* is important here, as results and possible unintended consequences are less under public control. Public institutions are not fully transparent in their work, but private research labs are even less so and, as they have to reach financial goals (return on investment, ROI), their behavior is profit oriented and might create a conflict of interest. A final, but important, problem is the making of futures. This means creating trends, ideas, and so-called windows of opportunities in order to push (consumer) markets. Trend opportunism (Rust) is not reliable for futures research because it is not transparent in its presumptions and objectives. Trend opportunism is full of plastic words, which sound good but have no meaning. Plastic words are like bullshit (Frankfurt). They lack substance and lead to useless trends. They are a void regarding possible futures.

(d) The last pillar refers to increased public knowledge. One of the positive effects of new and social media is the access to information (despite fake news, filter bubbles, and echo chambers, which I am not going to address here). Primarily, this is not knowledge, but information. The gap between experts and laypeople is getting smaller. Experts must explain in greater depth and articulate in a way that is understandable to a broader public. Regarding futures, this gap always used to be unreasonable because nobody knows the future. The individual concern is the relevant criteria regarding desired futures. Knowledge is also expressed by attitude, purpose, and conviction (belief). Insights exist by being concerned. Stakeholder dialogue, like round tables—an experimental WE—would be one idea for closing the gap and crossing borders. Responsible futures require all the perspectives of a democratic society, even if it takes more time and effort to design the participation. The commitment to a common future will be much higher, even *beyond price*. Using artificial intelligence (AI) is a really good example for closing the gap. This new kind of knowledge is widespread amongst the public. There are many users who work on a high level with AI (gaming, business actions (translation), simulation, etc.). The more we use AI, the better it gets. Computer simulation now has the status of robust knowledge and plays a major role in scientific discourse—the best example: climate change and global warming. Big data serves to evaluate huge amounts of information by pattern recognition (stochastics) and, therefore, more probabilities can be calculated to be approximately right (which is better than being completely wrong). Beck called this a reflective way of using scientific knowledge. AI is, in its inherent nature, both problem and answer.

Not-knowing is needed for better simulation to clarify all (scientific) presumptions but, behind the algorithm, cultural bias, risks of discrimination, and other prejudices, must also be transparent. If you do not discuss *not-knowing* in an adequate way, more mistakes will occur as unforced errors.

Proflexions to manage certain uncertainties

Terzic (2022: 17) points out the difference between *Future* and *l'Avenir*. Talk about possible futures is mostly dominated by *futures thinking*: having a plan, programs, or projects. We think of the future as a progress of technological solutions to shaping tomorrow. *L'avenir* is a word that opens horizons. It is *non-knowledge*, that which comes to us as uncertainty. *Not-knowing* is an attitude that accepts this kind of openness and uncertainty. The creation of futures takes more than planning, it also means to frame the unknown. This is what I call *future literacy.* What makes futures plausible is the responsible management of *not-knowing*, a *future ethics* (Jonas). This is why *non-knowledge* needs to be visible and understandable if it is to be explained.

Not-knowing means reversibility and keeping decisions in a state of loop learning, like a philosophy of the *second step* (Musil 1990: 735). It is the reflective capacity to learn by making errors and to keep this possibility of failure in mind. The art of the long view can be described as a sense of proportion (Bieri, 2017) and scale. You must be as precise as possible in order to estimate futures and tell stories about *not-knowing*. Future literacy means to have knowledge on a second level. You know that you do not know (Socrates) but you are evaluating all possibilities by having this in mind. *Non-knowledge* is best discussed in exchange with others who have multiple perspectives and different mindsets. *Not-knowing* requires keeping a distance to oneself and has a second level order to rethink and reframe futurism. Thinking this way means being subversive and not accepting plastic words or any other claim for future trends. It means being intellectually incorruptible (Bieri). *Not-knowing* must be accompanied by an ethical attitude and guidelines. The more you know, the more you can empathize with others. The art of the long view is, in a way, future ethics.

Proflexions, as a metaphor, relates to the words we use for future thinking. Perhaps a specific language is needed: sensitive, empathic, colorful, or vivid. *Fun to say*. This language must astonish and attract people's minds. Cory Doctorow dropped this statement during the *Sharing Desired Future*s conference in Linz 2023. Of course, plausibility is more important than easy understanding. However, using strong metaphors can help to illustrate the ideas. It is necessary to visualize fractures in future thinking and to make contradictions transparent and intelligible. Future scenarios should raise questions, encourage new thinking, and open the horizon for further steps. Responsible futures research (Opaschowski) is based on a transdisciplinary culture of trial and error (*thought experiments*) as well as of connecting and sharing issues (*network thinking*). *The fact that we are unable to speak precisely and with certainty about the future should not be an excuse for not wanting to say anything about it* (Tofler in Rust, 2009: 10).

Finally, there is one special form of *not-knowing: conscious unlearning.* This is a strong creative tool. Technological innovations are invented twice. First in a material sense; second in their cultural adaptation. *Conscious unlearning* makes reinventing technical solutions in various cultural adaptations possible. It is a powerful tool for reframing future scenarios, rejecting plastic words, and resisting trend opportunism. Unlearning is a capacity to rethink futures.

You will become more aware about your own narratives, unlearn your usual way of thinking, and reframe your mindset. But it is not only a question of leaving the path and disrupting path dependency. Unlearning has nothing to do with going far beyond looking for the next trend (to consume). It is more of an attitude of staying open-minded and, possibly, doing things the other way around. *Thinking out of the box.* It may be sensible not to stick to facts and figures. However, *future literacy* will look for accurate descriptions and the correct use of information. Asking good questions is one of the positive learnings from properly managing *not-knowing*. This will also be essential in staying away from easy and simple answers for possible futures, just knowing that there is so much *non-knowledge* that we must consider.

Understanding possible futures means forward-thinking reflection—*proflexions*.

I would like to thank Tina Reif for her way of understanding my thinking and for editing the English version.

References

Beck, U. 1986. ***Risikogesellschaft: Auf dem Weg in eine andere Moderne.*** Frankfurt a.M.: Suhrkamp.

Beck, U., & May, S. 2001. Gewusstes Nicht-Wissen und seine rechtlichen und politischen Folgend: Das Beispiel der Humangenetik. In U. Beck, & W. Bonß (eds.), ***Die Modernisierung der Moderne:*** 247-260. Frankfurt a.M.: Suhrkamp.

Bieri, P. 2017. ***Wie wäre es gebildet zu sein?*** Munich: Komplett Media GmbH.

Dahrendorf, R. 2006. Versuch und Irrtum: Das Prinzip Verantwortung im Kapitalismus. In W. C. Zimmerli, & S. Wolf (eds.), ***Spurwechsel: Wirtschaft weiter denken:*** 171-183. Hamburg: Murmann Verlag GmbH.

Förster, M., Herbert, S., Hofmann, M., & Jonas, W. (eds.). 2018. ***Un/certain futures – Rollen des Designs in gesellschaftlichen Transformationsprozessen.*** Bielefeld: transcript Verlag.

Frankfurt, H. 2005. ***On bullshit.*** Princeton: Princeton University Press.

Heintel, P. 2009. Zukunftsgestaltung. Ein philosophischer Essay. In R. Popp, & E. Schüll (eds.), ***Zukunftsforschung und Zukunftsgestaltung – Beiträge aus Wissenschaft und Praxis:*** 87-98. Berlin: Springer.

Hochmann, L. (ed.). 2020. ***Economists4future. Verantwortung übernehmen für eine bessere Welt.*** Hamburg: Murmann.

Jonas, H. 1979. ***Das Prinzip Verantwortung – Versuch einer Ethik für die technologische Zivilisation.*** Frankfurt a.M.: Suhrkamp.

Knott, M.-L. 2011. ***Verlernen - Denkwege bei Hannah Arendt.*** Berlin: Matthes & Seitz Berlin.

Krohn, W. 1997. Rekursive Lernprozesse – Experimentelle Praktiken in der Gesellschaft. Das Beispiel der Abfallwirtschaft. In W. Rammert, & G. Bechmann (eds.), ***Innovation – Prozesse, Produkte, Politik. Jahrbuch für Technik und Gesellschaft,*** Vol. 9: 65-89. Frankfurt am Main: Campus Verlag.

Lefort, C. zit. n. Charim, I. 2005: ***Probleme mit dem leeren Ort der Macht. TAZ,*** October 15. https://taz.de/!531775

Luhmann, N. 1991. ***Soziologie des Risikos.*** Berlin: de Gruyter.

Maturana, H. R., & Varela, F. J. 1986. ***The tree of knowledge: The biological roots of human understanding.*** Boston: Shambhala.

Mayntz, R., Neidhardt, F., Weingart, P., & Wengenroth, U. (eds.). 2008. ***Wissensproduktion und Wissenstransfer – Wissen im Spannungsfeld von Wissenschaft, Politik und Öffentlichkeit.*** Bielefeld: transcript Verlag.

Merton, R. K. 1973. ***The sociology of science: Theoretical and empirical investigations.*** Chicago: The University of Chicago Press.

Mittelstraß, J. 1996. ***An den Grenzen des Wissens – Philosophische Studien.*** Frankfurt am Main: Suhrkamp.

Musil, R. 1990. ***Der Mann ohne Eigenschaften.*** Reinbek bei Hamburg: Rowohlt.

Nowotny, H., Scott, P., & Gibbons, M. 2004. ***Wissenschaft neu denken - Wissen und Öffentlichkeit in einem Zeitalter der Ungewißheit.*** Weilerswist: Velbrück Wissenschaft.

Opaschowski, H. W. 2009. Zukunft neu denken. In R. Popp, & E. Schüll (eds.), ***Zukunftsforschung und Zukunftsgestaltung – Beiträge aus Wissenschaft und Praxis:*** 17-24**.** Berlin: Springer

Popp, R., & Schüll, E. (eds.). 2009. ***Zukunftsforschung und Zukunftsgestaltung – Beiträge aus Wissenschaft und Praxis.*** Berlin: Springer.

Popper zit. n. Fischer, E. P. 2024. ***Dialektik der Aufklärung 2.0*** [Blog entry]. Accessed online www.epfischer.com/dialektik-der-aufklaerung-2-0. Viewed January 25, 2024.

Prisching, M. 2004. Was ist das Neue an der Wissensgesellschaft. In M. Held, G. Kubon-Gilke, R. Sturn (eds.), ***Ökonomik des Wissens – Jahrbuch Normative und institutionelle Grundfragen der Ökonomik,*** Vol. 3: n.p. Marburg: Metropolis.

Rust, H. 2008. ***Zukunfts-Illusionen - Kritik der Trendforschung.*** Wiesbaden: VS Verlag für Sozialwissenschaften.

Schwartz, P. 1997. ***The art of the long view.*** Weinheim/Berlin: Bantam Doubleday Dell Pub. Group.

Shamiyeh, M. 2020. ***What plausibly makes the future plausible?*** Proposal for FWF *Connecting Minds.* Linz: University of Art and Design.

Staab, P. 2022. ***Anpassung – Leitmotiv der nächsten Gesellschaft.*** Frankfurt a.M.: Suhrkamp.

Steinweg, M. 2019. ***Proflexionen.*** Berlin: Matthes & Seitz Berlin.

Terzic, Z. 2022. ***Zukunft - Kunst des Ungewissen.*** Zurich: Diaphanes Verlag.

Wieland, W. 1982. ***Platon und die Formen den Wissens.*** Göttingen: Vandenhoeck & Ruprecht Verlag.

Willke, H. 1998. ***Systemisches Wissensmanagement.*** Stuttgart: UTB.

Wolf, S. 2010a. Philosophie des „nächsten Schritts": Politikberatung in der Wissensgesellschaft. In K. H. Schrenk, & M. Soldner (eds.), ***Analyse demokratischer Regierungssysteme – Festschrift für Wolfgang Ismayr zum 65. Geburtstag:*** 165-182. Wiesbaden: VS Verlag für Sozialwissenschaften.

Wolf, S. 2010b. Urteilskraft – ein alter Begriff ist neu zu denken. In: A. Gimmler (ed.), ***Vernunft und Innovation:*** 105-119. Munich: Fink Wilhelm GmbH + Co KG.

Wolf, S. 2013. Zukunftsideen in Gegenwartsdiskursen. ***Neues Archiv für Niedersachsen 1.2013:*** 128-150.

Zimmerli, W. C. 1988. Wandelt sich die Verantwortung mit dem technischen Wandel? In H. Lenk, & G. Ropohl (eds.), ***Technik und Ethik:*** 92-111. Stuttgart: Reclam Verlag.

Zimmerli, W. C. 1992. Lob des ungenauen Denkens Der lange Abschied von der Vernunft. In W. D. Rehfus (ed.), ***Der Taumel der Moderne:*** 13-27. Langenfeld: Bukowski.

Zimmerli, W.C. & Wolf, S. (eds.). 2006. ***Spurwechsel: Wirtschaft weiterdenken***. Hamburg: Murmann Verlag GmbH.

Photo: Erich Goldmann

RIEL MILLER
AUTHOR ON THE THEORY AND PRACTICE OF USING THE FUTURE TO CHANGE WHAT PEOPLE SEE AND DO
PARIS, FRANCE

BEYOND THE DEATH SENTENCE OF STRIVING FOR BETTER FUTURES: CAN HUMANITY HEAR THE UNIVERSE?

A primary feature of our time is that, despite numerous warnings and ever-more reliable evidence from multiple sources, humanity is failing to comprehend and manage its spiraling impacts upon the global system.
Farewell Alternative Futures?
(Richard A. Slaughter)

Just because our blithe monumentalist folly ended up changing the conditions to which we have been accustomed—and which served as guidelines for our habits and rules—, this does not mean that we can fix things or somehow acquire the power to control what we never controlled in the first place. The reproach, or admonition, lurking behind so many dire warnings—usually intended to incentivize compliance with some policy or changes motivated by the fear of cataclysm—is that: a) if you were better, you would not have committed such "bads" (repent and fly straight); and/or b) do not make the same mistake next time—learn from history. The entire "what-if" assessment and judgement depends on a heroic version of causality, outcomes, and change.

Oddly enough, it is pretty obvious that climate change is not some demonstration of our power. Just the opposite, it is a demonstration that we have no idea what we are doing and live in a universe that is not amenable to that kind of control. We are along for the ride, and the sooner we become at home with our home, the less we are likely to engage in the kind of insanity and horror that produces atomic bombs and the vampire frenzy of sucking oil out of the planet. Humans do not create the future, despite the narcissistic claims of Silicon Valley titans. Neither is our species nice or wise, nor is this universe.

So why not, instead of using the future to calculate our sins and redress our errors, change frameworks? What about applying our ability to imagine the not-past, not-present, to appreciate being, rather than a rat-race hell-bent on achieving pre-defined becomings? Reorienting our imagination so that it contributes to sensing and making sense of the emergent present, rather than obscuring it. Such a shift might not only reanimate the past as the present changes the meanings of what has already been. But, even more crucially, for people's peace of mind and confidence in a universe where the only certainty is uncertainty, it is a change that might enable us to become better at detecting and inventing difference as it constantly emerges. Adopting a strategy (yes, it is a goal) of becoming more futures literate makes both the past and the present more multi-dimensional, a living tapestry of differences.

In this way, difference in the emergent present, and the creativity it expresses, animates a joy in being—rather than posing a threat to pre-conceived becomings. Changing our relationship with the unknowable future also promises to alter the certainty with which people project zero-sum outcomes—the win/lose dualism of war and annihilation of the other. Humility and openness towards imagined futures defuse the inherently unverifiable accusations, the dueling speculations of looming death, hatred, and suffering, into considerations of how to manifest one's morals, ethics, and truths through what one does now. Relocating what matters to the present, combined with an enhanced ability to exalt difference, radically alters the implications of conflict. Disagreement, even fear, will not disappear. But, instead of conflating difference with all-or-nothing winning or losing, difference is grasped as the fuel of creativity, learning, and change. It is time to grow up and escape from the intransigent stasis of hatred. Indeed, this may be the biggest value added of futures literacy—the ability to step away from embodying conflict and despair with violence and, instead, to live the expression of shared struggles to discover, extend, and be different. Even to the point of embracing the generosity of gifting future generations with a vote of confidence that they will know how to handle the differences of their lives and to take as gentle inspiration the lightness of past generations on their shoulders.

Cool. Sounds like a plan. But how to make it happen?

Futures literacy—imagining an alternative to obedience and authority [1]

Imagine a world in which no human obeyed another human because of fear, or rank, or expected benefits. What an undesirable fantasy: Without the constraints and guiding forces of established authority, the continuity of known punishments and rewards, no one would work or acquiesce to the laws of land and property. Released from the authority of the boss, teacher, and leader, murder and mayhem would prevail. Even progress and order, not to mention the fruits of innovation and betterment through competition, would disappear without the majesty of entrenched authority and the authority of entrenched majesty. Furthermore, such a scenario is totally unrealistic, at odds with "human nature" and history. No one imagines such ridiculous worlds, do not give them a second thought.

The only thing is—people can and do imagine such worlds, across different cultures and languages. Regularly and consistently, when invited to wander in the non-probable and non-preferable imaginary landscapes of a Futures Literacy Laboratory (Carleton & Miller, 2023; Miller, 2018). Hundreds of these co-created "living laboratories"[2] have invited participants to embrace reasons and methods for imagining the future that go beyond the conventional obsession with colonizing tomorrow. All around the world, hailing from all walks of life, co-creators in Futures Literacy Labs apply their collective intelligence to imagining worlds that break the confines of today's prevalent and very ancient "monumentalist" and bureaucratic social orders. They imagine communities that function outside the box of millennia-old systems of authority and obedience, commandments and "preservationism," continuity and control.

Okay, you may say; unleashing the imagination from the confines of probability and teleology (pursuing goals) may be doable, but why bother? If imagined futures are not being used to prepare or plan for the future, what is the point? One answer is that an explicit awareness of the diversity of reasons and methods for imagining the future opens up a bridge or door to recasting the positionings of human agency, the vantage points for formulating our intentions and volition. Call it an escape hatch from the long-standing and ultimately self-annihilating arrogance of pursuing superiority over everything, from other humans to the universe that surrounds us.

---

1 Adapted from a forthcoming chapter in Roberto Poli's *Handbook of Futures Studies*, Springer, 2024.

2 UNESCO Map of Futures Literacy Laboratories conducted around the world: https://www.arcgis.com/apps/PublicInformation/index.html?appid=e8e24182c0204cbdae538afc2832fc97 (Viewed April 17, 2024).

Seduced and diminished by after-the-fact stories of heroic winners, those grand conquerors of tomorrow, paragon purveyors of monocultures of the imagination, is it surprising that, for the hum-drum, run-of-the mill everyday person, the wonder and joy evaporate? To be replaced by an alienation from creativity and mystery that obscures and/or obliterates the meaning of novelty, emergence, improvisation, and ephemerality. Denied the full power of our anticipatory capacities, being alive is reduced to making bets, picking winners. Perception is dilated down to the narrowest of apertures, the calculation of the probabilities of "being right." Prestige dissolves into legacy, the heavy hand of path-dependency, fear of difference, antipathy to change. Instead of cultivating the capacity and confidence needed to celebrate the unexpected, the creative gifts of a novelty-enabled universe, we build bastions of continuity, crafting the fragility and brittleness of continuity at all costs, refusing the agility of diversification, the dance of birth and death that are the only path to experimentalist resilience. We desperately seek the triumph of intelligence, oblivious to wisdom's other views.

As Michael Shamiyeh put it in 2018, "[...] it is important to conceive of the new as a welcome disruption of the old." His invitation to relocate difference, from the enemy of planning and certainty, to a source of inspiration and creativity, offers a clear rationale for futures literacy, a key ingredient of open design thinking. Enhancing the human capacity to be free is not a race for ultimate power and omnipotence, but an invitation to taste humility, experience an enhanced ability to sense and make-sense of difference, embrace change and ephemerality, live consciously with each other and with our universe, not against it. Granted; this is a speculative bet, one with no promise of a better future, only a wiser one, that contributes to strengthening common practices and shared learning experiences.

References

Carleton, T., & Miller, R. 2023. ***Futures literacy laboratory playbook: An essentials guide for co-designing a lab to explore how and why we anticipate.*** Paris: UNESCO. Accessed online https://www.researchgate.net/publication/373157930_UNESCO_Futures_Literacy_Laboratories_Playbook_2023_final. Viewed April 17, 2024.

Poli, R. 2024 (forthcoming). ***Handbook of futures studies.*** Elgar.

Shamiyeh, M. 2018. Neues als willkommene Störung des Alten begreifen. ***Der Standard,*** January 8. Accessed online https://www.derstandard.at/story/2000071532638/neues-als-willkommene-stoerung-des-alten-begreifen. Viewed February 15, 2024.

Slaughter, R. A. 2020. Farewell alternative futures? ***Futures,*** 121: 102496.

Photo: Erich Goldmann

CHRISTIN PFEIFFER

SENIOR CONSULTANT AT UNESCO SHS
AND COORDINATOR OF THE UN STRATEGIC
FORESIGHT COMMUNITY OF PRACTICE
ROME, ITALY

DEALING WITH THE FUTURE: EXPLORING WAYS TO REMAIN AMBITIOUS WHILE PUTTING A PIECE OF YOURSELF INTO THE FUTURE YOU ARE LOOKING FOR

The mission of the United Nations Educational Scientific and Cultural Organization (UNESCO) is to contribute to the building of a culture of peace, the eradication of poverty, sustainable development, and intercultural dialogue, through education, the sciences, culture, communication, and information. In its core function as a global laboratory of ideas, UNESCO has pioneered futures literacy and foresight since 2012. While our present day is marked by polycrises, we are confronted with deep and systemic challenges, but also numerous opportunities for the paradigmatic shift we need. Futures and foresight can make a significant contribution in this regard: anticipating emerging risks, opportunities, and trends has become crucial, while also boosting more participatory decision-making processes in all fields and enabling us to have a global view on the world and to be aware of our biases and blind spots. The empowering nature of futures and foresight has proven its clear potential to spread the feeling of agency within our society, and broadly supports action-oriented policymaking. With its network of 37 UNESCO Chairs, and in its role as coordinator of the recently established United Nations Strategic Foresight Community of Practice, UNESCO supports its 194 member states and UN agencies in building the capacity to scale their own foresight, co-create, and test new foresight approaches with the aim of contributing to positive social change that involves all stakeholders.

We find ourselves in the age of polycrisis—climate change, digital transformation with far-reaching consequences and risks for humanity generated by artificial intelligence, wars and armed conflicts, energy shortages that drastically impact our economies and lead to inflation and downturns, and a steadily growing level of social inequality. Young people—normally society's backbone for hope—feel lonely and cut off and fear for their long-term future. This inspired researchers in Poland to collect data, starting in 2016, for the *Dark Future Scale*,[1] which measures in five items the tendency to think about the future with anxiety and uncertainty. Yes, they started in 2016 and, therefore, before the dramatic outbreak of the COVID-19 pandemic, which turned our world upside down for some time. And yes, we live in a *VUCA World*[2] that does not allow for a linear determination of cause and effect. It is Volatile, as it constantly changes and unfolds in completely unexpected and sometimes dramatic ways that require the capability to adapt in advance; it is Uncertain, difficult to predict and simply so different from historical patterns and traditional forecasts; it is Complex, as problems appear to be multilayered, with far-reaching repercussions; and, finally, it is Ambiguous, offering multiple options that can lead to paradoxes and, sometimes, contradictory assumptions and deeply challenge our values and understanding of the global world order. Lately, this model has evolved into *BANI*—Brittle, Anxious, Nonlinear, and Incomprehensible, requiring us to respond with resilience and to nurture our abilities regarding empathy, improvisation, and intuition.[3]

---

1 The *Dark Future Scale* is a short form of the Future Anxiety scale, developed by Zbigniew Zaleski (1996). The *Dark Future Scale* is a short and reliable method for measuring future anxiety. "It offers a way to describe the subjective state of many people facing dangers and thinking of adverse events in their personal life as well as in a broader, global context" (Zaleski et al., 2019).

2 Based on the leadership theories of Warren Bennis and Burt Nanus, the VUCA acronym has been used since 1987 to describe or to reflect on the volatility, uncertainty, complexity, and ambiguity of general conditions and situations. Since 2015, the VUCA concept is very present in management and leadership studies, driven by the book *Managing in a VUCA World* by Oliver Mack, Anshuman Khare, Andreas Krämer, and Thomas Burgartz (2016).

3 This new approach has been coined by Jamais Cascio (2022). An interesting overview of VUCA versus BANI was prepared by Stefan F. Dieffenbacher in 2023, available at: https://digitalleadership.com/blog/bani-world/ (Viewed April 23, 2024).

But wait a moment—is that all?

Threatened from all angles, this might be the moment to pause and ask an important question: What is humankind's most precious resource? Neither gold, nor oil, nor data—most of us will easily agree.

Realizing that we are not the center of the universe, that we are descended from apes, and that we have a subconscious that we cannot control was bitter.[4] But is there a way to contain the fourth *insult to humanity,* either considered against the backdrop of *technology* (Indset, 2019),[5] as our algorithms are more powerful than our brains, or related to the advanced and nowadays difficult-to-limit levels of *interdependency* (Malleson, 2018)?

One constructive answer to the question around the most precious resource to humankind could be *meaning*. Meaning is what captivates and excites us, as we experience it with all our senses. And as we cannot make sense merely on our own, and despite the infinite challenges ahead, we are easily triggered to try the avenue of exchanging views on our anticipatory assumptions for a brighter future with others—the greater the variety, the better. In that vein, numerous players have understood the urgency of becoming creative and of offering ways to counter the *VUCA World* with *VUCA Thinking*,[6] which aims at strengthening Vision, Understanding, Clarity, and Agility as a means of adapting to change quickly and thinking beyond common boundaries.

Gabriela Ramos, UNESCO's Assistant Director General for Social and Human Sciences recently defined the crux of the matter: "there is an urgent need to enable a mind-shift and transcend the limitations of path-dependent thinking that led us to the current polycrisis" (UNESCO, 2023a: 2).

For more than a decade, UNESCO has put effort into the question of how to use the future to rethink the present and intensified work among all stakeholders to promote the ability to nurture hope and inspire constructive action among member states, institutions, and communities. Thanks to carefully prepared Futures Literacy Laboratories and foresight exercises, partners are experiencing how not to limit themselves to the contemplation and exploration of just one possibility. A key consideration here relies on the acceptance of the statement that the future does not (yet) exist and that, therefore, no data is available from the future that can reliably help us to predict. By probing into the full spectrum of futures (probable, desirable, but also preposterous) we learn how to reveal, challenge, and reframe our assumptions, which steadily contributes to the generation of new

4 In 1917, Sigmund Freud identified three insults to humanity: the cosmological, the biological, and the psychological (Freud, 1917).

5 Anders Indset, Die letzte narzisstische Kränkung, in: *Quantumwirtschaft – Was kommt nach der Digitalisierung* (2019), the related blog/website is also interesting: https://andersindset.com/de/das-wirken/die-letzte-narzisstische-kraenkung-der-menschheit/ (Viewed April 23, 2024).

6 Numerous players provide food for thought and reflection, among them the VUCA Learning Platform, available at: https://www.vuca-world.org/ (Viewed April 23, 2024).

knowledge and can help us to become agile in adapting to new situations and constantly changing circumstances. This requires sensible openness that enables us to shift our time horizon, democratize futures processes, and appreciate a participatory action-learning mode, in which improbable and unpreferred scenarios can also be touched upon without prejudice.[7]

Figure 1
A capability-based approach
© *UNESCO*

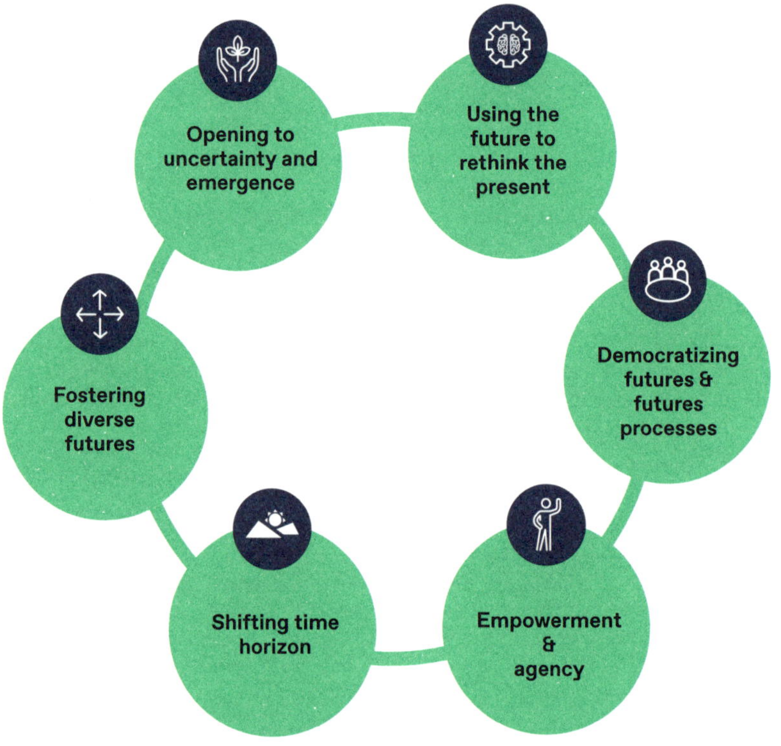

So far so good, it is no secret that nobody has a crystal ball. Many of us might have been engaged over the last year(s) in horizon-scanning, developing scenarios, and using abstraction and reframing techniques, and might even have paid attention to making those scenarios as inclusive as possible, by taking diverse stakeholders' views into account. But how can we train ourselves to expand our ability to cope with uncertainty and become resilient, to turn threats into opportunities or at least minimize damage?

7 More details are available at: https://en.unesco.org/futuresliteracy/about (Viewed April 23, 2024).3 This new approach has been coined by Jamais Cascio (2022). An interesting overview of VUCA versus BANI was prepared by Stefan F. Dieffenbacher in 2023, available at: https://digitalleadership.com/blog/bani-world/ (Viewed April 23, 2024).

Antoine de Saint Exupéry (1952) affirms that, as for the future, our task is not to foresee it, but to enable it. To a certain extent, this confirms that we need to experiment and to understand that we can fail when we accept not being able to predict, but must also learn to adapt quickly to change and to factor uncertainty and open-mindedness into our decision-making processes.

Working at an international organization like UNESCO, with its unique mandate to advance peace, sustainable development, and human rights by facilitating collaboration and dialogue among nations, I have no doubts about the power of collective intelligence to inspire and develop transformative ways forward. But let us become concrete and choose an example that fits the non-profit, social, and human sciences background, add global outreach, and pick a futures-related topic that is high on the international policy agenda today: intergenerational equity.

Intergenerational equity, solidarity, or justice, as stakeholders call it, has become an issue of major concern and media coverage, especially due to global protests regarding climate urgency. While it has many meanings, at least when it comes to nuances, and is approached differently by many cultures, it is a topic that has a clear relevance for today's decision-making processes, as well as an intrinsic correlation with a need to apply a long(er) term perspective. A quick check on the Internet confirms that weight has already been lent to this since 1997. The UNESCO Declaration on Responsibilities of the Present Generations *Towards Future Generations*, calls its member states to "ensure that the needs and interests of future generations are not jeopardized by the burden of the past, and to hand on a better world to future generations." The twelve articles reiterate important aspects on how to safeguard the fragile equilibrium that has to be maintained, referring to human rights and fundamental freedoms, including—among others—freedom of choice, non-discrimination, preservation of life on earth, protection of the environment, human genome and biodiversity, cultural diversity and heritage, development and education, and, finally, peace.

26 years later, the world appears to be even more complex, and the importance of futures work and foresight has gained great prominence in the UN ecosystem, as evidenced by the UN Secretary General's *Our Common Agenda Report* (2021), which emphasizes the need to promote and employ foresight for anticipatory governance, transformation, resilience, and fostering solidarity with future generations.[8] In response, the UN system has focused on the elaboration of a set of succinct principles that enshrine related values and serve as a basis for a shared understanding of the concept of future generations and intergenerational equity. Those *UN System Common Principles on Future Generations* were launched in May 2023, with the key goal to "ensure greater clarity on terminology and agree on a set of common values across the United Nations system for use across various contexts" (UN Chief Executive's Board on Coordination, 2023).

8 *Our Common Agenda Report* (UN, 2021) refers on multiple occasions to the importance of foresight and future generations. Check in particular Chapter III: Succeeding generations: shaping the future, 38-47.

Concretely, they invite us to:

1. Promote a vision for future generations based on human rights and equity
2. Pursue fairness between present and future generations
3. Recognize and foster an interconnected world
4. Think, plan and act with future generations in mind
5. Ensure meaningful representation of future generations and their interests
6. Foster open science, data and knowledge for the future
7. Foster a future-oriented organizational culture and capabilities
8. Strengthen inclusive partnerships and global cooperation.

While the effort certainly deserves praise, what we needed next was something substantial, something able to nurture the specific competences that would allow us to become better at all the aforementioned actions and feel more at ease.

It was in this vein that UNESCO and UN Global Pulse joined forces to design a pilot set of futures tools that help UN employees—at all levels of the hierarchy—to broaden their skills and advance the principles by concrete actions. Engaging with these tools is supposed to stimulate our capability to support the development of rich narrative scenarios, facilitate multi-layered dialogue about the future, and become aware of our biases, in order to become familiar with the roots behind our assumptions. What is better than having a useful toolkit at hand, which is able to help us foster different futures, shift the time horizon, and open up to alternative views of how drivers may play out in the future?

In this regard, it is worth mentioning recent efforts to decolonize our thinking and learning processes with the help of indigenous notions of time, space, nature, relationality, and knowledge and with the objective of truly democratizing futures processes, enriching global dialogue, and cultivating inclusion by developing a deeper appreciation of the other.[9] When participating in these efforts, people reported feeling a greater sense of individual empowerment and ability to change or at least influence their own future and assume responsibility, and felt encouraged to concentrate on those maybe small but precious details that can bring back hope.

Do futures exercises really have such power?

Before practicing ourselves, let us have a look at the *Futuring Peace in Northeast Asia* initiative, which showcased the way in which collective scenario building and testing could enable new avenues for the development of concrete recommendations for policymakers to emerge. The initiative explored pathways to a peaceful future for the region by relating to the role of youth. Among numerous other benefits, the project demonstrated how shared interpretations of historical legacies as drivers of futures can be created and how this can culminate in catalyzing present action in the interests of a preferred future.[10] On top of this, and by applying speculative design techniques, collective insights from the project have served as an inspiration to subsequently create "artefacts from the future." These inputs have provided interesting food for thought for strategic documents, including the recent policy brief *A New Agenda for Peace*, which deals with a broad spectrum of matters affecting our world at a crossroads, given its geopolitical transition and the "series of interlocking threats" (UN, 2023) that we are constantly faced with.

---

9 Numerous pieces are worth mentioning here. I shall take the opportunity to highlight UNDP's recent foresight brief entitled *Indigenous futures—Reimagining Development in Asia and the Pacific* (2022).

10 The project was initiated in 2021 by the United Nations Department of Political and Peacebuilding Affairs (UN DPPA Asia and the Pacific Division and the Innovation Cell) in partnership with UNESCO. Check available information at: https://projects.futuringpeace.org/NEA/methodology (Viewed April 23, 2024).

But back to our initial engagement to widen our capabilities by experimenting with futures while expressing our values. In the frame of intergenerational equity, UNESCO and UNGP are working together to define a preliminary set of focal areas in which training would be worthwhile:

- **Preparation and Planning,** defined as the capability to imagine and discuss probable developments or desirable future states when considering choices, setting priorities, and taking action,
- **Appreciating Novelty,** described as the capability to make sense of the newness arising from complex systems and of innovation related to change,
- **Temporal Empathy,** considered as the ability to empathize across time—past, present, and future—to appreciate the perspectives, needs, and priorities of the dead, the living, and the yet to exist,
- **Intercultural Awareness,** referred to as being aware of one's own cultural positionality and intersectionality while engaging with others to produce intergenerational equity,
- **Enabling Agency,** defined as being able to clearly see what you can do in the present in order to enable changes that may help current and future generations,
- **Long-Term Futuring,** described as the capability to think beyond immediate priorities or short-term futures, to imagine longer time horizons, and, finally
- **Advancing Equitability,** defined as co-producing equitable conditions for the present, the near future, and the more distant future, which entails taking actions today that advance equitability in all its forms and contexts.[11]

While this list is not exhaustive and, to a certain extent, subject to personal interpretation, the development of capabilities in these focal areas can crucially help the UN system to expand its stance toward the near and the more distant future beyond mere preparation and planning (UNESCO, 2023b). A set of tools, including a reflection exercise that stimulates structured conversation about partaking in futures-thinking activities, is offered to accompany our learning journey. Among the featured exercises, one can find some prominent approaches, such as the *Causal Layered Analysis* (Inayatullah, 2013),

11 All information on the project is available at: https://foresight.unglobalpulse.net/intergenerational-equity/ (Viewed April 23, 2024). In addition to the introduction, the description of focal areas, and the collection of tools, it is worth pointing to the feedback module.

The Thing from the Future (Situation Lab, 2014), or *Stranger Futures* (4CF, n.d.),[12] all presented and adapted to the specific background of intergenerational equity.

Would you appreciate a brief deep dive into one of the tools in order to get a flavor of what such an exercise can entail?

Let us look at Tool 5: *Active Futures Thinking*, which intends to stimulate dynamic engagement with your futures thinking by touching upon your own concerns about and images of the future. Inspired by the work of important futurists and researchers in the domain,[13] this tool fosters self-awareness about individual and collective anticipatory patterns through a guided three-step exercise. We start by mapping past and present futures against the backdrop of social, political, cultural, economic, technological, and environmental developments. With the help of selected retro images, a reflection on past people's anticipatory assumptions, compared with those that we make today, can spark an authentic discussion that is further nurtured in step two of the exercise, in which we reflect on patterns of change. What is your personal conception of time? Does this match with the one that our society applies and mainstreams? Does time have to be only linear? By triggering our flexibility, the future could be cyclical, but could also represent a spiral or a pendulum—concepts that require us to imagine a range of potential changes, discontinuities, and overall developments. When progressively associating examples with these words in your mind's eye, you can sense that this step is a crucial one that has the potentiality to shed light on substantive challenges to our current approach to decision-making and, therefore, deserves a reasonable allocation of reflection time! Last but not least, step three invites us to time-travel: after waking up 100 years from now, we look out of the window and are called to experience the new world with all our senses. Supported by AI-generated visual prompts, both individuals and groups can express their thoughts around emerging dynamics, risks, and opportunities as it becomes natural to us to explore how to enable positive change, driven by proper values (UNESCO, 2023c).[14]

Curious? Great! Please reach out, as running such an exercise multiple times with different groups provides the amazing diversity of insights that can unleash our collective intelligence and, in turn, ground humankind's most important value and reflect the *meaning* and sense-making capability of our species, which—at least for the moment—still confirms the distinctive character of humans versus mere algorithms. Finally, this could also be a modern interpretation of Herbert Spencer's appeal to remember that, while we are descendants of the past, we are parents of the future (Spencer, 1867: §34).

---

12 *Stranger Futures* is a strategy board game, developed by 4CF the Futures Literacy Company and designed for professional foresight applications, which requires the collective intelligence of participants in order to question assumptions regarding the future of a given area and to identify significant changes.

13 This tool is inspired by the work of Katie King & Julia Rose West, Sohail Inayatullah, Sirkka Heinonen & Juho Ruotsalainen.

14 Special thanks go to Irianna Lianaki Dedouli and Nicolas Balcom Raleigh, who largely contributed to its development.

References

Cascio, J. 2022. ***The BANI World,*** Keynote talk, Sri Lanka's International Research Symposium on Management [Video]. Accessed online https://www.youtube.com/watch?v=stBdyNBwfpU. Viewed February 16, 2024.

Dieffenbacher, S. F. 2023. BANI World: What is it and Why We Need It? ***Digital Leadership,*** September 3. Accessed online https://digitalleadership.com/blog/bani-world/. Viewed February 16, 2024.

Freud, S. 1917. A Difficulty in the Path of Psycho-Analysis. In: J. Strachey, A.

Freud, A. Strachey, & A. Tyson (eds.), ***The Standard Edition of the Complete Psychological Works of Sigmund Freud,*** Volume 17 (1917-1919): 135-144.

Inayatullah, S. 2013. ***Causal Layered Analysis,*** Sohail Inayatullah at TEDxNoosa [Video]. Accessed online https://www.youtube.com/watch?v=ImWDmFPfifl. Viewed February 16, 2024.

Indset, A. 2019. ***Quantenwirtschaft - Was kommt nach der Digitalisierung?*** Econ.

Mack, O., Khare, A., Krämer, A., & Burgartz, T. 2016. ***Managing in a VUCA World.*** Springer International Publishing.

Malleson, T. 2018. Interdependency: The fourth existential insult to humanity. ***Contemporary Political Theory,*** 17(2): 160-186.

Saint-Exupéry, A. de. 1952. ***The Wisdom of the Sands; Translated by Stuart Gilbert from the French Citadelle.*** London: Hollis & Carter.

Situation Lab. 2014. ***The Thing From The Future.*** Accessed online https://situationlab.org/project/the-thing-from-the-future/. Viewed February 16, 2024.

Spencer, H. 1867. ***First Principles.*** 2nd Edition. London: Williams and Norgate. Accessed online https://oll.libertyfund.org/titles/spencer-first-principles-1867. Viewed February 16, 2024.

UN. 2021. ***Our Common Agenda - Report of the Secretary-General.*** New York: United Nations. Accessed online https://www.un.org/en/content/common-agenda-report/. Viewed February 16, 2024.

UN. 2023. ***Our Common Agenda, Policy brief 9: A New Agenda for Peace,*** July 2023. Accessed online https://www.un.org/sites/un2.un.org/files/our-common-agenda-policy-brief-new-agenda-for-peace-en.pdf. Viewed February 16, 2024.

UNDP. 2022. ***UNDP RBAP Foresight Brief: Indigenous Futures.*** New York: United Nations Development Programme.

UNESCO. 1997. ***Declaration on the Responsibilities of the Present Generations Towards Future Generations.*** Paris: UNESCO. Accessed online https://en.unesco.org/about-us/legal-affairs/declaration-responsibilities-present-generations-towards-future-generations. Viewed February 16, 2024.

UNESCO. 2023a. ***UNESCO-PMU Symposium : towards evaluation frameworks for futures literacy and foresight (Report).*** MOST/2023/FLF/002. Paris: UNESCO. Accessed online https://unesdoc.unesco.org/ark:/48223/pf0000386130. Viewed February 16, 2024.

UNESCO. 2023b. ***Futures for Intergenerational Equity, Inception Report.*** Accessed online https://foresight.unglobalpulse.net/intergenerational-equity/wp-content/uploads/sites/4/2023/04/Report_1704.pdf. Viewed February 16, 2024.

UNESCO. 2023c. ***Futures for Intergenerational Equity, Active Futures Thinking Tool.*** Accessed online https://foresight.unglobalpulse.net/intergenerational-equity/wp-content/uploads/sites/4/2023/04/Tool5.pdf. Viewed February 16, 2024.

UN Chief Executives Board on Coordination. 2023. ***HLCP Paper on the United Nations System Common Principles on Future Generations***, May 2023. Accessed online https://unsceb.org/sites/default/files/2023-05/Advance%20Unedited%20-%20United%20Nations%20System%20Common%20Principles%20on%20Future%20Generations.pdf. Viewed February 16, 2024.

Zaleski, Z. 1996. Future anxiety: Concept, measurement, and preliminary research. ***Personality and Individual Differences,*** 21(2): 165-174.

Zaleski, Z., Sobol-Kwapinska, M., Przepiorka, A., & Meisner, M. 2019. Development and validation of the Dark Future scale. ***Time & Society,*** 28(1): 107-123.

4CF. N.d. ***Stranger Futures - Strategy board game.*** Accessed online https://4cf.eu/stranger-futures/. Viewed February 16, 2024.

STATEMENT

Photo: Roland Pelzl, Cityfoto

CLAUDIA REINPRECHT

AUSTRIAN FOREIGN MINISTRY
VIENNA, AUSTRIA

The world is in shambles, rattled and shaken by a heightened sense of insecurity, instability, and vulnerability in the Age of the Anthropocene. The seemingly untrammeled impact of polycrises and a profound perception of mistrust among major regions of the world, among and within communities, have shaken the very foundations of the international community of nation states. A lot of this distrust that permeates today's international discourse can be traced back to a mindset that looked at shaping the present by colonializing the future for the sake of a few (nations, transnational corporations, individuals). Time and again we have seen power centers emerge that have monopolized the images of the future and of what we as humans are capable of and should aspire to.

In view of this global crisis of trust, the United Nations increasingly refers to futures thinking and to the rights of future generations as novel conceptual ideas that should inform global governance with a view to better presenting a more desirable future for all. With the report *Our Common Agenda* (2021), out of which the idea of a "Summit of the Future" was born, the UN renewed its interest in working on futures literacy and strategic foresight within the United Nations. The Summit of the Future in 2024 is meant to be the global inflection point that will rethink global governance for a more equitable, intergenerationally fair, and sustainable world for both present and future generations. One key phrase is intergenerational equity—a concept whereby the United Nations is seeking to make the world a better place by embracing the futures of people today and of generations to come, especially as longer lifespans mean that four generations will be co-existing at any time. For change to happen, a key requisite is the capacity of all of us to be futures literate. Being futures literate means developing the capability to understand where the images of the futures come from through querying our own anticipatory assumptions and being able to imagine the futures that we want. The future has thus become a defining feature of a new paradigm in diplomacy and global governance as a means of ensuring the very raison d'être of the United Nations—peace and security, human rights, and sustainable development.

The past cannot be undone and the future is unknown. But we as humans can change and enter into a new, futures-literate paradigm by "giving people a sense of agency, intercultural awareness, considering the past and present, appreciating novelty, and temporal empathy" (UN Global Pulse, 2024). This paradigm includes the capacity to jointly imagine and communicate visions of desired futures in order to build our new world. The divisions among nations and within communities will not heal and we will not be able to tackle the big challenges of today and tomorrow unless we establish the global governance systems that enable us to imagine desired futures together.

References

United Nations. 2021. ***Our Common Agenda – Report of the Secretary-General.*** New York: United Nations. Accessed online https://www.un.org/en/content/common-agenda-report/#download. Viewed February 20, 2024.

United Nations. 2024. ***Summit of the Future: Multilateral solutions for a better tomorrow, 22-23 September 2024*** [Summit Website]. Accessed online https://www.un.org/en/summit-of-the-future. Viewed February 20, 2024.

UN Global Pulse. 2024. Using intergenerational equity to build solidarity across generations. ***Medium***, January 4. Accessed online https://medium.com/un-global-pulse/using-intergenerational-equity-to-build-solidarity-across-generations-087749105aba. Viewed February 9, 2024.

Photo: Erich Goldmann

JOSEF HARGRAVE

DIRECTOR AND GLOBAL
FORESIGHT LEADER AT ARUP
LONDON, UNITED KINGDOM

ENABLING DESIRED FUTURES AT ARUP

What is a desired future and why does it matter?

"It is not necessary to change. Survival is not mandatory." This quote from William Edwards Deming (1900-1993) feels like the motto of our time. Despite numerous initiatives, pledges, and a clear aspiration for more sustainable ways of living, we, as a global society, are nowhere near where we need to be to ensure a sustainable future. Greenhouse gas emissions, biodiversity depletion, and habitat destruction are all accelerating instead of slowing down. The consequences of our past and present actions, and inaction, are becoming increasingly evident and disruptive to our lives. This can be seen in the growing threat from extreme weather events such as floods and wildfires, the decimation of over a third of the world's arable land (Milman, 2015), and the growing rate of species extinction, with 70% of wildlife being lost in the past 50 years (Greenfield & Benato, 2022).

The result is a world that is increasingly less equitable, less livable, and less desirable for all. A world where survival is not guaranteed. For humans to thrive, our planet must thrive too. For this to happen, rapid and immediate action is necessary. But what does a better, or a *desired* future, look like? And why is it so hard for us to envision this, let alone achieve it?

Firstly, there is no universal understanding or agreement on the challenges that humanity faces or on the future we are collectively aiming towards. Personal preferences, requirements, divergent political views, varying levels of awareness, and the vast range of individual and collective expectations make consensus on a common vision improbable, if not impossible. These conflicting factors are well illustrated in the current discourse and inaction around the environmental crisis. While many see a 1.5-degree future as not only desirable, but essential, others question the legitimacy, relevance, and impact of this goal. We cannot effectively navigate a path towards a *desired* future unless there is a shared acknowledgement of what this future entails.

This lack of consensus should not stop us from working to develop our own understanding of what a desirable future is, or stop us from articulating this to others, especially in the context of business, design, and investment decisions. To enable progress, it is our responsibility to champion a positive vision and to demonstrate how it can be reached and the benefits it will bring for all of us. For Arup, this vision is a regenerative future, achieved through sustainable development. Establishing this definition facilitates the creation of a framework for change. The vision enables strategy; strategy enables planning; planning enables decisions; and decisions enable action. This "nested" logic of business transformation makes long-term strategic direction, investments, adaptation, reflection, and the development of new capabilities more targeted and effective. It embeds resilience and purpose into our organization and connects the future we want with decisions we need to make today. In defining this future, and being transparent about the pathway towards it, we invite our clients, partners, and the communities we work with to not only share in this vision, but also be a part of the required change.

Futures thinking at Arup

Any clear definition and articulation of a desired future needs to be paired with the collective exploration of strategies for how to get there. At Arup, futures thinking happens in a number of ways. It is embedded in our strategic planning, it is part of the way we deliver projects to clients, and it is a component of our corporate culture and mindset. A project that illustrates this is Arup's *2050 Scenarios*, which maps out plausible future scenarios of a more, or less, sustainable future. The scenarios facilitate discussion around how we can achieve planetary health in alignment with human health. These potential futures are intentional provocations and catalysts for debate. The scenarios provide a framework and starting point for discussion, which enable the exploration of different associated indicators, pathways, obstacles, and opportunities.

The 2050 scenarios were complemented by Arup's work *Reduce, Restore, Remove,* a framework for systemic decarbonization and focused climate action which maps out a plausible pathway *through* net zero. It highlights all the actions, options, and solutions humankind needs to consider, if we are to truly drive the emission reductions required to maintain the 1.5-degree goal, and thereby move us towards the Post-Anthropocene.

Figure 1: Arup's 2050 Scenarios: The four divergent futures—Humans Inc., Extinction Express, Greentocracy, and Post-Anthropocene—range from the collapse of our society and natural systems to the two living in sustainable harmony. © *Arup, 2019*

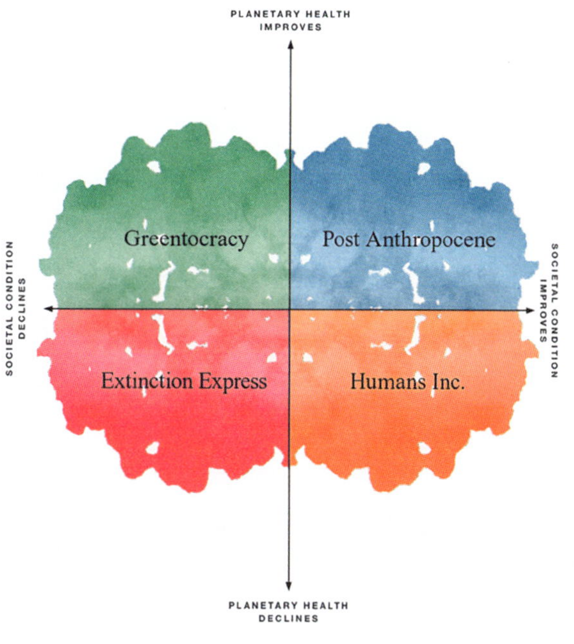

Futures thinking also contributes to a leadership and decision-making mindset that focuses on connecting the future to the present. This mission-oriented approach ensures that our leaders bring strategic and visionary thinking to all of our clients and projects. It supports both practitioners and investors in making the right design decisions today, which is essential in an industry built around long project lifecycles and extended timelines. Large infrastructure projects, for example, can take decades to move from inception to operation. Understanding the future operating context and potential challenges that these assets may encounter is critical to ensuring that resilience and adaptability are built in from the start.

New design paradigms to drive change

Strategies for reaching desired futures rely upon a fundamental shift in our current *design paradigms*. These paradigms are the systems of ideas and base assumptions that underpin and drive our desired future. An example of this is the transition towards the emerging notions of regenerative, multi-species, and nature-led design. These methodologies are about creating a pathway to a world where human and natural systems are not in conflict but co-exist and co-evolve in harmony. This is a world where everything humans use, consume, and build works within the *planetary boundaries*. A future that is positive for people, but also positive for the planet: A building that produces more clean water than it consumes, a new piece of infrastructure that regenerates the local biodiversity, or a structure that consumes more carbon than it emits. Nature-led and multi-species design consider that a project's "stakeholders" go beyond humans and include the wider natural world and overall health of the planet.

These are not new *paradigms*: Indigenous knowledge and practices have long respected ecological patterns and recognized the interconnectedness of all living beings. They provide a greater systemic understanding of our natural systems, of how humans disrupt them, and of the opportunities we have to regenerate nature.

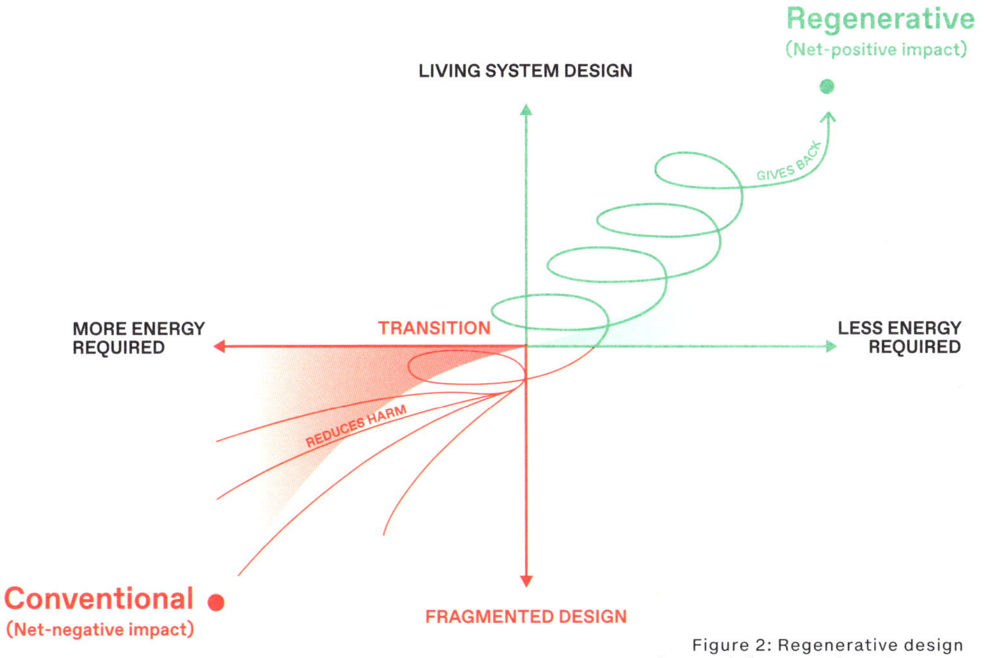

Figure 2: Regenerative design aims to deliver a pathway from net negative outcomes and planetary degradation to net positive outcomes and living system design. © *Arup (2024), adapted from Bill Reed (2007)*

Paradigm transitions are driving a multitude of new approaches and dialogues around how design practices must change to achieve more sustainable and regenerative outcomes for both people and the planet. A good example of putting this vision into practice is Amsterdam's "Habitat Royale." This is a planned 15,000-m² nature-positive residential building in the Zuidas business district that is due for completion by 2026. The proposal was developed by real estate developer KondorWessels Vastgoed and architect Mecanoo, in collaboration with Arup, BOOM Landscape, and Tenderboost. Nature-positive outcomes are achieved through the establishment of a wide range of microhabitats throughout the building's roof, open spaces, and facade. These provide space for a large variety of plants and animals, from birds and hedgehogs to local fauna and insects. This design approach doubled the amount of nature currently present on site. The use of timber means that the building acts as a carbon sink, while renewable energy infrastructure and the effective use of daylight maximizes on-site energy production and minimizes energy-related carbon emissions. Regenerative design is the vision, Habitat Royale is the contemporary manifestation.

Figure 3: Habitat Royale, a planned 15,000m^2 nature-positive residential building for Amsterdam's Zuidas business district. © *WAX*

A different world is possible. The COVID-19 pandemic has shown that, in a time of acute crisis a radically different way of life can emerge. One that is more local, more community-centric, less resource intensive, and more nature focused.

What is required is a clear and long-term vision of where we are going, strategies and pathways for "how" to get there, and a radical shift in ambition and assumptions. We believe that the best way to build a consensus on this collective vision is to articulate its benefits, demonstrate its potential, and inspire others to be a part of the journey. This is what we mean by shaping desired futures, and this is why Arup continues to invest in futures thinking and a futures mindset in everything we do.

References

Arup. 2019. ***2050 Scenarios – Four plausible futures.*** London: Arup. Accessed online https://www.arup.com/perspectives/publications/research/section/2050-scenarios-four-plausible-futures. Viewed January 29, 2024.

Arup. 2022. ***Reduce, restore, remove – A call to action.*** London: Arup. Accessed online https://www.arup.com/perspectives/publications/research/section/reduce-restore-remove-a-call-to-action. Viewed January 29, 2024.

Greenfield, P., & Benato, M. 2022. Animal populations experience average decline of almost 70% since 1970, report reveals. ***The Guardian,*** October 13. Accessed online https://www.theguardian.com/environment/2022/oct/13/almost-70-of-animal-populations-wiped-out-since-1970-report-reveals-aoe#:~:text=Earth's wildlife populations have plunged, pollute on an industrial scale. Viewed January 29, 2024.

Milman, O. 2015. Earth has lost a third of arable land in past 40 years, scientists say. ***The Guardian,*** December 2. Accessed online https://www.theguardian.com/environment/2015/dec/02/arable-land-soil-food-security-shortage. Viewed January 29, 2024.

INTERVIEW

Photo: private

SOHAIL INAYATULLAH

UNESCO CHAIR IN FUTURES STUDIES
BRISBANE, AUSTRALIA

The following interview with Sohail Inayatullah, professor, political scientist, and UNESCO Chair in Futures Studies at the Sejahtera Centre for Sustainability and Humanity in Malaysia, was conducted by Michael Shamiyeh. The aim of the interview was to understand how Sohail Inayatullah assists organizations and institutions in deconstructing their given narratives to develop the futures they wish to create. What does the process look like in concrete terms and what methods are used to reconstruct and communicate desirable futures? Professor Sohail Inayatullah is best known for introducing and pioneering the futures technique of Causal Layered Analysis, which uses a four-layered approach to bring about transformative change. He is on the board of numerous futures-oriented journals and is listed in the top two percent of the world's scientists as measured by the highest impact of citations.

Michael Shamiyeh (MS):
Let's start with your work with organizations and institutions. How do you go about it?

Sohail Inayatullah (SI):
First there must be interest. It can't just be us futurists pushing a particular product. There has to be general, indeed, compelling interest from someone in the organization, a champion. That tends to be someone who has taken a futures course or has heard a keynote. They get inspired and ask a futurist to come to their organization and assist/advise. And once the work starts, I ask them what their narrative is, not about the organization, but about this process they wish to engage in. For example, a few years back I had a project with a national law enforcement agency where, before we began, we created a shared story about the entire project, a narrative that helped us understand what could work and what the points of resistance might be. Instead of the typical and known focus on crime rates and new categories of crime, we instead used the story of a tsunami of crime arriving and the need to take the agency to higher ground, so that they would be safe and have a bird's eye view of the changes ahead. Each of the participants also chose a character for the project: one was the "machete wielder," creating the path to the new village. The other was the "white witch," suggesting appropriate spells—strategies to be used to ensure that the resisters understood the gravity of the change ahead and the need to move toward a predictive data-led crime assessment model. As we played with the narrative, it became clear that we needed a half-way resting point, given that law enforcement executives are reactive and find prevention/anticipatory work challenging. In terms of every engagement. I try to figure out: What's their story? How can I intervene in the process? Who are we, as

law enforcement, both at the surface level of the litany of news headlines and the deeper archetypical level? If this is done well, then the evaluation process later becomes easier. The evaluation is not only an objective process but a narrative process. Many just wish to use the checklist model—did we engage in foresight? How many meetings did we have? What were the forecasts? Did we have four scenarios and are thus now futures-proof? Evaluation from a narrative view is more focused on: How did their story—their identity and unconscious views of self and other—change significantly? Was their vision realized? Did they explore worlds they never even knew existed?

Understanding their narrative, my narrative, the characters we embody in these stories, helps create, I believe, a more successful project. Of course, within this framing, there can be utopias and profound moments of insights as well as tragedies, where the result of the futures work leads to a foundational destabilization of the organization.

MS: In other words, it is about telling and experiencing stories together that ultimately lead to change in organizations.

SI: Yes, we simultaneously exist in the imagined and real worlds—indeed, futures thinking is about working on multiple realities simultaneously. The purpose of narrative futures is to help shift the discourse, the institutional purpose, so new policies and strategies can result. For example, with the Asia Development Bank (ADB), their executive understood that the region was undergoing a dramatic shift, and that lending solely for infrastructure would not cut it, especially with the rise of the Chinese-led Asian Infrastructure Investment Bank. The ADB, as a development bank and as global experts, needed a new purpose. Over the past seven years they have transitioned to a new purpose, that of a knowledge bank. Then the key issue becomes, “But knowledge for what?” For the ADB, this is now framed as knowledge for climate change. The imperative is framed as the battle against climate change, how Asia will be central in this challenge toward renewables. But what is next? Work with policy leaders Susann Roth, Samantha Hung, and futurist Ivana Milojevic, suggests that the ADB becoming a gender bank could be the next organizing discourse. The rationale behind this vision is that gender equality is not only about social justice but also leads to prosperity.
This perspective can be flat or layered. Using Causal Layered Analysis (CLA), we developed an approach that moved from the head of the bank being a woman, to using feminist principals of inclusion and moving beyond GDP to empower women. This CLA chart captures the move from the politics of representation to the ethics of transformation (Inayatullah, Milojevic, & Hung, 2022):

	Today	Tomorrow
Litany	Gender is not bankable	Gender bank
System	Lack of dedicated resources Male-led governance Mansplaining Corporate targets without enough development impact	Standalone focused gender projects Dedicated trust fund Gender-equal or female-led governance Regular mandatory gender training for leaders/managers
Worldview	Decision-making without gender expertise	Gender-informed and justified decision-making
Metaphor	Counting women	Women Count

In this, the broader issues of moving from infrastructure to wellbeing are captured.

	Today	Tomorrow
Litany	GDP	Wellbeing
System	Man over nature	Just sustainability
Worldview	Prosperity	Prosperity, People, and Planet
Metaphor	Survival of the strongest	All Thrive

MS: What's the timeframe of such a process? You start with one or two people, as I understand, and they ask you to come in for a keynote or something like that, and then you go into depth. It's not just one day. We are certainly talking about a longer period here. What is the timeframe?

SI: Each group is different. I remember one group in the early 1990s. We explored food futures and I had suggested to them that they rethink their core offerings and move toward vegetarian food, like, for example, a vegetarian burger. I showed them the trend lines and suggested that dietary habits were changing. Seven years later, they introduced their first plant-based burger.
In the case of large organizations, it always helps if there is a champion at the top or near the top. Then futures thinking has a mandate. They can suggest skills and tools courses. They can suggest

conferences. They can fund transitional strategies from the current state to the future state. This can take from one to seven years as capacity is built, as strategy changes, and as a new purpose is created. Futures thinking thus informs the process in many aspects of the organization. And there is always resistance. This could be in the form of individuals being nervous that their own vision was being sabotaged or that funding for their own projects would end as the organization shifted. It could also simply be individual jealousy as to who is getting the most media attention.
In my own narrative, I have moved from planting seeds, to nurturing young trees, to creating a forest of foresight. For the young futurist, I remember the words of Jim Dator, when he suggested that, for the greatest impact, it is important not to be ideological but rather to see change/intervention as a hypothesis. In this sense, one is engaged but not manipulating or pulling levers—one is focused on what works, on the greatest good for all.

MS: Back to the process itself, you mentioned the use of metaphors to help people see themselves in a different, future role. Do you also take people back to the past to get a sense of what might have made them successful, made them comfortable, or made them move into a different future? Or is it just, as you said earlier, to get an insight into the possibilities of what might happen in the future?

SI: I use the Six Pillars process. The first part is mapping. Part of that mapping is the timeline. How did we get here? The past is honored, understood, the war stories told, and then we move onwards. We use the Futures Triangle to map the future. From there, we move to emerging issues—the disruptions. Then to scenarios, CLA, and backcasting. We conclude with the CLA of the self, or the inner stories that need to change. It is important to inquire into the current organizational metaphor and then move forward. With one group, they suggested that the current narrative was, "no appetite for change." Their preferred one was, "take a byte," which suggested implementing AI in their strategies and operations.

MS: You mentioned disruption scenarios. Can you give a more detailed picture of all the steps you go through when working with organizations?

SI: Okay, sure. If I have a day or two, the first thing at the facilitator level is to make everyone feel safe and make it clear—authenticity is a primary ingredient. For doing depth work, safety is important. In one two-day workshop, we had to stop on the second day as there was a conflict in the organization that was on the national news. We understood that the process had now become highly political, and no one felt safe about sharing stories and preferred futures. We wisely stopped the process.

MS: That seems to me to be an important point. How do you facilitate a conversation at eye level and without hierarchies when a manager is present? We know what happens when the boss is in the room, don't we?

SI: So that's the pre-work: if you want to do futures, it will be disruptive, it can be anxiety-producing. There are different organizational styles. Some prefer a top-down command-control model. Some prefer the participants to co-design their research questions. What the non-negotiable and the negotiable are has to be set. Lack of safety comes from confusion. Is this participatory, is it partially participatory, or is it really top down? Once everyone knows their role, the process can evolve. The way to ensure safety comes from the work of the late Rob Burke. He frames the futures journey as a learning journey. First is zero-loop learning, where there are good ideas but resistance is too great, so there is no change. Second is single-loop learning, where the good ideas merely become a checklist. Third, and more important, is double-loop learning, or learning through inner and outer questioning. This moves the discussion from the future out there to changing the core learning paradigm. Finally, narra-

tive learning asks us to change our core metaphor of self, other, and the organization. This, Burke suggests, can lead to profound change, as the story that we use to "see" the future has changed.
Once the learning dimension is explored, then the Six Pillars process begins. The goal is to map, anticipate, time, deepen, widen, and transform understandings about the future.

MS: And when do you start involving people who are not part of the process?

SI: Participation is built into the entire process, from co-design to the actual longer-term learning journey that emerges. We provide the methods and tools and the experience in doing futures. They bring their expertise, what they know best. The challenge in this is ensuring that the dialectics are respected, all views are heard, and we move forward.
I remember a decade back when we were working on the museums of the future. Everyone loved the idea of a co-created museum partly designed by young people, real time design, greener, et cetera, except one person in the room. And I could see that she was a resister and I said, "so, tell me what's bothering you." And because it was a safe space she said, "I have a PhD in curation, why are you going to let 13-year-olds curate my museum?" This became a fantastic conversation. The conclusion that emerged was designing content for museums that had experts and non-experts together. That seems simple, but to take 20 people to a new process, aha, that's our new product. The expert was happy. And the people who said "no, we need to do something else because things are getting boring," they were happy.
In another project focused on the futures of mental health, the moment of change came through the Sarkar Game—named after the world philosopher, P.R. Sarkar. The group was focused on how to anticipate depression and suicide. They quickly understood that if we wish to make a big difference we need to partner with Google or Microsoft or Facebook to develop early diagnostics prevention. And we can't just always be serving people who are already mentally ill, already about to commit suicide. We can't just only do front line; we must do prevention work. So that became very clear in a day and a half. They said, "aha, we need to re-partner, re-scale, do things differently." Then I ran the Sarkar Game, which is simple. We try to create a successful organization or civilization. Some people get tools. Some people get books. Some people get weapons. Some people get money. And if you do it well, participants invest in ideas, invest in good systems, invest in people, and you've made an amazing organization or civilization.
In this case, one of the warriors with the guns shot everyone in the room. It was a plastic gun, but she still shot everyone and then when we went to the CLA method, they said, "we actually can't do the inner work, because we're still in shock." Why did this happen? And the person who did the shooting, she stood up and said, "I'm the angel of innovation, the angel of mercy. I shot everyone because I understood you people want to do innovation, but none of you actually intends on implementing. I can tell." This came out and then there was this discomfort. So those are the things that happen in futures, unexpected things happen. I set this up earlier—if you're going to do a futures workshop, we can't predict the outcome, it is a learning journey. We will make it safe, you generally get new products and processes. But if you don't intend on following through, you may lose the best people and, within the workshop, you may see some issues.

MS: Let's stay with this topic for a moment. What does it take for people not only to understand the new, the not yet existing but possible in the future, but also to make sense of this future and actively want to help shape it? How do you make the leap from narrative to meaningful motivation that gets people involved? What tools can help you do this? Are we only talking about dialogue or do you also use images, etc.?

SI: I use CLA at that stage. We had one meeting with Edmund Rice Australia. They were an innovative, amazing group. There were forty or so educational leaders and ten students. So, we're looking at educational futures. And when we did the CLA, they said that Level 1 is "they tell us what to do, it's run by the ministry. It's a world view, a professor or teacher knows best." The metaphor was "one-size-fits-all." From the student viewpoint, the wish was for systems where their perspectives and input are included. And their preferred metaphor was tailor-made, personalized education. So now we have an old system and students with a new system and now we can negotiate. Then we did some skits. In this case, the students went further once they saw that they had been given space. Indeed, they ran a skit on the Tinder of education. Swipe left, teacher stays, swipe right, teacher goes. And suddenly this became funny, but also quite challenging. Is the role of the teacher to only meet the needs of the students? Do they have an administrative role? And there was this tension in the room. And the tension got resolved. They said, "okay, that's the current view. Those are the students' views. What's the view that integrates them?"
This was the initial CLA.

Students in 2030/2040	Today	Preferred Future
Litany	**Mandatory schooling** **Standardized, outdated, restricted**	**Flexible, unrestricted, global** **Everyone has access** **Relevant and adaptable**
System	**Segregated by status and gender. Restricted. Does not support individuality.**	**Students control learning** **Increasing drive to learn** **Increasing access to education**
Worldview	**Recall and strive for results rather than knowledge.**	**Knowledge is useful and adaptive.**
Metaphor	**One-size-fits-all**	**Tailor-made suit**

This was the new CLA once all parties were involved—the negotiated future.

Edmund Rice	Student	Principal	Integrated 2030/2040
Litany	Students know their needs	Traditional teaching and learning is best	Holistic - lectures, group work, and action learning - teaching and learning
System	Students design their education Fluid and flexible	Principals and teachers design education for a changing world	Social hubs anchor virtual learning Teachers as navigators and life gurus
Worldview	Student-led, artificial intelligence-enhanced education	Tradition-led education with some reforms	Technology plus place plus spiritual learning
Metaphor	Tinder of education	The authority	Life as learning: life as service

MS: Now the connection between CLA and embodiment or role-play becomes clear!

SI: Most of the games we use—the Sarkar Game, the CLA Game, the Conflict Transformation Game, all use role-play. Of course, it is best if the other perspectives are in the room but, when they are not, we need to role-play them to gain insight as to possible, plausible, and preferred futures.

MS: CLA therefore helps to not only gain a deeper understanding of the current situation, but also create a forward-looking picture of what could happen.

SI: Yes. Once we were involved in a two-day conference on disability in the future and when, as part of this, we did the CLA, the final story was from this person, Julie. She said: Today she is Julie, the blind girl who lives on the 3rd floor. The worldview is: Disability is a deficit. The system is: We can't access housing or roads. The data is: With this degree of disability you can't get work. The new metaphor was Just Julie, the worldview was ability, and the system was "city design like the Paralympics." And the data was no discrimination. So, as a group, we came up with a CLA and everyone said, "aha! when Julie speaks, you see it from her angle from now on": Don't call me Julie, the blind girl; call me Just Julie. CLA creates sense-making, creates a vision, creates movement.

MS: Is this a process that only takes place through conversation? You spoke earlier about role-playing games or even sketches that people make. What tools are we talking about when people in a group try to make sense of what is being talked about in the group? We know what happens when someone talks about something novel or shares ideas about a possible future. There's usually someone in the room who says, "I don't understand. What are we talking about here now?"

SI: There are two parts. One is, everyone learns differently. As much as possible, we try to ensure that there are multiple ways of presentation: text-based, skit-based, and personal perspective. What did you learn? What were your insights?
This leads to the next step. Once they've done this external CLA there is then, of course, what's the inner CLA? And this brings out the personal part. This can be shared or not shared. So, what's your story in the organization? As your organization changes, what's the better story? When we worked with SPC, the South Pacific Commission, their vision was a flotilla of canoes. Then we asked them, "if that's the new vision, the new story, what is each one of you in that story?" And then one person said, "I'm the one who makes the wool. I'm the one who navigates. I'm the one who finds the money for the making of the canoe." So, it is about getting clarity around role and purpose. With SPC, it started six years ago. They attended a workshop and we ran workshops for them.
And then many took our online course and now they have a compendium of South Pacific foresight work—using narratives from Fiji, from Samoa, from New Caledonia, from their own ways of knowing. They just keep moving forward, winning awards, and ensuring that futures thinking is being developed with local ways of knowing.

MS: How do you make sure that, after the workshop, the people involved actually move towards the future you've worked out? Isn't it the case that people like to fall back into their old patterns, into their familiar mental models?

SI: So, I think that's the perfect answer. With Rob Burke, we've tried to implement that, to see futures as a learning journey. Given that they have anxiety about the Monday morning question—"What is the business relevance?"—we have them present in the workshop. Say, there are ten executives: It's Monday morning, you have to present to your CEO or your board. Practice now in front of us to alleviate the anxiety as part of your learning journey. That's a method that really works well. Method 2, for example, which we did with the Queensland Crime Commission and just now with its local council, Maranoa Shire Council, is to link the process to your five-year plan. So, we do this, and the best ideas get picked up in the five-year plan. That's Method 2. Method 3 is about people development. Some people say, "well, I don't really care about the product or the plan. I want to make sure there's a new language of conversation."

The Monday morning question is critical in our work. This is the issue of relevance, of how do I use futures thinking when I go back to work. There are three ways to address this. The first is to have them teach futures to us during the course. To present their insights to us and the other learners as facilitators. This way, when they return to present to their Board of Directors or their CEO, they are prepared. The second, what we did last year with the Queensland Crime Commission and Maranoa Shire Council, was to link new ideas/projects/products to their five-year plan and long-term vision. The third is not so much about being futures-prepared or the plan but about really creating a new language of conversation in the organization on alternative and desired futures. A fourth way is a forward-facing process that I've enjoyed: anticipatory action learning, which I learned from Tony Stevenson.

Instead of the plan, participants create action learning projects that excite them, that they wish to create. This ensures novelty and experimentation. The key here is to ensure that these small projects have some seed funding, so that they can grow and possibly become centerpieces of the new future.

MS: Isn't it a problem that the work on the future is always delegated to a group that is then faced with the challenge of presenting the results to managers who were not initially involved in the workshop? In other words, unlike the employees, the managers had no opportunity to question their mental models of the world with regard to an alternative future. But they are the ones who decide on the alternative futures. What experiences have you had in this regard?

SI: So, one of the principles of good futures research is to ask, "Who is not in the room?" If the people who are going to make decisions are not in the room, then we know it may fail. If the people with wild ideas are in the room, then we have a greater chance of success because we have included outliers, novelty, and a 360-degree view of the future. So, futures design is about asking, "Who's not in the room? Who needs to be in the room?" It's really important that the champions are there. I know this from the Victoria Police, I run a program for inspectors. And they come with some amazing ideas. One was Citizen Forensics. Instead of waiting for the inspector to get to the crime scene, citizens already have some tools. They take some quick pictures. They do some initial work that gets sent to them straight away. So, that was interesting. Now, they came up with this. I've taken 300 or so inspectors through this process. And there are many who find futures work exciting, even if long-term issues aren't relevant to them... some say, well, I like it, but this is too far from me, so there must be a structural link from the futures course to the organization's actual future. We do this by linking the levels of the organizations, so that the ideas filter upwards. That link can also be person-based, i.e. ensuring that top level executives are there to play a part in nurturing younger leaders, in listening to their ideas.

MS: What experiences have you had in driving forward future initiatives? You mentioned that employees are involved in their operational work every day. Does future work need a free space away from day-to-day operations?

SI: I think you are 100% right. So, it's part of the design, it's not just the product from the workshop or the later intervention, but the deeper learning process about alternative futures. The product design is a different systemic process, where people have permission to search for emerging issues, weak signals. And they have permission to take one weak signal to fruition. Whether it's with an international organization, bank, or just a small organization—it has to be built in. Otherwise, everyone gets too busy because the present is always overwhelming. So, I think that's a systemic design. Now, I don't push it myself. For me, it's very clear: they have to own the space. We did one project for one university where they won a national award based on their scenario work. But the story did not end there. Once the Vice-Chancellor left, his deans left and the university became, I would say, more traditional, which is fine too. But those deans that left all started futures programs, they became executive leaders elsewhere. Then you could say, "well, the project was a failure, there was futures thinking but then the VC left and it stopped," or you can say that it was an amazing success, it led to other flowers growing. And that took 7-10 years. So, this is us not being so concerned about short-term success, but playing the long game.
This is us as futurists being clear about our narrative and vision. Here's my story in this. Here's the world I wish to see. And here's how I'm going to do it. That's meta-cognition. Because there will be resistance, people who don't like it. There'll be projects that fail all the time. Some will later rise like a phoenix. Some will lead to other projects. I can see the typology, but I can't predict on day one what's going to happen? Because humans are co-creating.

MS: Finally, what would you recommend to an organization that wants to look at its own future? What should they do and what should they pay attention to?

SI: I would first say, gain clarity on your own narrative in general and metaphor in specific. At rational and inner levels, who are you in this process? Second, I would also use the work of Jenny Brice. Her approach is to find the change agents. These are the leading edge, the creative minority, from 10 to 30%. Once you have them focused, then find the next 30%—they are looking for a vision, a purpose to work. Then be ready for the resisters or, as the late Pat Kelly would argue, the points of resistance (Futures Forum, 2017). These points could be anxiety, possible loss of work, or access to power. Either quarantine them or work with them to make the system more robust. Finally, there is a large group, up to 30%, who really just wish to be left alone. There is no need to waste attention or financial resources on them. With possible champions, I've learned through CLA to identify their core metaphors of themselves prior to the process. One managing director of a large bank wished to ensure her next board meeting went well. I suggested she discern each director's way of knowing the world first: Was it data? Theory? Connection? Once she figured this out, she could then pitch her ideas for the greatest impact.
To conclude, while I have focused on the metaphor or narrative aspects, equally important are the systems that create the stories. Currently we have a world system that is stuck. This is largely because the UN Security Council has granted veto powers to five and only five nations. There are no ways forward when issues of war and violence emerge. They count: others do not. While this may have made sense after WWII, it makes little sense now. This is the system issue. And we know very well that the five powers will not give up their veto ability. This becomes our

question, how do you transform the world when we resist foundational change? Strategic foresight merely wishes to enhance the power of the few over the many. I've argued here, as much as possible, for a more transformational approach, in which we co-design and change along with those whom we engage with. The goal is to move from Anticipation to Emancipation.

MS: Thank you for the interview.

References

Inayatullah, S., Milojevic, I., & Hung, S. 2022. Walking together: Gender equality futures 2042 in the Asia-Pacific Region. ***Journal of Futures Studies***, 27(2): 56-60.

The Futures Forum. 2017. ***Future sense now – The futures of women with Dr. Patricia Kelly*** [YouTube]. Available online https://www.youtube.com/watch?v=bfWCZ9syhic. Viewed June 5, 2024.

FUTURECASTING WITH DATA

Photo: Erich Goldmann

NICOLAS BALCOM RALEIGH

UNESCO CO-CHAIR OF LEARNING FOR TRANSFORMATION AND PLANETARY FUTURES, UNIVERSITY OF TURKU
TURKU, FINLAND

LEARNING AND TRANSFORMING WITH PLANETARY FUTURES

Introduction

We, the inhabitants of Earth, are living through a climate crisis. In 2023 alone, there was a record number of tropical storms, wildfires, exceptionally hot days, and other phenomena attributable to global warming (Ripple et al., 2023). The possibility of and need for an adequate response is widely discussed and climate action is being taken by an increasing variety of actors (IPCC Press Office, 2023). Underlying all these conversations and efforts is the larger question of how societies can transform themselves to fully address the multiple dimensions, causes, and impacts of climate change. This text offers one pathway toward this needed change: growing humanity's collective capability to produce, interpret, and discuss Planetary Futures—a form of "Futures Literacy"—in processes aimed at learning, meaning-making, and pursuing new ways of being.

Planetary Futures are proposed here as constructs of what living on Earth could be like in a time later than now. They can be produced in a variety of ways for a diversity of purposes, and take many forms such as models, images, scenarios, narratives, simulations, or even indicator systems. They can be general or specific, global or local, and cast onto any time horizon—short or long term. Importantly, very many of these planetary futures are populated with people and other living beings—either older versions of today's inhabitants of Earth or our descendants.

In this text, the term Planetary Futures refers to kinds of imaginaries which are flowing among us—either inherited from the past or invented in the present. These futures are often generated via anticipation aimed at planning and preparation, but are sometimes also sparked by engagement and struggles to make sense of arising novelty (cf. "anticipation for future" and "anticipation for emergence," e.g., Miller, 2018). Generating and conceiving of Planetary Futures entails dancing between the global and local scale and detailing general and specific phenomena. In today's world, as will be elaborated below, a variety of data-driven tools exist for the task. However, this text argues for the value of combining Planetary Futures built from data with contextually situated imagination informed by our inter-relations and concern for others.

A plausible Planetary Future motivates this text's core idea: within the next 5-10 years, climate impacts will culminate to such an extreme that all businesses, governments, and populations—even the most fossil fuel-dependent ones—will be highly motivated to address climate change at a sufficient scale to transform how humans utilize resources and relate to our ecosystems (cf. Berzonsky & Moser, 2017). However, to effectively change "how things work" so that humanity can fully adapt, mitigate, or otherwise respond to the massive transformations driven by Earth and humanity's intrinsically entangled and complex journey of "becoming," we will need more than our plausible Planetary Futures built from data (Wright, 2014). We will also need the capability to expand, vary, and diversify the kinds of Planetary Futures in use—adding the "appreciation of novelty" to the more common "planning and preparation" (cf. Miller, 2018)—as well as an increased capacity and willingness to collectively contextualize, discuss, and make sense of the lively embers of potential change in the present.

Planetary Futures

For as long as humans have been able to conjure them, futures have been imagined for various purposes on the basis of evidence found in the environment and collective memory. Some of these futures have had profound effects on how, over time, humans built social patterns as well as dynamics for relating to each other, to the rest of Earth's life, and to the many habitats and landscapes found on our common home: Earth.

The very earliest humans, in a plausible past, did not have the concept of a planet or know that they lived on one. Ancient astronomers started to raise attention to this idea. In the recent past, the convergence of several tools and conceptual leaps has made it common knowledge that we all live on a relatively small and unique planet called Earth. In the 20th century, we took many photos of our home[1] from low Earth orbit,[2] the Moon (NASA, n.d.), or from distant planets in our solar system (NASA, 2023). Images and reflections on "one small step"[3] and "a pale blue dot"[4] have offered pause and reflection about the preciousness of this locality in the vastness of space. Today, general knowledge about Earth is integrated in education systems and popular culture. Furthermore, media and cultural exchange allow for a sense of connection and common cause across distances. In the first decade of our current century, a combination of remote sensing (e.g., through satellites), Internet communication technologies, and big data have given billions of people instantaneous access to detailed information about any place, at any scale, via devices they carry regularly on their person. This contemporary setting offers several commonplace sources of what can be called a “planetary awareness”—a precursory ingredient to conjuring Planetary Futures.

Today, many billions of humans frequently use computing devices. We[5] could be called “Homo sapiens computare” (cf. “Homo sapiens faber,” etc.). For this large population of our species, computation capacity is closely coupled to cognition and perception. In other words, what “Homo sapiens computare” think, see, and do is mediated by their computational tools. Due to the extensiveness of computation in society, even those people and other living beings who never use computational augmentation themselves are inhabiting built environments, infrastructures, and mobility systems designed via computation, represented in computational systems, and monitored by others via networked devices. It could even be argued that computation—with all its required electromagnetic signaling (e.g., WiFi, satellite beams, cellphone coverage areas)—is becoming part of the “affordance landscape” (Walsh, 2014) for all of life on Earth. Speculatively, these computational affordances may have already co-constituted new repertoires of goals for both human and non-human life systems.

Among humans, the rise of “Homo sapiens computare” corresponds to a rising emphasis upon “computable data” as the core input needed to build compelling models of reality, including tools for comprehending the present state of various phenomena and systematically imagining its extension backwards and forwards through time. These simulations of past and future can be generated in increasingly sophisticated ways thanks to many converging advancements. One area of development is the increasing quantity of computable data—which is now vast and varied—pertaining to many aspects of our world including its physical planetary dynamics, habitats and ecosystems, human activities, individual beings, and more. Another angle of advancement is our increasing computing power combined with the invention of entirely new kinds of computation.

Today, the increasing volume and variety of computable data is met with more extensive and diverse computing power. Machine learning (ML) and artificial intelligence (AI) have enjoyed sustained attention over the past decades, and today there exist several projects, services, and products that are “blowing our minds” with their potential uses. Meanwhile, the race to build supercomputers continues—the fastest for 2023 being Frontier in the U.S. (1,194.00 TFlop/s), Fugaku in Japan

---

1 For a timeline, see https://en.wikipedia.org/wiki/Timeline_of_first_images_of_Earth_from_space, viewed November 21, 2023.

2 See Earth tab of International Space Station Galleries on https://www.nasa.gov/international-space-station/space-station-gallery/, viewed November 21, 2023.

3 Neil Armstrong said "One small step for man, one giant leap for mankind" as he stepped on the moon on July 20, 1969.

4 2 Voyager 1 took a photo of Earth on 14 February 1990 from more than six billion kilometers away. Carl Sagan made a moving reflection about the picture at a NASA press conference which he later published in his book A Pale Blue Dot (1994).

5 I typed this text on a computer, and you might be reading it on one.

(442 TFlop/s), and LUMI in Finland (309.1 TFlop/s; TOP500, 2023). Quantum Computing has also enjoyed sustained attention and, at present, many such machines are built, functional, and available to researchers and developers via Cloud-based service models (Dargan, 2022). Beyond these well-known computing trajectories, innovators are identifying ways to utilize photonics in device hardware, developing approaches to using DNA molecules for data storage (Rawat, 2023), and growing neurons to perform basic computational tasks (Ghosh, 2022). On top of these developments, computer engineers have speculatively proposed a next phase in computing—to follow conventional and quantum—which is initially being called Thermodynamic Computing and would be inspired by how "life computes" (Hylton, Thomas, Conte, & Hill, 2021). These advances are pushing the limits of what we presently know as computing and sparking novel ideas for the kinds of approaches to simulating Planetary Futures that could be produced and shared in the coming years.

Advanced computation is even being applied to help us situate our planet in the unfolding story of the cosmos. For example, a simulation called Uchuu plots the structural evolution of a cube of our universe, 9.63 billion light years per side. This simulated cube of the universe contains 2.1 trillion astronomical objects at the granularity level of a galaxy. It took a team of international researchers one Earth year and 20 million compute-hours of the supercomputer ATERUI II to produce. It enables exploration of the evolution of the structure of the universe from the Big Bang to now, including a plausible distribution of dark matter (NAOJ, 2023). This kind of application of advanced computing helps to locate our existence in a larger story of cosmological transformation, another useful ingredient for producing Planetary Futures.

The Uchuu example is impressive. Yet, arguably, people were able to build planetary models or contemplate our place in the cosmos long before our less-than-one-century-old computational era. Humans were able to predict seasons, invent calendaring systems, and notice changes in the heavens. However, computation has opened new approaches that can widen human perception and lead to new realizations. Based on data—recorded observations of phenomena—we can imagine plausible futures under the pattern of "based on X past evidence, we assume Y could happen" in a systematic and robust manner.

Examples of computationally derived Planetary Futures

There is no need to wait for future times to consider some remarkable examples of Planetary Futures produced from computable data. The following list gives a taste of the practical purposes to which they can be applied.

Neo-Carbon Energy. For these scenarios, energy systems were modeled and simulated by a research team at Lappeenranta University (Finland) for every major region of the world at a resolution of 30-minute time increments between 2015 and 2050. The simulation allowed the researchers to make a cost comparison between various energy-source mixes under a detailed set of assumptions. They found that in all scenarios, nuclear and fossil-fuel energy systems were the most expensive options, while renewable energy systems were the least.[6]

Quantitative COVID-19 scenarios. Various groups around the world produced COVID-19 scenarios during the COVID-19 pandemic. Notably, a research team at Washington University (St. Louis, Missouri, U.S.) produced and frequently updated a set of quantitative scenarios for nearly all the nations of the world. These scenarios projected quantities of new cases, hospitalizations, and COVID-19 deaths under various action scenarios (e.g., 80% wearing masks or 90% vaccinated). The typology of scenarios was regularly updated to reflect the latest available health policy recommendations.[7]

IPCC Climate Models. Climate scientists have built dozens of simulations based on historical weather data and an ever-improving understanding of Earth systems to project how climate change may unfold. The data upon which these climate change simulations are built are becoming increasingly comprehensive in terms of spatial and temporal detail and the variety of systems modeled. Several research teams around the world build these models, which are used to inform IPCC reports. The year 2100 is a common time horizon that has been used across several of these models for comparison (Climate Atlas, 2023). A recent study showed that the past projections from these models are highly credible (Buis, 2020).

6 See https://neocarbonenergy.fi, Internet of Energy, viewed September 6, 2023.

7 https://covid19.healthdata.org/, viewed November 21, 2023.
The team paused its activities in December 2022.

Big Data for Biodiversity. While it is common to discuss threatened or extinct species, the practice of counting populations of unique species is a key challenge in biology. Doing so often takes multiple modes of data collection, various spatial and temporal scales, and data-relevant forms of approximation. In one example, combining data from the citizen science app eBird with biologist field observations, researchers made an algorithm that estimated populations of 9,700 bird species to form a first-of-its-kind "bird census" (Cox, 2021). In another, space-based monitoring tools and data interfaces alert humans when a further species is in danger (Copernicus Climate Change Service, n.d.). Yet another example is a research project at the University of Helsinki which is developing and demonstrating biodiversity monitoring systems and data gathering standards (Life-plan Project, n.d.). Some researchers even propose the creation of an "Internet of animals," in which very many individual living beings are actively tracked (Larson, 2021).

Digital Twin Earth. Digital twins are often discussed as enablers of more efficient manufacturing or governance. Digital twins are computational models of actual entities—such as a factory assembly line, a building, a city, or even a person—which are continually updated with live data. The Digital Twin Earth project, supported by the European Space Agency and others, aims to create a similarly always-being-updated model of Earth and its many systems. Due to a variety of terrestrial and space-based remote sensing systems, many believe that such a system can be created. It would show real-time developments of climate change phenomena and build increasingly detailed projections at local and global scales (Rao et al., 2023; Voosen, 2020).

All computer simulations used for modeling reality or exploring scenarios—like the above examples for energy systems, COVID-19 cases, climate change, biodiversity, and the whole Earth—provide a basis for describing Planetary Futures, allowing people to connect potential local actions to global effects. In other words, they can drive perception of what is happening now and what could transform in the future.

Models and simulations like these are built from computable data that are translated into projections via algorithms. As beautifully concise as their numerical outputs are, these futures—like all others—are based upon assumptions about how various phenomenological processes interrelate. High-quality simulations are transparent about these assumptions (e.g., Neo-Carbon Energy, the IPCC Ensemble) so they can be subjected to scientific scrutiny and refined. In future, there could be simulations of Planetary Futures based on assumptions that are unreadable by humans due to the computing approach used to produce them.

Data-driven approaches to imagining Planetary Futures merit close attention because they serve as an evidence-driven basis for discussing present circumstances and potential transformations. Obviously, they are fueled by data from the past—even in the case of Digital Twins where "real-time" data (e.g., from microseconds in the past) are fed into the process. Because the future is, by definition, unknowable in advance, reliance on data from the past places a limit on what these systems can tell us about future changes. For example, relying on past data limits the extent and kind of novelty that can be produced—while truly transformational innovations will require new realizations about what can change and relevant ideas for action. We will likely need more than well-constructed programs and computational power to produce the kinds of insights about the future that are useful for reconfiguring how we relate to each other, the rest of life on Earth, and our common home.

Computationally produced Planetary Futures concerning climate change, energy systems, and biodiversity have contributed significantly to growing a collective awareness of significant issues, their potential impacts, and the need for action. However, this category of Planetary Futures has yet to inspire an adequately scaled, multi-level, coordinated, and impactful collective human response. In line with the thesis of this paper, a new collective capability is needed to close this motivation gap—the capability to invent and describe Planetary Futures, discuss them, interpret and explore their meanings, identify potential transformation, and innovate new ways of being together on Earth. Engaging in the development of such a capability offers pathways for augmenting the utilization of computationally generated Planetary Futures. These augmentations could catalyze much-needed transformational action.

Growing our capabilities to invent Planetary Futures and inspire transformational action

"Futures Literacy" is proposed as the capability to diversify, expand, and vary how and why we build and apply imaginary futures (cf. Miller, 2018; Conway, 2023). Understanding how Futures Literacy can be developed and applied is undertaken by a program of the same name from the UNESCO Social & Human Sciences Sector and a network of more than 40 UNESCO Chairs around the world. Futures Literacy is a capability for engaging with the diverse ways in which life builds, engages, and utilizes models of the future (Louie, 2010; Rosen, 1999). Humans, as a social species, frequently engage in Anticipation together—exchanging and inventing models of the future as needed to pursue goals.

Planetary Futures produced from computation and computable data give us increasing clarity on what has happened up to now and plausible ways things could develop in the future. Futures Literacy contextualizes approaches to engaging with the future as forms of Anticipation. It introduces the notion that there are other forms of Anticipation that could also be deployed. Seeking to grow Futures Literacy in relation to Planetary Futures does not aim to replace computational approaches to foresight but, rather, to include—and ensure the non-exclusion of—additional modes of engaging in a wider variety of forms of Anticipation, including via non-computational means.

Learning Futures Literacy can be uncomfortable. Most who begin developing it must locate their ideas with the help of familiar concepts and paradigms—a normal part of any learning journey. In a famous museum, large text informs visitors that (paraphrased) "to create the future, you must first imagine it." This is a commonly expressed idea and reflects a common form of Anticipation among people living in industrialized societies. The underlying "how and why" of this idea is "preparing and planning"—and follows the form of building models of the future for the purpose of formulating actions toward the future (cf. "Anticipation for Future," Miller, 2018). One of the key ideas in Futures Literacy which is most difficult to grasp is the idea that you can engage in Anticipation that is not about preparation or planning at all.

People who are growing their Futures Literacy also take interest in using this other form of Anticipation—so-called "Anticipation for Emergence" (cf., Miller, 2018). This form of Anticipation is about noticing and appreciating the novelty arising from our complex and transforming world. It is about struggling to see and interpret new phenomena or new ideas, or inventing new words to describe something yet-to-exist. It is about being able to do this noticing, appreciating, and struggling while avoiding the "solving mindset." It feels like improvising alongside "the becomingness" of our world.

Growing Futures Literacy is about toggling between these two kinds of Anticipation—about being able to build and apply models of the future for preparation and planning, while also leaving room for appreciating novelty. Experiences and exercises—big and small—can help a group to develop Futures Literacy. A well-established, efficient, and effective learning experience is a Futures Literacy Laboratory. Smaller exercises are also possible, such as experimental check-ins at meetings (Balcom Raleigh & Richards, 2022). In the following section, a simple exercise is offered to support such learning.

A small Futures Literacy exercise to support learning from Planetary Futures

Before reading the exercise in this section, it will be helpful to know its purpose (Why) and method (How).

In the field of information science, there are continuing discussions about the differences between Data, Information, and Knowledge. A common delineation is that Data can be compiled into information, Information can be built up into knowledge, and Knowledge can support the development of wisdom (Zins, 2007). However, quantum physicists and cosmologists raise the idea that our whole universe is made of something like information—from the quantum to the interstellar scale (cf. measurement as "causal intra-actions," Barad, 2007: 337). These notions imply that computable data can only deliver us a fraction of the rich information involved in our existence (cf. Lanier, 2011). An interpretation of these ideas is that the universe is filled with what can be called—for want of a better word—some kind of "pre-data." Applying this interpretation, when people use instruments like a powerful space-based telescope or research questionnaire to detect some phenomena, the target is imbued with this "pre-data" that, when mediated by the instrument, becomes encoded as data. Accessing the rich terrain of this "pre-data" can be a pathway to new realizations. Accessing this "pre-data" is the "Why" of this exercise.

To accomplish this exercise, imagination and reflective thinking will be used. Your mind is filled with pre-data. It can be accessed without computation, allowing for the exploration of your own intersubjective awareness of being alive, situated relationships to others, and hopes, fears, and other emotions related to the prospect of living in a transformed world. A non-computational process like this generates inter-personally meaningful futures. This is the "How" of this exercise.

Exercise—Situating Planetary Futures

1. Find a partner (or, do the exercise now and share with someone else later).

2. Quietly reflect. Imagine a child you know who is 10 years old or younger.

3. Add 35 years to their age. Imagine this child has grown into a middle-aged adult.

4. Reflect on the state of climate change in this future: Is Earth hotter? Has society radically transformed itself and addressed it in time? Something else?

5. Imagining this future, answer this question: What does this person you know do on a regular basis to encounter and appreciate novelty?

6. When you and your partner are finished—share what you imagined with each other.

After trying this exercise, you will have produced a contextually unique Planetary Future, populated with someone you know who is doing something interesting, maybe even novel. This exercise can enable many kinds of images, thoughts, and feelings. Two intended outcomes are, first, to de-generalize the future and situate it within the context of one's own relationships and life experiences; and, second, to intertwine subjective knowledge and perception with ideas inspired indirectly by more general data-driven models of the future.

The question in Step 5 of this exercise serves as a reminder: Novelty happens and will continue to happen in the future. By imagining how a person in the future encounters "the new" and the approach they take in order to include it in the enrichment of their life experiences, it is possible to invent a practice for appreciating novelty which could plausibly be developed in the present. It raises productive questions about how Anticipation for Emergence could receive more of our attention: What practices of appreciating novelty can be adapted by individuals and collectives? How could children and youth invent their own practices? How can we participate in "becoming with" ongoing transformations while passing something useful forward to the upcoming generation? Inquiring into reflective questions like these after doing this exercise supports learning from Planetary Futures.

Conclusions

While we cannot know the future, computable data and advances in computer modeling and simulation have made it possible for us to have a better understanding and awareness of our current circumstances and their plausible potential developments. These computer-generated forms of Planetary Futures contribute significantly to the case for climate action. Yet, because they are built from data recorded in the past, they are limited in how well they can help us appreciate novelty in the present and future. By combining computable data with other ingredients for imagining futures—such as intersubjective, situated, and relational inputs—we can expand our perception of transformation and close the motivation gap for addressing climate change. By combining awareness of the implications of computationally driven models of Planetary Futures with inspiration from our own relationships and sense of being, we can spur much-needed transformative innovation. Growing societal Futures Literacy—the capability to diversify, expand, and vary how and why we use futures—can help us invent, share, and discuss meaningful Planetary Futures that support learning and transforming with the aim of the collective survival of all of Life on Earth.

References

Balcom Raleigh, N., & Richards, M. 2022. ***12 Tasty futures literacy recipes for sustainability innovators**** [Blog Post]. UNESCO Chair in Learning for Transformation and Planetary Futures, March 15. Accessed online https://unescochair.utu.fi/12-tasty-futures-literacy-recipes-for-sustainability-innovators/. Viewed March 5, 2024.

Barad, K. 2007. ***Meeting the universe halfway: Quantum physics and the entanglement of matter and meaning.*** Second Printing. Durham: Duke University Press Books.

Berzonsky, C. L., & Moser, S. C. 2017. Becoming homo sapiens sapiens: Mapping the psycho-cultural transformation in the anthropocene. ***Anthropocene***, 20 (December): 15–23.

Buis, A. 2020. Study confirms climate models are getting future warming projections right. ***NASA Global Climate Change***, January 9. Accessed online https://climate.nasa.gov/news/2943/study-confirms-climate-models-are-getting-future-warming-projections-right/. Viewed March 5, 2024.

Climate Atlas. 2023. ***Climate change projections: How computer models help us understand climate.*** Climate Atlas of Canada. Accessed online https://climateatlas.ca/climate-change-projections. Viewed March 5, 2024.

Conway, M. 2023. EP 170: FuturePod conversations - Riel Miller and Maree Conway. ***FuturePod***, October 23. Accessed online https://www.futurepod.org/podcast/ep-170. Viewed March 5, 2024.

Copernicus Climate Change Service. n.d. ***Biodiversity***. European Centre for Medium-Range Weather Forecasts, on behalf of the European Union. Accessed online https://climate.copernicus.eu/biodiversity. Viewed November 20, 2023.

Cox, L. 2021. World is home to 50bn birds, 'breakthrough' citizen science research estimates. ***The Guardian***, May 17. Accessed online https://www.theguardian.com/environment/2021/may/18/world-is-home-to-50bn-birds-breakthrough-citizen-science-research-estimates. Viewed November 20, 2023.

Dargan, J. 2022. 13 Quantum cloud computing software companies in 2022. ***The Quantum Insider***, May 3. Accessed online https://thequantuminsider.com/2022/05/03/13-companies-offering-quantum-cloud-computing-services-in-2022/. Viewed March 5, 2024.

Ghosh, P. 2022. Lab-grown brain cells play video game pong. ***BBC***, October 12. Accessed online https://www.bbc.com/news/science-environment-63195653. Viewed March 5, 2024.

Hylton, T., Thomas, M., Conte, T. M., & Hill, M. D. 2021. A vision to compute like nature. ***Communications of the ACM***, 64(6): 35-38.

IPCC Press Office. 2023. ***Urgent climate action can secure a liveable future for all.*** IPCC Press Release 2023/06/PR, March 20. Geneva: IPCC. Accessed online https://www.ipcc.ch/2023/03/20/press-release-ar6-synthesis-report/. Viewed March 5, 2024.

Lanier, J. 2011. ***You are not a gadget: A manifesto.*** Reprint. New York: Vintage.

Larson, C. 2021. Scientists hail golden age to trace bird migration with tech. ***AP News***, June 10. Accessed online https://apnews.com/article/business-birds-technology-science-environment-and-nature-03234b4ba-5506dae02e6dcd16e3c33de. Viewed March 5, 2024.

Lifeplan Project. n.d. ***Lifeplan: A planetary inventory of life*** [Blog entry]. University of Helsinki. Accessed online https://www.helsinki.fi/en/projects/lifeplan. Viewed November 20, 2023.

Louie, A. H. 2010. Robert Rosen's anticipatory systems. ***Foresight***, 12(3): 18-29.

Miller, R. 2018. Sensing and making-sense of futures literacy: Towards a futures literacy framework. In Miller, R. (ed.), ***Transforming the future: Anticipation in the 21st century:*** 15-36. London: Routledge.

NAOJ. 2023. ***Largest virtual universe free for anyone to explore.*** NAOJ: National Astronomical Observatory of Japan. Accessed online https://www.nao.ac.jp/en/news/science/2021/20210910-cfca.html. Viewed November 21, 2023.

NASA. n.d. ***Apollo 8*** [Blog Entry]. NASA Science. Accessed online https://www.nasa.gov/mission/apollo-8/. Viewed November 21, 2023.

NASA. 2023. ***Voyager 1's pale blue dot*** [Blog entry]. NASA Science. Accessed online https://science.nasa.gov/resource/voyager-1s-pale-blue-dot/. Viewed September 4, 2023.

Rao, Y., Redmon, R., Dale, K., Haupt, S. E., Hopkinson, A., Bostrom, A., Boukabara, S., Geenen, T., Hall, D. M., Smith, B. D., Niyogi, D., Ramaswamy, V., & Kihn, E. A. 2023. Developing digital twins for earth systems: Purpose, requisites, and benefits. ***ArXiv***: 2306.11175.

Rawat, S. 2023. Is DNA data storage ready for data centers? ***SynBioBeta***, November 7. Accessed online https://www.synbiobeta.com/read/is-dna-data-storage-ready-for-data-centers. Viewed March 5, 2024.

Ripple, W. J., Wolf, C., Gregg, J. W., Rockström, J., Newsome, T. M., Law, B. E., Marques, L., Lenton, T. M., Xu, C., Huq, S., Simons, L., & King, Sir D. A. 2023. The 2023 state of the climate report: Entering uncharted territory. ***BioScience***, 73(12): 841-850.

Rosen, R. 1999. ***Essays on life itself.*** New York: Columbia University Press.

TOP500. 2023. ***Highlights - June 2023: 61st edition of the TOP500*** [Blog entry]. Accessed online https://www.top500.org/lists/top500/2023/06/highs/. Viewed March 5, 2024.

Voosen, P. 2020. Europe builds 'digital twin' of earth to hone climate forecasts. ***Science***, 370(6512): 16-17.

Walsh, D. M. 2014. The affordance landscape: The spatial metaphors of evolution. In G. Barker, E. Desjardins, & T. Pearce (eds.), ***Entangled life: Organism and environment in the biological and social sciences:*** 213-236. Dordrecht: Springer Netherlands.

Wright, K. 2014. Becoming with: Living lexicon for the environmental humanities. ***Environmental Humanities***, 5: 277-281.

Zins, C. 2007. Conceptual approaches for defining data, information, and knowledge. ***Journal of the American Society for Information Science and Technology***, 58(4): 479-493.

STATEMENT
CHRIS LUEBKEMAN
LEADER, STRATEGIC
FORESIGHT HUB,
ETH ZURICH
ZURICH, SWITZERLAND
Photo: Erich Goldmann

The future is a peculiar place. Many of us spend our professional lives bridging the gap between what we perceive in the present and what we envision could unfold in a future.

Utilizing methods spanning from the analytical to the constructive and even to the wildly creative, the essence of our work lies in my realization that, when it comes to the future, there exists no absolute right or wrong, that the answer to most questions is a resounding **"it depends."**

It all boils down to the context; the nature of the question(s) posed, the cultural backdrop in which one operates, the level of detail which is compelling, and the intricacies of the futures one endeavors to comprehend. When examining the forces driving change, different groups will invariably select different drivers. This divergence is characterized not by correctness, but by context. It is intriguing to witness how disparate groups across the globe, when confronted with the same set of drivers, rank them differently based on their unique perspectives. Again, therein lies no definitive right or wrong; only the imperative to comprehend and engage with, and within, a context. **It depends.**

The exciting part of our profession is that we have both the opportunity, and, I believe, the responsibility, to challenge a group's assumptions about their chosen drivers. I find it quite useful to think of the 60-30-10 rule: 60% of the drivers should be expected, 30% of the drivers should be unexpected, and 10% should be unknown to the group with whom one is working. I believe that this ratio enables us to challenge their preconceptions and propel conversations forward in a meaningful way. Helping them to see that ... **it depends.**

In assessing the current global drivers of change, it is easy to succumb to a sense of despair. I find myself meandering between hope and despair at an ever-increasing amplitude. I am also convinced that it is my duty to foster a mindset of positive possibility. In the midst of what is arguably the most dynamic decade in human history, we can feel the deep dynamics of global, regional, and local change at work. This is why I founded [y]our2040, an inspiring community-based think-do tank focusing on ideating, developing, and implementing positive regenerative futures.

We believe in the transformative power of innovation, collaboration, and the relentless pursuit of excellence. Looking ahead to 2040, a decade poised between the Sustainable Development Goals and the UN Climate Targets, we believe in a world of limitless opportunities.

Our collective mission is to co-create visions of a positive, pragmatic, and plausible world—**THE** paramount goal that merits our concerted efforts. In the relentless pursuit of positive possibilities, [y]our2040 stands committed to weaving a tapestry of hope, driven by collaborative visions and a shared dedication to shaping a future that transcends the bounds of the imagination. This may sound lofty, but only by embracing the diverse drivers of change within their unique contexts can we navigate the evolving landscape of change to foster a collective determination to inspire transformative narratives for a flourishing world. Our future generations are depending upon us to do so.

EVA BUCHINGER

SOCIOLOGIST AT THE
AUSTRIAN INSTITUTE
OF TECHNOLOGY (AIT)
VIENNA, AUSTRIA

Photo: Erich Goldmann

FUTURES THINKING: ANTICIPATING SOCIETY'S EMBEDDING OF NEW & EMERGING TECHNOLOGIES

Future technological societies: Sharing facts

"The future is open"—Popper reflected, yet Heidegger reminded us that technology may remain crucial.[1] Justifying investments in research and innovation thus requires the anticipation of the societal embedding of new and emerging technologies (EC 2023, 2021, 2020; OECD 2023; UNESCO 2023, 2021, 2015). Societal embedding acknowledges that manifold factors are driving innovation, whereby technical (artifacts and techniques) and societal (economy, politics, law, science, ethics, public sphere) developments are conditioning each other. Some of these factors can be collected and condensed in the form of empirical evidence and shared as facts.

In a recent initiative called TechEthos,[2] we conducted a horizon scan and collected and condensed facts to identify new and emerging technologies with high economic and ethical relevance, i.e., where substantial challenges for societal embedding are expected. Beginning with scanning 150+ technologies, we prepared factsheets for 16 shortlisted technologies based on quantitative and qualitative

---

1 For reflections about "the future is open," see Popper (1991/2007 and 1993/2007), for the notion that we are chained to technology, see Heidegger (1949/1977), for the idea that modern societies are inherently technological, see Ellul (1954/1964), and for the relevance of new and emerging technologies for the green and digital transition, see, e.g., IPCC (2023), OECD (2022, 2023).

2 TechEthos receives funding from the EU H2020 research and innovation program under Grant Agreement No 101006249.

analysis. These factsheets were used by more than 100 experts in an assessment in order to single out three technologies for further analysis—climate engineering (CE), digital extended reality (XR), and neurotechnologies (NT)—for which refined factsheets were produced and shared with partners and clients (Porcari et al., 2021; Buchinger et al., 2022). Each of these refined factsheets delivers a description of forthcoming technology applications, key ethical issues, and expected economic, policy, legal, and public impacts.

Figure 1: Technology factsheets: socio-economic and ethical impact © *TechEthos*[3]

3 Source: https://www.techethos.eu/resources/factsheets/ (Viewed April 18, 2024).

4 For the stories, their background, and their expert and citizen enrichment, see Adomaitis, Grinbaum, & Lenzi (2022), Bernstein & Mehnert (2022), Buchinger et al. (2023), Umbrello et al. (2022).

Desired futures: Sharing stories

For anticipating the societal embedding of new and emerging technologies, facts are important, but not sufficient. The future is open and therefore we cannot predict what will happen. We can just speculate about possible and plausible alternative futures. And for this, stories are an adequate approach. While stories may to some extent be inspired by data and analysis, their value unfolds especially in dealing with the desires and concerns of individual stakeholders, and in coping with uncertainties, surprises, contingencies, and possible not-knowing ("wild cards," "black swans," "unknowns") (Schoemaker, 1995; Peperhove, Steinmüller, & Dienel, 2018; Taleb, 2007).

In the above-mentioned TechEthos initiative, we created stories (scenarios) about alternative anticipations of the societal embedding of technologies. Here are some examples:[4] For climate engineering, the stories contrast natural solutions (values: post-materialism, environmentalism, non-anthropocentrism) with technological solutions (values: materialism, anthropocentrism) for carbon dioxide removal. In digital extended reality, one of the stories describes a future where almost all white-collar (i.e., non-physical) workers working from home are required to use VR helmets, vast rural spaces have been repopulated, and families have become bigger in size. In one of the neurotechnology stories, the narrative is about a car accident in which each driver is wearing a neuromodulation brain-computer interface and, following which, drivers, manufacturers, and regulators have a hard time deciding, respectively, how to accept responsibility.

Figure 2: Playing the *TechEthos game: Ages of Technology Impact* © *TechEthos*

All stories were shared and enriched in visioning workshops with experts from various fields. To reach out to the desires and concerns of the wider public, we conducted “world councils” in six European countries. To facilitate citizen engagement in enriching the stories, the *TechEthos game: Ages of Technology Impact* was developed and played by more than 300 participants, including vulnerable groups. We learned as a result that, across the technologies, three values are prioritized by citizens: equity, reliability, and the health of people and the planet. Equity concerns the just distribution of benefits and burdens associated with innovation, as well as processes used for decision-making. Reliability concerns whether a technology functions as intended, delivers the promised outcomes, ensures safety, and minimizes unintended, undesirable, or adverse side-effects. The health of people and the planet refers to the creation and implementation of technologies that have a minimal negative impact on the environment and human health while promoting biodiversity and ensuring a healthy society and ecosystems.

Framed futures: Sharing briefs

Our work speculates about futures and supports stakeholders in research, policy, and strategic decision making, and, thus, contributes to the possible framing of futures. This is also true for the TechEthos initiative, which is based on the learnings of multi-stakeholder engagement (Cannizzaro et al., 2023; Seedall et al., 2023; Hiney & Vleugel, 2023; Vinders & Howkins, 2023). For researchers from academia and industry, for research ethics bodies, and for policy makers we scanned ethics criteria, guidelines, and frameworks, made suggestions for their enhancement, and drafted specific policy briefs with key messages for the ethical governance of new & emerging technologies and for the enhancement of the respective EU legal frameworks. The framings and briefings have been shared via social media, webinars, consultations, and events.

References

Adomaitis, L., Grinbaum, A., & Lenzi, D. 2022. ***TechEthos Deliverable D2.2: Identification and specification of potential ethical issues and impacts and analysis of ethical issues of digital extended reality, neurotechnologies, and climate engineering.*** TechEthos Project Deliverable to the European Commission. Accessed online https://zenodo.org/records/7619852. Viewed February 20, 2024.

Bernstein, M. J., & Mehnert, E. W. 2022. ***Policy note: Analysis of expert scenarios addressing ethical implications of selected technologies.*** TechEthos Project Deliverable to the European Commission. Accessed online https://zenodo.org/records/7615250. Viewed February 20, 2024.

Buchinger, E., Bernstein, M. J., Nishi, M., Mehnert, W., & Csabi, A. 2023. ***TechEthos Deliverable D3.4: Anticipation of societal embedding of new and emerging technologies: Using scenarios to explore public awareness and attitudes in climate engineering, digital extended reality and neurotechnologies.*** TechEthos Project Deliverable to the European Commission. Accessed online https://zenodo.org/records/10200667. Viewed February 20, 2024.

Buchinger, E., Kienegger, M., Zahradnik, G., Bernstein, M. J., Porcari, A., Gonzales, G., Pimponi, D. & Buceti, G. 2022. ***TechEthos technology portfolio: Assessment and final selection of economically and ethically high impact technologies. Deliverable 1.2 to the European Commission.*** TechEthos Project Deliverable to the European Commission. Accessed online https://zenodo.org/records/7590422. Viewed February 20, 2024.

Buchinger, E., Mehnert, W., Csabi, A., Nishi, M., Bernstein, M. J., Gonzales, G., Porcari, A., Grinbaum, A., Adomaitis, L., Lenzi, D., Rainey, S., Umbrello, S., Vermaas, P., Paca, C., Alliaj, G., & Whittington-Davis, A. 2023. ***TechEthos Deliverable D3.1 Multi-stakeholder evolution of TechEthos scenarios on ethical issues in climate engineering, digital extended reality and neurotechnologies.*** TechEthos Project Deliverable to the European Commission. Accessed online https://zenodo.org/records/10676415. Viewed February 20, 2024.

Cannizzaro, S., Bhalla, N., Brooks, L., Richardson, K., Francis, B., & Lenzi, D. 2023. ***TechEthos Deliverable D5.3: Suggestions for the revision of existing operational guidelines for climate engineering, neurotechnologies and digital XR technologies.*** TechEthos Project Deliverable to the European Commission. Accessed online https://www.techethos.eu/suggestions-for-the-revision-of-existing-operational-guidelines-for-climate-engineering-neurotechnologies-and-digital-xr-technologies/. Viewed February 20, 2024.

EC. 2020. ***Strategic foresight report: Charting the course towards a more resilient Europe.*** Brussels: European Commission. Accessed online https://commission.europa.eu/strategy-and-policy/strategic-planning/strategic-foresight/2020-strategic-foresight-report_en. Viewed February 20, 2024.

EC. 2021. ***European Research Area Policy Agenda – Overview of actions for the period 2022-2024.*** Brussels: European Commission. Accessed online https://commission.europa.eu/system/files/2021-11/ec_rtd_era-policy-agenda-2021.pdf. Viewed February 20, 2024.

EC. 2023. ***Horizon Europe: Programme guide.*** Brussels: European Commission. Accessed online https://ec.europa.eu/info/funding-tenders/opportunities/docs/2021-2027/horizon/guidance/programme-guide_horizon_en.pdf. Viewed February 20, 2024.

Ellul, J. 1954/1964. ***The technological society.*** Toronto: Vintage Books. (Translated from the French original "La Technique ou l'Enjeu du siècle").

Heidegger, M. 1949/1977. ***The question concerning technology.*** New York/ London: Garland Publishing (Translated from the German original "Die Technik und die Kehre, Holzwege, und Vorträge und Aufsätze").

IPCC. 2023. ***Climate change 2023 synthesis report: Summary for policymakers.*** Geneva: Intergovernmental Panel on Climate Change. Accessed online https://www.ipcc.ch/report/ar6/syr/downloads/report/IPCC_AR6_SYR_SPM.pdf. Viewed February 20, 2024.

Hiney, M. ,& Vleugel, M. 2023. ***TechEthos Deliverable D5.5: Complementing the ALLEA European Code of Conduct for Research Integrity.*** TechEthos Project Deliverable to the European Commission. Accessed online https://www.techethos.eu/complementing-the-allea-european-code-of-conduct-for-research-integrity/. Viewed February 20, 2024.

OECD. 2022. ***Going digital to advance data governance for growth and well-being***. Paris: OECD Publishing. Accessed online https://www.oecd-ilibrary.org/science-and-technology/going-digital-to-advance-data-governance-for-growth-and-well-being_e3d783b0-en. Viewed February 20, 2024.

OECD. 2023. ***OECD Science, Technology and Innovation Outlook 2023: Enabling Transitions in Times of Disruption.*** Paris: OECD Publishing. Accessed online https://doi.org/10.1787/0b55736e-en. Viewed February 20, 2024.

Peperhove, R., Steinmüller, K., & Dienel, H.-L. (eds.). 2018. ***Envisioning uncertain futures: Scenarios as a tool in security, privacy and mobility research.*** Wiesbaden, Springer.

Popper, K. R. 1991/2007. Against the cynical interpretation of history. In K. R. Popper (ed.), ***All life is problem solving:*** 105-115. London/New York: Routledge. (Translated from the German original “Gegen den Zynismus in der Interpretation der Geschichte”).

Popper, K. R. 1993/2007. The necessity of peace. In K. R. Popper (ed.), ***All life is problem solving:*** 139-144. London/New York: Routledge. (Translated from the German original “Von der Notwendigkeit des Friedens”).

Porcari, A., Pimponi, D., Gonzales, G., Buceti, G., Buchinger, E., Kienegger, M., Bernstein, M., & Zahradnik, G. 2021. ***TechEthos Deliverable D1.1: Description of selected high socio-economic impact technologies.*** TechEthos Project Deliverable to the European Commission. Accessed online https://zenodo.org/records/7590310. Viewed February 20, 2024.

Schoemaker, P. J. H. 1995. Scenario planning: A tool for strategic thinking. ***MIT Sloan Management Review,*** 36(2): 25-40.

Seedall, C., Lindemann, T., Klar, R., & Tambornino, L. 2023. ***TechEthos Deliverable D5.4: Criteria for ethical review by research ethics bodies (RECs) in emerging technology research.*** TechEthos Project Deliverable to the European Commission. Accessed online https://www.techethos.eu/criteria-for-ethical-review-by-recs/. Viewed February 20, 2024.

Taleb, N. N. 2007. ***The black swan: The impact of the highly improbable.*** New York: Random House.

Umbrello, S., Vermaas, P., Paca, C., Alliaj, G., Whittington-Davis, A., Jouvenot, F., Bernstein, M. J., Mehnert, W., & Buchinger, E. 2022. ***TechEthos Deliverable D3.2: Tools to develop and advance scenarios dealing with the ethics of new technologies.*** TechEthos Project Deliverable to the European Commission. Accessed online https://www.techethos.eu/tools-to-develop-and-advance-scenarios-dealing-with-the-ethics-of-new-technologies/. Viewed February 20, 2024.

UNESCO. 2015. ***Ethical perspective on science, technology and society: A contribution to the post-2015 agenda.*** SHS/YES/COMEST-8EXTR/14/3. Paris: UNESCO World Commission on the Ethics of Scientific Knowledge and Technology. Accessed online https://unesdoc.unesco.org/ark:/48223/pf0000234527. Viewed February 20, 2024.

UNESCO. 2021. ***Report of the world commission on the ethics of scientific knowledge and technology (COMEST) on the ethical implications of the internet of things (IoT).*** SHS/COMEST-Ext11/2021/2 Rev. Paris: UNESCO World Commission on the Ethics of Scientific Knowledge and Technology. Accessed online https://unesdoc.unesco.org/ark:/48223/pf0000375304. Viewed February 20, 2024.

UNESCO. 2023. ***Report of the world commission on the ethics of scientific knowledge and technology (COMEST) on the ethics of climate engineering.*** SHS/COMEST-13/2023/1 REV. Paris: UNESCO World Commission on the Ethics of Scientific Knowledge and Technology. Accessed online https://unesdoc.unesco.org/ark:/48223/pf0000386677. Viewed February 20, 2024.

Vinders, J., & Howkins, B. 2023. ***Enhancing EU law on climate engineering, neurotechnologies, and digital extended reality: Policy Briefs.*** TechEthos Project Deliverable 6.2 for the European Commission. Accessed online https://www.techethos.eu/enhancing-eu-law-emerging-technologies/. Viewed February 20, 2024.

DIETMAR OFFENHUBER

PROFESSOR OF DESIGN /
PUBLIC POLICY AND URBAN AFFAIRS
NORTHEASTERN UNIVERSITY
BOSTON, UNITED STATES

Photo: Erich Goldmann

DATA DILEMMAS: THE MATERIAL AND THE IMAGINARY

How can we make a future plausible that does not yet exist? In the realm of planning and policy, the answer is usually through data—with so-called evidence-based methods that create scenarios that can be evaluated and compared. Administrative data from diverse areas are synthesized into metrics designed to support decisions and measure success. These metrics are then visualized in real-time dashboards designed to inform the decisions of policy makers. And yet, it seems debatable whether these metrics, data visualizations, and dashboards really do such a good job at making futures plausible—their track record is rather mixed.

In many ways, data dashboards are not always the best basis for decision making. A recent study from the Brookings Institute concluded that most dashboards ultimately fail to meaningfully shape strategic decisions (Donahue, Fleming, & Parilla, 2023). One reason is that the metrics employed in these dashboards implicitly contain assumptions about a desirable future, leading to preemptive conclusions and self-fulfilling prophecies. Based on their embedded worldviews and their assumed causal mechanisms, metrics often imply certain scenarios and desired outcomes, which are then merely confirmed by data analysis.

In administrative practice, working with data rarely resembles scientific processes or experiments. Data collection is often merely an afterthought or serves as a justification for decisions that have already been made. Data work can give rise to a bureaucratic narrowness that is more concerned with following a prescribed process than exploring what data may indicate. But strategic decisions about desired futures require more than a justifiable process—they require imagination, and they require the critical examination of assumptions that are taken for granted. This begins with common assumptions about the nature of data. Are they plain facts or subjective interpretations, neutral observations or clues that invite speculation?

In this short chapter, I want to make three points:[1]

1. Our commonly used concept of data is flawed for the purpose of making futures plausible.
2. Recent developments in the field of artificial intelligence (AI) require us to rethink this traditional notion of data.
3. I will conclude by proposing an alternate perspective on data that addresses some of these shortcomings.

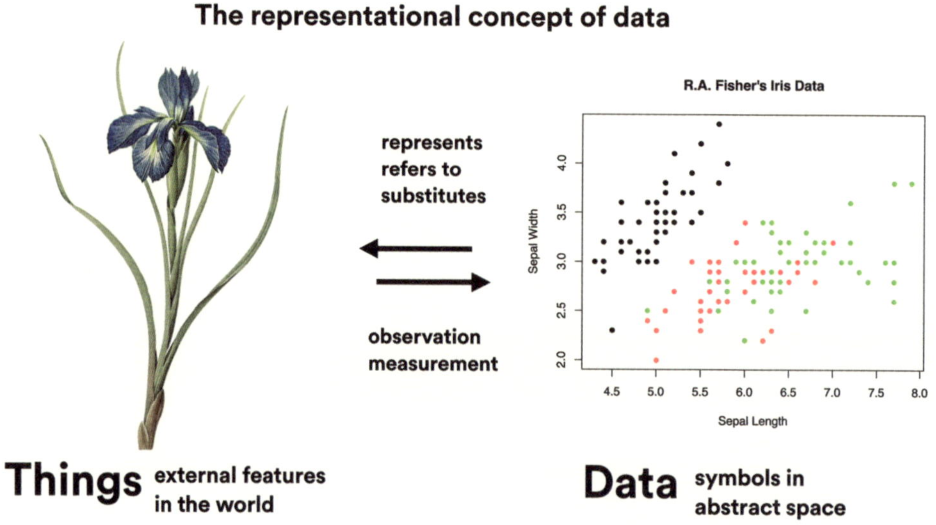

Figure 1: The representational concept of data: data as references to things in the world. © *Offenhuber*

1 These arguments are further elaborated in Offenhuber, 2024.

Data as representations

The traditional concept of data can be summarized as follows: A *datum* is a reference that points to a thing in the world. This thing can be physical or abstract. It has certain features that can be measured or described, features that are selected on the basis of aspects that are considered important. Once a dataset exists, it can be used to substitute the thing. Used in its place, the dataset can be taken apart, transformed, or aggregated. We can describe this model as the representational concept of data (see Figure 1).

While this concept may seem straightforward, there are several problems with it. First, not every datum is a representation of something in the world; data are often generated as placeholders, intermediate results, or by-products of some computational process. Even more problematic is the role of data as surrogates: Collecting data involves many simplifications, judgments, and often arbitrary decisions. But once a dataset exists, we tend to forget its history and the assumptions and simplifications that went into creating it. The question of how exactly it relates to the thing in the world fades into the background.

This oblivion leads to a disconnect between datasets and the world that data are supposed to describe. In this relationship, the world is assumed to be static, which, of course, is never the case. Data, on the other hand, are considered abstract, which is also not the case: data are always physical entities.

While such issues of representation have been debated in academia for some time, I will proceed to an emerging phenomenon that challenges the representational model in perhaps more obvious ways: the phenomenon of synthetic data. Synthetic data are artificially generated data that mimic information gathered from real-life observations. They do not represent any specific object or phenomenon, but could plausibly do so.

The weirdness of synthetic data

Synthetic data serve two primary purposes: firstly, as a substitute for observational data when privacy concerns limit data sharing; and, secondly, as a tool to produce training data for machine learning models and, particularly, to prepare them for rare scenarios that are unlikely to occur in the real world. Artificial data for simulation and mathematical experiments have been around for some time, but as with many other recent developments, generative AI has made things particularly weird. MIT Sloan estimates that, by the end of 2024, 60% of all data used in training and data analytics are going to be generated by AI (Lucini, 2021).

In the first and most common use case, synthetic data are used in place of a real data set that cannot be shared for privacy reasons. The synthetic dataset aims to mimic all the correlations and patterns of the original dataset, making it statistically indistinguishable without replicating any of its records. In addition, the synthetic data model can correct for known biases, fill in missing information, and scale up the dataset—in short, create an idealized version of it, like a Photoshopped portrait. It is noteworthy that the US Census Bureau, whose data are considered the gold standard for US demographic information, is currently considering distributing synthetic data to address privacy concerns and to fill data gaps.

The second use case involves generating training data for models designed to predict rare events for which there is no good real-world data: detecting rare forms of cancer despite a lack of real-world data due to restrictions on sharing patient information; training software for autonomous vehicles to prevent accidents; or correcting for inherent biases in training data due to missing information. In the first example, AI image generation can be used to generate plausible variations of brain tumor images; in the second, footage from games and virtual environments can be used to simulate potentially dangerous events; and in the third, new artificial images are introduced to cover missing cases and expand the variability in the training dataset. In all three examples, the goal is not to generate perfectly realistic training data, but to generate training data that measurably improves the performance of the trained model.

Most of the training data used in AI today are already partially synthetic. A common technique is automatic labeling, which involves describing the contents of an image that can then be used as a ground truth reference for training. While early datasets such as ImageNet[2] were manually labeled by crowd workers, newer and larger datasets are labeled by other AI models that may have originally been trained on ImageNet. Data inpainting techniques involve the creation of entirely fictional data to fill gaps in existing datasets. The brain tumor dataset may be created by generative AIs that paint tumors into healthy brains, creating images that are then used to train other models to detect brain tumors. This circularity may seem unsettling, and its implications may not yet be well understood, but it is nevertheless a widespread practice.

Both use cases are remarkable departures from the idea that data factually represent reality. In the first case, the data mimic but do not represent real-world situations: No record in a synthetic population dataset corresponds to a real individual. The representational relationship is intentionally vague, based on plausibility and similarity. The departure in the second case is even more extreme. One is struck by the lack of realism in some synthetic training data sets: cartoonishly distorted faces, crudely modeled 3D environments, and unconvincing image editing. These distortions are partly deliberate, due to the aim of making the trained models more versatile and allowing them to abstract and ultimately deal with unfamiliar situations.

It should not be ignored that synthetic data have many problematic epistemological, ethical, and social aspects. Synthetic data may

---

2 See https://www.image-net.org (accessed April 4, 2024).

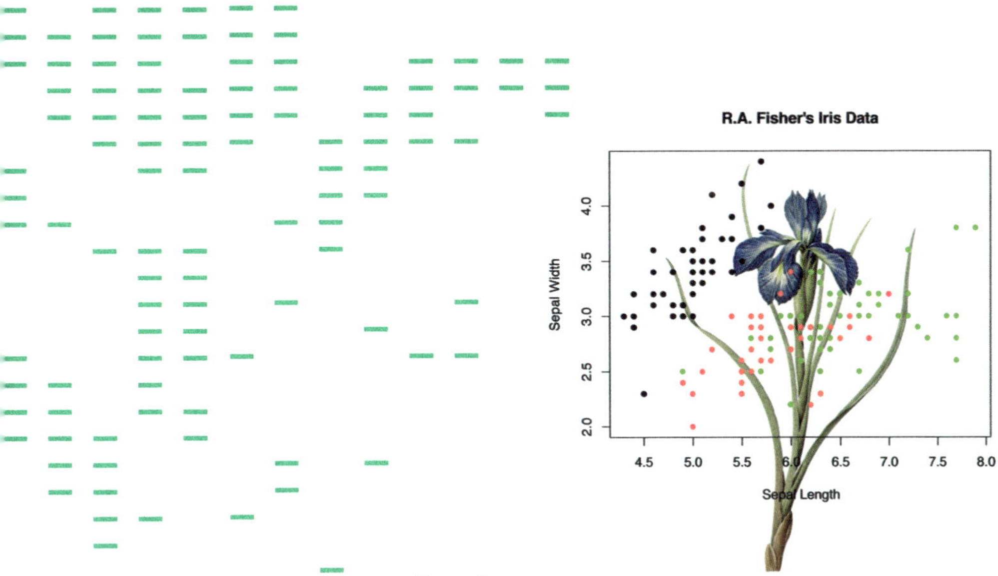

Figure 2
Data as material things and parts of a phenomenon
© *Offenhuber*

Data as parts of **Phenomena**

be able to scale up a small dataset and correct for biases. However, it should be clear that this process does not magically increase the amount of information; in fact, it decreases it. Synthetic data do not describe a real population but merely the distributions of the derived model. Creating seemingly relevant data out of thin air is nevertheless a tempting proposition. Some AI startups offer synthetic data for sensitive purposes including pricing home insurance. Even the US Census Bureau has come under scrutiny from social scientists who point to cases where synthetic data may not be accurate enough, such as the drawing of congressional districts or the estimation of the impacts of COVID-19 on marginalized groups.[3]

What are data in these cases, if not descriptive facts? If anything, synthetic data are counterfactual: They capture possibilities, imagined scenarios, and black-swan events, but they decidedly do not represent existing features of the world. They are not entirely arbitrary either, since they have a measurable effect on a trained model. Synthetic data are not defined by what they represent, but by what they do. This is a second departure from a traditional understanding of data, since data no longer precede their application but are defined by their purpose.

Synthetic data allow us to view data from a different angle. Precisely because of, rather than despite, their shortcomings, they force us to consider the wider context of data generation. This allows for a more comprehensive perspective on data, not just as factual records, but also as speculative tools for envisaging potential future scenarios.

3 See https://www.ipums.org/changes-to-census-bureau-data-products (accessed April 4, 2024)

Data as embodiments

A second area in which synthetic data challenge the representational model is the often-opaque process of synthetic data generation, especially when artificial neural networks (ANNs) are involved. Based on current knowledge, ANNs are not decomposable. They are similar to a baked cake, which cannot be separated back into its ingredients.[4] The training data are not recoverable, nor can the embedded algorithms that evolved during the training process be easily analyzed. One cannot disassemble them to neatly observe their internal workings; one can only run them and observe their results.

Whether and to what extent ANNs build generalized, interpretable internal representations of their training data is still an active matter of research. But much seems to suggest that they do not represent but, rather, embody information. The difference between representation and embodiment can be illustrated by a device like the wind tunnel, which can be seen as an analog computer that calculates turbulence. The wind tunnel does not produce numbers, it embodies the phenomenon. To obtain numerical results, one has to measure the trails of smoke or smudges of colored oil disturbed by the wind. While ANNs produce numbers, it is not clear what exactly they represent—other than being intermediary artifacts that are involved in the generation of output that can be evaluated. Supporting this analogy, AI researchers have developed techniques that treat the ANN almost like a natural phenomenon—they poke its different parts, see how they respond, and map the results (Olah, Mordvintsev, & Schubert, 2017).

Can we talk about data only after the turbulence in the wind tunnel has been measured and translated into a table of numbers? Or, as I would argue, can we consider the smoke trails themselves as a form of material data? The concept of data can be defined in many ways, but if we take a broader view that includes this turbulence, then we no longer have the separation between data and the world it supposedly represents. Data becomes an embodied artifact resulting from a material process. The *datum* is no longer a description, but part of a phenomenon that encompasses not only the wind, but also the entire apparatus, the mathematical formulas that guided its design, and, ultimately, the observer (see Figure 2).

Figure 3: *Staubmarke* (dust mark)—material visualizations of air pollution, Dietmar Offenhuber 2018 © *photograph by Frank Kleinbach*

Post-digital approaches to presenting evidence

There are many examples of artists, citizen scientists, and environmental activists using material data to advocate for a desired future. They have found that, when it comes to presenting evidence, it is best to go to the source of data and emphasize its material nature. Digital data visualizations may brandish the visual language of rational objectivity, but they have become so commonplace that they often fail to impress with their sophistication. Instead, they often raise suspicion: "The graph looks nice, but where does the data come from? Oh, it was not collected by a scientific agency but by a group of amateurs who have an axe to grind? I don't buy it." After a decade in which advocacy groups and activists eagerly adopted the digital crafts of data analysis communication, we can now observe many of them coming back to more analog methods. These post-digital practices focus on what data alone cannot show: its own origin. By laying out material evidence and walking the audience through its material interpretation, they try to stay as close to the phenomenon as possible.

The practice of pedestrian and bicycle advocates of documenting "sneckdowns," a contraction of the phrase "snowy neckdown," serves as a simple example. "Neckdown" is a term used in traffic engineering to describe bulb-shaped sidewalk extensions that are added to roads to help slow down traffic.[6] When fresh snow builds up, some areas of the road remain untouched by traffic, forming a similar kind of sidewalk extension. Activists interpret these snowy areas as proof that vehicle traffic does not require as much space as transportation planners claim and as an indication of areas that could be returned to pedestrian use. They share images of "sneckdowns" on social media, annotated with proposals on how these areas could be redesigned for a more pedestrian-friendly urban future. The remarkable thing about this simple example is that the activists do not engage transportation engineers through their native medium—plans and simulations—but through simple observations that cannot be easily dismissed by calculations and technical guidelines. The "sneckdowns" are not only a medium of communication but also the outcomes of a natural experiment. The former can be contested through rhetoric, the latter much less so. Finally, finding "sneckdowns" is also an engaging activity that lends itself to participatory citizen science approaches much more than numerical simulations. Observing an *autographic* process of self-inscription allows participants to experience causality.

---

4 Credit for this metaphor goes to Denisa Kara.

5 I examine this question and discuss some of the following examples at length in Offenhuber, 2023.

6 See https://en.wikipedia.org/wiki/Sneckdown (accessed April 4, 2024)

In 2018, I was invited by a citizen sensing initiative in the German city of Stuttgart to test a similar approach. Stuttgart is struggling with air pollution, partly due to its topographical setting and to its heavy industry, which includes some of the largest German car companies. Particulate matter, fine dust suspended in the air, is a major subject of public controversy between the city and citizens' groups. Their differences about how to interpret sensor data often come down to the technicalities of measurement and the placement of sensors and their distribution across the city. However, none of these contested technicalities are reflected in the data itself. The invisible dust pollution is measured in plain numbers, whose meaning and contextual relevance is difficult to assess beyond comparing them to a threshold value. But while particulate matter is invisible, it accumulates on all surfaces in the city. Using a pressure washer, I created visual marks by cleaning specific parts of a surface in a public space, a technique often described as "Reverse Graffiti." The resulting marks (see Figure 3) make it possible to estimate the amount of accumulated dust and, by gradual disappearing, record the re-accumulation of this dust over time. I wanted to invite questions such as: "Do areas with consistently high sensor readings show a stronger dust patina?" Of course, this is not an accurate method of measuring dust, and observers were quick to point out what the method accomplished and failed to accomplish. However, this kind of critique was the goal of the intervention, to allow a debate about a material process of measurement that is normally concealed, carried out by electronic sensors in black boxes, and whose reductive measuring technique is affected by its own shortcomings but hidden from scrutiny.

As a final example, I would like to invite you to take a glimpse of the unfolding climate crisis by visiting the Grossglockner, Austria's highest mountain (see Figure 4). From a large observation deck accessible by car, a funicular train once transported the visitor directly onto the ice of the *Pasterze*, the largest glacier in the eastern Alps. Now, the train covers only a third of the distance to the glacier lake, which formed in 2010 and contains remnants of ice. The path to the lake is lined by occasional signs that mark the extent of the ice in the corresponding year: 1960, 1975, 1990, 2013, and so on. The path is a striking, visceral example of data embodiment: The history of the glacier is visualized through its absence. Symbolic data is present in the form of signs, contextualized by its environment. One starts to observe the slopes of the mountain differently; for example, by searching for traces of past ice, similar to the bleached shorelines of an empty water reservoir. The extent of the missing ice is not only measured by comparing two lines in an infographic but by the hiker's stamina and breath as they traverse the long and steep path. And yet, symbolic data plays an important role: I found myself thinking about how I would have experienced the situation if someone had secretly moved or disturbed the historical markers: One can lie with the help of traces even without manipulating them—just by framing them differently.

The meaning of data—whether symbolic, synthetic, or material—depends on its context. Material data reflects interactions within the physical world, yet part of this context is inaccessible. Data is a snapshot of a past that cannot be fully reconstructed; it can never completely reveal its original story. But in its temporality there also lies an incorporeal, speculative component. Data implies unknown futures, and its full significance rests on potentials that exist beyond its immediate context. To unlock these potentials, we require critical reflection, speculation, and creative imagination.

Figure 4: Pasterze glacier, Grossglockner: Historic marker of the 1960 glacier position at the exit from the funicular train. © *Offenhuber*

References

Donahue, R., Fleming, P., & Parilla, J. 2023. How local leaders can upgrade their regional economic dashboards for a new era of place-based policymaking. ***The Brookings Institution***, May 4. Available online https://www.brookings.edu/articles/how-local-leaders-can-upgrade-their-regional-economic-dashboards-for-a-new-era-of-place-based-policymaking/. Viewed February 6, 2024.

Lucini, F. 2021. The real deal about synthetic data. ***MIT Sloan Management Review***, October 20: Reprint # 63217.

Offenhuber, D. 2023. ***Autographic design: The matter of data in a self-inscribing world.*** Cambridge, MA: The MIT Press.

Offenhuber, D. 2024. Shapes and Frictions of Synthetic Data. ***Big Data & Society***, 11(2): 20539517241249390.

Olah, C., Mordvintsev, A., & Schubert, L. 2017. Feature visualization. ***Distill***, 2(11): e7. Available online https://distill.pub/2017/feature-visualization/. Viewed February 6, 2024.

Photo: Erich Goldmann

WEI LIU

ASSOCIATE PROFESSOR,
FACULTY OF PSYCHOLOGY,
BEIJING NORMAL UNIVERSITY
BEIJING, PR CHINA

DONALD, TELL US HOW: FUTURECASTING PRINCIPLES FOR EMPOWERING HUMAN-CENTERED DESIGN

WEI LIU, XIN XIN, YANCONG ZHU, DI ZHU, RUONAN HUANG

Introduction

Donald Norman's impact on human-centered design (HCD) is unparalleled. His contributions have profoundly influenced our perspective and methodologies in the field. A cognitive psychologist by training, Norman has broadened the reach of invaluable insights into human behavior and cognition, reshaping how we approach user experience. His seminal works, particularly on the psychology of everyday things, are cornerstones in the literature that elucidate the vital connection between usability and user experience (UX) (Kuo, Tseng, & Yang, 2019; Stappers, Sleeswijk Visser, Keller, Visser, & Keller, 2014; Leifer & Steinert, 2011). His formulation of the four HCD principles has been particularly transformative (Norman, 2019), offering guidance in creating solutions that resonate with users both emotionally and functionally. These principles underpin our educational philosophy, influencing how we approach and teach HCD (Norman & Verganti, 2014).

Our journey has been richly informed by Norman's expertise, through various interactions ranging from academic discussions to global forums and online engagements. These experiences have deepened our understanding of HCD and reinforced our commitment to educating future practitioners. Here, we invite you to explore with us the transformative power of HCD and design thinking, guided by Norman's enduring principles, and to dive into the futurecasting principles that enable us to envision and shape a more human-centered world.

This paper narrates our journey as influenced by Norman, covering diverse interactions from educational settings to global discussions and online platforms. It emphasizes the essential blend of theory and practical application in a broader user-centered context. Central to this discourse, we introduce our 4E principles—Experience, Empathy, Exploration, and Evaluation—and dive into the concept of futurecasting. This approach allows us to project forward-thinking scenarios and craft strategies for a world increasingly focused on human needs and perspectives. Our work celebrates Norman's enduring impact, his inspiration of a forward-looking approach that transcends conventional design thinking and places a stronger emphasis on futurecasting and its role in enhancing human experiences.

Interacting with Donald Norman

Our path in design education has been significantly enhanced by our interactions with Donald Norman. Since 2010, these engagements have shaped our understanding and application of design principles. Particularly impactful were the on-site Q&A sessions in our classrooms (see Figure 1), where his direct engagement with students demystified complex concepts and linked them to practical design challenges. These interactions underscored the value of merging theory with practice, a key aspect of our educational philosophy. At the International Association of Societies of Design Research (IASDR) conference, our discussions with Norman on various design topics, in which he underlined his dedication to connecting design theory with practice, were enlightening. Additionally, his webinars and online seminars have kept us abreast of the latest in design thinking and HCD, deepening our grasp of his principles and their practical applications.

Figure 1: The on-site Q&A interactions with Donald Norman conducted in our classrooms. © *Wei Liu et al.*

Norman's insights have profoundly influenced our teaching approach. His focus on the emotional dimension of design has inspired us to embed empathy and user-centeredness in our curriculum (Desmet, Xue, Xin, & Liu, 2023). We have integrated his principles of designing for people, addressing root causes, systems thinking, and iterative learning into our programs. Our interactions with Norman are milestones in our journey, constantly reinforcing our dedication to leading in design education and nurturing a new generation of HCD practitioners. Engaging with him has not only deepened our knowledge but also shaped our approach to teaching UX, as we remain committed to inspiring future designers with the same passion and adherence to HCD principles.

The significance of futurecasting

As we navigate an ever-evolving landscape, futurecasting has emerged as an invaluable tool that provides a unique vantage point for anticipating and shaping the future that transcends the traditional boundaries of everyday things (Shamiyeh, 2016). This strategic approach empowers professionals and visionaries across fields to create innovative solutions that resonate with evolving needs and aspirations, ensuring their work continues to enhance lives while pushing the boundaries of possibility (Chen, Zhu, Qiao, Wang, & Zhang, 2023; Zhu, Tang, Liu, & Qi, 2022). Futurecasting concretizes and communicates visions of possible alternative futures, playing a pivotal role for several reasons.

Anticipating Needs. A key advantage of futurecasting lies in its ability to anticipate needs before they are explicitly articulated. By closely monitoring emerging trends and societal shifts, practitioners in various fields can proactively identify latent demands and preferences. This foresight enables the crafting of solutions that not only meet current requirements but also align with future expectations, ensuring that innovations remain relevant and responsive.

Fostering Innovation. Innovation sits at the core of progress, with futurecasting serving as a key driver in this area. It encourages forward-thinking individuals to explore unconventional ideas, experiment with new technologies, and challenge existing paradigms. By envisioning future scenarios and potential challenges, futurecasting stimulates groundbreaking innovations that can redefine industries and user experiences.

Adopting a Human-Centered Approach. Despite its forward-looking nature, futurecasting remains firmly rooted in human-centered philosophy. It emphasizes understanding human behaviors, values, and emotions, ensuring that innovations are deeply aligned with human needs and desires. Futurecasting helps to concretize and communicate visions of possible alternative futures. It envisages their impact on individuals and societies.

Promoting Adaptation and Resilience. In today's dynamic world, adaptability and resilience are invaluable. Futurecasting triggers the ability to anticipate disruptions and adapt swiftly. By envisioning various future scenarios, practitioners can develop strategies that are flexible and robust in the face of unforeseen challenges, ensuring that solutions thrive in an ever-changing environment.

Shaping Ethical Considerations. Futurecasting extends beyond envisioning what *can* be done to what *should* be done, encouraging a contemplation of the ethical implications of innovations in future contexts. By considering potential ethical dilemmas and unintended consequences, it promotes proactive measures to ensure that advancements align with societal values and ethical standards.

Norman's HCD principles

Donald Norman's extensive experience and insights have been distilled into four fundamental principles that underpin HCD. These principles provide a solid foundation for designers and innovators to create solutions that effectively resonate with and address people's needs. Norman's HCD principles offer a comprehensive framework for crafting human-centric designs that emphasizes empathy, deep problem understanding, a systemic approach, and continuous iteration as a way of guiding designers to create more meaningful and effective solutions.

Design for People—All the People Who Are Affected. The essence of HCD lies in its emphasis on people: end-users, customers, and all affected individuals. This principle underscores the importance of empathy and understanding diverse needs, behaviors, and preferences. It involves comprehensive user research, early engagement with potential users, and continuous feedback integration. By centering solutions around people, these solutions are tailored to genuinely meet expectations and improve overall experiences.

Solving the Correct Problems—The Causal Factors, not the Symptoms. This principle encourages a deeper examination beyond obvious issues, focusing on identifying and resolving underlying causes. And this approach ensures that solutions are not just superficial but address the real problems at their core. Applying this principle effectively requires in-depth analysis and systems thinking, leading to impactful and lasting solutions.

System Thinking–Everything Is Part of a System. HCD goes beyond isolated solutions, considering the broader systems they operate within. This principle highlights the importance of understanding how various elements within a system are interconnected and the wider effects of decisions. It encourages a holistic view of how solutions integrate into larger ecosystems, promoting seamless integration while being mindful of unintended consequences.

Learn and Modify–Nothing Works as Planned. This principle recognizes that the development process is continuous and true perfection is a progressive journey. It promotes a culture of constant learning and adaptation that focuses on regular testing and feedback analysis and has the flexibility to modify and advance on the basis of real-world experiences and user insights, ensuring that solutions continuously evolve and improve.

The authors' HCD principles

In our journey through the dynamic landscape of HCD, we have refined a set of guiding principles over eight years of teaching, practice, and collaboration with industry leaders like Porsche and Apple. These principles, known as the 4E principles: Experience, Empathy, Exploration, and Evaluation (see Figure 2), have become the cornerstone of our approach, aligning closely with Norman's foundational HCD principles.

Figure 2: The 4E principles: Experience, Empathy, Exploration, and Evaluation. © *Wei Liu et al.*

Experience. At the core of our principles, Experience focuses on creating memorable and meaningful interactions. This principle emphasizes understanding and enhancing an individual's journey through various contexts and fostering emotional connections, not just with products or services but with the world at large.

Empathy. Empathy is a key element that fosters deep understanding of the needs and desires of and challenges to others. It is about stepping into another person's shoes and viewing the world from their perspective, and is integral to effectively addressing and solving problems.

Exploration. Exploration drives innovation by encouraging a push beyond conventional boundaries. It involves embracing curiosity and divergent thinking, and is an iterative process, fostering creativity and new ideas across various disciplines.

Evaluation. Evaluation emphasizes the significance of research and data in any process. Encouraging a hypothesis-driven approach, this principle ensures that outcomes are impactful and meet the intended needs and goals.

The 4E principles harmonize with Norman's HCD principles, enhancing the overall framework. Each principle resonates with Norman's concepts of focusing on people, solving the right problems, systemic thinking, and continuous learning and modification, thus creating a comprehensive approach across various fields. The evolution of the 4E principles from theoretical constructs to practical tools was significantly propelled by collaborations with global corporations. These partnerships provided real-world contexts for applying and refining our principles. This journey underscored the interconnectedness of the 4E principles with Norman's principles, showcasing their practical application in creating impactful solutions across diverse areas.

Transformative UX foundation course

Launched in 2015 by Beijing Normal University's Faculty of Psychology, China's first master's program in Applied Psychology with a UX specialization has been a trailblazer in shaping UX education in the country (Liu, Lee, Gray, Toombs, Chen, & Leifer, 2021). Central to this program is the UX Foundation Course, which is designed to immerse students in HCD principles and offers a thorough understanding of UX. This course has evolved substantially over eight years, transitioning to a project-based curriculum that intertwines psychology, design, technology, and business. This transdisciplinary approach, emphasizing hands-on industry projects, bridges academia and industry, enriching students' learning with real-world experiences. Collaborations with over 20 leading companies have led to significant research contributions and innovative design solutions that have been recognized by awards such as the First Prize for Teaching Graduate Students at Beijing Normal University. This course has thus established itself as a crucible for future UX professionals, equipping them with the skills to thrive in the digital era.

Drawing from our rich experience, we present below a series of guidelines for effectively futurecasting and enhancing the reach of educational innovations. These guidelines offer a strategic roadmap for embedding forward-looking methodologies into educational frameworks, aiming to not only adapt to evolving landscapes but also actively shape the future of learning and development.

- **Transdisciplinary Integration.** Merging psychology, design, technology, and business to bridge gaps in China's UX education.
- **Project-Based Learning.** Engaging students in real-world projects to boost their skillsets and employability.
- **Psychological Insights in UX.** Integrating psychological theories into UX design provides practical tools for understanding user behaviors and needs, applicable across various sectors.
- **Comprehensive Curriculum Development.** Expanding beyond the UX Foundation course, we have created an extensive curriculum that includes physical product development and service system design, thus enriching the educational spectrum.
- **Innovative Educational Models.** Extending our curriculum to K-12 and higher education, we equip students for future professional challenges and opportunities.

- **Wide-Ranging Industry Impact.** Influencing diverse fields such as automotive design, finance, and education, our course content contributes to sectoral advancements.
- **Global Perspectives.** Collaborating with international experts and leading universities like Stanford, Purdue, and MIT, we infuse our UX education with a global perspective.

Conclusions

Our journey, deeply influenced by Donald Norman, has significantly enriched our practice and understanding of HCD. His foundational HCD principles have been a guiding force in our endeavors, shaping our approach to creating user experiences that are both emotionally resonant and practically effective. Our varied interactions, from classroom teaching to global forums and online discussions, have reinforced the crucial link between theory and practice. Embracing futurecasting, as highlighted in this paper, we are inspired to foresee and shape a more human-centered world, addressing both present and emerging needs (Ohashi, Auernhammer, Liu, Pan, & Leifer, 2022). Norman's legacy continues to inspire our exploration and expansion in HCD. With our 4E principles, we aim to shape a future where design profoundly and positively impacts human experiences, guided by the enduring wisdom of a true pioneer in the field.

References

Chen, D., Zhu, M., Qiao, Y., Wang, J., & Zhang, X. 2023. An ergonomic design method of manned cabin driven by human operation performance. ***Advanced Design Research,*** 1(1): 12-20.

Desmet, P. M., Xue, H., Xin, X., & Liu, W. 2023. Demystifying emotion for designers: A five-day course based on seven fundamental principles. ***Advanced Design Research,*** 1(1): 50-62.

Kuo, H. C., Tseng, Y. C., & Yang, Y. T. C. 2019. Promoting college student's learning motivation and creativity through a STEM interdisciplinary PBL human-computer interaction system design and development course. ***Thinking Skills and Creativity,*** 31: 1-10.

Leifer, L. J., & Steinert, M. 2011. Dancing with ambiguity: Causality behavior, design thinking, and triple-loop-learning. ***Information Knowledge Systems Management,*** 10(1-4): 151-173.

Liu, W., Lee, K. P., Gray, C. M., Toombs, A. L., Chen, K. H., & Leifer, L. 2021. Transdisciplinary teaching and learning in UX design: A program review and AR case studies. ***Applied Sciences,*** 11(22): 10648.

Norman, D. A. 2023. ***Design for a better world: Meaningful, sustainable, humanity centered.*** Cambridge, MA: MIT Press.

Norman, D. A. 2019. The four fundamental principles of human-centered design and application [Blog post]. ***JND.org,*** July 23. Accessed online https://jnd.org/the-four-fundamental-principles-ofhuman-centered-design-and-application/. Viewed April 4, 2024.

Norman, D. A. 2005. Human-centered design considered harmful. ***Interactions,*** 12(4): 14-19.

Norman, D. A., & Verganti, R. 2014. Incremental and radical innovation: Design research vs. technology and meaning change. ***Design Issues,*** 30(1): 78-96.

Ohashi, T., Auernhammer, J., Liu, W., Pan, W., & Leifer, L. 2022. NeuroDesign-Science: Systematic literature review of current research on design using neuroscience techniques. In J. S. Gero (ed.), ***Design, Computing, and Cognition'20***, Conference Proceedings: 575-592. Cham: Springer.

Parmentier, D. D., Acker, B. B. Van, Saldien, J., & Detand, J. 2021. A framework to design for meaning: Insights on use, practicality and added value within a project-based learning context. ***International Journal of Technology and Design Education,*** 31: 815-838.

Shamiyeh, M. 2016. Designing from the future. In W. Brenner, & F. Uebernickel (eds.), ***Design Thinking for Innovation: Research and Practice***: 193-219. Cham: Springer.

Stappers, P. J., Sleeswijk Visser, F., Keller, A. I., Visser, F. S., & Keller, A. I. I. 2014. The role of prototypes and frameworks for structuring explorations by research through design. In P. A. Rodgers, & J. Yee (eds.), ***The Routledge Companion to Design Research***: 1-13. London: Taylor & Francis.

Zhu, Y., Tang, G., Liu, W., & Qi, R. 2022. How post 90's gesture interact with automobile skylight. ***International Journal of Human-Computer Interaction,*** 38(5): 395-405.

INTERVIEW

Photo: Erich Goldmann

ANGELA WILKINSON

SECRETARY GENERAL AND
CEO OF THE WORLD ENERGY COUNCIL
OXFORD, UNITED KINGDOM

The following interview with Angela Wilkinson, Secretary General and CEO of the World Energy Council, was conducted by Michael Shamiyeh. The interview's aim was to understand how the World Energy Council establishes its credibility among various interest groups and pioneers new ideas for a better future and, specifically, how the World Energy Council is pushing for global energy transitions and what methods are being used. Dr. Angela Wilkinson has more than 30 years' experience of leading and managing global strategic transformation processes, such as today at the World Energy Council or previously at Royal Dutch Shell and Oxford University.

Michael Shamiyeh (MS):
In a recent interview, you said that citizens need to find their role in the energy transition and that time, CO_2, and credibility are the keys to change. How can we understand your statement in concrete terms and how is credibility in particular linked to citizen participation?

Angela Wilkinson (AW): I think most people, citizens, are no longer looking for experts or their leaders to tell them what the future will be. They're looking for leaders to help and enable them to achieve a better life for themselves and their children. Let me start there.
The long history of future thinking, before the advent of scientific forecasting, was characterized by utopian thinking and prophecy, and the roles of oracles and visionaries. Who can know the future and what does a more desirable future look like? But I think that, these days, everybody has a vision of what "better" looks like. And not all those visions are the same. So, one of the challenges is, first of all, what are our common interests in the future and how do we make leadership judgments that will make for a better future? When it comes to energy transitions, which is really the action agenda of the World Energy Council, it's even more challenging because I get a sense that energy futures thinking has become stuck in the competition of techno-economic assessment and the polarization of political ideologies. That it's all about who's got the best technical assessment, who's got the best data, who can make the best projections, whose truth is better than everybody else's?
On the one hand, we can say, "Great, we've increased the diversity of our capabilities in future thinking." But we're not able to close the gap between the future we want and the present we're standing in. So, my emphasis in making better energy futures happen is on closing that gap between the future we desire—knowing that there's no single vision, but there's a common direction—and where we stand today, recognizing that situations and starting points also differ. And to do that, we have to engage with diversity and differences—a pluralism of participatory futures interventions.
We have to recognize that there are multiple pathways, that the journey is not a predictable straight line but a challenge of turning the corner. It's actually about experimentation, co-creation, and sustaining collaboration with "others," about drawing attention to time, carbon, and trust, for example, when I was talking about energy transitions.

Some people expect that there's going to be some instant energy transition. It's actually a decadal process that will go faster and slower depending on alignment and collaboration—"how to" make energy transitions happen depends on "with whom." We may know how to technically transition away from fossil fuels, but we lack the political know-how to do this in an orderly, just, and equitable way. Maybe we can accelerate the pace of decarbonization, but we certainly can't complete an energy transition overnight or all in one go. A moonshot can put a person on the moon, but the best way to succeed is by humanizing energy to enable the hundreds of thousands of smaller steps that need to be taken.

Carbon—ultimately what we're trying to do is avoid a climate change crisis by transitioning away from the unabated burning of fossil fuels.

But energy transition is about more than carbon. We have to pay attention to other planetary boundaries and structural inequalities—we need to manage connected challenges—energy security, affordability, and sustainability—for orderly transitions to progress.

And we can't just focus on swapping old technologies for new and substituting renewable for fossil supplies. It's also about wider and wiser uses of energy. There are a billion people in the world who lack any access to electricity and billions more don't have enough energy for decent lives. There are even more people who can't afford to maintain their use of modern energy supplies. Hence, it's not just about carbon. And trust is an enabler that's fast becoming the binding constraint in making faster, fairer, and more far-reaching energy transitions happen. We can't achieve this energy transition on our own, no single country, company, city, or community. So, we have to align diverse needs and interests and cooperate with "others." In short, how "we" got to here, won't get "us" to there! Many new ways of aligning are available. Collaborating is not straightforward. International cooperation is a choice. There is no lack of technology—or money. The biggest challenges we face are about trust and making "choices" about the "how-tos" and the "with whoms." Top-down, consensus-driven commitments are not easy to translate into reality. And a new world order is emerging. These days we have to recognize that, whilst there is global common sense about the necessary direction of change, there is no agreement about the ideal pathway, and multiple pathways will be needed. Collaboration with "others," cooperation across borders and fuzzy system boundaries, a lack of full consensus: despite our differences, our best hope is to move forward together by leading and learning with each other and engaging with diversity as a source of innovation.

MS: How does this work? Now we're at the point. This is exactly what I'm fascinated about. You say that many new and different stakeholders are involved. It's not just the government anymore. It's not even a single company. It's multiple sectors. It's leaders at all levels of society. It's even different countries. So how do we set up a successful collaborative process? How does the World Energy Council do that in very practical terms?

AW: We [at the World Energy Council] are the world's first and most diverse and distributed energy leadership community. Leadership for us is about the practical actions involved in co-creating a better energy future with the common goal of enabling 10 billion better lives and a healthy planet. We are a community of communities, so we're looking for what we could call network leverage effects, forging shared understanding whilst respecting that every part of our community is in a specific situation.
We are headed in the same direction, from different starting points and with diverse capabilities for change-making.
Our direction is to accelerate the decarbonization of societies—and the energy systems on which we all depend—with resilience and justice. Our focus is on humanizing energy to make faster, fairer, and more far-reaching energy transitions happen in all parts of the world.
And to do that, we have to engage with what we call the new energy innovation ecosystems and new power system shapers. And we have to remember that energy systems include people. We tend to talk about energy in terms of technology and money or in terms of the supply side of the system. But actually, what the future of energy [looks like], the contours, even what the specifics are, are quite clear: It's going to be a more flexible, user-centric, decentralized system with increasingly electrified end uses. The outlook for new and shifting demand is one of the biggest sources of uncertainty and it's also clear that we will need more demand-driven solutions because users' needs and situations are increasingly diverse—geographically, technologically, and demographically.
Starting points and pathways vary across the world—there's no one-size-fits-all approach. We exist to help these diverse communities of energy transition leadership interests lead with and learn from each other. They share perspectives and best practices, but we don't have a top-down, consensus-driven change-maker program. We look at how change in energy systems happens at the level of a city. How does change happen at the level of a country? How does change happen at the level of a value chain? These are different ways of organizing for system change. We share learning and adapt our practices as we go. We're pragmatic and practical. We're not ideological. We recognize that not everything works the same way everywhere. We need to engage with the pull of societal transformation, not just the push of technological innovation, to ensure that any overshoot is a blip—and experiments in institutional re-design and policy innovation are also needed on this journey.
We have a change-maker toolkit for energy transition-leaders, which is designed for convening power and collaborating for the common good and developed by our community for *their* use. We are not an assessment report production factory, not a policy prescription shop. We have horizon scanning and sense-making tools: the World Energy Issues Monitor, World Energy Pulse Survey series, and World Energy Transition Radar. We have a policy performance and pathfinder tool—the World Energy Trilemma Index, and a set of archetype scenarios. By using these tools in combination with our exceptional power to convene with multiple stakeholders from across and beyond our world energy leadership community, we have developed agile and flexible capabilities for managing connected challenges in specific situations and learning how to move forward together, sharing with each other what works or not. We need to maintain a sense of realistic hope. We are learning how to achieve net zero and beyond in a warmer, wobblier, and weirder world. Incremental improvements are not enough. Engaging in a socially messy change-making process which turns a corner towards a new and better future is possible, but if and only if we are willing to drop the heavy model-based tools of projectable and predictable futures that we have come to rely on. We cannot rely on a big global technology moonshot. Only 11 men on the moon so far and the costs were a much smaller burden than the trillions of dollars needed every year for energy transitions. Reliable and affordable energy transitions will take the form of hundreds of thousands of smaller steps, which coproduce a system

of systems changes. Actions will blur the boundaries of silos, sectors, and political borders: and even though energy system boundaries are fuzzy, how the "system" is framed can be a source of conflict. What we need is a more critical approach to systems thinking, combined with a participatory approach to futures making and a humble approach to learning about the system as we make change happen.

MS: Are these tools somehow designed for the different communities, levels, and stakeholders in terms of applicability? Do you differentiate whether you are providing tools for a company manager, an executive, or an ordinary citizen who is simply concerned about his or her own house or apartment and asks what he or she can do for the energy transition? In other words, do you simply make these tools available on your website or do you have employees who address the respective communities? How can we imagine the process of spreading the idea you have just presented to us in practice?

AW: We talk about a scalable and flexible toolkit. If I take something like the World Energy Trilemma Index, it was a framework that was designed to recognize that energy and sustainable development are connected challenges. That's how we framed it in the action agenda in the 1980s. The many different parts of our community—some of them are policymakers, others are CEOs, some are ordinary academics, others are energy users, buyers or whatever—came together and said "well, how do we know what good performance looks like in securing more energy for sustainable development?" And they started to share insights from around the world about what good energy transition performance means. They developed this integrated approach and framework for managing connected challenges called the World Energy Trilemma Index: it helps direct attention to the evolving trade-offs and emerging synergies between the simultaneous dimensions of energy security, energy equity, affordability, and environmental sustainability policies. There is also attention to national context and an emphasis on quality of governance.
The framework measures performance in all these dimensions and, while it can be used to rank and compare countries, it's best used to learn about what is working or not in enabling year-on-year progress. But we also know that more digital data and new metrics are emerging that would allow us to evolve the framework and extend its use to cities and regions and real-time data analytics. Hence, we want to make the framework more scalable and flexible so that we have the ability to support multi-stakeholder conversations and collaborations at the global, national, sub-national, and city levels. Maybe we'll get it onto a mobile phone app with real-time data that people can use. It's a way of connecting the dots between people and challenges without being so comprehensive that it's incomprehensible. And that's the challenge that we have found with the United Nations Sustainable Development Goals. There are so many metrics, so many ways of making connections that things become incomprehensible. The Trilemma Index is our way of tracking and guiding performance. It's ultimately the world's GPS system for energy transitions: How do we know whether we're doing well? And if we combine trilemma and scenarios, we can support future-mindful pathfinding.

MS: Based on your experience, you probably also encounter people who have doubts about the need for a radical energy transition. How do you deal with this? How do you manage to change their mental models of the world?

AW: First of all, decarbonization and energy transition have become two of the most common terms in the last decade. But when people use them, they often mean different things. So, let's start right there: For the hardline climate activist, energy transition means no coal, oil, or gas! Just stop using fossil fuels now. However, stopping supply without transforming demand is a recipe for a different kind of crisis. It won't deliver an orderly, inclusive to equitable energy transition, even though solar and wind resources are freely available everywhere. We frame the problem as "how to" enable more energy for climate resilient, sustainable development with justice and without overshooting other planetary boundaries. We believe the framing of "net zero and beyond" energy transitions is more realistic and practical than a "green only" global energy transition. Our framing is in line with the one adopted by the COP 28 meeting: to transition away from fossil fuels in a just, orderly, and equitable manner for net zero by 2050.

MS: So, we're initially dealing with different perspectives, aren't we?

AW: Yes, we have to start off with a conversation about the purpose of energy transition and clarify that ends and means are different. For us, it means ten billion better lives on a healthy planet, right? That's the vision. That's the ultimate goal. That's what it looks like. What does ten billion better lives on a healthy planet look like? I ask people, what does it smell like? What does it taste like? What does it feel like? Right? What does it sound like? Because then you start to articulate what this future looks like, there are multiple pathways for translating this vision into reality. Then you can say: Where are we now compared with where we need to be? How can we close the gap? Now, there are people who do that quite technically, like the International Energy Agency. They use their technology road mapping and their policy assessments in a backcasting process to identify preferred pathways to net zero by 2050. And we've looked at all their reports and those of others producing climate-energy scenarios and outlooks and what we find missing from all these roadmaps is *people* and huge uncertainties about new and shifting energy needs and demands. To engage and mobilize more people and diverse communities we need human-centric stories of energy transition and to develop a new genre of participatory scenarios which help them understand *their* roles and choices, including choices for aligning collaboration and cooperation with "others" at speed and scale. This represents a more distributed and democratized approach to energy futures thinking than currently exists. So, we are also trying to refresh and reframe our World Energy Scenarios approach to meet this challenge of encouraging people to tell their own stories of energy transition in ways that help them to engage with their future visions and reveal and test their assumptions about what is preferable, plausible, and possible. We can't hope to succeed if we rely on current approaches of top-down futures, corporate scenarios, and universal policy prescriptions.
We have a partnership with BBC Story Works: We're collecting people-centric stories of communities, households, cities; people telling their own stories of where they are in their energy transition, where they're headed, and what the challenges are.
We have to have a combination of top-down visioning but bottom-up engagement and empowerment if we're really going to make this work.

MS: You mentioned the BBC. Can you be more precise now in terms of what's really happening in this process, in the democratization of the future vision of energy? How does it work, how did you set it up, what's the time frame, etc.?

AW: When people talk about a net-zero energy system, they mean a net-zero greenhouse gas emissions energy system by 2050, and then last year some more commitments were made about tripling renewables by 2030, doubling energy efficiency by 2030. Multiple goals, connected challenges. They can be both abstract and overwhelming.
So, what we do with the BBC is ask all our member organizations and communities to tell us an inspiring story of a community-led and/or place-based energy transition. We have stories from mayors about their cities, from workers about their companies, from energy users—big industries, SME businesses, and households. It's the "who" and the "how to" at the same time, the challenges and the benefits. We collect these cases and they're turned into wonderfully accessible stories by

a master storyteller, the BBC. The BBC reaches audiences of ordinary people in over 100 countries and tells stories in a language that's accessible.
These stories come from places like Mongolia, Peru, Taiwan, Japan, Saudi Arabia, the UK, and Australia. The Taiwan story is poetically told in a local narrative form. These stories of how diverse leaders and their communities are making their energy transitions happen inspire others to have a go too. People want to play their part, to get engaged, and to benefit from this process, and not see it as something foreign, prescribed, and remote.

MS: Thus, it's stories that help people to make sense of it all and promote enactment.

AW: Making sense of themselves and helping them understand that they have agency. It's not empowerment, because then we would have to give them some power. They have agency, they just don't realize *how* they can exercise it. So, this gives them a way of exercising their agency.

MS: Now you are pursuing this strategy in your role on the World Energy Council. Given your experience at Oxford and also at Shell, would you generally see this approach as the most successful strategy for reframing people's mental models? Instead of trying to change someone from the perspective of an expert, get him or her to listen to the stories of others to see how people in Mongolia or wherever approach transitional issues.

AW: My interest in the future has always been as a safe space that helps us to think about how the present could be different and how we would change it. So, I've always been interested in impact rather than methodology. Unfortunately, the futures field ties itself up to death with methodology and talks too little about impact.
So, I am an unashamed idealist and I want to make the world a better place for my children and for other people's children. I think that's what human progress means. Does the next generation benefit from what this generation does? So, I'm interested in stories where people have made change happen and the role that the future played in helping them do that. And if you don't have a vision of better, how do you know whether you're making any progress? You ultimately have to envision better, right? But you must have an understanding of where you stand in the present and what that means, what options for taking action do you have available, otherwise we're wishful thinkers and dreamers who can't make change happen. The options open to a household are different to the options open to a business leader, or policymaker.
But all of them are future shapers, and democratizing energy systems is what we're doing. The future of energy is going to be shaped much more by demand than just by supply-side choices. Because we're decentralizing the system. So, the future of energy is becoming more decentralized. We stopped trying to do predictive forecasting in the World Energy Council in the 1970s because we didn't think that it was playing a part in making change happen. In fact, it was doing the opposite. It was giving people a reason not to make change happen: paradoxically, because they were either optimistic or pessimistic about the future. But you couldn't change it. They weren't really trying to change it. What we're trying to do now is change the future *and* learn about the energy system by changing it: not knowing the energy system first, but learning about the system by changing it.
And we have to change it from every possible perspective. From the householder to the supplier, from the transmission to the electrification part, to the molecule part. That's what we're doing. We are creating a conversation about making the future happen and changing the energy system that we all depend on.

MS: So there is a method then, this conversation about stories, right?

AW: Yes. Actually, the future is first and always a story (Betty Sue Flowers). I'm a big subscriber to that. It can be expressed

in numbers or narratives or images, but it's a story. And whoever controls the story controls the future. And people understand that these days. They don't want a single person or entity controlling that story. They want to be co-creators of that story. They want to play their part. They want their children to play a part as well. So if it's a story, how do we express stories as people, as human beings?
We still express stories to each other through conversation. That's through communication and conversation, not discussion. Discussion comes from percussion, and it means to bang things. So you bang the argument backwards and forwards to see who's right. That's a discussion. Conversation means that we have different ideas and we turn them over together to try and find something new and different that we can all live with.
Experimentation is a big thing. Nobody knows how to achieve a global energy transition. We've never done it before. So, we are in the era of experimentation. This means that we have to learn to deal with failure and success. And it means that nobody has the right answer. But we can avoid repeating mistakes because we can find out what works and what doesn't.
Energy is a very technical area and the jargon of the energy professional is quite exclusive. So, we have to change that. We have this "humanizing energy" aspect, which asks us how we tell stories in the language that people tell stories in. How do we talk about energy in the way users and producers of energy can engage with it? Not how do we tell stories about energy for experts or leaders alone.

MS: So, there are two things I take away from this interview: it's about building community as a way to move forward, and it's about conversation. And yet there seems to be a third aspect—exploration—which means we learn by changing the future. So, would you go so far as to say that it is not important to have a clear picture of where we are going, but only a rough, vague idea? We need an energy transition, but how we achieve it is uncertain. We will explore it as we move forward. Would you agree with that?

AW: I don't think *anymore* that we have a fully-fledged picture of the future and a clear plan that says it's A, then B, then C, right? I don't think that's the way that we've learned to do futures. I think we have a sense of direction and an understanding of what's good and bad. We have a judgment and aesthetic to deploy. So, we have normative futures, always.
There are good futures and there are bad futures, but we also have possible and plausible futures, right? Can we or can't we get there? What's possible and what's not? What's plausible in terms of being realizable through our action, rather than just through luck or good fortune?
So, a few years ago we wrote, "What did we learn from all these practices?" And we wrote, "The five principles of realistic hope," and that's what we work with. The first principle is about diversity, about who is in the room. Not just can we put all women, children, or whatever in the room, but how do we activate diversity? *Activating* diversity is the challenge, not just having a lot of different people at the table. But how do you engage them effectively? And the way we do that is through dialogue. Dialogue is about exchanging our understanding of where we stand in the present and where we're going in the future and how we can get there.
And the third principle is experimentation because there's no path to follow. You have to make it. You have to blaze the trail as you go along. The fourth principle is systems thinking. You know you can't change energy by just thinking about renewable power because, at the moment, we have a lot of investment in renewable power generation, but we haven't connected it to where we need supplies. You've got to think about the whole system, right? You have to be careful about your system approach as well.
We've come through an era of quantified systems thinking. We've come through an era of soft systems thinking, and now we're in an era of critical systems thinking. Because how we set the boundaries of the system depends on who we legitimize as being in or out of that system, and this takes us back to that first point of who's in the room, right?

So we've got to have critical systems thinking. And the fifth principle is futures framing. What is the purpose with which we are looking at the future? Are we looking at the future so that we beat all those other people that we don't like? We're competing with them, right? Is it competitive or is it much more collaborative? If it's collaborative, then we are going to have a different way of interacting with everybody. For me, collaboration is one of the biggest words that gets used in energy transition, "We need more collaboration." But it is also one of the most misunderstood areas because the way we're going to collaborate in the next couple of years is going to be very different from the way we think collaboration works. It's not about different people coming around the table: you work really hard and you get to a consensus and then you implement it. We don't have time for that. We're going to have different people coming together. They're going to have different visions and different ideas. We're going to have to do some bold experimentation and we're going to learn as we go, and we have to keep making progress, even if we don't like the other people at the table.
We're going to have to stop blaming them when things go wrong because the problem is not that somebody else has a different opinion from us. The problem is our shared responsibility for the fact that we aren't able to change a system that we can't see.
That's what we're talking about. How do we make faster, fairer, and more far-reaching energy transitions happen? Knowing that there are multiple pathways, starting points, and stakeholders involved. That's why I have a lot of conversations now with Adam Kahane about the way he's moving towards stretch collaboration, because we have to work with people who are different from us, who don't think or see things the same way, because we still all have to work for the common good and make change happen. I think the futures of collaboration are the most interesting futures at the moment for sharing desired futures, because that word collaboration is not a method, it's not a fight between methodologies, it's about who in practice can really make collaboration between very different interests occur and be sustained over decades, because an energy transition process isn't done quickly.

MS: Thank you for this wonderful synopsis! Did we miss an aspect?

AW: Well, just one last piece. I think, it was about 20 years ago, there was a guy called Claudio Ciborra who wrote a book called *From Control to Drift*. It made a great impression on me at that time because often when you're looking at people who do future thinking, they all know that you can't control the future, but actually they're quite controlling about the way they do their future.
Claudio—God rest his soul, he died years ago. But I've always been interested in this emphasis we place on stability and control. The modern disease is: If there isn't stability and control, then there's only chaos and anarchy. There's nothing in between. And yet complexity comes along and tells us that you have chaos *and* stability, that your order emerges from chaos. So, we know something is changing and I think there's a big word at the moment that's becoming more pronounced, and this is emergence.
And I think that the aspect of capability with which futures practitioners now have to help people is: How do we build *emergent* capability rather than the predictive and anticipatory capability that we used to talk about? So, it's emergence. The easiest way to think about this is the way that people talk about flocks of birds and the murmuration: You actually have no centralized authority guiding anything, but each of them knows how to make an adjustment.
That's my view of how energy futures thinking needs to evolve—more engaging, participatory, and democratized—rather than global, top-down prescription. Humanity is a swarm of interdependent individuals with forms of collective intelligence. This distributed intelligence is key to being agile and adaptive. It's like the murmuration of birds, patterns that suddenly emerge and change the direction of the whole. We are learning how to make

faster, fairer, and more far-reaching—net zero and beyond—energy transitions happen with a new story of emergence, distributed actions, fast and slow changes. We are raising big questions about choices in aligning diverse cooperation and collaborations. We are not trying to predict or control the future. We are supporting new forms of collaboration and cooperation that are essential in transFORMing energy for ten billion better lives and a healthy planet.

MS: It's sensing and leading from the emergence, I think, in working with the people, right?

AW: Absolutely.

MS: Thank you for this terrific interview.

FUTURECASTING WITH FICTION

CORY DOCTOROW

SCIENCE FICTION AUTHOR, ACTIVIST, JOURNALIST, AND BLOGGER
LOS ANGELES, UNITED STATES

Photo: Julia Galdo and Cody Cloud (JUCO)

SCIENCE FICTION IS A LUDDITE LITERATURE

What do science fiction and Luddites share?

A key book contribution: "Science Fiction is a Luddite Literature," kindly provided to us by Cory for this volume, could not be published here for copyright reasons. However, the QR code below will take you directly to the text on his website.

In his text, Cory raises the question of the fundamental relevance of science fiction. Known for destroying textile machines in early 19th century England, the secret society of the "Luddites" serves as Cory's example to show it is less about what technology can achieve and more about the social conditions that determine its use. The Luddites were doing de facto what science fiction authors essentially do, namely taking a (new) technology and imagining all the different ways it could be used or misused.

Michael Shamiyeh

Article published on January 3, 2022 at https://locusmag.com/2022/01/cory-doctorow-science-fiction-is-a-luddite-literature/ (Viewed March 28, 2024).

Photo: Erich Goldmann

CAROLINE BASSETT

PROFESSOR, FELLOW OF CORPUS CHRISTI COLLEGE CAMBRIDGE, AND DIRECTOR OF CAMBRIDGE DIGITAL HUMANITIES
CAMBRIDGE, UNITED KINGDOM

EXCEPT IN SCIENCE FICTION? WHY YOU CAN GET THERE FROM HERE

You'd like to see into the future. Maybe you want some reassurance that what's ahead isn't going to turn out to be a dead end, perhaps a dead earth. Maybe you want to find a way to design alternative futures that feel plausible or find reasons up ahead to be hopeful now—we need some sense of having a future to live at all—even if some of us are cheated of that future in the end, or if it disappoints or betrays us. Whatever your motive, you have a problem; you'd like to see into the future, or visit it, study it from the inside, but you can't see how to get there from here. Time travel doesn't exist after all, except maybe in science fiction. *Except in science fiction*; the implication is that fictional travel doesn't count—"don't take this seriously, it's not for real"—that kind of thing. But in this article I'm taking this kind of time travel seriously. I'm arguing that science fiction enables travel—not only to the future, sometimes into parallel worlds, or into fictional pasts, but at any rate out to places beyond our current horizons—and its usefulness for future studies will be explored here.

The aim is to consider what it is to design futures with the help of science fiction, to ask what kind of time travelling may be undertaken as the door to the future dilates.[1] This entails inquiring into the terms of the travel undertaken (how far, how near, how entangled, how expensive, or at what cost), the barriers to entry (what kind of writing, or auditing, or viewing, takes you there, what kind of engagement is demanded), or the methods of engagement (science fiction methods or texts). It also entails asking what kind of stay you might have, who might be travelling with you—and what might be brought home.

The proximate focus of this discussion is AI, which currently looms so large on the horizon that it threatens to occlude all else. So something should also be established here: why focusing in on technology itself—on AI or other technologies claiming to be exceptional in their own times—is not the best way to understand technological futures as techno-cultural futures. Let's start with that:

---

1 The phrase comes from science-fiction writer Robert Heinlein.

Technology predicting its own future?

New technologies have a way of suggesting that they can predict their *own* futures—and ours alongside theirs; we'll tag along, so to speak. It is popularly assumed that AI will develop along already largely determined pathways—increasing growth, increasing capacity, increasing "intelligence", increasing influence in a world increasingly automated—and that this will be the case, even if the pace of development might be radically uneven, characterized by sudden jumps but also by moments of deceleration. This teleological view of AI sees its endpoint as something like Artificial General Intelligence, or even The Singularity. The kinds of fears that some of those making this stuff articulate in warning letters to the media, public recantations, or calls for regulation, seem to confirm this; behold the handmaids of AI, the tech industry, continuing to develop AI while claiming its future is beyond them, to be revealed. A further twist is this; AI is, in a sense, a tool that works in and with the future, calculating probabilistically: Given this training and working with this prompt, what letter might follow this one, or what word, or what token. This is what a Large Language Model (LLM) does, after all. It bets on the tiny futures that it makes.

If AI lives in the future, if AI is the future, if AI is a reliable indicator of what the future will be, and if we can also use AI as a predictive tool to think about coming futures, which we increasingly can, then why do we need science fiction and its time shifts to help us understand, predict, or engage with AI-driven futures? The case made here is that science fiction is useful as a counterforce. It can weigh in against the technological determinism that tends to characterize thinking about new technologies and that encourages teleological views of where they will take us, in the end. It can also help us to distinguish between the potentials of a technology and how this technology is shaped by the social and economic contexts within which it is made.

Why does this matter? In my view, the circulating imaginings of AI, largely shaped by market-driven imaginings reflecting current needs, reliant on timescales depending on investment priorities and short-term performance indicators, and constrained by the need to sell a vision that is competitive, sell us short. Science fiction can help make the case that the AI future doesn't have to be given by technology or contained by the technologies that the market gives us and promises to give us in the future—or *as* the future. The latter may fuel powerful popular imaginings, address mass markets, and flow across national boundaries and claim to be global, but these technologies are often less universal than they claim. Certainly, they are dominated by Western viewpoints and temporal perspectives (for instance: What does it mean to be included or excluded "in" this or that "generation" of a technological culture?) (Arora, 2019). We can employ science fiction—with its capacity or potential to open genuinely new horizons and to think more ambitiously and, paradoxically, more realistically, about the future—as a counterweight to the realism, short-termism, and parochial dreams of the market. All of this makes science fiction a powerful tool for futurecasting. Shortly before her death, the science-fiction writer Ursula Le Guin argued for the importance of fiction in the coming hard times. She called for *"writers who can see alternatives to how we live now and can see through our fear-stricken society and its obsessive technologies to other ways of being, and even imagine some real grounds for hope. We will need writers who can remember freedom. Poets, visionaries—the realists of a larger reality."*[2] Le Guin's realists need to be consulted to help shape possible futures.

Understanding AI: Technology or storytelling?

To think about the differences between how technology predicts its future and how science fiction might do it, let's compare what CHAT might say about itself with what science fiction might say about AI, with our goal in both cases being to elicit information about AI futures. This isn't where I ask CHAT to identify its future trajectory through the production of some sort of essay of its own—it's far too unsmart to know, and it doesn't mean what it says. But it *is* worth asking if investigating CHAT's current capacities, reading its entrails perhaps, might offer pointers to where AI is going next. One problem, however, is that AI is "taciturn." Bruno Latour, the sociologist of technology, once called technology obdurate (Latour, 1991). At the risk of being anthropomorphic, it could be argued that CHAT is stubbornly silent, obscuring its own convoluted methodology: We can't see under its smooth surface. Of course, it would be possible to explore not entrails but industrial/scientific predictions about the expected rise in capacity of the LLM algorithms on which CHAT is based. We know that its younger siblings will outstrip it radically, at least if the current trajectory continues. But does a number that predicts "by how much" an AI technology grows in processing power tell us much about what we want to know—about what more power for an AI might *mean* culturally or socially? This sets aside the question of whether predictions of future growth are in any way accurate, given, for instance, that technology intervenes in its own growth curves, and in complex ways. Turning "to the thing itself" can be important as a reminder that representation is not everything—that materiality intervenes and shapes what is made techno-culturally—but it has its limits in terms of thinking about possible futures, or even making them plausible.

CHAT may well be suggestive in helping us think through some issues circulating around AI and the future; by, for instance, giving us previews of what it might mean to deal with alien agency, or to live in a

2 Ursula Le Guin, speech to the National Book Foundation, 2014 (The Guardian, 2014).

world increasingly shot through with artificial agents. However, it isn't much help in thinking through some other questions. For instance, how to make plausible, or enable the design of, various forms of future life, enabled by AI, including forms that are diverse, non-standard, not normative. This might include addressing what it means to contemplate a radical extension of automation so that cognitive labor becomes, in many spheres, a thing of the past, or considering changes in memory and asking how we may contemplate a society in which all knowledge is available just-in-time? More prosaically, how can a society, or multiple societies, operate/co-operate when the old means whereby authenticity or authority or even identity were recognized—the masthead, the passport, the photograph, the voice, even the fingerprint—have broken down in an age of deep fakes and multiple agents.

Another way to explore AI futures is by time travelling with science fiction. Oddly enough, this doesn't necessarily mean staying right on the cusp of the now. There are resources for the future in fiction that deal with AI but date from well before its recent resuscitation following its winter sleep.

We could, for instance, listen to the Minds of intelligent ships, passing each other in the impossibly long nights of the universe of Iain M. Banks's *Culture* novels, and passing the time by discussing their human cargo; co-citizens, hugely under-powered, fleshy, puny, meat machines. "Look at these humans," say the ships, "how could such glacial slowness even be called *life*?"[3] As we listen in, we might wonder whether this is how we will be discussed, with vague benevolence, slight distaste, and a kind of amused forbearance, by the future beings that we may create (or that we are creating now, whether we know it or not). Listening to the ships produces a peculiar sense of overhearing some other future form of life, not ours; one whose humor is alien—the peculiar ship names, for which the Minds are famous, suggest a cosmic sense of humor somewhere beyond us.

Beyond these existential registers, and possibly more useful in relation to futures thinking as a practical project, the *Culture* novels enable the sustained exploration of worlds characterized by abundance, where full automation is standard, bodily augmentation and fluid gender forms might be negotiated in new ways, and protagonists encounter the problems that long life might produce. Meanwhile, the *Culture* itself, the central society within the novels, pre-configures what a society beyond money—or forms of alienated exchange—might look like and how social power and division might persist, take new forms, and be challenged in new ways.

In the *Culture* novels, these possibilities are not raised in the abstract, nor as puzzles, but emerge as they are lived, and in worlds that are made real, albeit in fiction. There are no recipes here, no certainties, no injunctions (except perhaps against stupidity, which might include the stupidity of war, artificial scarcity, and unfreedom), and yet, for many, Banks's works are important for thinking the future.

3 *Look* at these humans! How could such glacial slowness even be called *life*? An age could pass, virtual empires rise and fall in the time they took to open their mouths. (Banks, 1996: 180)

I'd suggest that this is precisely because they are not blueprints, do not constitute finished plans, and cannot be taken as demands but, rather, let us *rehearse* something, or stage and play out some forms of life or some aspects of possible future cultures. These include forms of life and ways of living collectively with AI that we may wish to use to design a culture for ourselves ahead of time. The risk is that if we don't do this, we may have to live in societies deeply influenced by AI that are *without* design, or imagined by others, or only by the powerful.

Of course, it's not only the science fiction of Banks, nor the kind of tech-interested space operas that his work is sometimes associated with, that offer a resource to help us design the future, or make it plausible, through their fictional realization and ideas that are concerning (or alluring) in relation to the possibilities of AI. Consider Octavia Butler's *Lilith's Brood* trilogy (2023), which is regarded as a founding text of Afro-Futurism, although it perhaps pre-figures it. Amongst the issues rehearsed here are issues around memory and its externalization. Butler creates an earth in which literature, art, music, built architectures, and other forms of the cultural heritage of humanity (a heritage that includes the violent and uneven relations that produced it) are regarded as irrelevant by colonizers. What they see as important and valuable is the genetic heritage of a race, which is literally to be absorbed. The narrative is an invitation to explore a new/old form of colonization, or to ask how biotech might play out—if we are not careful.

Or think about contemporary apocalypse science fiction, which takes collapse as inevitable, or even boring; "let's start with the end of the world...get it over with and move on to more interesting things" says N.K. Jemisin (2016) at the opening of one of her *Broken Earth* novels, which goes on to explore how to live in ruins. Or consider how the banal science fiction of the current moment might be informing. Kazuo Ishiguro's *Klara and Sun* (2021), for instance, explores everyday worlds in which intelligent agents are recognized as having personalities but are not accorded rights, although they may be rewarded for good behavior and loyal servitude. Klara, the robot assistant at the heart of Ishiguro's novel, battered and redundant, and having damaged herself to donate her essence (or at least her brain matter) to her owner, is deemed to deserve her slow junkyard fade.

These examples point to how science fiction can offer a response to possible technological futures in ways that technology itself cannot. They also begin to suggest that this response is somewhat specific to *science* or *speculative* fiction, when compared with literature or fiction in general. So what makes science fiction good at thinking about the future with technology? Is this just because, to put it crudely, it has technology in it, or because technology is its subject matter? In my view, that's not it. To explain why, it's necessary to look harder at what defines science fiction. A warning, however: Eons have been spent arguing over this and what is written below is just one view.

There are multiple disputes about the precise definitions of science fiction versus speculative fiction, and arguments about science fiction versus fantasy continue, while new genres including the New Weird blur these lines even further. I am tempted to follow Terry Eagleton (2013) and suggest that, as with literature in general, you can't easily distinguish it from a laundry list, but you probably know it when you see it. The trouble with this is: Whose vision of what is seen should be believed? Feminist science fiction and non-Western science fiction have often been excluded on this basis. Something better is needed. Here, the work of Darko Suvin is key. Suvin (1979) argued that science fiction's capacity to pitch us into the future, its force and power as a cultural tool, perhaps rests on two characteristics that define it as science fiction. The first is epistemological gravity, by which he meant that the worlds in science fiction utilize internally coherent science. For instance, a form of faster-than-light travel (FTL) works consistently throughout the universe of the *Culture* novels—and exceptions are catered for via subliming, and the weakly god-like. Suvin argued that epistemological gravity is coupled with cognitive estrangement (and here he was leaning into Brecht). Science fiction pitches us out of our world, defamiliarizes us, and opens us to experiencing the new; or to accepting new horizons. This is why and how we seem to be able to travel to, and experience, impossible worlds, worlds made of advanced technologies, and to rehearse how they might be.

The crucial point here is that science fiction does not deal in real science, but with scientific realism, as writers and theorists including Mark Bould and the novelist China Miéville have argued (2009). In other words, science fiction uses imaginary technology and science, and deals with these realistically, rather than invoking "magic" and the irrational, to constitute its worlds. But this of course does not mean that it is "doing science" and it is not developing technology either.

Accepting this view has consequences for how science fiction might be understood to relate to technology. The division to be drawn here is between seeing science fiction as inventing the future and seeing it as a resource or methodology that enables the rehearsal of possible forms of future life. It is often assumed that science fiction is useful for futurecasting because it can *invent the technologies* of the future, leap-frogging the usual expense and bother of more standard forms of industrial/scientific development. Putting it like that, perhaps we can already see why the idea of being able to use science fiction to invent technologies, to dig nuggets out of the loam of imaginary worlds like treasure seekers in children's novels, may seem desirable, but is not viable and is vanishingly rare. Science fiction doesn't rely on inventing *real* technology or science but on a particular kind of realism. The *Culture* novels do not give us faster-than-light travel, nor do Butler's novels give us advanced genomic techniques, though they variously rely on these "technologies" to create worlds within which plots emerge and narratives unfold and which may inform us how to set out to design regulation for future genomic thinking, or think through cultural claims, or invent possible futures.

Does this mean that science fiction isn't as useful to futurecasting around technological futures as is claimed? Or that the worlds that it produces are further from science or tech than they seem?

On the contrary: To argue that science fiction does not invent technology doesn't mean that science fiction isn't interested in or specifically invested in science/technology issues, or that technologists are not influenced by science fiction. There is traffic in both directions between science and tech circles and fictional science fiction writers, producers, and world-makers. But this mutual influencing between science and literary production doesn't turn on a parallelism between "making up" technologies in fiction or in a lab and is, in any case, only one loop or strand in a much larger and more complex series of exchanges between making and writing, technology and other cultural forms (Bassett, Steinmueller, & Voss, 2013).

So how *is* science fiction a resource? Or a tool for futures thinking? If its role is not to let us jump ahead into the future and bring back treasure? Two possibilities present themselves, both of which are useful. The first is to think about science fiction as it is found in the world as a resource, a huge globally dispersed resource that offers us multiple worlds within worlds and reaches both before and after the proximate technologies that we are faced with, and which we may use as a means of thinking through and rehearsing engagements with the technological. This is what I have explored here. The second proposition, which develops out of this, is to think about how science fiction may also be used as a method; speculative design and theory fiction, for instance, lean on this. My own sense is that both of these approaches to futurecasting with science fiction may be useful. One of the powerful ways in which science fiction can and is generating a response to the kinds of futures different people want from AI is by offering an alternative to industrial visions and their foreshortened timescales. This is the greater realism of which Le Guin spoke—and which she rightly says we need. In the end, utopian thinking is more radical, and more realistic, than the enchantment offered by the constantly renewed prospect of continued growth. For whom we time travel matters.

Ends.

References

Arora, P. 2019. ***The next billion users: Digital life beyond the west.*** Cambridge, MA: Harvard University Press.

Banks, I. M. 1996. ***Excession.*** London: Orbit.

Bassett, C., Steinmueller, E., & Voss, G. 2013. ***Better made up: The mutual influence of science fiction and innovation.*** Nesta Working Paper 13/07. London: Nesta. Accessed online https://www.nesta.org.uk/report/better-made-up-the-mutual-influence-of-science-fiction-and-innovation/. Viewed February 15, 2024.

Bould, M., & Miéville, C. (eds.). 2009. ***Red planets: Marxism and science fiction.*** London: Pluto Press.

Butler, O. E. 2023. ***Lilith's brood (Imago, Dawn, Adulthood rites).*** London: Headline Ltd.

Eagleton, T. 2013. ***How to read literature***. London: Yale University Press.

Guardian, The. 2014. Ursula K Le Guin's speech at the National Book Awards: "Books aren't just commodities." ***The Guardian,*** November 20. Accessed online https://www.theguardian.com/books/2014/nov/20/ursula-k-le-guin-national-book-awards-speech. Viewed February 15, 2024.

Ishiguro, K. 2021. ***Klara and the sun.*** London: Faber and Faber.

Jemisin, N. K. 2016. ***The fifth season: The broken earth, book 1*** (Broken Earth Trilogy). London: Orbit.

Latour, B. 1991. On technical mediation. ***Common Knowledge,*** 3(2): 29-64.

Suvin, D. 1979. ***Metamorphoses of science fiction: On the poetics and history of a literary genre.*** New Haven: Yale University Press.

Photo: Erich Goldmann
IRINI PAPADIMITRIOU
CREATIVE DIRECTOR
AND CURATOR
RIYADH, SAUDI ARABIA

FUTURE PERFECT? TELLING BETTER STORIES ABOUT AI AND TECHNOLOGY

Today we are part of a world of too many futures. We are obsessed with forecasting, futurisms, and conversations about "shaping the future." Anxiety-filled, uncertain, unstable, optimistic, technological, utopian, exciting, hopeful, scary, dystopian, what is the future, and what does it mean to make or design it? And while we are obsessed with the future, whose future are we talking about, and who decides what it is?

Living in uncertain and challenging times can make it overwhelming or difficult for many of us to think about any kind of future. Even though we have been going from crisis to crisis for a while now, asking "what kind of futures we want," and having the power to influence the future could not be more pressing. But what does making the future mean at a time when the world feels so bleak, in a present that for many people is dreadful? How can we take control and create a future we want, when most of us feel disempowered or unable to imagine different worlds?

In art and culture, we have long encountered impressions, reflections, or imaginations and visions of futures, worlds, and narratives beyond what we see and know. From a perfect imaginary world in Thomas More's *Utopia*, which either hoped for a better future or satirized a chaotic present, to the apocalyptic worlds in Hieronymus Bosch's *Garden of Earthly Delights,* which presents the fate of humans taken by lust, to Mary Shelley's vision of the end of civilization in *The Last Man*, to William Heath's or Robert Seymour's satirical illustrations of a changing world gripped by technological progress in the early 19th century, artists have long been expressing their ideas and hopes, but also anxieties, about potential futures. While questioning and challenging the status quo or societal norms and obsessions, artists have also been predicting and inventing new ideas and views of tomorrow, while often reminding us how our actions in the past and present will affect coming generations, and how current injustices will continue to be replicated into the future.

Since the advent of the Industrial Revolution, we have been racing towards worlds defined more and more in technological terms. Society, through the ages, has envisioned technological futures, machines that could transform us and our world and fulfil our fantasies, and machine-like versions of humans. Since ancient times, humans have envisioned the possibility of automation and artificial intelligence as a means of not only advancing people and society, but also realizing ambitions and dreams. Very often, new technologies and, today in particular, artificial intelligence, have featured in most conversations concerning our future, promising us "fixed," liberated, and problem-free worlds, and radical new futures made of Silicon Valley dreams. Technologies like artificial intelligence can indeed offer us great potential and be used as creative tools for reaching new directions and possibilities, but a big obstacle is that these technologies are being built on the basis of profit and exploitation rather than for their potential to enable us to view, understand, and connect with our surroundings, the planet, and the universe, in different ways, and collectively. The way we understand AI today is either as a savior tool and a corporate-hyped response to society's challenges, or as something that will drive humans to extinction. From thinking of it as a force for good to imagining its dark or even unsettling side, our relationship with technology has always been a complex one. But thinking about AI in these terms is narrow minded, although this is obviously also not surprising, because our experience of it, from corporate techno utopian products to the way it is depicted in popular culture and the media, is pretty much framed along these lines.

Today, AI is everywhere and, whether we realize it or not, it affects all of us. But while AI is part of everyone's lives, not everyone is part of it or can shape its narratives.

The aforementioned prints by Heath and Seymour, made in the 1820s, were a response to and a reflection of the heated debates in British society in the early 19th century about the *March of Intellect* or the *March of Mind*, which addressed rapid industrialization and the shift of social status. This was a period of opportunities and possibility for those championing progress and new ideas but also, according to others, a period of transformation that could bring more damage. The caricatures in the *March of Intellect* present futuristic scenes depicting

Figure 1: *March of Intellect* by William Heath, 1829 *© CC BY-NC 4.0/ Wellcome Collection*

fast travel vacuum tubes, flying machines, or mechanized domestic servants. But, in reality, these transformative technologies and industrialization meant a loss of control for workers, a reshaping of economies, and new social structures. In the futures and the transformative technologies that we create today, AI is—to paraphrase Matteo Pasquinelli in *The Eye of the Master* (Verso, 2023)—the continuation of the process of dispossession of knowledge from labor; AI is the "capitalization of collective knowledge into new apparatuses, into the datasets, algorithms, and statistical models of machine learning."

And as we have become more obsessed with AI, creating a society that learns to rely on machine-based decision making and automation, we are adapting ourselves to AI processes, perceiving the world through a machine-like rather than human lens and slowly becoming a society that thinks or behaves more like a machine. But while AI can be a creative and powerful tool, AI discourses and trajectories have mainly been driven and monopolized by corporations and dominant voices, focusing on profit, quantification, and surveillance, and replicating and reinforcing societal injustices and racialized and gendered ideas, rather than enabling the revolutionary futures that we expected.

From ancient depictions of mechanical servants such as those of Philon of Byzantium, the Greek engineer of the Hellenistic Period, to terror-arousing androids in medieval literature, from Captain William Henry Richards' early 20th-century robots Eric and George, to today's robots, bots, and smart assistants, our attitude to and perception of technology and machines has not changed very much. Machines—usually anthropomorphic—are created to take the role of romanticized obedient helpers and servants, building on previous master-slave narratives while feeding our imagination with horror stories of machines that rise and eventually eliminate humans. Futuristic machines like these tell us more about our present condition than about what we might want for our futures. Indeed, the future that one can see in such technologies is a future where things stay pretty much the same as what we know so far.

What knowledge is gained from the innumerable AI-generated images saturating the world today: AI-enlightened, hyped projections, and images of the future? What is new about a future created from endlessly recycled content?

What if we could free technology from corporate narratives and have the power to reimagine it as a tool for collaboration, creativity, and resistance, rather than obstruction? We have been creating AI in the same way that we think about futures and everything else, from a human centric, narrow perspective that prioritizes growth and profit. Have we been thinking about and developing technologies and AI for the wrong reasons and, hence, limiting their potential? As James Bridle argues in *Ways of Being* (2023), "rather than being a tool to further exploit the planet and one another, artificial intelligence is an opening to other minds, a chance to fully recognize a truth that has been hidden from us for so long. Everything is intelligent, and therefore—along with many other reasons—is worthy of our care and conscious attention." What if we rethink or reframe technology itself and our approach to it, not as something fixed and to be controlled, but as hackable, adaptable, and possible to change?

What if AI was a tool for creating more equitable worlds?

What if, to paraphrase Ursula K. Le Guin (2019), we thought of technology as a carrier bag, a recipient and container of collective stories and ideas, rather than a singular, dominant story?

And what if more of us had the power and opportunities to shape technology and the future, rather than consuming the technologies and futures provided by a small group of people?

These and many more "what-if" questions have recently become starting points in our practice at FutureEverything, an organization that—working across art, technology, and action research—has been enabling collaboration, placemaking, and critical conversations. In these processes, we have been bringing people together to co-develop and co-create new ideas and alternative visions for the future in response to current events and urgent social and global issues. From contemporary society's obsession with technology, AI, and automation to climate change, environmental disruption, and injustice, at FutureEverything we have been exploring some of the most urgent questions of our age through participation, public engagement, and inclusive, playful approaches. We strongly believe that art can be an important catalyst for enabling critical conversations and engaging people in collective action.

Through public engagement and collaboration facilitated by artistic interventions, we have seen how art can influence and open up new ways of thinking and acting; but it can also enable new perspectives and responses to challenges, helping us explore alternative ideas.

While being predominantly an art organization, a lot of our work takes place in non-art domains and public spaces in both the UK and internationally, and with diverse organizations, partners, and people, from arts, academia, the tech industry, and business, as well as local government, community groups, and, of course, artists.

And contrary to what the name might suggest, FutureEverything's purpose is not to predict any futures, but to create spaces and conditions for critical thinking and creative ideas, and for imagining alternative futures and how the status quo could be different.

Although we cannot know for sure what the future world will be like, we can try to understand, influence, and shape parts of it and, rather than feeling powerless, work toward social change.

As an art worker, I often ask myself: What is the role and obligation of art institutions and curators like myself in contemporary society and what can art can do in times of crises, uncertainty, and division? Living in a technocentric world, I often wonder how cultural institutions can address and engage with challenges in an age of accelerated technological applications and quantified societies; an age of digital bureaucracies and monitoring and profiling infrastructures that not only replicate but also augment existing inequalities, racism, and unfairness. If art belongs to or should belong to all, what does this mean in terms of opportunities and limitations, power and powerlessness? Maybe art, creative exchange, and collaboration can help us to shift dominant narratives, making place for us to focus on technology's potential for social good and ethical values and reimagine a society for all.

The world through the algorithmic lens and, if AI's taking over, who's looking after me?

Two separate projects and case studies, both starting with the opening statement and the understanding that AI is omnipresent, ask whom AI serves and whether it sees and treats everyone the same, while also questioning the current landscape and exploring how this could be shaped if we bring different voices to the conversation.

You and AI: Through the Algorithmic Lens, an exhibition and public program commissioned by Onassis Stegi, took over a public park in the heart of Athens, Greece, bringing critical conversations about AI as a present-day reality into the public space (FutureEverything, 2021). The objective of the exhibition and program was to challenge perceptions about a technology that we falsely perceive as intelligent and autonomous, and to examine how AI systems are constructed and by whom, and their impact on society. But, most importantly, the exhibition asked and invited us to reimagine these technologies for the better.

Questioning the increasing implementation of these systems and their impact on human subjectivity in social, working, and democratic contexts, exhibition artworks were encountered across Pedion tou Areos Park, a space for public gathering and leisure, but also a former army training ground and, in other words, a fitting parallel to AI's origins in military applications and use as an instrument of power and exploitation. The exhibition unfolded through thematic areas, investigating AI in the context of civic space, democracy, and digital bureaucracies, AI as a lens through which we are being seen and we see the world—can we believe what we see?—questioning whether it is we who control technology or the machine that controls us, and the meaning of intelligence in AI.

In artistic installations presented in the park such as Mushon Zer-Aviv's *The Normalizing Machine*, we are invited to reflect on algorithmic prejudice and social normalcy, and question how machines come to define what is "normal." Participants are asked to select the face that looks most normal from a line-up of previously recorded participants, while the machine analyzes their decisions and adds them to its aggregated algorithmic image of normalcy. *The Normalizing Machine* points out prejudices in algorithmic systems such as facial recognition and makes a strong case for how these technologies not only lead to new levels of surveillance, but also re-establish previously abandoned pseudo-scientific systems based on racist stereotypes such as physiognomy, i.e., judging a person's character based on physical attributes and facial features. Physiognomy goes back in time, from ancient Greece to the studies of Giambattista della Porta in the 16th century and Johann Casper Lavater in the 18th century. But it became particularly popular in the assessment of mental health in the 19th century, when it was championed by criminology and forensics theorists such as Alphonse Bertillon and Cesare Lombroso.

Figure 2: *The Normalizing Machine* by Mushon Zer-Aviv © *Lucinda Grange*

Conversely, *Zizi—Queering the Dataset* by Jake Elwes, while inviting us to consider bias, responds to the lack of diversity and representation in the training datasets used in machine learning and facial recognition systems, which are dominated by normative faces and identities. The work disrupts training datasets, injecting them with drag or gender-fluid faces. What appears in front of us is the possibility of neural networks being different from what we think of as a representative identity.

In another section of the exhibition that asks whether AI could enable different understandings of the world and non-human intelligence, artists like Anna Ridler in *Circadian Bloom* explore the concept of time from the perspective of flowers. Using complex algorithms and working with a machine that can keep time at an atomic level, the artist shows a series of plants that are also able to keep time, blooming at the appropriate point of the day.

Figure 3: *Zizi—Queering the Dataset* by Jake Elwes © *Stelios Tzetzias for Onassis Stegi*

In 2023, we worked with the Science Gallery London, bringing together researchers from across King's College London, artists, technologists, patients, and young people to develop *AI: Who's Looking After Me?*, an exhibition and season of public events revolving around questions of ethics and care in a society obsessed with automation and AI applications (FutureEverything, 2023). Going a step further than typical AI art exhibitions, *AI: Who's Looking After Me?* focused on diverse perspectives and lived experiences, showing the need for a multiplicity of voices, peoples, backgrounds, and knowledge—when it comes to designing AI systems—and for moving away from the usual media narratives of hype and doom.

Collaborative projects such as *Does AI Care?*, by Sofie Layton with young adults who had experience of cancer and researchers from the Wellcome/EPSRC Centre for Medical Engineering, discussed experiences of care, cancer, and AI, while considering how technological developments may shape patients' experiences.

In *Between the Lines*, Sarah Selby, in collaboration with Beyond Detention, The Dickson Poon School of Law, King's College London, Twist Bioscience, and individuals navigating the UK immigration system, highlights bureaucratic systems and the risk of using algorithms and machine-based decision making within immigration and justice services that further marginalize individuals and reduce them to statistics. The project explores DNA storage technology as a way of embedding the stories of individuals and impacting these back into the systems that govern them. Testimonies by individuals subjected to the UK border regime are encoded into synthetic DNA, which is then mixed into writing ink and inserted into pens distributed to UK immigration control administrative workers.

Figure 4: *Between the Lines* by Sarah Selby © *Phil Wilson*

How do we put responsible, transparent, and inclusive AI into practice and who should be involved in AI regulation? Participatory events throughout the season empowered people to question how AI technologies, embedded in our lives, shape us and society. *AI: Who's Looking After Me?* called attention to the urgent need to address questions around the fairness and transparency of AI systems, while enabling conversations about AI governance and ethics and bringing together people from different backgrounds and sectors. It also made a case for the need for art and artists, as catalysts in creating spaces for different stories to be heard, and for different ideas to be shared and realized. Art can indeed help us dare and imagine possibilities; it can help us see ways to envision change and rediscover positive futures.

References

Bridle, J. 2023. ***Ways of being. Animals, plants, machines: The search for a planetary intelligence.*** Dublin: Penguin Books.

FutureEverything. 2021. ***You and AI: Through the algorithmic lens.*** Available online https://futureeverything.org/portfolio/entry/you-and-ai-through-the-algorithmic-lens/. Viewed February 6, 2024.

FutureEverything. 2023. ***AI: Who's looking after me?*** Available online https://futureeverything.org/portfolio/entry/ai-who-is-looking-after-me-exhibition/. Viewed February 6, 2024.

Le Guin, U. K. 2019. ***The carrier bag theory of fiction.*** Ignota Books.

SOPHIA BRUECKNER

FUTURIST ARTIST, DESIGNER, AND ENGINEER
DETROIT, UNITED STATES

Photo: Erich Goldmann

TEACHING CRITICAL OPTIMISM: SEVEN LESSONS FROM A DECADE OF SCI-FI PROTOTYPING

As an artist (formerly a software engineer), my path to futures research differs from most of the futurists that I have met. I grew up surrounded by my dad's extensive science fiction book collection, which I ravenously consumed, even though it was certainly not age appropriate. To this day, sci-fi dystopias haunt my dreams. For the last 12 years, I have taught Sci-Fi Prototyping, a course combining science fiction, extrapolative thinking, building prototypes, and technology ethics at MIT, Harvard, the Rhode Island School of Design, Brown, and the University of Michigan. After teaching hundreds of students from all disciplines, I have learned that most people struggle to imagine futures that are neither naively optimistic nor extremely pessimistic, and that it is the inability to imagine a full range of possibilities that prevents people from building desired futures.

Before I became a professor, I worked as a software engineer for five years. I left to pursue art and design when I realized that I was not building the future that I wanted. I went to the Rhode Island School of Design's Digital+Media MFA program, where the future of technology was much discussed. In the same way that Apple said, "There's an app for that," I could say, "There's a sci-fi story about that," in response to any of my classmates' ideas. This happened so much that people urged me to teach a class on it. In 2011 at RISD, I taught my science fiction class for the first time to a group of undergraduate and graduate artists and designers, where we read and watched a whole lot of sci-fi as a means of inspiring art and design projects. Since then, I have taught it nearly every year to artists, designers, architects, engineers, and scientists. Every year, I rewrite the syllabus to reflect what's going on in the world and tune it to my students' interests. My Sci-Fi Prototyping class and my students' work have been featured by *The Atlantic, Wired, Scientific American, Smithsonian Magazine,* NPR, and others.

After many iterations of this course and having seen numerous student projects go beyond simplistic utopian or dystopian visions, I have collected seven insights on how to teach people to constructively imagine a range of possible futures and communicate these to others.

1. Science fiction teaches extrapolative thinking.

Most people think science fiction is about the future whereas it is really about people's hopes and fears in the present. Science fiction authors extrapolate current trends into the future and imagine what will happen when these scale up. They speculate on the consequences of these trends, both good and bad, if they continue unchecked. Ursula K. Le Guin said that "Science fiction is not prescriptive; it is descriptive." During the Cold War, many sci-fi stories focused on the apocalypse and space travel. Following the discovery of CRISPR, many sci-fi stories were written about biology and genetic engineering. Recently, many more stories are being written about artificial intelligence. Frederik Pohl said, "A good science fiction story should be able to predict not the automobile but the traffic jam." Often dystopian, sci-fi stories speculate on the future of technologies while also exploring where they go wrong.

2. People don't learn about the scale of consequences the way they learn about efficiency and cost.

As a young software engineer for Google, I experienced for the first time the unintended consequences of my own design decisions at an enormous scale. Fresh out of undergraduate school, I designed and built some of the most popular apps in the world, most of which had many millions of users. Google was much smaller at that time, and our team had no dedicated customer support staff. I received all of my users' emails directly. When I developed a new feature that helped my users, I was flooded with effusive, grateful emails. When I was required to make changes that my users did not like, I was overwhelmed by angry messages from frustrated people who had structured their entire days around our product. As a computer scientist, I learned about scale but only related to speed or cost. I had not learned anything about the scale of how my design choices could impact people's lives.

Science fiction stories can teach designers and makers of all kinds how to think about the scale of the consequences of even a small design choice. I use science fiction and extrapolative thinking to teach young designers and engineers to think about how the consequences of one seemingly tiny design choice might scale with frequency of use, number of users, and time used, etc. The *Black Mirror* episode "Nosedive" is a perfect example of taking one simple technology, the star rating, and speculating on the negative consequences of scaling up the number of users, the frequency of use, and the time used. In this episode, people's every interaction is star rated by others as a means of determining their social standing and even where they are allowed to live. Any time a student has an idea for a future technology, I ask them to extrapolate in the same way, and I want them to take this way of thinking into their future workplaces. Another hard lesson from my time as a software engineer was that whenever something has already been launched into the world, it becomes extremely hard to reverse. If more people could learn the extrapolative way of thinking that sci-fi authors excel at, we could possibly prevent or at least mitigate many of the unintended negative consequences of the things we build.

3. Science fiction is like an ethics class for designers and engineers.

People who earnestly want to make cool and helpful things often do not want to think about unintended negative consequences. Though their work might heavily impact the most intimate aspects of people's lives on a daily basis, designers, engineers, and entrepreneurs are not usually required to take an ethics class like doctors and psychologists. However, these people will often be very excited by the idea of making projects inspired by science fiction. Once exposed to lots of science fiction, it is difficult to avoid talking about the dystopian futures that these stories so often portray. With practice, generating new ideas comes with automatic consideration of negative consequences, and sensitivity to consequences does not prevent one from being able to generate new ideas with optimism.

Figure 1: Sci-Fi Prototyping student Bechara Maalouf speculated on the future of birthdays once the Earth runs out of helium, a finite resource. Critiquing humankind's tendency to try to solve problems with unnecessary new technologies, he created birthday balloons that are held aloft by drones. © *Bechara Maalouf*

4. Science fiction stories bridge disciplines.

People from STEM fields and humanities fields struggle to understand each other. Even people in different sub areas within these two groups struggle to understand each other. Each discipline comes with its own unique vocabulary and set of priorities. Science fiction stories give us common references and a common vocabulary that allow people from extremely different disciplines to communicate and work with each other. This is useful both when one has students from different disciplines in one classroom and when one has people from different disciplines working together on a team.

5. Science fiction illustrates the importance of diversity.

Every year, I ask my students to read *Fast Times at Fairmont High* by Vernor Vinge and *Immersion* by Aliette de Bodard, two sci-fi stories that speculate on the future of augmented reality. Vinge's vision centers on a dystopian sort of efficiency and suggests that AR might allow for greater individual freedom of expression. De Bodard's vision speculates on a future in which AR perpetuates colonialism, racism, and conformity. Why are their visions for the future of this technology so drastically different? I ask my students to research each author's life. Vernor Vinge is a white American man and formerly a mathematics and computer science professor. Aliette de Bodard is a female computer engineer of French and Vietnamese descent (Vietnam was formerly colonized by France). Both of these authors' personal backgrounds are clearly reflected in their visions for the future of AR technology. Both of these authors' visions are informative and valuable when considering how to design AR technologies. Given that people's ability to envision the future is so influenced by their own life experiences, reading science fiction stories by diverse authors, side-by-side, clearly illustrates the need to include diverse people when imagining unintended negative consequences. This means diversity of race, gender, class, nationality, age, ability, education, etc. and even types of diversity of which we are not yet aware.

6. Experiential/tangible prototypes are necessary.

In the fields of art and design, speculative prototypes are often not experiential. They are meant to convey an idea, look real, and provoke discussion. However, people aren't always very good at predicting how they will feel if something exists, no matter how polished a presentation, video, or non-interactive model might be.

Early on in my teaching career, I had a group of students who had the idea of connecting an EEG headset with a handheld model of a brain. Their goal was to make lights flash in the handheld brain model driven by the EEG headset. I was not very excited by their presentations of the idea as I had seen many projects like this before. However, actually interacting with their prototype was surprising and unforgettable. When you wore the headset and held the brain yourself, you experienced a sense of affection and nurturing towards your own mind, a gentleness that was similar to holding a baby. When someone else was wearing the headset while a different person held the brain, it felt uncomfortably intimate. There was no way to read someone's thoughts by looking at the flashing lights, and later the students revealed that the wireless communication did not work and that the flashing of the lights was random! Even though the prototype was not fully functioning, it was experiential enough to bring unexpected and intense emotions to the surface. I use this example to illustrate why I require my students to make their ideas as experiential as possible, even if this means just acting something out.

Figure 2: Sci-Fi Prototyping students imagined an artifact shaped like a brain that, when held, flashed lights in response to EEG readings. Though the prototype only flashed lights randomly, people sensed surprisingly strong feelings of intimacy and discomfort, as if they were invading someone's privacy. © *Sophia Brueckner*

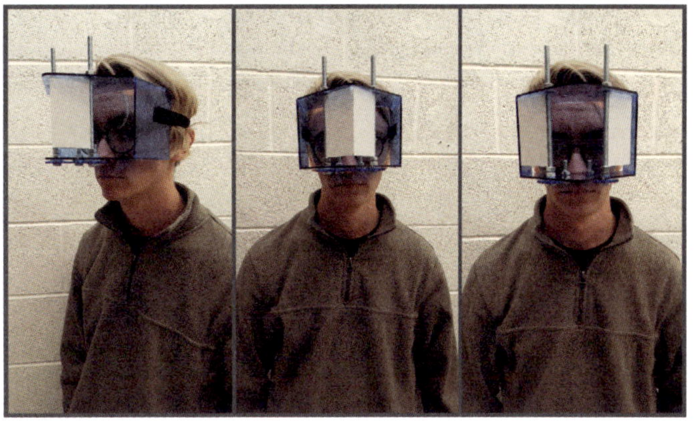

Figure 3: Sci-Fi Prototyping student Sam Bertin speculated on how augmented and virtual reality technologies might be used to mediate conversations. He created a wearable that can block out the face of either a speaker or any distracting surroundings, depending on who is speaking and what is being communicated. An experiential prototype that explores the implications of the future of VR/AR does not necessarily need to be implemented using those technologies. © *Sam Bertin*

7. We need medium to light gray thinking instead of black-and-white thinking.

The ability of people to envision the future tends to fall between two unhealthy and unconstructive extremes. On the one side, there are those who are blindly optimistic about technology. This attitude is sometimes termed "technosolutionism," the naïve idea that every problem can be solved with technology. At the other extreme, some are so critical of technology that they adopt an unrealistic Luddite attitude and avoid technology altogether; or they assume that a dystopian future is inevitable and, as a result, become passive. Neither of these extreme attitudes avoids what I see as the preventable negative consequences of many of today's technologies.

Instead of either clinging to or oscillating between these extremes, I believe that we need to cultivate what I call a *critically optimistic* approach. Critical optimism navigates between these two extremes, encouraging an earnest hopefulness that also incorporates a healthy dose of criticality. What futures are possible, which are probable, and, most importantly, which might be *preferred*? What steps might we take to move towards a preferred future?

I often say that instead of black-and-white thinking, we need more medium to light gray thinking. I ask people to honestly reflect upon their position on the spectrum of pessimism to optimism and to consider where they really want to be.

Ultimately, my teaching is focused on eliminating passivity in my students, whether as a maker of default design choices or as a passive consumer of technologies and ideas. I want my students to graduate with a critically optimistic attitude: to be hopeful and to be sensitive to possible consequences so that they can deliberately shape the future instead of just letting it happen to them and to all the others who might be affected by their design choices.

Figure 4a, 4b and 4c:
Illustration by © Shannon Yeung

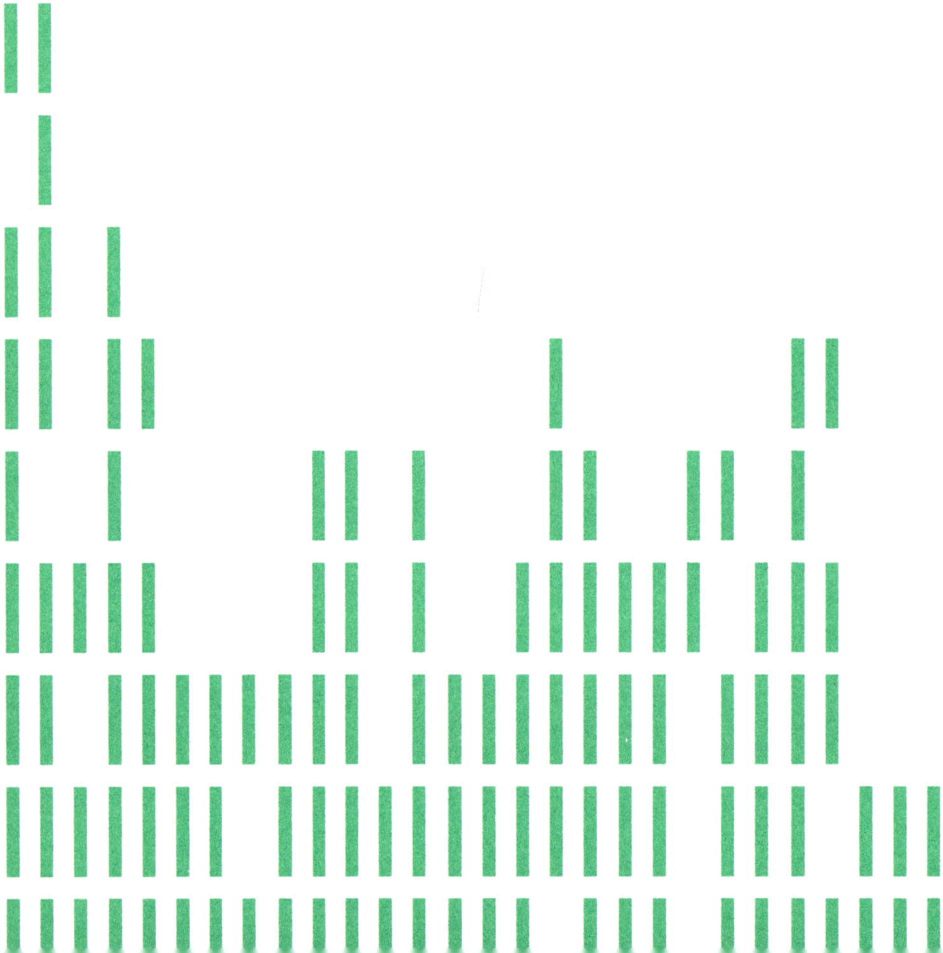

Run your own tiny sci-fi workshop

Inspired by the two-page short story, *Answers to a Questionnaire* by sci-fi author J. G. Ballard (1991), I created this exercise to introduce students to a sci-fi, extrapolative way of thinking. It works, even if you do not consider yourself to be a writer, and it often results in great project ideas. I recommend working in groups of three to five people.

1. Pick a current technological/societal trend.
2. Thinking about this trend, ask a "what-if" question. What if this trend continues X years into the future? What if there were X times as many users? What if people use this X more times per day? Extrapolate on the trend.
3. Take 15 minutes to write out answers. Delete the question, and the answers are your tiny sci-fi stories.
4. Share the answers with your group and discuss.
5. Do three rounds of this. For the first round, do one-sentence answers, then three-sentence answers, and finally one-paragraph answers.

As well as the answers often providing excellent ideas for projects, you should also pay attention to whether you lean towards being dystopian or utopian when thinking about the future of technology. Discuss this with your group, and share your favorite stories on social media using #tinyscifi.

References

Ballard, J. G. 1991. Answers to a Questionnaire. ***New York Times,*** March 24: 17. Accessible online https://www.nytimes.com/1991/03/24/opinion/answers-to-a-questionnaire.html. Viewed February 5, 2024.

Photo: Erich Goldmann

STATEMENT

STEFAN WALLY

PARTICIPATORY FUTURISM,
CEO OF THE ROBERT JUNGK LIBRARY
FOR FUTURE STUDIES
SALZBURG, AUSTRIA

STEFAN WALLY AND CARMEN BAYER

"It is worth preparing for the future mentally without committing oneself too early and too bindingly,"[1] wrote the futurologist Robert Jungk in his 1990 editorial in *ProZukunft*, referring to the major changes in Eastern Europe (Jungk, 1990: 2). He criticized how we all too often merely react instead of thinking and planning ahead. Even today, we are confronted with multiple trouble spots and challenges, the overcoming of which requires communities to be able to imagine alternative futures in order to not only adapt but also actively work on possible new futures with all those affected. Together with Norbert Müllert, Robert Jungk developed the instrument of the future workshop (*Zukunftswerkstatt*). The aim is to enable democratic imagining and the shaping of the future.

Both futurecasting and the future workshop deal with images of the future and emphasize how important it is to experiment with ideal states and utopias. In contrast to futurecasting, however, the utopia only represents the middle section of the future workshop, framed by the introductory criticism phase, in which problems within existing structures are collected, and the final realization phase. Concrete project ideas should emerge from the utopias. The aim of this model is to free oneself through imagination from current, critically scrutinized constraints, thus mobilizing the imagination to create new realities. The interplay between intuitive-emotional and rational-analytical thinking plays an important role in this process. The interaction between these two types of thinking has proven to be fruitful, time and again.

In addition to the methodological guidance for creative thinking, Robert Jungk's future workshop also requires the involvement of all those who are affected by the topic of the workshop in order to ensure that every perspective and all experiences have their place. This aspect illustrates Jungk's aim of using future workshops to "make up for the mass prevention of imagination"[2] (Jungk & Müllert, 1989: 27). Future workshops should enable the wishes and ideas of the many to flow into planning processes at an early stage. The scale of the projects created in the workshops can range from the small-scale restructuring of a team to large-scale projects.

---

1 "Es lohnt sich, die Zukunft geistig vorzubereiten, ohne sich deswegen zu früh und zu bindend festzulegen."

2 "massenhafte Phantasieverhinderung wieder gut zu machen"

The combination of methods can create new qualities if carried out conscientiously: Futurecasting can be embedded in the utopia part of a future workshop in order to, for example, make it easier to approach alternative strategies by using storytelling during the utopia phase. Alternatively, a future workshop can also continue to work with the results of the futurecasting. In this case, it is a good idea to swap the criticism phase for an inventory in order to check which conditions already exist for the visions developed. The utopia part could be used to change perspectives and develop the idea further. Finally, ideas are examined and project plans developed in the course of implementation. Such or comparable work with both methods is in the spirit of Robert Jungk. He was keen to use the future workshop to create a lively method that adapts to people's needs.

References

Jungk, R. 1990. Editorial: Die Unvorbereiteten. ***ProZukunft***, 4(1): 2. Accessed online https://www.prozukunft.org/fileadmin/user_upload/magazine/1990_1.pdf. Viewed January 29, 2024.

Jungk, R., & Müllert, N. R. 1989. ***Zukunftswerkstätten – Mit Phantasie gegen Routine und Resignation.*** Munich: Wilhelm Heyne Verlag.

Photo: *Sarah Beier*

CARMEN BAYER

SOCIOLOGIST AT THE ROBERT JUNGK
LIBRARY FOR FUTURE STUDIES
SALZBURG, AUSTRIA

DAVID A. KIRBY
PROFESSOR OF SCIENCE,
TECHNOLOGY, & SOCIETY
CAL POLY UNIVERSITY
SAN LUIS OBISPO, UNITED STATES

USING DIEGETIC PROTOTYPES TO CREATE A FUTURE WORTH LIVING IN

Work in the history of technology has shown that technological development is never pre-determined or inevitable. There are many obstacles that can impede or alter the development of a potential technology, including a lack of funding, public apathy over the need for the technology, public concerns about potential risk from a technology, or just a fundamental belief that the technology will not work. One of the best ways to jumpstart technical development is to produce a physical, working prototype. Working prototypes, however, are time-consuming, expensive, and may not even work. Prototypes always require initial funds. But to obtain these funds scientists and engineers need to show funders that the technology works. But that requires a prototype, which requires initial funds, which requires a prototype, which leads to a vicious circle that hinders technological development. Even with a working prototype, there is still the hurdle of trying to convince the public that they need or want the technology. To overcome these issues, scientists and engineers have begun using fictional narratives as an alternative to producing real-world prototypes.

In my research, I found that scientists and engineers who work as science consultants for major motion pictures have an unprecedented opportunity to create realistic depictions of nascent technologies within a fictional world—what film scholars refer to as the diegesis—with the intention of reducing anxiety and stimulating desire in audiences to see these potential technologies become realities. Fictional depictions of future technologies that entice public support for technological development are what I refer to as “diegetic prototypes” (Kirby, 2010). Diegetic prototypes foster public support for potential or emerging technologies by establishing the need for, harmlessness and viability of these technologies. Science consultants craft diegetic prototypes and enhance their realism by influencing dialogue, plot rationalizations, character interactions, and narrative structure. Popular cinema provides scientists, engineers, and designers the opportunity to promote their visions of technological futures in the hope that these visions become self-fulfilling prophecies. Diegetic prototypes are in essence what I term “pre-product placements.” Just as with a real product placement, the goal of a pre-product placement is to instill a desire in the audience for these products, but the only way for audiences to get these pre-products is to support their development.

Diegetic prototypes, in fact, have a major advantage, even over true prototypes: In the diegesis—in the fictional space—these technologies exist as "real" objects that function properly and which people actually use and interact with in ways that suggest possibilities for these technologies. Diegetic prototypes are most effective when they already exist as a commonplace technology within the fictional world. In those cases, the extraordinary becomes ordinary and, therefore, seems possible. But diegetic prototypes are not just about stimulating desire for undeveloped technologies. These cinematic depictions of future technologies also demonstrate to mass public audiences the possible use and consequences of these technologies. Their placement within a narrative and a fully developed world establishes for audiences how these technologies can be used to develop more equitable, sustainable, and livable societies.

Diegetic prototypes have proven to be an effective tool for generating public support for a wide range of technologies including computer interfaces (Ernst, 2019; Kirby, 2010; McDowell, 2019), health care technologies (Cardoso, 2020), mechanized armor (Spennemann & Orthia, 2022), and the artificial heart (Kirby, 2010). In this paper, I will utilize Disney's animated film *Big Hero 6* (Williams & Hall, 2014) to show how a fictional narrative within a visual medium can incite technological development by highlighting the possibilities of a future technology. The collaborations between the filmmakers and their roboticist consultants demonstrate the goals of a diegetic prototype and how the consultants helped shape the depiction of technologies in the film to meet these goals. I also discuss the construction of diegetic prototypes in two space-based films, *Interstellar* (Nolan, 2014) and *The Martian* (Scott, 2015), which were made after the retirement of the Space Shuttle program in 2011. The case for developing technologies for space travel is difficult to convey to the public since space travel involves hard-to-define benefits alongside easily understood challenges and risks. This discussion will illustrate how scientists and engineers helped filmmakers construct narratives in major motion pictures that were aimed directly at convincing the public that supporting space travel was a moral and spiritual necessity.

Huggable robots vs. metal monsters: *Baymax* as a diegetic prototype in *Big Hero 6*

Big Hero 6 usefully illustrates the goals and components of a successful diegetic prototype. In fact, the breakout character of the film, the soft medical robot Baymax, *is* a diegetic prototype. During pre-production the filmmakers were searching for a new type of robot for their film, one that had not been seen on screen before (Palmeri, 2014). One of the film's directors, Don Hall, took a research trip to Carnegie Mellon University's Robotics Institute, where he met with roboticist Chris Atkeson and his research team (Aitoro, 2015; Blair, 2014). Atkeson's group was developing a novel type of robot that utilized vinyl to create soft medical robots (see Figure 1). The idea of a gentle, soft medical robot as a character appealed to Hall because it was so different from previous movie robots, who were almost always made of metal and were frequently scary. Once he decided to go with a soft medical robot for Baymax he asked Atkeson and his group to serve as consultants for *Big Hero 6*.

Figure 1: An inflatable vinyl robotic arm that helped inspire Baymax's design at Carnegie Mellon University's Robotics Institute.

(Accessed online https://commons.wikimedia.org/wiki/File:Inflatable_Robotic_Arm.jpg. Viewed April 24, 2024.)

For his part, Atkeson was thrilled to participate in the film's production. He needed to convince the public and potential funders to support the development of soft medical robots. From his perspective, the film could play an important role in overcoming the obstacles impeding the development of soft medical robots by publicly demonstrating the possibilities of his group's embryonic technology. Essentially, he and his team were helping the filmmakers create a diegetic prototype that could stimulate a desire in the audience to see soft medical robots become a reality. To overcome ethical, safety, and technical apprehensions about these robots, Atkeson had to establish the following in this diegetic prototype: 1) the medical *necessity* of the technology, 2) the *harmlessness* of a technology involved in health care, and 3) the *viability* of soft robots. Atkeson and his team clearly believed that this film was an important public relations opportunity. So, they helped *Big Hero 6*'s filmmakers construct a character, Baymax, and a narrative that overtly addressed these three concerns.

An important scene in the film, and the key scene for Atkeson's diegetic prototype, is the introduction of Baymax. In this scene, the protagonist Hiro is visiting the research lab of his older brother Tadashi, who is a student at the San Fransokyo Institute of Technology. Tadashi is showing Hiro the soft medical robot, Baymax, whom he created to serve as a personal healthcare companion. To demonstrate Baymax's capabilities, Tadashi slightly injures Hiro by pulling a piece of tape off his forearm. Baymax successfully diagnoses the injury ("a slight dermal abrasion") and provides an appropriate treatment (an antibacterial spray with Bacitracin) (see Figure 2). Hiro tries to trick Baymax by claiming that he is allergic to Bacitracin. Baymax does not fall for this, however. The robot tells Hiro that he is not allergic to Bacitracin, but that he is allergic to peanuts. Hiro then praises Baymax's coding, his skeleton, and his method of movement. The exchange ends with Tadashi telling Hiro that Baymax is "going to help a lot of people." The scene not only created a memorable and beloved Disney character, but also served as a dream pitch for every roboticist working on soft medical robots.

Figure 2: In this screengrab, Baymax provides an accurate diagnosis of Hiro's medical condition.

This scene illustrates that the roboticists were excited to work on the film because it distinctly achieves a diegetic prototype's three goals of establishing a technology's viability, necessity, and harmlessness. One concern about soft robots, including soft medical robots, is that they are not feasible, given how different their mechanics would be from traditional rigid robots (Iida & Laschi, 2011). Rigid robots move using conventional motor-driven actuators that involve gears and pistons, but that mechanism is not suitable for the movement of soft robots. Soft robots require actuators that would be smaller, softer, and deformable and, yet, they would also still need to be able to generate the same amount of movement and force as a rigid robot. In *Big Hero 6*, Hiro's analysis of Baymax's structure and machinery specifically counters these critiques about the viability of soft robots. Hiro raves about Baymax's "killer actuators" and is told that they allow the robot to lift over 1,000 pounds. Hiro also calls attention to Baymax's ultralight skeleton framework, which Tadashi tells us is made of carbon fiber that is "even lighter" than titanium. By the scene's end it is clear to Hiro, and to the audience, that soft robots are mechanically viable.

For *Big Hero 6* to be a successful diegetic prototype it also had to convince audiences that developing soft medical robots is a necessity. Many roboticists believe that medical robots could solve what is known as the "care crisis" (Riek, 2017). Expanding elderly populations in many countries are increasing the need for healthcare services just as the number of caregivers is diminishing (Chew, 2017). But there is significant public resistance to the use of medical robots (Maibaum, Bischof, Hergesell, & Lipp, 2021; Sparrow, 2016; Stahl & Coeckelbergh, 2016). Both patients and health workers are concerned about the potential for robots to de-humanize patient care. There is a perception that medical robots will be like the scary metal robots seen in most science fiction movies and that they will provide cold, impersonalized care. In fact, Atkeson argues that an obvious design for a medical robot is that of a "giant spider," whose multiple appendages would allow it to undertake tasks simultaneously and would make it more stable (Anonymous, 2014). According to Atkeson it is not unreasonable for people to fear a future in which they are cared for by a "big honking metal monster." For him, this leads to the logical question: "When you're old, do you want to be taken care of by a giant spider?"

Atkeson and other proponents believe that the public would be willing to accept medical robots if they were soft robots because these would have a less intimidating appearance and their interactions with frail patients would be gentler. As Atkeson says, "old people today probably wouldn't go for the giant spider [robot], but they would go for Baymax." Baymax's introduction scene in *Big Hero 6* was designed to highlight the need for soft medical robots in healthcare by emphasizing Baymax's unthreatening and patient-friendly nature (see Figure 3). When Hiro comments on Baymax's vinyl exterior, Tadashi tells him that he was "going for a non-threatening, huggable" design. Hiro reinforces this perception by saying that Baymax looks like a "walking marshmallow." He then goes on to poke and prod Baymax, demonstrating his softness and pliability. The scene also highlights Baymax's gentle demeanor with his sensitive, reassuring voice and his promise to keep working until told that his patient is "satisfied with your care." Tadashi's final line in the scene conveys a clear message to the audience about the desirability of developing this technology: "He's going to help a lot of people."

Figure 3: The soft medical robot Baymax is depicted as unthreatening and patient-friendly in this screengrab, in which he provides his patient with a lollipop.
© *Chris Williams & Don Hall, 2014*

Much of the public's resistance to medical robots comes from a fear of turning over one's healthcare to a robot that is not beholden to the Hippocratic Oath's directive to "do no harm." One key concern about medical robots and medical AI is that they will be prone to misdiagnosis (Aronson, 2022; Wu, Xu, Bai, Chen, Gao, & Jiang, 2023). That concern is partially addressed in the Baymax introduction scene, with Tadashi telling Hiro that the robot has been "programmed with over 10,000 medical procedures." But for this diegetic prototype to be successful it would not be enough to just have Baymax provide a correct diagnosis for Hiro's condition. Most people understand that medical robots will be able to provide accurate diagnoses most of the time. The concern for patients is that a medical robot's AI could become confused and prone to misdiagnosis if a patient, whether intentionally or unintentionally, provided the machine with incorrect information. This is why the scene included Hiro attempting to trick Baymax into a misdiagnosis about his supposed allergy to Bacitracin (see Figure 4). Despite receiving faulty information Baymax still came up with the correct conclusion about Hiro's health status. Atkeson hoped that this scene left the audience with the belief that it would be safe to leave their health in the hands of a robot.

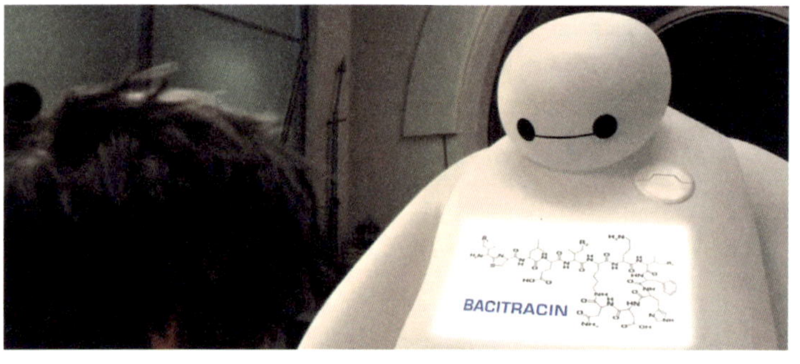

Figure 4: Hiro unsuccessfully tries to convince Baymax that he is allergic to Bacitracin in this screengrab. *© Chris Williams & Don Hall, 2014*

Atkeson and his team were betting on the fact that his diegetic prototype would create a desire amongst the public for soft medical personal care robots in the real world. Within the film world, a soft medical robot worked properly, was safe, and would save lives. Why would audiences not want to see Baymax become real? Atkeson took advantage of the audience's new desire for a real soft medical robot by providing them with an easy way to support development of the technology. He set up a website devoted to public fundraising built around the idea of making Baymax, or "at least a useful healthcare companion robot" real (Atkeson, 2014) (see Figure 5). Atkeson's goal of creating a soft medical robot also benefitted from the dozens of media articles discussing his consulting work on the film. Each of these articles reiterated the points made by the diegetic prototype that there was a need for these robots, that they were technically feasible, and that they were trustworthy. But it was still the diegetic prototype that best conveyed these themes to audiences.

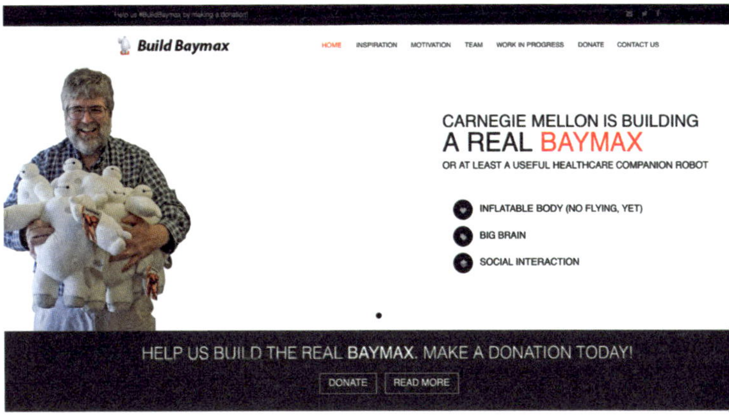

Figure 5: Website created by roboticist Chris Atkeson to raise funds for the development of a real-world soft medical robot. *© Chris Atkeson, 2014*

Through its plot, narrative, dialogue, and visuals, *Big Hero 6* made something unfamiliar and potentially frightening seem safe, desirable, and attainable.

Diegetic prototypes and the promotion of space travel in *Interstellar* and *The Martian*

The number of resources required to overcome the physical and technological obstacles to human space travel have made it challenging for space advocates to convey the necessity of space travel to the public. Space travel as a technological development has no obvious social benefits, an extremely high price tag, severe technological limitations, and high risk factors. The public needs to believe that it is worth investing time and resources in transcending the limits that keep us Earthbound, whether physical, economic, psychological, social, cultural, or spiritual. Diegetic prototypes embedded within mainstream movies made with the assistance of scientists and engineers have proven to be a very successful way of convincing the public that developing the technological capacity for space travel is a worthwhile endeavor. The success of this promotional strategy explains why scientists and engineers have worked as advisors on movie productions over the last one hundred years. But a diegetic prototype that previously worked to spur technological development may not work subsequently as political, social, and economic contexts change. This is why scientists' and engineers' advice to filmmakers about space travel has shifted as humanity's hopes for and anxieties about technology have changed over time.

Prior to the Moon landing in 1969, cinematic stories about space travel contained themes about American technological and, thus, ideological supremacy; stories about the military threat that the Soviet Union would pose if it reached the Moon before America; and stories that tied space travel to the American frontier. After the Moon landing, proponents of space travel in the 1970s through the 1990s had to change their storytelling tactics and instead promoted messages touting space travel as the way to solve social or environmental problems on Earth through colonies on Mars or space stations. After the retirement of the Space Shuttle in 2011, none of the previous justifications for space travel would convince the public to continue supporting its development. For the American public, the Space Shuttle had become a cultural icon because it represented the next stage in the evolution of space travel after the Apollo era (Billings, 2013). But the end of the Space Shuttle program marked the end of one manned spaceflight venture without a certain, foreseeable replacement vehicle for the first time in NASA's history. The problem for space travel enthusiasts is that it seemed to the public as if America had given up on space travel. The retirement of the Space Shuttle required scientists and engineers to consult on films to help tell new stories whose messages focused on the need for humanity to keep reaching for the stars.

The Space Shuttle program's retirement had a major influence on *Interstellar* (Nolan, 2014). The film's opening shot unsubtly sums up the story's overall message with the title "Interstellar" superimposed over a shot of a toy Space Shuttle sitting on a bookcase covered in dust (see Figure 6). The film is set in a near future where climate change has decimated the world's environment and resources, especially food, have become scarce. Most people in this society not only consider space travel to be a low priority, *but also believe that the misplaced funding of space travel has contributed to Earth's problems.* They wonder why we bothered funding something as frivolous as space travel when there were so many Earthly problems facing humanity, including poverty and environmental degradation. *Interstellar*'s narrative refutes this idea by depicting space exploration as humanity's only salvation. Public opinion in this fictional world prevents the government from openly funding NASA, so the organization has been driven into hiding underground, where it functions as a secret band of rebels trying to save the Earth. The audience learns that the world's atmosphere has become too saturated with nitrogen and that humanity's only hope involves NASA developing interstellar travel.

Figure 6: The opening shot of *Interstellar* is a pretty unsubtle message of a toy Space Shuttle covered in dust in this screengrab. © *Christopher Nolan, 2014*

Given NASA's heroic role in the film it is not surprising that the organization was keen to work with the filmmakers (Zakarin, 2014). But the organization only undertook some minor consulting work for the film by providing permissions, and astronauts for the actors to consult with (Pearlman, 2014). What separates *Interstellar* from most space travel films made in the 2010s is that its primary science consultant was not associated with NASA. The film's director Christopher Nolan hired physicist Kip Thorne as his primary scientific consultant and Thorne's role was so significant that he is credited as an executive producer. In fact, Thorne came up with the initial story idea for *Interstellar* because he believed that a major Hollywood film would help convince the public to endorse his notion of using wormholes for interstellar travel (Clery, 2014; Smaglik, 2014). The whole film is essentially a feature length argument for the development of wormhole technologies, with all the appropriate elements of a diegetic prototype. There is an overwhelming need for the technology (to escape an ecologically damaged earth), the technology is basically harmless (the astronauts survive the process), and wormhole travel is shown to be viable (the technology takes them across the universe). The film essentially provides audiences with the ultimate reason for wanting to see this fictional technology turned into a real technology: The protagonist saves the future using wormhole travel and, without it, humanity would have become extinct.

Many people considered the Space Shuttle's grounding as symbolic of a larger anti-science movement developing in the US (Billings, 2013). The creators of *The Martian* (Scott, 2015) wanted to fight against this trend by producing a story they considered a "love letter to science" (Lussier, 2015). The film's screenwriter Drew Goddard considered the story to be a "religious movie" in which the "religion is science." Unsurprisingly, NASA was eager to collaborate on the film and they became involved from the beginning of its production

(Bradley, 2015). At the time of the film's production NASA had just experienced the biggest decrease in its budget since 1971 (Handberg, 2014). The organization was struggling to convince the US government to provide the funding needed to make space exploration a priority again. A major part of NASA's strategy for convincing the government to increase their funding was to provide support for Hollywood movies that treated astronauts and space travel in a reverential manner. The film's narrative shows heroic NASA astronauts using science to solve problems even in the direst situations—such as being stranded alone on Mars. That single message ensured that NASA was interested in participating in the film's production and promotion. What guaranteed NASA's full involvement was the fact that the story featured the kind of scientific mission that the organization wants people to think it should be undertaking.

The film's primary science consultant, NASA's Director of Planetary Science Jim Green, was excited to work on the film because he believed that it would inspire the public to support a human mission to Mars and, ultimately, the terraforming of the planet (Stuart, 2015). Green helped filmmakers' design narrative elements that made terraforming look feasible and straightforward. One key plot element, for example, involves stranded astronaut Mark Watney using a few potatoes meant for a special Thanksgiving meal to grow an entire crop of the vegetable (see Figure 7). Watney essentially functions as a one-person terraforming operation who demonstrates to the audience how food could be cultivated and grown on Mars. For Green, the movie serves as a high-profile diegetic prototype that shows audiences "a vision of a future [that] we can step into and make happen" (Saey, 2015). From Green's perspective, the ultimate goal of *The Martian* is to make people believe that a human-led mission to Mars is not science fiction but a real vision of the future.

Figure 7: Mark Watney's ability to feed himself for months using a few potatoes demonstrated the ingenuity of NASA astronauts in this screengrab from *The Martian*. *© Ridley Scott, 2015*

Conclusions: Creating a future for all

Diegetic prototypes result in "happy endings" for designers trying to fund their yet-to-be-developed technology. The presentation of a nascent technology within a cinematic framework can convince audiences of the validity of ideas and create public excitement about seeing these technologies become realities. Fiction's lack of constraints and filmmakers' creative assistance provide an open, "free" space to put forward speculative conceptualizations; they also embed these speculations within a narrative that treats these ideas as already actualized within a social context. The key to diegetic prototypes is that they allow designers to visualize *specific* methods and technologies within the social realm of the fictional world. Filmmakers and/or designers can use the narrative and visual framework of cinema to contextualize and model potential futures for their technology, whether this is medical, robotic, space-based, or from any other area. Because of its visuality, cinema offers an ideal vehicle for establishing a technology's necessity, viability, and benevolence within society. Disney Studios provided Chris Atkeson and his robotics team the opportunity to demonstrate that his designs for soft medical robots *could* work, and the narrative provided reasons why the public should *want* it to work. Likewise, several films in the 2010s afforded proponents of space travel the chance to establish new justifications for supporting human space travel in the light of political, cultural, and social changes in the 1990s and 2000s.

The utility of the diegetic prototype is not limited to big-budget Hollywood motion pictures, nor is it limited specifically to movies. Any medium can be used to create diegetic prototypes, as long as it allows for fully conceived characters to interact with potential technologies in specific scripted scenarios. In fact, diegetic prototyping has been adapted and expanded by those who engage in the practice of design fiction and who wish to create socially conscious technologies (Bleecker, Foster, Girardin, & Nova, 2023). Design fiction highlights the power of storytelling in generating desire for a specific future as well as exploring the meaning and consequences of that future. Most importantly, fictional frames show us how to envision a more livable, ethical, and inclusive future by providing a lens for exploring the social, ethical, and cultural implications of nascent technologies. Diegetic prototypes embedded within fictional stories provide a lens for exploring the potential social impacts and unforeseen consequences of technologies before they are even considered for development. Deploying diegetic prototypes is a useful approach to exploring people's potential lived experiences with household technologies or they can also be used to assess the societal impact of large-scale technologies meant for urban infrastructure. By utilizing diegetic prototypes, designers can help create a future worth living in.

References

Aitoro, J. R. 2015. DARPA goes Disney thanks to 'Big Hero 6'. ***Washington Business Journal,*** 19 November. Accessed online www.bizjournals.com/washington/blog/fedbiz_daily/2014/11/darpa-goes-disney-thanks-to-big-hero-6.html. Viewed October 16, 2023.

Anonymous. 2014. 'Big Hero 6:' The science behind Baymax, Disney's big, soft robot. **NBC News,** 5 November. Accessed online www.nbcnews.com/tech/gadgets/big-hero-6-science-behind-baymax-disneys-big-soft-robot-n240241. Viewed October 16, 2023.

Aronson, J. K. 2022. Too much healthcare—technology. ***British Medical Journal,*** 378. Accessed online www.bmj.com/content/378/bmj.o2102. Viewed October 16, 2023.

Atkeson, C. G. 2014. ***Build Baymax,*** Carnegie Mellon Robotics Institute. Accessed online www.cs.cmu.edu/~cga/build-baymax. Viewed October 16, 2023.

Billings, L. 2013. Wowing the public: The space shuttle as a cultural icon. In R.D. Launius, J. Krige, J. I. Craig, & N. Allen (eds.), ***Space shuttle legacy: How we did it and what we learned***: 299-321. Washington, DC: American Institute of Aeronautics and Astronautics.

Blair, E. 2014. The challenge of 'Big Hero 6:' How to make a huggable robot. ***NPR,*** November 7. Accessed online www.npr.org/sections/alltechconsidered/2014/11/07/362030044/the-challenge-of-big-hero-6-how-to-make-a-huggable-robot. Viewed October 16, 2023.

Bleecker, J., Foster, N., Girardin, F., & Nova N. 2023. ***The manual of design fiction.*** Venice Beach, CA: Near Future Laboratory.

Bradley, R. 2015. Why NASA helped Ridley Scott create 'The Martian' film. ***Popular Science,*** August 20. Accessed online www.popsci.com/why-nasa-helped-ridley-scott-create-martian-film-and-what-means-future-sci-fi-space-movies. Viewed October 21, 2023.

Cardoso, M. A. 2020. The influence of science fiction in healthcare technology. ***Avanca Cinema Journal,*** 2(4): 803-808.

Chew, C. M. 2017. Caregiver shortage reaches critical stage. ***Provider,*** 43: 14-16.

Clery, D. 2014. The theoretical physicist behind *Interstellar.* ***Science,*** 346(6211): 800-801.

Ernst, C. 2019. Natural user interfaces and the imagination of post-industrial warfare: A brief look at *Blade Runner 2049.* ***Interface Critique Journal,*** 2: 243-250.

Handberg, R. 2014. Human spaceflight and presidential agendas: Niche policies and NASA, opportunity and failure. ***Technology in Society,*** 39: 31-43.

Iida, F., & Laschi C. 2011. Soft robotics: Challenges and perspectives. ***Procedia Computer Science,*** 7: 99-102.

Kirby, D. A. 2010. The future is now: Diegetic prototypes and the role of popular films in generating real-world technological development. ***Social Studies of Science,*** 40(1): 41-70.

Lussier, G. 2015. The screenwriter of *The Martian* explains why being stranded on Mars is a "spiritual" experience. ***Gizmodo,*** October 1. Accessed online gizmodo.com/the-martian-screenwriter-says-its-a-religious-movie-bu-1733865987. Viewed October 17, 2023.

Maibaum, A., Bischof, A., Hergesell, J., & Lipp, B. 2021. A critique of robotics in health care. ***AI & Society,*** 37: 467-477.

Marvin, R. 2015. Space-age wonder through the retro futuristic lens of 'Tomorrowland'. ***Medium,*** May 22. Accessed online medium.com/@rjmarvin1/space-age-wonder-through-the-retro-futuristic-lens-of-tomorrowland-cf5d-d802378e. Viewed October 17, 2023.

McDowell, A. 2019. Storytelling shapes the future. ***Journal of Futures Studies***, 23(3): 105-112.

Nolan, C. (Director). 2014. ***Interstellar*** [Film]. Paramount Pictures.

Palmeri, C. 2014. *'Big Hero 6' turns Godzilla into a lovable Disney robot.* ***Bloomberg,*** *October 31. Accessed online* www.bloomberg.com/news/articles/2014-10-31/-big-hero-6-turns-godzilla-into-lovable-disney-robot#xj4y7vzkg. Viewed October 17, 2023.

Pearlman, R. 2014. 'Interstellar' actors sought space tips from real NASA astronaut. ***Space.com,*** November 7. Accessed online www.space.com/27691-interstellar-actors-astronaut-advice.html. Viewed October 17, 2023.

Riek, L. D. 2017. Healthcare robotics. ***Communications of the Association for Computing Machinery***, 60(11): 68-78.

Saey, T. H. 2015. It's sci-fi, but the new movie 'The Martian' has a lot of real science in it. ***Science News,*** September 22. Accessed online www.sciencenews.org/article/martian-entertaining-science-fiction-rooted-fact. Viewed October 17, 2023.

Scott, R. (Director). 2015. ***The Martian*** [Film]. Scott Free Productions.

Smaglik, P. 2014. Media consulting: Entertaining science. ***Nature***, 511(7507): 113-115.

Sparrow, R. 2016. Robots in aged care: A dystopian future? ***AI & Society***, 31: 445-454.

Spennemann, R., & Orthia, L. 2022. Technology through Film: Diegetic prototypes in the Iron Man trilogy. ***Arbeiten aus Anglistik and Amerikanistik***, 47(2): 225-242.

Stahl, B. C., & Coeckelbergh, M. 2016. Ethics of healthcare robotics: Towards responsible research and innovation. ***Robotics and Autonomous Systems***, 86: 152-161.

Stuart, S. C. 2015. How a NASA physicist helped bring 'The Martian' to life. ***PCMag,*** October 3. Accessed online www.pcmag.com/news/how-a-nasa-physicist-helped-bring-the-martian-to-life. Viewed October 17, 2023.

Whalen, A. 2016. Tomorrowland NASA liaison Bert Ulrich tells us how science fiction inspires the future. ***Cosmoso,*** May 25. Accessed online cosmoso.net/tomorrowland-nasa-liaison-bert-ulrich-tells-us-how-science-fiction-inspires-the-future/. Viewed October 17, 2023.

Williams, C., & Hall, D. (Directors). 2014. ***Big Hero 6*** [Film]. Walt Disney Pictures.

Wu, C., Xu, H., Bai, D., Chen, X., Gao, J., & Jiang, X. 2023. Public perceptions on the application of artificial intelligence in healthcare: A qualitative meta-synthesis. ***BMJ Open***, 13(1). Accessed online bmjopen.bmj.com/content/13/1/e066322.full. Viewed October 16, 2023.

Zakarin, J. 2014. NASA's movie and TV guru explains how Hollywood goes to space. ***Yahoo! Entertainment,*** November 3. Accessed online www.yahoo.com/entertainment/nasa-movies-tv-shows-about-space-101691248232.html. Viewed October 17, 2023.

MARK T. KEANE

CHAIR OF COMPUTER SCIENCE
AT UNIVERSITY COLLEGE DUBLIN
DUBLIN, IRELAND

PLAUSIBLE FUTURES: COGNITIVELY BALANCING COMPLEXITY, CORRO-BORATION, & CONJECTURE IN FUTURECASTING

Introduction

When we attempt to predict the future, to forecast or futurecast, irrespective of the methodology adopted, we will always be cognitively limited by the mind's biases, design limits, and previous experiences. At the end of the day, any attempt to predict the future rests on core cognitive abilities, such as imagining the unexpected and recognizing what is and is not plausible and what might be surprising. Without these fundamental cognitive processes, no individual or society can hope to gauge what an uncertain future might bring. The central argument of this paper is that successful predictions of the future, the ones that are more likely to actually occur, need to be plausible and, yet, unexpected. By plausible, I mean that these predicted futures need to be something that could actually happen (not radically different than proposals in future studies, e.g., see Fischer & Dannenberg, 2021; Ramírez & Selin, 2014). By unexpected, I mean that they also need to be imaginative conjectures, in the sense of being something that is new, something that might, actually, have never happened before. However, balancing plausibility and conjecture is non-trivial. According to cognitive theories reviewed here, the assessment of the plausibility of a futurecast requires some assessment of the complexity of the projected future, and some corroboration of the proposal from prior experience (see Connell & Keane, 2004, 2006). However, successful forecasting also requires imaginative conjecture, imagining unexpected things that might never have occurred before.

Unfortunately, as we shall see, recent research shows that people are quite poor at imagining the unexpected, they are very conservative in what they imagine and often fail to consider "really" unexpected things that might occur. Interestingly, this means that the conservative assessments of the unexpected that people commonly make are more plausible, as they tend to rely on objects/actions/events that actually occur quite commonly. However, it also means that their forecasts involve less conjecture, they may lack inventiveness and the innovation required to truly imagine what might occur in the future. So, cognitively, forecasters need to observe plausibility but also stretch it a bit, to counter their natural conservatism in predicting the unexpected. In short, a balance needs to be struck between plausibility and conjecture that can probably only be made with conscious effort and reflection.

In the remainder of this paper, I quickly review the relevant research areas on expectations about the unexpected (see section 2), on how people judge surprise (see section 3), and on the roots of plausibility (see section 4). Then, I try to bring these literatures together with some suggested guidelines for avoiding our inherent cognitive biases in attempting to create plausible futures (section 5). Finally, I conclude by outlining a working example of futurecasting in agriculture, to show how these proposals might be implemented in practice (section 6).

Expectations of the unexpected

Although thinking about the future and prospective thinking have been studied in psychology, this research has tended not to focus on how people think about the unexpected future, how they think about the events that occur in the future that we did not expect. Quinn, Keane, and colleagues did just this, collecting over 10,000 responses from people in a program of research that recorded their predictions of the unexpected for everyday scenarios (e.g., going shopping, gardening, doing an exam, buying a car; see Quinn, Campbell & Keane, 2019, 2021; Quinn, Ford & Keane, 2022; Quinn & Keane, 2021, 2022).

Table 1 shows one such scenario about Louise going clothes shopping, along with the different instructions given to different groups of

Lousie Shopping Scenario

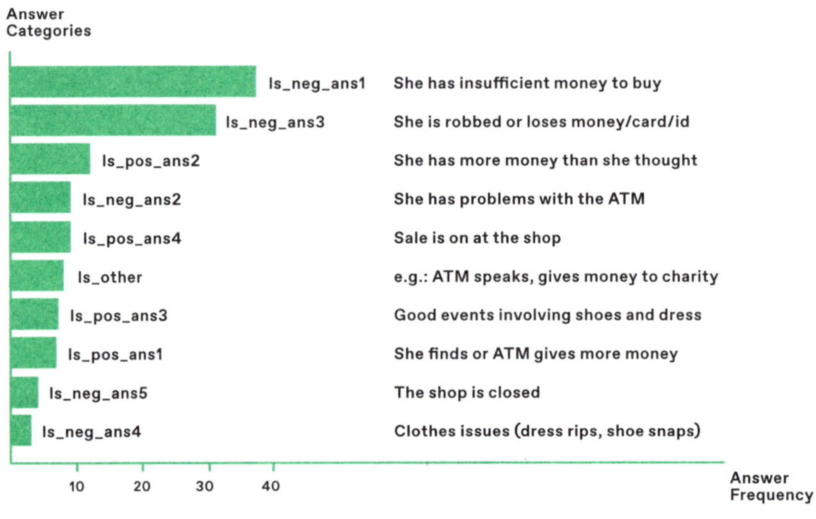

Table 1: Louise Shopping Scenario & the instructional variants used in different conditions of the experiments by Quinn et al. (2021)

participants in one of the studies (involving hundreds of participants). Three main variables were examined in this series of studies, manipulating (i) the instructions given to people in thinking of the unexpected (e.g., telling them "something unexpected happened, what?" or "something good and unexpected happened, what?" or "something bad and unexpected happened, what?", (ii) the *valence* of scenarios (e.g., scenarios varied to have a positive or negative sentiment), and (iii) the *controllability* of events in the scenarios (e.g., whether the main actor is in control of events or not). There are three main results from these studies of relevance to future thinking.

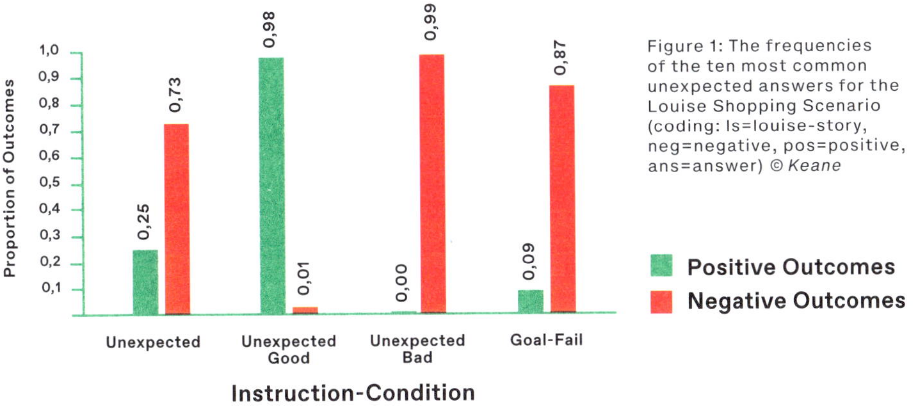

Figure 1: The frequencies of the ten most common unexpected answers for the Louise Shopping Scenario (coding: ls=louise-story, neg=negative, pos=positive, ans=answer) © *Keane*

People Think the Unexpected Is Mainly Bad. People do not have a good idea about what is "really" unexpected, they have a negativity bias in imagining unexpected events (see the "neg" answers in Figure 1). Figure 2 shows the typical overall response patterns seen when people are asked to think about the unexpected. In the Unexpected condition, where people are simply asked to "think of the unexpected," the majority of them report negative outcomes (73% of responses), even though they have no problem thinking of positive outcomes (98% of responses) when they are asked to "think of unexpected good" things (see Unexpected Good in Figure 2). So, their natural inclination is to think of the unexpected as negative, even though they know about good outcomes. Obviously, when they are asked to "think of unexpected bad" things (see Unexpected Bad in Figure 2) they also mainly report negative outcomes (as they do for Goal-failure instructions, see Figure 2).* Parallel effects occur for an uncontrollability bias that has complex interactions with valence that I will not elaborate further here (see Quinn & Keane, 2022 for details).

* Quinn et al. (2021) also show that this negativity bias can be somewhat mitigated by the valence of the initial scenario statement; if the initial scenario is positive, then the unexpected outcome will be negative, but if the initial scenario is more negative, then positive outcomes are increasingly mentioned (though negative outcomes still tend to dominate overall).

$$\text{plausability} = 1 - \text{implausability}$$

$$\text{inplausability} = \frac{\text{complexity}}{\text{corroboration} - \text{conjecture}}$$

Figure 2: Valence of unexpected events, reported as positive and negative outcomes, in the four instructional conditions of Experiment 1 © *Quinn et al., 2021*

People Are Poor at the Unexpected. Furthermore, the bad future outcomes they imagine tend to be quite "expected"; they tend to think of the *expected unexpected* rather than "really unexpected" happenings and they tend to agree with one another in their answers. For example, in the Louise Shopping Scenario, people propose "unexpected" outcomes that are really quite expected. Figure 1 shows that the main answers given typically involve commonplace plan disruptions to a shopping expedition; for example, (i) she has insufficient money to buy the clothes she wants (ls_neg_ans1), (ii) she has problems with getting money from the ATM (ls_neg_ans2), (iii) she is robbed or loses money/card/id (ls_neg_ans3). Furthermore, people tend to agree on these "expected unexpected" outcomes; these three answers account for over 70% of the responses made to this story (see Figure 1) and similar patterns occur for other scenarios tested. From one perspective, treating unexpected events in this way makes sense, in that it is adaptive. As Leake (2014) argues, people build up schemas for common disruptions to everyday plans whether they experienced them personally or vicariously. It makes sense to note, record, and generalize what commonly occurs, as it will be more likely to be the disruption you actually encounter in the future. However, as a basis for thinking about really unexpected things, this strategy is flawed; it will not lead us to consider truly unexpected outcomes, the ones that may be the most useful in futurecasting (e.g., that when Louise gets to the store, there is a flash mob doing a synchronized dance). Indeed, this tendency to be conservative about the unexpected seems to be deeply ingrained; people persist with these sorts of answers even when they are instructed to "think of something bizarre and unexpected" (see Quinn, Campbell, & Keane, 2019).

People Discount the *Unexpected* Unexpected. Indeed, even when people know about possible outcomes that are truly unexpected they often discount them, for a variety of reasons. For example, at the beginning of the COVID-19 pandemic, as governments moved to implement lockdowns and mask-wearing, many people were surprised, finding the measures unexpected. Yet, there were many readily available historical cases that should have made these responses more expected (e.g., the Chinese experience with SARS in the 2000s, and the Spanish Flu in 1918). People were told about these pandemics and what happened in them, but seem to have discounted them because they either thought that such things would only happen in a far-away country (i.e., not in my country) or happened a long time ago (i.e., not with our modern medicine). In short, most of the time the unexpected-unexpected appears not to be available, people will simply not think of it at all (without interventions) and even when it is available they may discount it as unlikely to occur. In the next section, I consider related phenomena in the area of surprise that again show surprising events that can be familiar and unfamiliar (i.e., somewhat unexpected and very unexpected).

Familiar & unfamiliar surprises

In trying to imagine an interesting and novel future, it sometimes helps to use surprise as a heuristic; if I can think of something that really surprises me or you, then perhaps I am on track to identifying something of interest. However, here again, there is evidence that people can be stumped by the truly unexpected. Foster & Keane (2015, 2019) found that surprising events can be familiar surprises or unfamiliar surprises (echoing the expected/unexpected unexpected distinction).

Foster & Keane (2015) proposed a sense-making theory of surprise called the metacognitive explanation-based (MEB) theory of surprise. When people encounter something surprising, they say "how could that have happened?" This pause for thought triggers an attempt to explain the surprise, to resolve it; in essence, to make it not surprising anymore. In a series of experiments, Foster & Keane (2015) showed how surprise judgements differ in how easily they can be resolved, some surprises are more difficult to resolve than others. Consider one of the scenarios used in these experiments. Imagine, one day you are walking home and discover that your wallet is missing from the back pocket of your jeans. You would be surprised, but also have some ready explanations for what might have occurred (e.g., "I may have left it in a shop I just visited," "I might have been pickpocketed," "I might have dropped it"). Now, imagine you are walking home and discover that your belt is missing from the waist of your jeans, the one you distinctly remember fastening that morning. Again, you would be surprised, but in this scenario few explanations present themselves (the only plausible one we could think of was leaving one's belt in the security area at the airport). The first scenario more commonly occurs and, as such, people have ready-made explanations for resolving the surprise experienced. The second is uncommon and, as such, it is hard to explain, accordingly hard to resolve, and much more surprising to people.

In short, there are familiar and unfamiliar surprises, where the former are resolved by working off stored knowledge about common disruptions and the latter appear to have little available relevant knowledge. Indeed, it was also found that when people were asked to explain these events, they tended to agree much more on their explanations for familiar surprises than those for unfamiliar ones (i.e., common knowledge was available for the former but was not available for the latter). So, again, we see that people are hampered when they need to consider truly unexpected things, in this case in their comprehension of the unexpected rather than the production of the unexpected. Furthermore, Foster & Keane (2015) showed these impediments can be somewhat mitigated; subtle changes to a scenario can cue less-available knowledge and decrease the surprisingness of the unfamiliar cases (e.g., if mention was made of going through airport security in the belt scenario). So, this shows that potentially useful knowledge can be found if an appropriate cue or context can be provided. This proposal echoes older proposals in creative thinking and insight problem solving. In the 1960s, the synectics brainstorming technique (Gordon, 1961) proposed elaborating almost random ideas around a focal topic with a view to eliciting creative ideas. Similar ideas occur in psychological models of insight, where the contents of working memory are said to cue new problem-spaces, making new operators available that overcome impasses in problem solving (e.g., see Keane, 1985, 1989; Ohlsson, 1984, 1985, 1992).

These results effectively parallel the findings on familiar (i.e., expected unexpected) and unfamiliar unexpected events (i.e., unexpected unexpected). Familiar surprises tap stored knowledge about common disruptions (e.g., someone stole my money) and are judged to be less surprising, they are responses to expected-unexpected outcomes. Unfamiliar surprises are very surprising because supporting knowledge cannot be found to make sense of them (i.e., having no idea how your belt disappeared). Effectively, they present people with the unexpected-unexpected outcomes that they are not equipped to handle. As such, they show us another perspective on how poor people are at dealing with the truly unexpected. In the next section, we consider other work on plausibility and on how it completes the set of cognitive processes that act together in forecasting.

The roots of plausibility

Thus far we have considered the psychological evidence around the difficulties people have in considering the future. In this section, we consider a final set of cognitive processes around the assessment of plausibility. As we shall see, any useful futurecast or projection of the future needs to be plausibility-tested to determine its potential usefulness.

Connell & Keane (2004, 2006) proposed a theory of plausibility that they modelled computationally and tested in several psychological experiments. This theory, the Knowledge-Fitting Theory, maintains that there are three main components that people assess when considering the plausibility of event descriptions: (i) complexity, (ii) corroboration, and (iii) conjecture. Stated simply, a plausible story is one that corresponds well to our prior experience (it fits our knowledge and is *corroborated* by it), it should be simple rather than *complex* (fewer steps), and it should avoid too much *conjecture*, invented objects/actions/events that were not given in the initial description of a situation.

Consider an example in which we imagine I am a murderer and am trying to cover my tracks with a plausible alibi. In one of Raymond Chandler's (2000) famous crime novels, when the femme fatale asks Marlowe what they should tell the police after a murder, he replies "well the most plausible story we can tell is the truth, what actually happened, maybe we should start with that?" A plausible alibi needs to have a high level of corroboration and a low amount of conjecture and to be a simple, low-complexity story.

So, a good alibi needs as much *corroboration* as possible. I should say that I did the things I always do (e.g., I left my office at the usual time, took my usual route home, and went to bed early), where the account is corroborated and corresponds to past experience. Indeed, it will also help if my account has points of actual corroboration (e.g., someone saw me at the office or my wife greeted me when I got home), where there is direct support for the truth of some of the events. Second, the alibi will be better if it is *simple* rather than *complex*, if it has fewer steps or convolutions; for instance, the account will get less plausible if I say, "Oh, halfway home, I realized that I had forgotten my laptop, so I went back to the office to pick it up...and *then* I went home." Third, the alibi will be more plausible if there are not too many *conjectures*, invented steps, objects, and actors; for instance, if I say I stopped at a shop and someone broke into my car (that's how those fibers got on the seat, they were from the robber). The problem with conjectures is that they need to be substantiated and when the police cannot find corroboration for them they often find the murderer.

Connell & Keane (2004) tested several aspects of this theory in a series of experiments where people were shown simple descriptions of events and asked to make plausibility judgements under carefully controlled conditions (e.g., word frequency and word coherence were carefully controlled). Furthermore, they also modelled these results using a precise formula for characterizing plausibility and implausibility (assuming one could represent the knowledge using graph-based representations). As such, these ideas could guide how plausibility might be more accurately and comprehensively assessed in real-world situations, such as futurecasting. It is to this proposal that I turn in the next section of this paper.

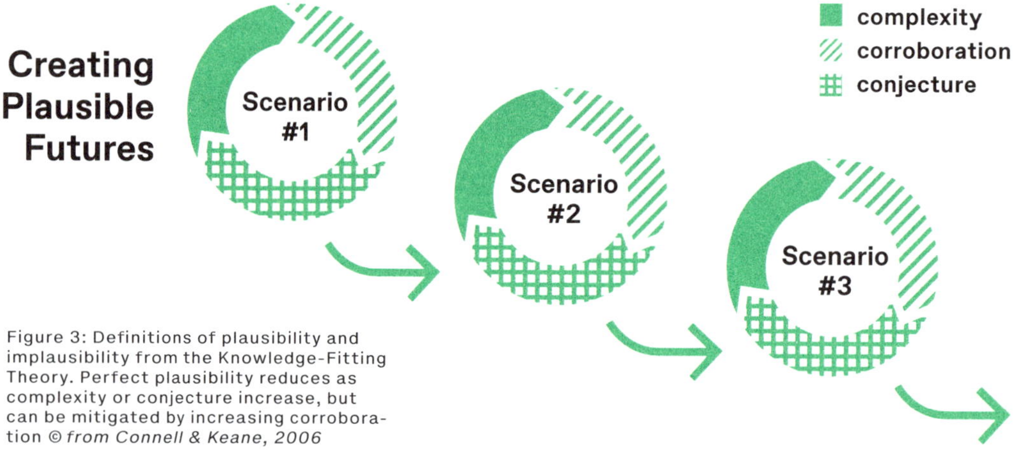

Figure 3: Definitions of plausibility and implausibility from the Knowledge-Fitting Theory. Perfect plausibility reduces as complexity or conjecture increase, but can be mitigated by increasing corroboration © *from Connell & Keane, 2006*

Thinking about plausible futures

When we consider forecasting, futurecasting, or scenario planning we are essentially trying to imagine a plausible future, but one that imaginatively goes beyond what one would readily expect (Fischer & Dannenberg, 2021; Ramírez & Selin, 2014). Here, I have tried to highlight some cognitive findings to provide some psychological insight into how people predict and imagine the future. In this section, I try to distill what we have learned from this work into a set of cognitive proposals for optimizing future thinking by individuals and groups. This is just an initial sketch of how this might be done, but it may nevertheless prove useful. As a use case, I will try to apply these ideas in a simulated futurecasting scenario for the future of dairy agriculture. But, first, I will start with some lessons that we should perhaps take from the research reviewed.

From a cognitive perspective, a very coherent picture emerges from the reviewed work with respect to prospective thinking, surprise, and plausibility. Across these psychological studies we see that our prior knowledge is good at dealing with the *near* unexpected, it can allow us to assess the familiar unexpected and explain familiar surprises. However, these adaptive cognitive strategies for dealing with the familiar unexpected and familiar surprises leave us poorly equipped for dealing with "really" unexpected events. So, "really" unexpected things can completely blindside us; we are totally surprised by these events and have few resources to explain them (e.g., the COVID-19 pandemic). As such, many people will respond very badly to such events, they will find them upsetting, they will feel threatened, they will experience a failure to understand and an undermining of their "normal" world. Such responses are also probably not uncommon in organizational contexts, when "really unexpected" disruption occurs and may well account for the resistance from staff to the airing of uncommon futures.

To imagine the truly unexpected we need to recruit another set of cognitive processes, those often associated with creativity, imagination, and leaps that go beyond the solid reality of the current world. We need to somehow entertain uncommon conjectures about future possibilities that might never occur or are completely foreign to us. It is my belief that many foresight and futurecasting methods try to provide constructs and interventions to do just this, to help people get beyond the constraints of their prior knowledge and expectations, and to elicit more creative understandings. In the next, and final, section, I sketch how the ideas reviewed here might supplement such activities with appropriate interventions.

Figure 4: Cycles for creating plausible futures where Scenario #1 is proposed and plausibility checked (assessing complexity, corroboration, and conjectures) before it is extended further with more unexpected ideas (the yellow arrow to Scenario #2), before that scenario is, in turn, plausibility checked and so on to Scenario #3 and further cycles. © *Keane*

Sentence Type	Louise Shopping Scenario
Goal	Louise wants to shop at an expensive clothes store.
Additional Information	She is wearing her favourite dress and matching shoes
Plan-Step	Louise draws money from the ATM.

	Instructions
Unexpected	Then, something unexpected occurred. What do you think happened?
Unexpected-Good	Then, something unexpected and good occurred. What do you think happened?
Unexpected-Bad	Then, something unexpected and bad occurred. What do you think happened?
Goal-Fail	But Louise does not shop at the expensive clothes store. What do you think happened?

Figure 4 shows a proposed workflow in guiding people's thinking when developing futurecasts. The proposal here is to have successive futurecasting cycles where futures are imagined, vetted for their plausibility (assessing their complexity, corroboration, and conjectures), and then explicitly extended further into the unknown on a second cycle, before entering another plausibility-checking stage, before entering a third cycle and so on (and then stopping when people are satisfied with the results). Let us concretize this by assuming we are trying to futurecast for the dairy farming sector to meet environmental regulations and sustainability targets.

Supporting future-casting: Agri scenarios

In the last few years, we have been developing a suite of AI technologies to ameliorate the future of the dairy sector in Ireland (Delaney, Greene, Shalloo, Lynch, & Keane, 2022; Kenny et al., 2019; Riaboff et al., 2022; Ryan, Guéret, Berry, Corcoran, Keane, & Mac Namee, 2021; Pakrashi et al., 2023; Temraz, Kenny, Ruelle, Shalloo, Smyth, & Keane, 2021). The Irish dairy sector largely uses what is called a pasture-based system; this is a system where, given a mild climate, cows can be left outdoors for most of the year and fed on grass pasture rather than being housed in sheds for most of the year and fed on transported feeds. This system has the potential to be sustainable as feed is lower-carbon and locally-sourced, mixed swards may allow a reduction in the use of artificial fertilizers (i.e., nitrates), and animal welfare can be generally better. Pasture-based systems involve quite complex grass management where herds are rotated over multiple paddocks (fields), with carefully timed cuttings of silage for winter feed and well-planned decisions on calving. Although this pasture-based system has the potential to be a zero-carbon system, it still has issues with pollution (i.e., nitrates polluting waterways) and greenhouse gas emissions (i.e., cows produce methane as they digest grass). Also, low margins, market volatility in the sector, and emerging climate challenges often make technological innovation too expensive (e.g., sensing systems may be too expensive for farmers). While, environmentally, the sector is under pressure from environmental regulation, in many parts of the world these businesses are one of the last bulwarks against rural depopulation and the decline of rural communities.

Governments worldwide are currently exploring futures for this sector, largely with the aim of meeting climate challenges and emerging environmental targets. In a first cycle, assume that we consider three future scenarios: let us call them the *culling*, the *luxury food*, and the *coupled-systems* scenarios. Each is briefly sketched out below:

- **Culling Scenario.** The sector could be forced to directly meet environmental targets and restrictions using the simple but somewhat brutal strategy of reducing herd numbers via restrictive licensing and/or funding farmers to leave the sector.

- **Luxury Food Scenario.** The sector could become a luxury food sector, ceasing to be a provider of cheap, staple, foods such as "ordinary" milk, cheese, and meat, and, rather, moving up the value chain to being an expensive, high-value supplier of luxury products.

- **Coupled-Systems Scenario.** The sector could be forced to directly meet environmental restrictions but supported to innovate around the better coupling of its systems. For example, in many countries, the current producer system (mainly independent farmers) is quite de-coupled from the processing system (the food factories, the processors), which can have long-standing inefficiencies. Better sensing technology around production systems could help reduce environmental impacts, track milk properties at farm-level, and provide better early-stage information for later-stage, in-factory processing. E.g., lactose levels in milk vary based on grass quality at different times of the year and have significant effects on the downstream processing of the raw product; higher-lactose milk is better for cheese production, a change of production that requires major in-factory re-organizations of machinery and processes. A tighter coupling between producers and processors using advanced sensing technologies and state-of-the-art modelling could dramatically improve the sector.

Having proposed these alternative futures, we might plausibility-check them, looking at their complexity and the corroboration available for them, and asking which aspects of them involve conjecture. In a first step, the real task is to unpack the initial proposed scenario to assess whether it is actually feasible, to find concrete or analogous evidential support for it, and to identify the conjectural parts of it that have no support (ironically, although the latter may make the scenario less plausible, they may be good sources of more imaginative ideas about the future). Consider a putative first cycle assessment for each scenario:

- **Culling Scenario.** This scenario appears to be highly plausible as, on the face of it, it is simple and corroborated. Governments have intervened before in agri-sectors to radically alter production and shift efforts to other activities (e.g., in the 2000s, the sugar beet industry in Ireland effectively closed due to EU quotas, and farmers were compensated to stop growing beets). Also, the administrative mechanisms for this sort of intervention exist already. Arguably, however, it is too close to our current world, it has very little unexpectedness (few conjectures), and it is so plausible it lacks creativity. Currently, it is also politically unacceptable as it would speed rural depopulation and is strongly resisted by the farming lobbies. Indeed, it is so plausible it is hard to imagine how it could be elaborated further in more creative directions. It is almost too well-founded in past practice.

- **Luxury Food Scenario.** This scenario is somewhat more creative. It is also plausible by virtue of having been done before in this industry, though its plausibility is partly mitigated by being somewhat more complex. Some high-quality cheeses command luxury prices, though the proposition usually rests on limited production and more expensive processing steps (e.g., long and/or specialized maturation steps). In the Irish context, something like this has already been done for butter from grass-fed herds (see Kerrygold or Le Beurre d'Echiré) and A2 milk products are following a similar path. However, the proposition is not simple from a practical perspective; creating premium brands, targeted marketing, and establishing a consumer base are non-trivial. These aspects of the scenario are, perhaps, the ones that require further elaboration in a second cycle of futurecasting that would, for example, stretch the ideas around brand creation in food products into some new space. A more creative set of conjectures might be found around a healthy-food scenario, where specific, new health benefits for a food are discovered and promoted. However, this scenario is still very firmly within the realms of the probable. We are still running on the rails of past experience rather than pushing the creative envelope. Also, this and the previous scenario obviously do not avail of current technological advances (e.g., in SmartAg). They are operating with old know-how.

- **Coupled-Systems Scenario.** This scenario, in comparison with the others, stretches the current state of things much more, it seems much more creative but, accordingly, suffers on plausibility; it is much more complex, it involves a lot more conjecture, and is less well supported by previous cases (e.g., technology adoption in this sector has traditionally been slow: Palma-Molina et al., 2023). Here, we might search for corroboration from analogous cases of technology adoption in other sectors (e.g., the use of smartphones on farms in sub-Saharan Africa to access market data and sell products). However, this also means that the scenario is potentially ripe with unsupported conjectures that could be pursued in an elaboration of the scenario in a further futurecasting cycle.

So, let us assume that we accept some of the current implausibility of this scenario and continue to push it further by elaborating certain aspects. Perhaps the biggest impasse to the adoption of advanced sensing systems on farms is cost, profit margins in farming make for conservative investment in such technologies; however, if the sensed information is very valuable to the processors then such costs could be shared or, indeed, paid for completely by processors, and/or farmers could be paid for these data-gathering tasks. In this way, a new income source for the producer systems could be introduced that would also increase their profitability. Indeed, this coupling of systems could be pushed further; recent research has shown that many milk quality traits for individual cows can be predicted from routinely-available milk spectra (Frizzarin, et al., 2021). So the use of this data-gathering as a source of income for farms could be extended to provisions for governmental environmental agencies, perhaps building a novel early-sensing or monitoring network. If we take these more elaborate conjectures into a second cycle, these proposals should then be submitted to a second round of plausibility checking. This gets more challenging as we move further away from current practice, but such assessments could be made speculatively, perhaps together with further invention to take us to a third cycle of plausibility checking (see Figure 4). In this way, one can imagine a progressive set of repeated cycles that could take us psychologically and in a guided way closer to potentially better and more inventive (but plausibly grounded) outcomes as we imagine possible futures.

Conclusion

In this paper, I have tried to advance a psychological perspective on futurecasting to elaborate some of the psychological processes that people must rely on when they think about future plausibilities. From this research, I have tried to extract several key psychological steps that people need to engage in when carrying out these activities (i.e., assessing complexity, corroboration, and conjectures) in order to push them more towards the unexpected, but perhaps an unexpected that is also grounded in prior experience, without being too grounded to be unimaginative.

Acknowledgements

This paper emanated from research funded by Science Foundation Ireland (SFI) to the Insight Centre for Data Analytics (12/RC/2289-P2). For the purpose of Open Access, the author has applied a CC BY copyright to any Author Accepted Manuscript version arising from this submission.

References

Chandler, R. 2000. ***The Big Sleep and Other Novels.*** London: Penguin UK.

Connell, L., & Keane, M. T. 2004. What plausibly affects plausibility? Concept coherence and distributional word coherence as factors influencing plausibility judgments. **Memory & Cognition,** 32(2): 185-197.

Connell, L., & Keane, M. T. 2006. A model of plausibility. ***Cognitive Science***, *30*(1): 95-120.

Delaney, E., Greene, D., Shalloo, L., Lynch, M., & Keane, M. T. 2022. Forecasting for sustainable dairy produce: Enhanced long-term, milk-supply forecasting using k-nn for data augmentation, with prefactual explanations for xai. ***Case-Based Reasoning Research and Development, 30th International Conference, ICCBR 2022, Nancy, France, Proceedings***: 365-379.

Fischer, N., & Dannenberg, S. 2021. The social construction of futures: Proposing plausibility as a semiotic approach for critical futures studies. ***Futures,*** 129: 102729.

Foster, M. I., & Keane, M. T. 2015. Why some surprises are more surprising than others: Surprise as a metacognitive sense of explanatory difficulty. ***Cognitive Psychology***, 81: 74-116.

Foster, M. I., & Keane, M. T. 2019. The role of surprise in learning: Different surprising outcomes affect memorability differentially. ***Topics in Cognitive Science***, 11(1): 75-87.

Frizzarin, M., Gormley, I. C., Berry, D. P., Murphy, T. B., Casa, A., Lynch, A., & McParland, S. 2021. Predicting cow milk quality traits from routinely available milk spectra using statistical machine learning methods. ***Journal of Dairy Science***, 104(7): 7438-7447.

Gordon, W. J. 1961. ***Synectics: The development of creative capacity.*** New York: Harper.

Keane, M. 1985. Restructuring revised: A theoretical note on Ohlsson's mechanism of restructuring. ***Scandinavian journal of psychology***, 26(1): 363-365.

Keane, M. 1989. Modelling problem solving in Gestalt 'insight'problems. ***The Irish Journal of Psychology***, 10(2): 201-215.

Kenny, E. M., Ruelle, E., Geoghegan, A., Shalloo, L., O'Leary, M., O'Donovan, M., & Keane, M. T. 2019. Predicting grass growth for sustainable dairy farming: a CBR system using Bayesian case-exclusion and post-hoc, personalized explanation-by-example (XAI). In ***Case-Based Reasoning Research and Development, 27th International Conference, ICCBR 2019, Otzenhausen, Germany, Proceedings:*** 172-187.

Leake, D. B. 2014. ***Evaluating explanations: A content theory.*** Hove, UK: Psychology Press.

Riaboff, L., Shalloo, L., Smeaton, A. F., Couvreur, S., Madouasse, A., & Keane, M. T. 2022. Predicting livestock behaviour using accelerometers: A systematic review of processing techniques for ruminant behaviour prediction from raw accelerometer data. ***Computers and Electronics in Agriculture***, 192: 106610.

Ohlsson, S. 1984. Restructuring revisited: I. Summary and critique of the Gestalt theory of problem solving. ***Scandinavian Journal of Psychology***, 25(1): 65-78.

Ohlsson, S. 1985. Retrieval processes in restructuring: Answer to Keane. ***Scandinavian Journal of Psychology***, 26(1): 366-368.

Ohlsson, S. 1992. Information-processing explanations of insight and related phenomena. In Keane, M. T., & Gilhooly, K. J. (eds.), ***Advances in the psychology of thinking***: 1-44. London: Harvester Wheatsheaf.

Ramírez, R., & Selin, C. 2014. Plausibility and probability in scenario planning. ***Foresight***, 16(1): 54-74.

Ryan, C., Guéret, C., Berry, D., Corcoran, M., Keane, M. T., & Mac Namee, B. 2021. ***Predicting illness for a sustainable dairy agriculture: predicting and explaining the onset of mastitis in dairy cows.*** AAAI-21 Workshop on Explainable Agency in AI (XAI).

Pakrashi, A., Ryan, C., Guéret, C., Berry, D. P., Corcoran, M., Keane, M. T., & Mac Namee, B. 2023. Early detection of subclinical mastitis in lactating dairy cows using cow-level features. ***Journal of Dairy Science***, 106(7): 4978-4990.

Palma-Molina, P., Hennessy, T., O'Connor, A. H., Onakuse, S., O'Leary, N., Moran, B., & Shalloo, L. 2023. Factors associated with intensity of technology adoption and with the adoption of 4 clusters of precision livestock farming technologies in Irish pasture-based dairy systems. ***Journal of Dairy Science,*** 106(4): 2498-2509.

Quinn, M. S., Campbell, K., & Keane, M. T. 2019. The expected unexpected & unexpected unexpected: How people's conception of the unexpected is not really that unexpected. ***Proceedings of the 41st Annual Conference of the Cognitive Science Society, Montreal***: 2627-2633.

Quinn, M. S., Campbell, K., & Keane, M. T. 2021. Do we "fear for the worst" or "Hope for the best" in thinking about the unexpected?: Factors affecting the valence of unexpected outcomes reported for everyday scenarios. ***Cognition,*** 208: 104520.

Quinn, M. S., Ford, C., & Keane, M. T. 2022. People's reports of unexpected events for everyday scenarios: Over 1000 textual responses, human-labelled for valence/sentiment, controllability and topic category. ***Data in Brief,*** 44: 108545.

Quinn, M. S., & Keane, M. T. 2021. Three datasets reporting unexpected events for everyday scenarios: Over 9000 events human-labelled for overall valence/sentiment, topic category, and relationship to the initial goal of the scenario. ***Data in Brief,*** 35: 106935.

Quinn, M. S., & Keane, M. T. 2022. Factors affecting "expectations of the unexpected": The impact of controllability & valence on unexpected outcomes. ***Cognition,*** 225: 105142.

Temraz, M., Kenny, E. M., Ruelle, E., Shalloo, L., Smyth, B., & Keane, M. T. 2021. Handling climate change using counterfactuals: Using counterfactuals in data augmentation to predict crop growth in an uncertain climate future. ***Case-Based Reasoning Research and Development: 29th International Conference, ICCBR 2021, Salamanca, Spain:*** 216-231.

ARI POPPER

FOUNDER AND CEO, SCIFUTURES
LOS ANGELES, UNITED STATES

THE IRON FIST AND THE VELVET GLOVE: "THE FUTURE SIMULATOR"

We know that communicating a future vision that results in meaningful action is challenging.

This is because the future is:

- Complex
- Vague
- Technical
- Abstract
- Emerging

Furthermore, organizations like our Fortune 500 clients are prone to inertia and are risk averse. Yet, what made them successful in the past will not necessarily make them successful in the future. The usual approach of drowning people in trend reports and "Powerpointing" them to death with dry strategic visions will never result in meaningful action.

Neuroscience has shown that strong emotion leads to action (Zak, 2015). So, for the future content that you create to be effective, to *motivate behavioral and organizational change*, it must create epiphanies.

Content about the future, therefore, needs to be:

- Emotive
- Human
- Tangible
- Visceral

The "Iron Fist" and "Velvet Glove"

A future inspired and communicated by immersive narratives (the "Velvet Glove")—yet grounded in robust research, facts, trends, and science (the "Iron Fist")—allows credible concepts and transformative approaches to emerge, be embraced, and be understood.

Our experience over the past 12 years, working with a large roster of Fortune 100 clients like JP Morgan Chase, Coca-Cola, L'Oreal, etc., has taught us that you need both the Iron Fist and the Velvet Glove if you want this work to result in meaningful action.

Our clients' preferred futures are not plucked randomly out of the air. The Iron Fist is the credible backbone that consists of extensive research and is shaped by a well-thought-out and co-created strategic vision through workshops and working sessions with our clients. These futures are shaped, finessed, and refined, in close collaboration with our clients' key stakeholders. The strategic vision should fit with the goals, objectives, and values of our clients' organizations. Interestingly, deciding on preferred future visions forces our clients to get a clearer sense of what they "want to be" and this often means them letting go of what they "don't want to be". But the essential point is this: Any future vision must be well-grounded in research and be credible. It must have a strong research backbone with broad stakeholder buy-in. The danger of not having an Iron Fist foundation is that the entire credibility of a future vision can vanish like a castle in the sky.

If the Iron Fist represents the head (intellect, logic, analysis, and rigor) the Velvet Glove represents the heart. We are emotional creatures who make many decisions from the heart or, as the social psychologist Jonathan Haidt states, "The emotional tail wags the rational dog." This does not stop when we enter the workplace. As Yuval Harari notes, "Humans think in stories, we try to make sense of the world by telling stories." For this future content to change behavior, it is vital that the Iron Fist is wrapped in a Velvet Glove of emotion and stories. The Velvet Glove is the spoonful of sugar that makes the medicine go down.

The Velvet Glove is usually a high-fidelity narrative execution. This could be illustrated short stories, a graphic novel, or an experiential first-person video (more about this below). Narratives that are effective create a strong emotional connection with the characters, build genuine empathy with their dilemmas, and showcase how our client's future products or services can solve these problems. A well-executed Velvet Glove should make the viewer feel inspired and moved...literally "moved" to take meaningful action. *When it is all said and done, if this work doesn't result in meaningful action, it is a waste of time and resources.*

The elastic band

However, keep in mind that communicating a future vision is much like stretching an elastic band...If you pull too far into the future, the band snaps (and you lose everyone and hurt yourself). Yet, if you do not pull enough, lack of tension results in lack of progress (and nothing changes). Understanding and navigating this tension is the key to success in the work we do.

One way to address this tension is through using a "Now, Next, Future" approach. We gain acceptance by showcasing near-term, actionable solutions as the "Now," and inspire Next" and "Future" initiatives as plausible but transformative evolutionary developments through immersive storytelling.

The above is the essence of science fiction prototyping and the SciFutures approach that we developed for large organizations.

Example: The future simulator

A recent real-world example of this approach was the creation of what our clients called the *future simulator*. This future simulator was a highly successful part of a larger project and its goal was to bring our client's preferred future to life in order to accelerate genuinely transformative innovation.

After conducting extensive research into the signals and forces of change for our client's businesses (studying emerging technologies, startups, patents, research interviews with experts, etc.) we formed a strategic vision of what our client's preferred future could look like. This research then led to the ideation of a host of immersive narrative devices to bring that future to life. The result was an immersive experiential lab that showcased the research (the Iron Fist), using narratives and immersive experiences (the Velvet Glove).

A key asset in this lab was the future simulator.

Imagine walking into a shipping container but all the walls of that container are covered in screens. Now imagine those screens showing a story, of the near future using live action, where you are the main character. Importantly, the scenes were shot in first person Point Of View, so you, the viewer, embody the main character. Now imagine the engaging narrative stopping and asking for your feedback at key moments, like in the "choose your own adventure" novels of the past. The scenes progress on the basis of your direct input. This is what we delivered for a Fortune 500 consumer packaged goods company.

Figures 1, 2, 3, and 4
© *SciFutures Inc.*

Emotions lead to action

While, on the surface, the video seemed simple, it was not simplistic. The narrative strategy (Iron Fist) was developed from a huge database of research content and the use cases and narrative choices were based on real consumer needs and tensions. The future simulator (Velvet Glove) was a short but highly immersive narrative experience, yet it managed to effectively communicate a visionary future, in an immersive and personal way, that changed the culture and the belief of what is possible. It was highly effective in creating a personal and emotional connection with the ways that our client's customers could experience their products and services in the future. This resulted in instant epiphanies with our client's preferred future.

While several immersive future assets and experiences were created for our client in this lab, we learned from the client that the future simulator was most successful at creating rapid organizational transformation. It helped transform a rigid and risk-averse culture by inspiring belief and motivating a series of transformative R&D workstreams. These workstreams were directly inspired by the simulator as it provided a clear and accessible mental heuristic for this large traditional company to align against. It became a powerful North Star. In fact, it became so useful that this experience became an essential new employee orientation tool to understand their overall vision and strategy for the future.

At SciFutures, we have learned over the past decade that creating a preferred future vision requires both the Iron Fist and the Velvet Glove. It is vital to pull at the head strings *and* the heart strings. The skills for achieving this are varied and diverse: To create a credible Iron Fist, you need excellent researchers, synthesists, and strategists; to create a compelling Velvet Glove, you need gifted storytellers, visionaries, creatives, and producers. And to ensure that this work aligns and is accepted by the client, you need strong consultants who are genuine trusted advisors. When this work is delivered well, we have seen, time and time again, that it creates rapid and meaningful change.

References

Zak, P. J. 2015. Why inspiring stories make us react: The neuroscience of narrative. ***Cerebrum***, 2: 26034526. Accessed online https://pubmed.ncbi.nlm.nih.gov/26034526/. Viewed February 16, 2024.

INTERVIEW

Photo: Erich Goldmann

ALEX MCDOWELL

CREATIVE DIRECTOR,
PRODUCTION DESIGNER,
PROFESSOR, WORLDBUILDER
LOS ANGELES, UNITED STATES

The original interview, conducted by Michael Shamiyeh and Bolko von Oetinger, delves into Alex McDowell's distinctive world building approach. McDowell, a designer and creative director in narrative media, views world building as a versatile framework for diverse narratives. The aim is to explore how this method can be applied beyond film or games to tackle real-life challenges and communicate alternative futures effectively.

Michael Shamiyeh (MS): Alex, what do you mean by world building?

Alex McDowell (AMD): Everything we build starts with storytelling. Not linear, as it is often understood, but storytelling as a method of communicating across a vast field. Traditionally, the storyteller was a central hub; the one who gathers stories and disseminates them horizontally, from person to person within a community, for the hunter-gatherer, the child, or the elder to make sense of the world around them. Increasing knowledge generates more stories, and now these are passed vertically through generations, accruing and distributing knowledge as they go. For this narrative system to be effective and to weave these evolving stories it needs networks of storytellers through space and time and needs to be accessible. Complex ideas can be translated into comprehension through metaphor, conveyed by the language of the senses; dance, music, and art.
As a visual and narrative designer, I am focused on creating shared language. The craft of design is powerful because our work can be shared across boundaries on multiple platforms for multiple audiences. The design space is an agile hub responsible for converting complexity to comprehension, whether in wayfinding, empathy, or immersion, and for provoking evolutionary change.
In world building we are creating new design systems that are intimately engaged with translation, understanding the intent and implementing the answers to the provocations and questions that kick-start each world.

MS: The way you talk about world building is very abstract. When you talk about a platform, what do you mean in concrete terms?

AMD: Perhaps a simple example is this. Around 1440, Gutenberg designed the printing press. His invention revolutionized the distribution of text, but it shifted the power of oral storytelling to written literature. Mass production effectively fixed the text and elevated the single author. Whether in literature, art, architecture, theater, or music it created a proscenium relationship between the idea and the audience. A single author cannot build a holistic and evolutionary world. World building creates a multi-dimensional container that demands a network of creators to co-create revolutionary outcomes and a coherent logic. Inside this container a limitless number of stories can be woven to allow many participants to negotiate the complexity of a world in the same way that we negotiate the world outside our door. It returns us to the space-time network of oral storytelling, helping us again to make sense of the world around us. In part it is a legitimate response to Yuval Harari's question: "...How can we prepare ourselves and our children for a world of ... unprecedented transformations and radical uncertainties...?"
World building creates a platform for multiple disciplines to work together in many languages, to share knowledge, and to create outcomes for immersion, evolution, and change. Traditionally, it's unfamiliar for us to work outside our own discipline, but it's fundamental to world building that it dissolves these boundaries. As this emerging discipline develops, it creates a multidisciplinary and agnostic platform for collaboration, and as a design platform it allows us to focus on building tangible outcomes.
In 2009 we collaborated with partners who were building a project for multiple participants who did not share a common language. By creating a shared visual

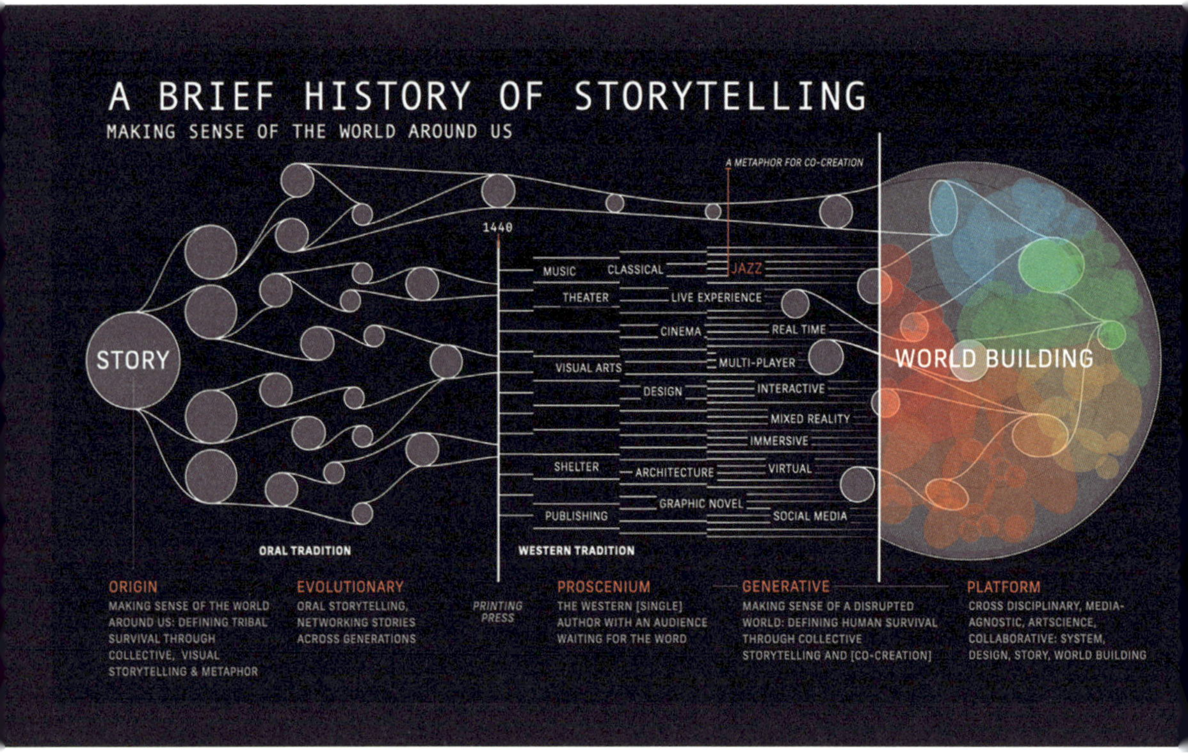

Figure 1: A brief history of storytelling
© *Alex McDowell*

"Humankind is facing unprecedented revolutions, all our stories are crumbling, and no new story has so far emerged to replace them. How can we prepare ourselves and our children for a world of such unprecedented transformations and radical uncertainties...?" Yuval Noah Harari, 2018, *21 Lessons for the 21st Century*

From the beginning of human history, storytelling developed to make sense of the world around us. Oral storytelling translates real-world experience, through metaphor, into cautionary tales or compelling mythology accessible to all. A growing network of storytellers passes these narratives within and between communities and across generations, where the aggregated and evolving knowledge becomes foundational to our ability to survive. But with the invention of the printing press in 1440, Western story tradition shifts to the single author, with narratives published in formats easy to distribute but locked in linear and non-evolutionary formats, whether in writing, art, architecture, or music. For the past 600 years, the West has become habituated to the proscenium, the author on stage, the rest of us in the audience.

World building provides a shared, collaborative platform for co-creation, for a world whose "unprecedented transformations and radical uncertainties" require a return to the tradition of woven narratives and non-linear distribution.

platform in the form of film, illustration, and animation, we allowed the participants to not only step inside a tangible vision of something that didn't yet exist, but also intimately understand what they were building because they were immersed in the outcome. Despite different languages and cultures, the client always asks that a vision transforms into an outcome. We can convene dozens of experts from multiple disciplines around the world-building table, but to collaborate they need to understand each other before they can become an influential force for change.

MS: We are already talking about two different applications of world building. In movies, for the development of fictional but coherent worlds, and in real-life situations for, for example, the collaborative development of possible futures. Let's stay in the domain of the real for a moment. How far do you think you can move into the future without losing people in the process?

AMD: When we step into the future it is fictional by definition, but in world building, whether for movies or to create real-world change, it has to be based in a deeply researched reality. So, one of the processes of world building is an intricate dive into all the factors that connect to make a world real. To first explain our approach to the real, let me use a movie! In the film *Minority Report*, unusually, there was no script at the start of production, and the usual framework of a linear narrative was not there to build from. But because the director was Steven Spielberg, he asked us to build a world that they could pull the script from.
In film, regardless of what the script describes, the designer needs to dive deep past the descriptions laid out in the linear narrative into all possible versions of that world to create the narrative design that most truthfully frames the story and the characters. When we design a movie, we don't know where the camera is going to look, or where the actors are going to move; by building a spherical world we know that any possible narrative will be

supported. The film audience must completely subscribe to the vision. They cannot be taken out of the world at any time, so the interior logic of the world is important. Every aspect of a world is connected to another. Actions reverberate throughout, whether the world you're building flows through the past, present, or future. What matters is that it shares a coherent set of rules and logic that allows any kind of narrative to be spun out from it. Everything has a place in the world.
The real world makes the same demands. A holistic system like world building will frame the strategic action while also reflecting the intricate network of human needs, breadth of conditions, variables, and possible outcomes in the time and space of each unique set of provocations. We need experts, stakeholders, and inhabitants to help us gain knowledge of every world we are building, so we can develop the highest level of intricate detail. We have worked with hundreds of different people with their own areas of expertise, everything from mobility to weapons, from advertising systems to furniture and new technologies, to earth sciences, biology, anthropology, media, manufacturing, politics, urban development, architecture, mapping, language... All of those elements rely on us to gather information and then bring it back to the hub. This kind of storytelling navigates within gathered knowledge to discover the pathways of the stories that evolve from the inhabitants of that world.

MS: What about disruptions? From your explanations, one might assume that the worlds you have created are coherent, without upheaval. But we know that our world is not without disruptions, for example, the pandemic. What does it take for people to find your future worlds plausible?

AMD: Plausibility is always determined by the strength and depth of the human narrative. The diverse narratives motivated by any world are how you first test the world. Disruption is an inevitable by-product when investigations are prompted or directed by diverse and opinionated sources.
The real world integrates coherence and disruption. I think of our story development process as a constant negotiation between predictability and upheaval. Imagine you are driving on a road through a small town. The town is solid, it is made of architecture with history, footprint, materials that

we have researched before we set out. The road is a constant, the characteristics of the vehicle and the way you drive are subject to rules. At high level, the human behavior in the town tracks over years without much change. But from your car you can see or imagine a disparity of wealth, arguments and escalating violence, a new birth with all its unpredictability, the impact of an earthquake, cultures clashing, or integrating, and disease. Everything is defined by the human narratives flashing past your eyes and senses; at ground level, chaos and logic go hand-in-hand.
We need to build credibility for the world before that detailed level of investigation can answer our questions: How will this develop? How will that transform? How does that evolve? What if? Why not? We have to take the same steps in any kind of storytelling when we want to engage a human audience; we have to allow them to believe in it absolutely. Whether it is an unfamiliar reality, science fiction or fantasy, it has to have a coherent core.

MS: Logic and consistency seem clear to me, especially with regard to the question of details, particularly in films. The question that now arises for me and that is familiar from the real world is that of acceptance. What do I mean by that? We know from architecture that, when designers have very precise ideas about the future, be it in the form of urban utopias or the like, people often don't see themselves in this future. In other words, it is the designer's future, but not the one that the people concerned might imagine. How do you see this?

AMD: I think that the processes are identical. What is common is that you have people at the center, and you are not following single stories. I'd argue that the failed utopian cities are often, maybe always, the product of a single author. There's no linear narrative in architecture (except perhaps in the architect's mind), or the street, or in nature, and there's no linear narrative in developing a world. A film may portray a linear narrative but it is within a spherical world, and it needs that holistic context to create an immersive experience for the audience. And we know that that world could support many different stories. If it has had the time and resources to be dense, deep, and broad enough there are hundreds of different stories to be told within it.
In that sense, although Steven Spielberg didn't know what he wanted to do with the world, rather than preempting it all in a script he was able to enter a future Washington DC and all it provoked as it developed, and prototype the ways in which the yet unbuilt world would work to support his narrative.
Similarly, in the real world, whatever the scale and challenges that you are being presented with, you must assume that the core of the story will work from multiple different viewpoints and behave differently for different people.
The way we understand the world is by interrogating the needs of people who are going to live in it, or their children, or what their imagination can conjure. Then we can say to our partner client that these people you want to engage in your vision, these are their expectations. This is the new context of the world and how your product will reverberate throughout their lives. And we can give you feedback on a future that doesn't yet exist because we have already lived in it. We can collectively understand how to step inside a time-space that does not yet exist. To achieve that, our work is to understand the framework in which these human stories might exist and understand the individual and disparate human needs. We can't know what disruptors will come. What we do know is that disruption is a part of the weave of development and can be core to strengthening believability.

Bolko von Oetinger (BVO): How would you compare your approach to traditional market research, because in market research people could go to Panama City or to Chicago, and they could look for risks of heat or risks of tornadoes? They would probably get all the data and statistics. In addition, they could develop a story on how life will develop in these cities. So, what's the difference from your approach?

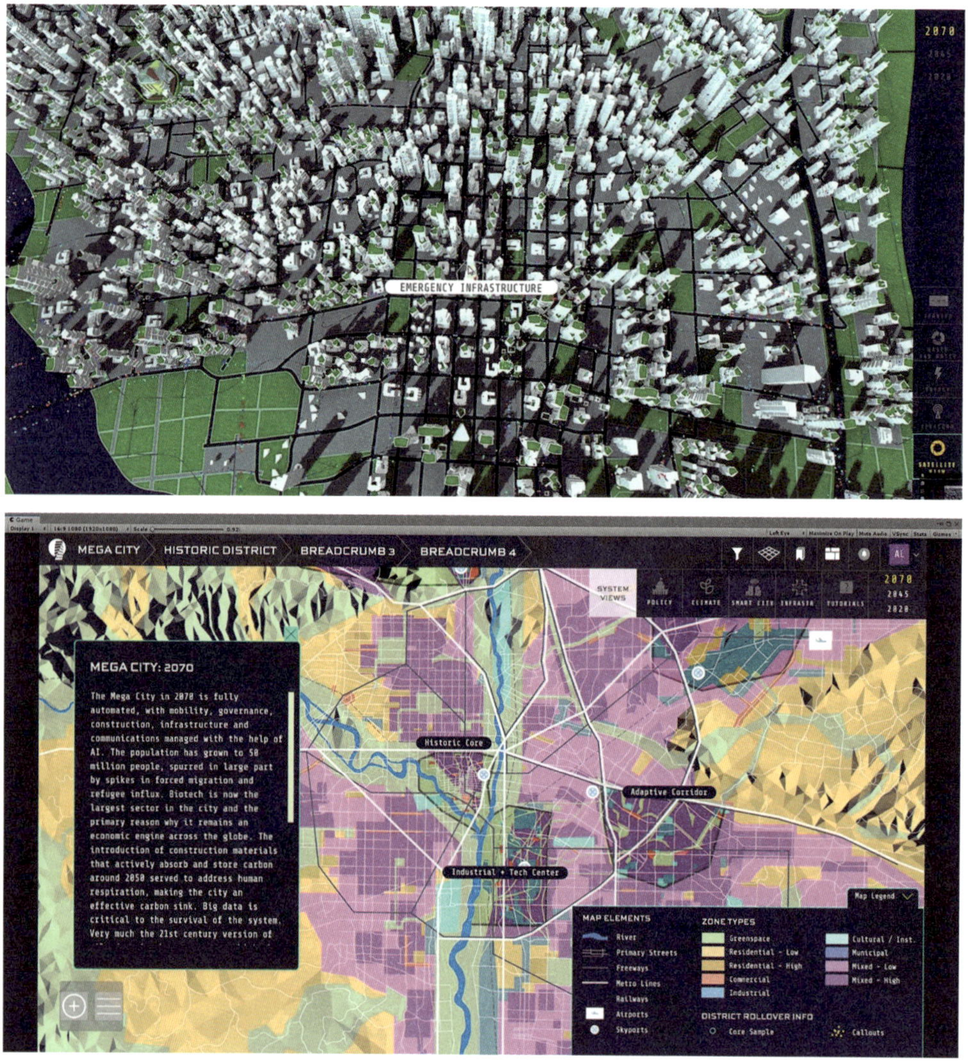

Figure 2-5: Caption ASCE (American Society of Civil Engineers) project: Future World Vision
© image courtesy of the American Society of Civil Engineers

For the American Society of Civil Engineers project "Future World Vision," the choice of a game engine platform as the basis for the exploration of a future city by student engineers allows an interactive integration between world building, engagement with plausible futures, and shared experience. Within the Unity game model, the user begins to move through the scales of the city, from the Global View, to the City View. At this level, tags respond to interactive choices of infrastructural systems. The viewer remains autonomous, able to "fly" over the city and respond to data from multiple viewpoints.

At the subsequent level, the narrative of the city becomes apparent. The user gains deeper access and connection to the aspects and issues throughout the city via the context of storytelling.
At the same time, the experience is contextualized with levels of accessible data, at this scale based on the data's impact on different zones of the city.

As the user descends into the city, different categories and levels of data become accessible through the lens of three future time periods. Accessible for each analysis are narrative, informed context, and the ability for the user to comment.

The highest level of detail, the human scale, is the “Street Corner.” Because this project was designed to prototype urban futures in 50- and 75-year futures, the insights delivered in relation to changing conditions in climate, infrastructure, urban planning, land use, construction, and materials can be best appreciated through the human lens. It points to the multiple connections within the ecosystem of the city that impact the daily reality of the population, in the same way as a street corner gives a snapshot of the intersection of inhabitants and infrastructure.
These micro-environments give data-driven forecasts and insight into macro-city trends while remaining accessible and empathetic in a way that traditional methods of collecting and distributing data in urban planning do not.

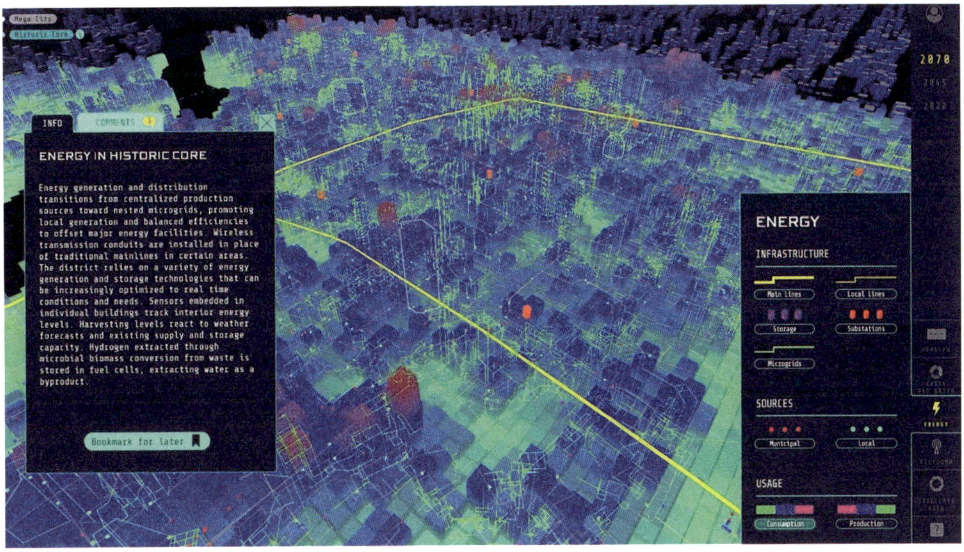

AMD: Again, storytelling is at the heart of it because it demands a relationship with the human at street level and an empathetic understanding of the factors that drive social groups, communities, or individuals, rather than the extraction of high-level data and the application of this to the 200-page analysis and report. Storytelling allows human narratives to evolve and listens to them, and world building projects those human narratives into the distant- or near-future to understand the ways in which those stories will play out. World building develops an understanding of data as empathy.

We recently completed a project about the future of civil engineering, where we were initially brought in after a "global strategy consulting firm" had delivered a futurecasting report. We suggested to the client that a report based on data and statistics might not produce an accurate vision of the future, partly because instead of assuming disruption it's following trends. It works very well at a high level but extracting data from different areas and then assimilating them into giant stacks of spreadsheets, text documents, post-it notes, and PowerPoints does not tell you about the stories that drive the world.

In the project that developed from that discussion with the American Society of Civil Engineers, representing more than 160,000 members, we created a set of immersive, narrative environments built in a game engine that allows hundreds of people and their stories to represent the future. The ways in which people behave could be examined as a living breathing system. And that system could be disrupted. We built an interactive platform that provokes undergraduate students to proactively make changes and see how they reverberate. We're connecting to a city as a living organism. That's the fundamental difference between world building and market research; once you're embedded in it, it becomes evolutionary. You can come back to it repeatedly and have the narrative lenses in place to extrapolate 25, 50, or 75 years into the future and thread back to see it reverberate in the present, at multiple scales, answering questions.

Provoked by the Alaska State Department of Education, Our Future Ancestors asks "What if Our learning systems reflected Our community and culture?" This story-gathering website project, guided by Experimental Design's studio and executed largely by Inuit designers, has developed a new platform for the voices of Alaskan Indigenous tribes who have used their cellphones to write, narrate, capture, and geolocate their stories about Indigenous education locally and across Alaska. From the network of 229 tribal villages and 23 languages, there are over 500 stories (and growing) that respond to the core question.

Addressing both the future and a deep cultural history, individual stories accumulate as an expanding narrative space that the community owns as a living system. We design this system to be a self-sufficient tool in the hands of the community, one that continues to develop with an ever-deepening accessible set of lenses that can now start to drive that future vision of education. A global repository of stories shared for the first time across a unique culture becomes a different kind of analytic or quantifiable data that does not conflict but supports the narrative and those recounting it.

What do humans need? How do we connect to the actual requirement or engagement of people in their own future and in their own narrative? There is an enormous repository of data contained in the human condition that can be accessed in tight vertical slices that reveal daily lives and their development told through hundreds of cyclical stories. These narratives impact their environment and, in turn, their environment impacts them.

MS: Let us briefly summarize: World building is now being applied by you in two, if not three, different ways. On the one hand, you create a future world with experts, which is then populated by others, such as Steven Spielberg with characters such as Tom Cruise in his story. On the other hand, you interview people, such as the Indigenous people in Alaska, and use their stories to create the world they want. How do you manage to take an essential step into the future? In the latter case, are they not calling up what is already known?

AMD: There's no fixed solution or fixed outcome. What is known is just a part of the arc into multiple pathways into the future, like the sankofa bird that flies forward while looking backwards, its past drives its future. If a world works, it allows you to enter it from different viewpoints. As soon as we step into this five-dimensional container of volumetric space, time, and the flow of stories, all those narratives coexist and interconnect. I can look at myself or my grandparents or those not yet born running through that world and see how it impacts them or myself.
The fact is that we don't deal with fixed worlds. There will constantly be disruptors in this world, but there are frameworks as large as containers within which they operate.

MS: Would you agree that the difference between your understanding of world building and scenarios is that you create a container in which different kinds of stories can develop? Furthermore, you look at this world with a holistic view and back it up with emotionally appealing visuals.

AMD: Yes, it's a holistic view. The container of a world is based on deep research that is at least a third of the work of any project because, unless we know the world intimately, we can't start to build it. Then we have to determine the best way to visually present it.

MS: So it's the visual/tangible that immerses people in the story, is that where you see the difference from scenarios?

AMD: Our work is to allow people to step inside an experiential world, to live in it and understand it holistically. We're no longer viewing from the outside. We're building the world and then viewing it from the inside; from a human viewpoint. The focus is less on the visuals than on the full range of tangible, empathetic, sensory movement through the world that we can experience as participants because we are given the keys and prompts to enter the world.
If you allow your imagination the freedom to believe this world exists, then you can step inside it and imagine yourself inside it, and then you can begin to understand it. We're putting the onus on the client to help us build the world, partly because they own the context, they know their vision much better than we do, but also so they can understand how the world relates to them, directly. We are saying that we will work together to build a world based on the knowledge that you the client have and on the capabilities that we the storytellers have. But it's only going to work if it's believable enough to live within it and to understand the difference between that future-present world and your world in the present.
We say that you extrapolate forward in order to thread back to the present. When we're building these worlds, we are being asked to reframe the present through storytelling. It comes back to the idea of the holistic. There is no single scenario. Every scenario connects to another to reflect the complexity of the world around it and to become a system that can produce anything to reflect that world. If you can imagine it, you can build it.
We often use the metaphor of a street corner in the city because if you stand on any street corner and survey it you can understand it at human scale. Data analysis, scenario planning, are high level at best, and you are never stepping inside the human experience. Our methodology is to understand the language at the center through the integration of, and immersion in, the stories. We understand that if we step outside our front door there is a network of relationships within the context of where we live. And if we set that up for many places, whether it's in different cities, or on two different street corners, or in districts inside the city, then we're getting an intimate knowledge of each intricate and intimate set of relationships and how they all connect to one another. They are vibrant and always evolving. Scenario planning isn't going to create the world. The world must be built first.

BVO: In the world building process, you describe the world in the singular, just one world. Take *Minority Report* as an example; given the ambiguity of the data, you might have come up with several different worlds. So, how do you manage the process of one or several worlds?

AMD:
I guess I'd differentiate between multiple choices within the context of a single world and different worlds. In *Minority Report*, for example, we were making different choices within the context of a single set of parameters, a single world. Every world is a container for multiple layers of narratives. These layers may start as self-contained and distinct, but they become robust because they develop conflicting interactions that have to exist under a single set of underlying rules. In fact, the more ambiguity or conflicting data there is, the more the world develops longevity and can deliver richer outcomes. The world evolves a foundation of holistic logic by being widely interrogated, which means that conflicting viewpoints reinforce its ability to support their demands.
As an example, and a metaphor: If we were to develop an urban planning model for a client, we would look at the vast number of narratives that it has to support, balancing the often widely disparate requirements of its population with the reality of its infrastructure. This single world is perfectly capable of supporting countless outcomes. We talk of this as a series of verticals or street corners, whose stories can deliver consistent data whether interwoven or distinct.
It's another important part of the definition of world building. Within the logic and rules of a single world there are multiple nodes; you can investigate the bottom of the ocean, or you can send a rocket to Mars. The more you interrogate the world, the more interesting and useful it becomes. A world as a living system can be useful for decades. One can investigate a continuous range of different demands and find crystal clear solutions because they coexist within the framework of a coherent logical system.

MS: Back to the process. How does it actually work? You choose a time horizon, interview a number of people on the topic, and then go back to your office and develop the world extracted from the stories. When you're done, you present the world you've created to your client, right?

AMD: We need a broad range of expertise because we need to understand how this world works. A lot of the exciting work emerges when we get two or three experts together who've never considered the problem before and are forced to generate new ideas, while we are tracking and gathering data and identifying the missing knowledge that we know is out there but must be found. We provoke and try to disrupt the way people think about their everyday lives and working narratives because disruption is a fundamental part of our survival.
We're asking people to think from a different viewpoint. It's a part of our gathering process that we ask questions to change the way some of our experts support their own practice.

MS: Have you experienced any setbacks with your clients using this method? We know from scenario planning practice that when scenarios about the future are developed far away from the decision-makers, they don't catch on. In other words, because they were not part of the research, they could not rethink their mental models of the world in the way that you do in a long research process. Have you had any experience of this?

AMD: When I meet with a client, my introduction to the context of our work is that I know nothing and that they are essential partners. The client may not understand how to put the pieces together in a way to answer the questions that they're asking. But they are the experts, the intermediaries who own the knowledge that we need. We bring our expertise of crafting a translation from complexity into comprehension. When we start a project, we have no preconceptions. While we know nothing, everything we do opens new discoveries and more knowledge. Only by this kind of joint discovery can we get revelations from a client who is stepping into a world

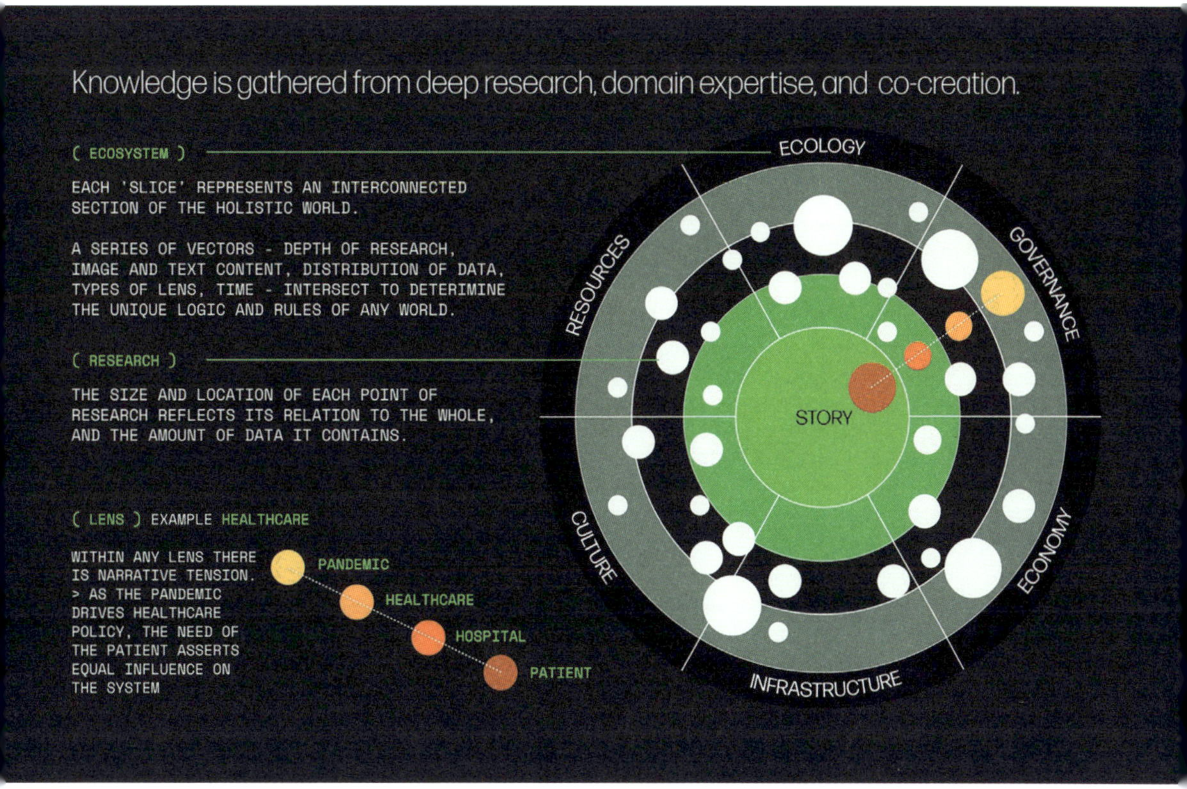

Figure 6: The Mandala © *image courtesy of Alex McDowell, Experimental Design, 2022*

The Mandala system is foundational to world building practice. It provokes the stakeholder to consider an intricate weave of interconnected factors in a defined and coherent world, and it stimulates deep research and triggers the spherical conditions that drive the logic that deliver the insights that frame the narratives that deliver the multiple outcomes of a defined brief.

The illustration demonstrates the basic framework of the Mandala for any world under development. Its concentric rings represent the scales of insight at City level, District level, and Street Corner level and the narratives each scale provokes and represents.

At Street Corner level, the lived experiences of the inhabitants—their stories—are as fundamental to the data landscape as the metrics of their environments. For world building, this balance emphasizes that qualitative data from stories complements quantitative environmental data.

Figure 7: Volvo "ROAM"
© *image courtesy of Volvo, 2023*

In an evolving collaboration with Volvo, we envision a near future where, instead of producing vehicles, the company produces *safety*, worldwide. This provocation initially led us to a broad sweep of social media, gathering narratives connected to the vehicles but in cities that are in some form or another hard for cars to negotiate. The investigation uses the enthusiasm for the company's values around safety as a Trojan horse to dive into a discussion of the need for safety in cities that are fundamentally unsafe. ROAM produced globally networked and unique "street corner" stories that provide inspiration for a reimagined future where safety is recentered and globally distributed. It delivers powerful new stories on a company-facing website densely packed with interviews and fictional social media posts.

they didn't know existed. Their participation in the building of the world gives us important information that steers the way that world develops.

MS: What you do is a kind of translation service, a translation of stories heard into visuals and tangibles, right? This approach is very reminiscent of the work of architects, whose results are often very different despite the same underlying starting points. Let's think of the functionalist city Brasilia or, in contrast, the liveliness of New York. How do you ensure that you don't paternalistically counsel a particular solution or future?

AMD: The failure of Brasilia and other utopian cities are fascinating subjects for world building. How do you make any client's metaphoric vision of a "utopian city" into an achievable success?
In 2016 I met with Kilian Kleinschmidt who had only recently left his position as "mayor" of Za'atari refugee camp, which opened in 2012 and quickly became the largest camp for Syrian refugees in the world. He asked a fundamental but unsolvable question. Why are refugee camps not the future of cities?
Through the lens of world building practice, we need to understand the relations between the elements that shape the universe of a refugee camp: geography, biology, migration, culture, politics, architecture, psychology, the multiplicity of interwoven narratives, and how the elements interact at different scales, redefining the limits of design and narrative as a tool to comprehend and fundamentally change our world.
World building enables us to sculpt imagination into existence but also to comprehend the complexity of our world. Focusing on the idea that refugee camps could become cities of the future, our grand challenge is to make it possible for world building to address the dynamics, relationships, and intricacies of a generic near-future refugee camp. Could a cross-disciplinary group of experts set about creating a world that would disrupt and reinvent urban development from the ground up, and literally place essential human stories at the center of provoking change?
Can we create a viable world by retrofitting a history stemming from a future before it exists?

MS: Thank you, Alex, for this insightful conversation!

The interview was reorganized and rewritten by Margaret Chandra Kerrison.

FUTURECASTING WITH MATTER

Photo: Erich Goldmann

ELLIOTT P. MONTGOMERY

SENIOR STRATEGIC FORESIGHT
SPECIALIST, AUTODESK
NEW YORK, UNITED STATES

IN PRAISE OF VACUUMS

The ideas of a researcher at the National Center for Atmospheric Research and a ten-year-old in Bushwick Brooklyn may be vastly different, but their thoughts about futures can have striking similarities. In my countless collaborations on foresight with folks from these walks of life and many others, I've found people to be both excited and at the same time confused by the premise of futures; a terrain that's at the same time familiar and unreachable. In this text, I will respond to this paradox by proposing a process for bridging this gap. I make the case for inverting the common foresight practice of imagining futures first and then populating those futures with details and artifacts. I suggest practitioners attempt to visit futures by physically channeling the future through embodied movement and interactions before deciding on the details of such a future, in order to tacitly project its contents. I'll put forth a scaffold of elements necessary to do this work well. I call it "Tacit Foresight."

Over the years I've spent working in foresight, I've had the privilege of discussing futures in a multitude of contexts, and five common ideas have surfaced time and time again. From these conversations, I've developed a working definition of what futures are and what they do.

Futures are social constructs of a later time, that help people do some or all of the following:

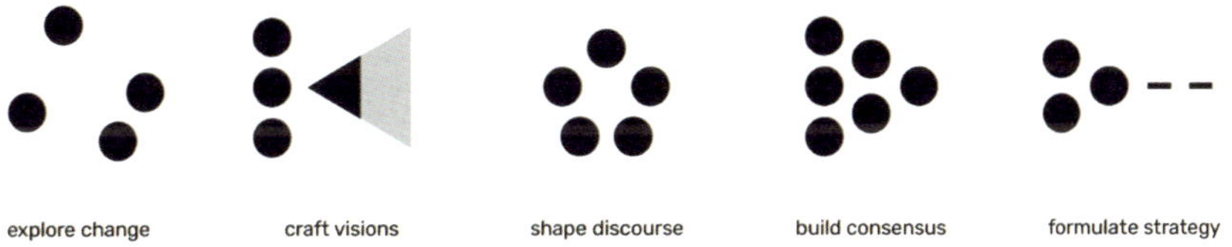

Figure 1
© Elliott P. Montgomery

People use futures to explore change, and this could be in the context of research labs, think tanks, or movies & entertainment, science fiction, etc.

In cyclical fashion, existing futures can serve as the basis for crafting new visions; through reference, juxtaposition, critique, extension, projection, etc., into unimagined futures, often crystalized in concrete ways.

People use futures to frame conversations, provoke new types of engagement, teach and learn in educational settings as well as in communities and organizations.

People use futures to convince, coalesce, evangelize, advocate, and energize groups in a certain direction. This can be seen in political contexts and lobbying efforts, but also in grassroots movements and innate social behavior.

While futures are not strategies, they can help people through the use of approaches like strategic foresight, and offer insights that drive toward strategies or plans.

If futures are indeed social constructs, their range is then determined by knowledge and imaginative capacity. Futures are shaped by the subjective limits of people's ability to envision what happens next. Futures hinge on people's experience of plural pasts and alternate interpretations of our present. People rarely hold ideas of futures as one crisp time horizon but, rather, as a blurry range ahead.

Narrative Futures Cones

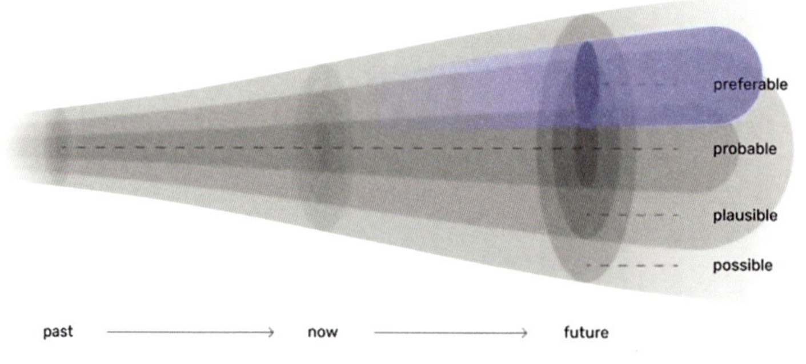

Figure 2
© Elliott P. Montgomery

I've attempted to visualize some of these understandings of futures, to provide an alternative to earlier visual representations that suggest a singular present, linear past, and infinitely expanding futures that terminate cleanly at some specific juncture. I've developed the Narrative Futures Cones visualization, which emphasizes plurality and humanity in a social understanding of futures.

I've synthesized these premises out of my foresight practice, teaching, and research, but my work is also informed and influenced by these same premises. I'll describe several projects which illustrate ways this circular relationship exists. I'll conclude this essay by situating some of this work as a proposition for an emerging form of practice.

Provocations for Times Square

This project was a collaboration with the Times Square Alliance in New York City, MFA Transdisciplinary Design Students at Parsons School of Design, and my colleague Radha Mistry. The project started in Times Square, a district that holds powerful social significance on top of a complex past. The "crossroads of the world" is a commercial icon and a cultural center that stands on a former red maple swamp. It was called the "thieves' lair" in the 1800s and considered seedy and dangerous through the 1970s. Today, as urban centers bend under driving forces including ecological crises, changing forms of work, retail, culture, and economic disparity, the crossroads will continue to transform. In this project, our group worked with the Times Square district as a context to explore ecological change, new economies, and social shifts.

The work started with collective signal scanning, followed by focused research on a specific issue and, subsequently, fabricating hypotheticals. Groups of students developed propositions through experiential and situational media, including simulations, enactments, and artifacts. The groups' work took on elements of role play, live action, and immersive or pop-up qualities, moving out of the gallery context that speculative design has traditionally occupied.

The work culminated as a "tour of futures" through Times Square. The "tourists"—Times Square Alliance employees, university faculty, and curious onlookers—were invited to walk through the district and, every so often, encounter an instance of the future, intermingled with the present.

One group was role-playing as a startup offering subdermal implants that capture the body's unused thermal energy as a currency that can be passed on to children as an heirloom. Legacy Energy's fictional technology suggested that corporations might be willing to offset your living expenses in exchange for onboarding the implanted device.

Another group was recruiting laborers to train for mining projects on the moon—suggesting that the facade of glamor surrounding space travel will succumb to earthly wealth and income gaps and the associated divide between "essential workers" and the leisure class.

A third group was conducting scent surveillance—ensuring safety by using robotic smell technology.

Figure 3
© Elliott P. Montgomery

Figure 4
© Ella Rocker, Anna Pierce, Cheenar Shah

One group was posing as urban biologists monitoring the breeding grounds of GMO plastic-eating insects that were being introduced to New York City.

And yet another group was taking readings of emotional health to grant people shopping privileges—those with riskier emotional profiles were not admitted to high-end and family-friendly shopping areas.

After the project, I talked with students about the experience. One of them told me that the most difficult part of the project was just conceptualizing a fully furnished future. Over the course of the project, the students traveled to Times Square several times to try out versions of their ideas. This particular student said that the first few times they went to test their prototypes, they couldn't "get to the future." After several attempts though, they hit an "imagination flow state." They reached a future and, once they were there, they were able to live in it, move around in it, and this was necessary to understand it and bring members of the public with them. They were able to experience what their future "felt" like, and what they needed to let go of from the present.

Figure 6
© *Aloma Antao, Natalie Chester, Camille Girard, Jeremy Siwik*

Figure 5: © *Giselly Mejia Zapata, Maria Otero, Cas Esteve, Jasmine Jensen, Jungmin Lee*

Figure 7
© *Shanshan Duan, Kenichi Kawamura, Giulia Donatello, Ye Tian*

The Extrapolation Factory—99¢ Futures

For over a decade I've been running a practice called The Extrapolation Factory with my collaborator and co-founder Chris Woebken.

The practice is a research studio through which we develop and test new modes of engagement with design and participatory futures. Our first project was called 99¢ Futures. We asked a group of willing participants to picture the merchandise one might find in a dollar store in a future, and then, going through a custom four-step process, we collectively materialized those artifacts and stocked them on shelves in an actual dollar store in Brooklyn, NY, for shoppers to find.

The Extrapolation Factory—Alternative Unknowns

Another project I did through The Extrapolation Factory was conducted in collaboration with New York City's Emergency Management Office.

In Alternative Unknowns, Chris and I brought together a group of designers and practitioners to imagine how New York might prepare for a future emergency situation. This was in 2015 and, in a meeting with our counterparts at Emergency Management, they said they'd like us to explore the implications of a pandemic. In order to envision what might possibly happen, we decided to create a simulation room in which we would try out different approaches to dealing with a future pandemic.

Our recruited designers and practitioners were invited to create speculative objects that might offer new ways of managing our fictional pandemic. The collection of speculative objects was placed within the simulation room, ready for use. We then worked with four trained actors to improvise through our pandemic, each time interpreting the speculative objects as turning points in the vignette. We ran through the same pandemic four times, each one was improvised in real time without a plan for where they'd go. Some outcomes were positive, but others were tragic. We wrapped up the project with a roundtable discussion with the staff from Emergency Management to figure out what we'd just done, and what they might take away from the experience.

The Extrapolation Factory—Metro Test Zones

The last project I'll share was also developed at The Extrapolation Factory. This project challenged what we think of as parks in New York City, invoking the countless neglected medians, grass patches, and other green urban commons that aren't considered parks. Regardless, these sites provide important respite, pathways, food, materials, and shelter for residents. In this project, we attempted to focus on the changing nature of NYC's green urban commons.

We gathered a group of 20 subject matter experts and community leaders and invited them to work through a process to imagine how the green urban commons in NYC could be different in our futures. With our group of landscape architects, biologists, journalists, actors, and employees of the NYC mayor's office, we spent a day developing nine different loose concepts, and then reconvened several weeks later.

Between these two meetings, my team built an outdoor simulator environment and assembled a collection of props. When the group returned, we entered the space, and through improvisational role play, we attempted to live in each of our nine variations of our futures, trying to feel out the futures in an embodied manner. Each one unfurled in interesting and unexpected ways and allowed our futures to be manifested through our behaviors and our interactions with each other, with artifacts, and with the space, as opposed to having a fully-formed future pre-defined for us to experience.

Tacit Foresight

Elise Boulding once said, "We cannot work towards a betterment we cannot imagine" and practitioners often take this stance in futures; to build a better future, one needs to imagine it first.

For a long time, I was convinced of this, but I'd like to question the logic. Some of Boulding's contemporaries were inverting this paradigm. The Situationists critiqued the capitalist use of stuff to mediate our social relations. They had the goal of creating novel situations that disrupted patterns of familiarity, seeking a "revolution of everyday life."

Around the same time, Franz Erhard Walther was situating the people engaging with his work as active agents. His work would only come to exist once it had been activated. His work's task was to empower those people who were engaging, breathing life into his vessels as they became the material. Walther and the Situationists were actually tapping into the ways human brains work. The brain predominantly processes abstract notions with the linguistic system, while concrete notions are processed with the sensorimotor system.

Following Boulding, foresight methods often lead practitioners to imagine futures first, and then populate those futures with details and artifacts. Only then is it possible to invite others to experience these futures. I want to make the case for the inverse approach, in which practitioners attempt to visit futures by physically channeling the future through embodied movement and interactions before deciding on the details of a future, in order to tacitly project the contents of a future.

Building on these observations of the past, on my years of experiments with Chris at The Extrapolation Factory and on lessons learned from teaching with Radha at The New School, I've surfaced four key insights which I'm proposing as a scaffold of elements necessary to do this work well.

I call it "Tacit Foresight."

Figure 8
© Elliott P. Montgomery

First, Tacit Foresight calls for voids. Voids are stripped-down spaces that eliminate the unwanted residue of our current moment, enabling participants to project a range of future contexts and situations. A void can simply be an empty room, or an elaborately constructed simulation space. What's important is that it satisfactorily frees participants from the imaginative confines of our current world long enough to channel what's inside. The second set of elements is the vessels. These are the proverbial containers onto which participants can project symbolism and multiple meanings, in real time. Vessels can be unrecognizable objects, placeholder items, or artifacts without strong social symbolism, allowing a participant to instantly envision the object serving any number of purposes that weren't predicted beforehand. Third, the Tacit Foresight approach calls for contributors to interject their perspectives, or voices. A Tacit Foresight exercise necessitates active invitations for participant construction and the co-creation of futures in real time. A simple microphone can easily serve as an invitation for participants to voice their perspective, but other solicitations of co-creative contribution will do. Fourth, the recipe calls for variations; the repeated attempts to move through futures with subtle differences in each round. This iterative repetition of interactions leverages our sensorimotor system in addition to our linguistic system, allowing for the development of new procedural memory as we channel possible futures into an embodied state.

I believe Tacit Foresight offers a new and useful way to invert participatory foresight processes, by animating futures as a way to begin imagining them, instead of the inverse. Tacit Foresight provides a complementary approach to the traditional work of staging foresight processes, which prioritizes elaborately plotting experiential futures before manifesting them.

Sometimes, it may just be necessary to visit a future first, and then work on imagining it.

TIME'S UP

LABORATORY FOR THE
CONSTRUCTION OF EXPERIMENTAL
AND EXPERIENTIAL SITUATIONS
LINZ, AUSTRIA

© Time's Up

EXPERIENTIAL INSIGHT: WHEN WE DO, WE UNDERSTAND

Suppose it is Monday and you have been requested to have some insights about Rome on Friday, for a discussion around lunchtime. Your work, domestic duties, and other responsibilities will be taken care of for the next three days, and you have two options: You can stay in a quiet hotel with a pile of books, travel guides, a complete collection of Fellini's films, and all the other media you want. Or you can get on the fast train, be there tonight, where a friend of a friend will show you around, including taking you to her cousin's wedding on Wednesday, then get back in time for the discussion on Friday.

Which of these will give you more insight? The reason we prefer to travel somewhere, rather than just read about it, is to get the ineffable experience of being there. The smells. Proprioception. The claustrophobia, the way rubbish bins work, how people breakfast—lunch—and dine, what happens on the streets, what happens almost out of sight. A documentary or a statistical analysis might have its place if we cannot join Sea Shepherd for a tour to the Antarctic Ocean or we need details of the fisheries' catches in the eastern Mediterranean, but insight is often well supported through direct experience.

This is the core understanding that *Experiential Futures* leverages. The experience of a possible future helps to create insight about the lived possibilities of that future. An experience can lead us to understand why, in spite of the numbers, the future being discussed does not match our values, our preferences, the life we wish to be living. Perhaps the smell of the air as it might be someday can help understand the life experience of living in a polluted city far more powerfully than the mere numbers (Superflux, 2017). Experience trumps data for impact.

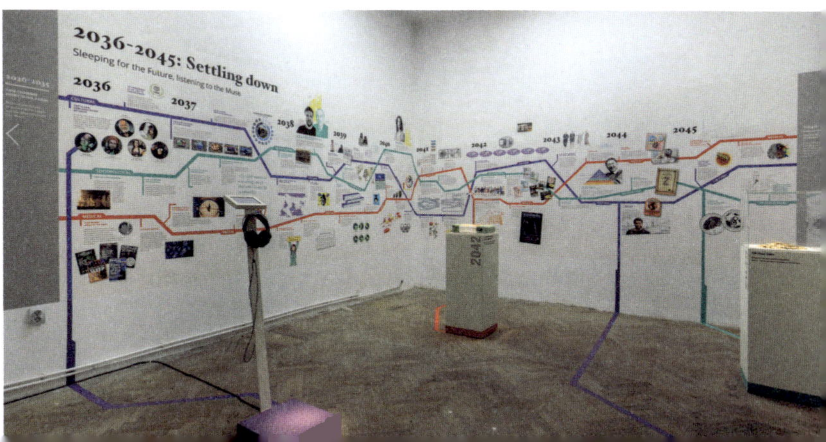

Figure 1:
Work Upside Down
© Roland Vaczi, 2021

Foresight / hindsight / insight

At the symposium, we enjoyed Alexander Mankowsky's question of "Where are your grandchildren in this scenario?" or even: Where are your grandparents? Where are the normal people, not the smart-suited C-suite apparent success stories but the actual stories of the actual us?

In our work, we focus on the everyday. The things normal people have, use, and live with. This is not to say that we are mundane or unexcited, although we gladly accept the term mundane for the type of futures we want to explore (Foster 2013). Everyday life, like the future, is where we (will) spend most of our lives. The futures of peak experiences are a lot less insightful than the futures of everyday life (Vaneigem, 1994).

In discussions of the future, there is often too much utopia or dystopia. Both are rightfully pooh-poohed, but utopian thinking offers a way to approach desire and experimental attitudes (Schaper Rinkel, 2020). Beauty can arise in the midst of horror. Even during the Holocaust/Shoah, love bloomed and desired children were created, despite the danger and futility of it all. We cannot avert our eyes from the climate catastrophe (Extinction Rebellion, 2019; IPCC, 2022), the destruction of oceanic and other ecosystems (Dryden and Duncan, 2022; Heinze et al., 2021), yet we at Time's Up want to create imaginations and experiences of lives that can be well lived in these scenarios. Our technique is to interweave dystopian and collapse scenarios with utopian, progressive, and even radical fragments: Ecosystem collapse necessitates universal societal basic services; energy decline demands wealth redistribution; the destruction of coastal living spaces affects rich and poor, creates awareness of the necessity for migration, and the welcoming of new neighbors, whether from the Netherlands or Namibia.

We remind ourselves and others that "we are no futurists" (Time's Up et al., 2023). We do not claim to have great futuring insights and robust techniques that are able to help organizations or individuals imagine and formulate plans, strategies, and even coherent visions for their futures. Whether our "no future" resonates with Jim Dator or the Sex Pistols is almost beside the point, except that this difference relates immediately to the questions of what we can know about the future as opposed to whether we are allowed to even imagine futurity for ourselves. We agree with the former (Dator, 1995) and demand that we, and anybody else who cares to, can and should have the ability to think out loud about possible and preferred futures. The likes of Margaret Thatcher have indoctrinated us with "TINA: There Is No

Alternative" and too many in society have come to accept this (Fisher, 2009), which is probably what the refrain "No future—No future—No future for you" from the Sex Pistols' "God Save the Queen" meant. The self-appointed Realists have worked out how the system works for them, and they claim that any other ideas are necessarily unrealistic; naïve, woolly-headed, or even insane. They want things to stay as they are because that is how they derive their success. And they have the power to enforce that, as the world continues its descent into imbalance and destruction, collapse and disruption.

Hegemonic power does not want uppity citizens calling its patterns of exploitation into question. It wants people who are happy with the choice architecture they have been supplied with (Trentmann, 2017) and who continue to follow the cynical advice that "no matter who you vote for, a politician wins." By merging restricted and designed choices with an awareness of the pointlessness of those choices (Coke or Pepsi?) all agency around activity is removed. The Malvina Reynolds song "Little Boxes" alludes to the re-creation of power differentials, scrabbling to be a little bit less far down in the heap. These structures work to shore up the power and arrogant comfort of those who find themselves at or near the top of the pile.

Futures Literacy is a core competency to escape these restrictions of choice architects, one of the tools with which to say "mu" to the questions posed. "Mu" is an un-asking of the question (Pirsig, 1974) and, as we know, many strengths are to be had in the asking of powerful questions (Vogt, Isaacs, & Brown, 2003) as opposed to the choice between two equally meaningless responses. Constructing processes and facilitating them as exercises to enable and encourage imaginative futures-thinking awakens an awareness of and desire to imagine further, to imagine harder (Bleecker, 2023). Futures Literacy enables us all to delve into more nuanced discussions than optimists or pessimists, who expect that things will go well or badly regardless of what they do. When we at Time's Up undertake a *futuring exercise*, we use those futures muscles to imagine the implications of actions, large and small, and to underscore our agency in making changes in the world. From passive optimism or pessimism, an active hope can emerge, enabling and encouraging action in the world (Macy and Johnstone, 2012). Futures Literacy, as we understand it, is the ability to imagine several possible trajectories for various parts of the world and to see them all as possible, or at least as equally worthy of being entertained. An old saying, often falsely attributed to Aristotle, notes that one mark of an educated mind is the ability to entertain an idea without necessarily believing it. This is one of the characteristics of a futures-literate mind. Entertaining several possibilities for possible futures, without believing any of them in particular, is a valuable skill. Being able to investigate and flesh out the details and intricacies of those scenarios to imagine what is worth fighting for and against. Recognizing which elements to encourage and which to let fade, is worthwhile. This is not to claim that scenarios fall into the good or the bad, and perhaps the ugly. Most scenarios, at least most of those that are relevant, will combine elements that are preferable and those that are not. The scenarios intertwine utopian strands that help mitigate, compensate for, or react against dystopian elements.

We sometimes even admit *there is no way out*. In 2022, Time's Up addressed this premise in perhaps one of the more tightrope experiences of our series of futuring exercises. We set the controls for the heart of the sun before swerving to make the comet trail curve, just in time. It is no cozy task to facilitate a group that is coming perceptibly close to tears or panic. As discussed above, we have always assumed a certain degree of collapse; perhaps not the Dark Mountain (Hine and Kingsnorth, 2009) level but at least the level of a Better Catastrophe (Boyd, 2023). The intermingling of utopian and dystopian, the dance above the chasm on a tightrope of humanity and socially progressive desire; this is where the realistic and more useful scenarios are likely to emerge. In this case, the relief as we swerved from collapse to adaptation was palpable.

Our work revolves around creating experiences of possible futures. One method uses the power of immersive physical narratives (Time's Up (ed.), 2014) as a way to create fragments of possible futures that can be explored as physical spaces. The other method involves facilitating workshops for interested groups where multiple scenarios are constructed and artifacts within these scenarios are imagined as part of a storyworld embedded with character and structure. Both of these methods invoke the combined approaches of structure and imagination that Julian Bleecker identifies as the main forces for experiential futures (Bleecker, 2023). When structure and imagination work simultaneously, they can intertwine in a dance that allows deep insight to emerge.

Figure 2: Medusa Bar, Turnton Series
© *Elisa Unger, 2019*

Turnton imagines a world in 2047 (Time's Up, 2017). A world in which the implications of the careless misuse and manipulation of ecological systems have come home to roost, where a climate disaster is unavoidable and underway. In opposition, we propose that humanity responds to this ecological dystopia with sociopolitical utopian changes. Turnton is experienced as a walk-through future, an immersive installation, including spaces such as harborside bars, museums, public squares, travel agencies, factories, ships, laboratories, rehabilitation units, and flooded cellars.

We find ourselves in the year 2047, in the streets of the harbor of an indeterminate small coastal city somewhere in Europe called Turnton. Pollution levels have boomed, ocean ecosystems have collapsed, the land, the water, and the air are filled with poisons emitted a century ago. Climate change, the result of a decidedly lax response to warnings and evidence, has gained momentum: Weather extremes are commonplace, with floods, droughts, and the most severe storms we can imagine. The coastal regions have gone from being the beautiful playgrounds of the rich to dangerous abandoned zones suffering from rotting algae and the decomposing bodies of a few fish in the collapsing ecosystems as jellyfish and slimes take hold.

In Turnton, Time's Up imagines that humanity responds to this ecological dystopia with sociopolitical changes that appear utopian. We have developed a melding of several emergent positive opposition proposals to impede the ecological slide. We must take up the slogan “Change was our only chance” as something serious, something that is not just undertaken by small groups trying to “prove a point” but becomes normal, widespread behavior. Cooperation replaces Competition, the learned behavior of *homo economicus* morphs into *homo reciprocans*, the cooperative human. A world where the reality-denying mantras of neoliberalism and unconstrained growth are replaced by the maxims of mutualism, where free trade is moderated to support crucial social goals without falling into some nationalistic protectionism, where economics is about a better world and a better life.

Economic success focuses on satisfying human wants and needs in a way that is fair and respects resources, with quality of life and the common good as its goals. Sustainability in raw materials, energy and transport, trade, production, and work practices orbit around environmental protection, human rights, distribution fairness, and working standards. Thus, migration becomes a non-issue, transnational settlement and mobility are normal and well organized, new arrivals are welcomed and included as new neighbors. Not only ecological but also cultural, social, and economic diversity is recognized as an asset. Nothing is too big to fail, and experiments are welcome. Solutions that were ridiculed in the last decades as being politically, economically, or technically utopian, unimplementable or naïve, have gained the upper hand in Turnton.

The image of the docklands, the city of Turnton, and the surrounding society in this speculative future is incomplete; not a prognosis, only a proposal. We mix and match concepts and signals that we know with a playful portion of fabulation and poetic speculation to obtain a possibility worth contemplating. We look into the preferable and not just the pessimistic probable, imagine a future worth living despite all that might befall us, a good life for all. We invite an audience to join us in imagining more of the incomplete picture.

When we look at Turnton, we clearly see the levels of Stuart Candy and Jake Dunagan's *Experiential Futures Ladder* (2016). Let us discuss it as if it were a linear process. We start with the *Setting*, the *when* and *what* that is being examined for a futuring development. We develop a *Scenario* using various futuring techniques. Then we determine a *Situation* in which the future scenario can unfold and thus be experienced. These situations are built. We then build the *Stuff* that is designed and created for the experience. The menu at the Medusa Bar in Turnton is part of the *Stuff* in the *Situation* of the bar, in a *Scenario* developed from a *Setting* of European coastal life in 2047. However, we see that there is a stage that is implicit in their work that is valuable to expand upon. *Storyworld* is the result of the process of fleshing out the space between a scenario and the situations in which we will create experiences.

Figure 3: Town Square, Turnton Series
© *Elisa Unger, 2019*

We understand storyworld to be the result of *worldbuilding*. Regarded as a vital part of futures understanding (Raven and Elahi, 2015; Stackelberg and McDowell, 2015), worldbuilding can, however, lead to the problems of top-down world determination and corporate-friendly imposed futures of commercial foresight (Bleecker et al., 2022) or the "stomping foot of nerdism," where worldbuilders feel the need to share their entire world (Harrison, 2007). It is the responsibility of designers and practitioners to ensure that these lurking dangers do not threaten the project.

Figure 4:
Adapted Experiential Futures Ladder
© Time's Up

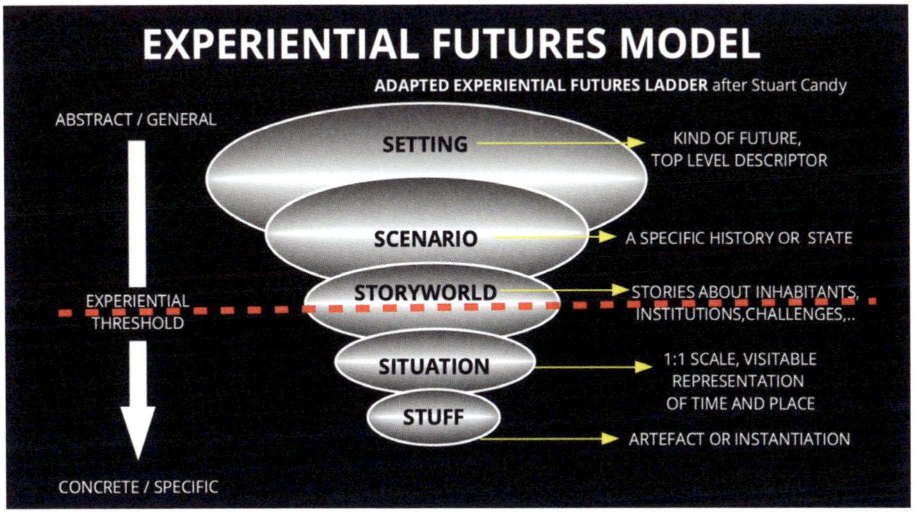

We use many techniques for worldbuilding. One technique we have repeatedly resorted to in our futuring exercises is based upon Matthew Richter's Four Cs (2004): Characteristics, Components, Characters, and Challenges. The *Characteristics* are the properties of the world: smell, feeling on the street, climate, political temperature, perceived levels of safety. *Components* are what make up the world, from tools and technologies to organizations and infrastructure. *Characters* are the people and personalities, perhaps including roles and jobs, artificial intelligences, talking whales. Lastly, *Challenges* include the things that are (still) hard, whether it be the climate catastrophe, the boredom of fully automated luxury communism, diseases, fossil fuel smugglers, etc. To these we have added the fifth C of *Competencies*, which we have found useful in terms of what people have learned to do. Sometimes we ask "Which competencies do characters have and which tools and components do they use to deal with the challenges emerging from the characteristics of their world?" We have many smaller questions to assist participants in thinking about these aspects.

These formal and almost didactic processes of storyworld creation are not meant to be prescriptive. Rather, they are meant to enable questions and thinking out loud among groups of participants in a futuring exercise. The question "So, who's got a good idea?" sets such high expectations that it paralyzes creative thought. Many facilitators will know the excited hubbub that accompanies open-thinking processes, where the excitement of exploration has overcome the fear of some idea not being good enough. When it works, no one knows who originally suggested an idea because it has been bounced around and molded by many in the group, so that it has no actual owner anymore.

We note that the experiential futures (experiental futures ladder) is by no means a linear process description. While we might decide a setting and develop one or more scenarios, the process of developing the storyworld will deepen the scenario and the stuff will enrich the storyworld, modify the situations, and deepen the scenario once again. Some practitioners even go so far as to start with the stuff, say a box of breakfast cereal, and develop from there to find a scenario within which the box makes sense, a form of futures archaeology.

The two experiences of futures, the immersive environment and the imagining process, are valuable and, in many senses, orthogonal and complementary. The experience of being in a scenario as an immersive "walk-through future" can make insights possible that are enabled by the lack of apparent objective distance. Surrounded by a possible future, immersed in a political rally (Candy, Dator, & Dunagan, 2006) or a verbal bar room tiff (Time's Up, 2017), the compulsion to say "this cannot happen" is reduced. Even if only as theater, it *is* happening. The experience of being facilitated through a creative and open-ended, even goal-free, imagination process, enables one to experience the simplicity yet the subtlety of creating imaginations of the future. Both of these experiences, we strongly believe, enable us to imagine, share, and then be able to create desired futures, not just for some, but for everyone.

Acknowledgement

This text is part of Curiouser and Curiouser, cried Alice: Rebuilding Janus from Cassandra and Pollyanna (CCA), an art-based research project from Design Investigations (ID2) at the University of Applied Arts Vienna and Time's Up. It is supported by the Program for Arts-based Research (PEEK) of the Austrian Science Fund (FWF): AR561.

References

Bleecker, J. 2023. ***It's Time to Imagine Harder: This Reader's Guide to The Manual of Design Fiction (Part 1 The Artifact).*** Near Future Laboratory.

Bleecker, J., Foster, N., Girardin, F., & Nova, N. 2022. ***The Manual of Design Fiction.*** Near Future Laboratory.

Boyd, A. 2023. ***I Want a Better Catastrophe: Navigating the Climate Crisis with Grief, Hope, and Gallows Humor.*** New Society Publishers.

Candy, S., Dator, J., & Dunagan, J. 2006. ***Four Futures for Hawaii 2050.*** Paper presented at the "Hawaii 2050: Charting a Course for Hawaii's Sustainable Future" Kick-off Summit at the Dole Cannery, Honolulu, August 26. Accessed online https://www.researchgate.net/publication/253641086_Four_Futures_for_Hawaii_2050. Viewed May 20, 2024.

Candy, S., & Dunagan, J. 2016. The Experiential Turn. ***Human Futures,*** December: 26-29.
Dator, J. 1995. ***What Futures Studies Is, and Is Not.*** Hawaii Research Center for Futures Studies.

Dryden, H., & Duncan, D. 2022. Climate Disruption Caused by a Decline in Marine Biodiversity and Pollution. ***International Journal of Environment and Climate Change,*** October: 3413-3435. Extinction Rebellion. 2019. ***This Is Not A Drill: An Extinction Rebellion Handbook.*** Penguin UK.

Fisher, M. 2009. ***Capitalist Realism: Is There No Alternative?*** Zero Books.

Foster, N. 2013. The Future Mundane [Column]. ***Core77***, October 7. Accessed online https://www.core77.com/posts/25678/The-Future-Mundane. Viewed January 22, 2024.

Harrison, M. J. 2007. Very Afraid [Blog post]. ***Uncle Zip's Window***, January 27. Accessed online https://web.archive.org/web/20071013105409/http://uzwi.wordpress.com/2007/01/27/very-afraid/. Viewed January 22, 2024.

Heinze, C., Blenckner, T., Martins, H., Rusiecka, D., Döscher, R., Gehlen, M., Gruber, N., et al. 2021. The Quiet Crossing of Ocean Tipping Points. ***Proceedings of the National Academy of Sciences***, 118 (9): e2008478118.

Hine, D., & Kingsnorth, P. 2009. ***Uncivilisation: The Dark Mountain Manifesto.*** The Dark Mountain Project.

IPCC. 2022. ***Climate Change 2022: Impacts, Adaptation, and Vulnerability.*** Cambridge University Press.

Macy, J., & Johnstone, C.. 2012. ***Active Hope: How to Face the Mess We're in without Going Crazy.*** New World Library.

Pirsig, R. M. 1974. ***Zen and the Art of Motorcycle Maintenance: An Inquiry into Values.*** Morrow.

Raven, P. G., & Elahi, S. 2015. The New Narrative: Applying Narratology to the Shaping of Futures Outputs. ***Futures***, 74 (November): 49-61.

Richter, M. 2004. Structured Sharing - 4Cs. In Thiagarajan, S. (ed.), ***Play for Performance: Seriously Fun Activities for Trainers, Facilitators, Performance Consultants, and Managers.*** Workshops by Thiagi, Inc. Accessed online https://thiagi.net/archive/www/pfp/IE4H/march2004.html. Viewed January 22, 2024.

Schaper Rinkel, P. 2020. ***Fünf Prinzipien für die Utopien von Morgen.*** Picus Verlag.

Stackelberg, P. von, & McDowell, A. 2015. What in the World? Storyworlds, Science Fiction, and Futures Studies. ***Journal of Futures Studies,*** 20 (2): 25-46.

Superflux. 2017. The Future Energy Lab [Blog post]. ***Superflux.*** Accessed online https://superflux.in/index.php/work/futureenergylab/. Viewed January 22, 2024.

Time's Up. 2017. *Turnton Docklands*.

Time's Up. 2022. ***Beautiful Gestures & Utopic Fragments*** [Blog post]. ***LOOSE DIARY,*** April 25. Accessed online https://loosediary.wordpress.com/2022/04/25/beautiful-gestures-utopic-fragments/. Viewed January 22, 2024.

Time's Up (ed.). 2014. ***PARN: Physical and Alternate Reality Narratives.*** TU Press.

Time's Up et al. 2023. ***Futures Brought to Life: We Are No Futurists.*** University for Applied Arts Vienna.

Trentmann, F. 2017. ***Empire of Things: How We Became a World of Consumers, from the 15th Century to the 21st.*** Penguin UK.

Vaneigem, R. 1994. ***The Revolution of Everyday Life.*** Rebel Press.

Vogt, E. E., Isaacs, D., & Brown, J. 2003. ***The Art of Powerful Questions: Catalyzing Insight, Innovation, and Action.*** Whole Systems Associates.

SHAHAR LIVNE
CONCEPTUAL MATERIAL DESIGNER
EINDHOVEN, NETHERLANDS
Photo: Erich Goldmann

METAMORPHISM

Figure 1: © *Shahar Livne Design*

Figures 2 and 3:
© *Shahar Livne Design*

In a post-plastic future, where the only place to extract petrol-based plastics will be from nature in a new hybrid form, plastics will regain a new value, far beyond the way we see them in our current time. Metamorphism is an ongoing research and design project that speculates on a future in which plastic waste further permeates Earth's surface and its natural systems; on how it could one day blend with natural matter to become an entirely new extractable resource.

Figure 4: © *Design Academy Eindhoven Photograph by Ronald Smits*

Figure 5: © *Alan Boom*

Figure 6:
© *Shahar Livne Design*

To a certain extent, this scenario is already in effect. In 2014, researchers discovered rocks on Hawaiian beaches that were formed by both sand and plastic waste. They dubbed these new rock formations "plastiglomerates."

Environmental changes, deforestation, and the spread of man-made pollutants are inevitably threatening the existence of natural materials and transforming nature as we know it. At the same time, new natural materials that are the result of environmental contamination are emerging, and man-made materials such as plastic are proliferating in our surroundings.

Lithoplast is the result of thousands of years of natural metabolism and its encounter with the "golden spike" of humanity, plastics. Lithoplast is a new speculative raw material that can be processed in a similar way to clay and is acting as an ultimate symbol of the transformation of matter and the inevitable shifts between nature and culture.

In this project, I explore how people experience a form of matter, which is originally regarded as synthetic, as a possible new natural material and how the qualities of the material can be a basis for design.

NICKLAS LARSEN

SENIOR ADVISOR AND HEAD OF ARTS AND CULTURE AT THE COPENHAGEN INSTITUTE FOR FUTURES STUDIES (CIFS)

COPENHAGEN, DENMARK

EMBODYING FUTURES: THE TRANSFORMATIVE POWER OF EMBODIED LEARNING EXPERIENCES

Can we truly recognize future potentials contained in the present if visions are painted only with words? Or does genuine revelation reside within the immersive and sensory encounters of art, design, and creative storytelling?

To say that the body is an indispensable component of any human experience seems self-evident, intellectual or otherwise. Yet, for too long, the importance of physicality has been neglected by cognitive sciences. It is worth remembering that our most basic form of learning is pre-verbal and sensorial, with the body playing a crucial role in shaping our understanding of the world. In the quest to comprehend and engage with futures ahead, the power of embodied learning shines forth as an untapped, transformative, and compelling learning modality that counters the crisis of imagination (Mulgan, 2020) that leaves us with only a few domineering images of the future.

Speaking to a gathering of newfound friends, colleagues, and mentors in the field of futures studies at the Sharing Desired Futures event in Vienna in 2023, I mused over the significance of embodied experiences and learning; how they can drive action toward desirable futures. My thoughts were mirrored in a phenomenal panel: Ari Popper from Sci-Futures shared his strategic approach to aiding organizations through science fiction prototyping, rehearsing the future through immersive stories and soulful experiences in a manner that can perhaps best be described as epiphany-inducing. Mary Flanagan introduced principles from her game designs, suggesting that giving people agency and making them face dilemmas heightens immersion, cultivates empathy, and can provide grounds for shedding prejudice. Finally, Stefanos Pavlakis highlighted that transformational experience design implies co-creation in developing stories that suspend and transcend existing patterns of order, and, if done right, these can help us embody the change and behavior we wish to see.

This paper will dive further into the research and the anecdotal and empirical evidence, suggesting that our bodies and emotions play a crucial role in the learning process, while also drawing on my experience as a futures practitioner in educational and cultural environments.

The inadequacies of reading and writing

Conventional education, which is heavily reliant on reading and writing, the reproduction of past facts, and the inheritance of knowledge, has inherent shortcomings when confronted with comprehending the multifaceted nature of the future. While reading and writing are valuable tools for transmitting information, they often limit our understanding to the confines of text-based representations. The complex and dynamic nature of the future requires more than the passive absorption of words on a page; and, as a result, we increasingly see a shift towards active engagement and immersive experiences in learning environments and cultural outlets.

Embodied learning recognizes that our bodies and emotions are integral to the learning process, enabling us to bridge the gap between theoretical knowledge and real-world application. By challenging the dominance of reading and writing in education, corporate environments, or elsewhere, embodied learning opens new avenues for grasping the essence of what lies ahead. It empowers learners to embrace uncertainty and envision a future that goes beyond the limitations of text-based narratives. This also contrasts with traditional trend reports, which often fail to fully capture the dynamic and multi-faceted nature of potential futures. They are often fixated on the deterministic extrapolation of past trends and can lead to a narrow and myopic view of the future, overlooking the complexities and uncertainties that shape it, and failing to explore the potential of emergent possibilities and what it means to be human.

Disclaimer: *I am not disregarding the need, role, and potential for literature in fostering imagination and anticipatory processes, rather, I am trying to shed light on how we might enhance this potential.*

“Embodiment is the future”

Mark Walsh, the organizer of the 2020 Embodiment Conference, passionately proclaimed that “Embodiment is the future.” The conference, possibly the largest online event of its kind, featured over 1,000 speakers spanning 10 days and drew more than 500,000 attendees, who were eager to explore the forefront of embodied learning. In broader terms, proponents of embodiment theory reject the notion of a divide between the mind and body. They view these elements as inseparable, mutually dependent entities, emphasizing their function as an interconnected, communicative network. Consequently, they give prominence to the body’s role in traditionally abstract domains of the mind, including perception, cognition, memory, decision-making, and learning (Clughen, 2023).

At its core, this transformative pedagogy recognizes that learning is not solely a mental activity but a holistic experience that involves physical awareness and emotional engagement (Nguyen & Larson, 2015). The fundamental principles of embodied learning revolve around active participation, sensorial activation, and immersive interactions. By incorporating movement, touch, and visceral experiences, learners are encouraged to force a deeper connection with the subject matter, fostering critical thinking, creativity, and, potentially, even empathy. The rise of innovative pedagogies and transformative learning has also been the center of discussion in international organizations. Specifically, the OECD has developed pedagogical principles for embodied learning which emphasize the integration between body and mind in the learning process and the interconnectedness between movement and concepts. They highlight that action and thought occur simultaneously, with science and art mutually supporting each other. Moreover, the OECD’s principles underscore the interrelation between reality and imagination. Ultimately, the principles reinforce the notion that human consciousness is shaped through the integration of the lived body (Paniagua & Istance, 2018).

As such, it becomes clear that embodied learning transcends traditional classroom or whiteboard methods and embraces experiential encounters, simulations, roleplay, and artistic expressions to internalize knowledge and encourage meaningful reflection. Through this approach, individuals not only gain a profound understanding of the material, but also develop a sense of agency in shaping their own learning journey. From my experience, however, it is necessary to establish psychological safety in order to be able to take proper intellectual risks and overcome the barriers that accompany potentially awkward or uncomfortable situations, where the need for improvisation amongst peers or strangers in embodied work can cause a sense of friction. But remember: It is in moments of friction, more than in seamless experiences, that we store wisdom, related to the future or otherwise.

Through this, the conventional notion of knowledge creation is challenged as a purely cognitive pursuit when we acknowledge that, by engaging in physical and tactile experiences, learners can escape theoretical abstractions and connect with knowledge through movement, touch, and visceral encounters, paving the way for a more holistic and profound learning experience.

Our future selves and cognitive dissonance

Our future selves remain unfamiliar to us, and this is not a figurative statement—it is a neurological observation supported by FMRI studies. When we attempt to envision our future self, our brain behaves oddly, ceasing to treat it as a self-image and instead treating it as an entirely separate individual.

When we think about ourselves, a region of the brain called the medial prefrontal cortex (MPFC) becomes active. However, when we contemplate others, this activation diminishes. If we perceive little in common with the individuals in our thoughts, the MPFC becomes even less active. Numerous brain-imaging studies have corroborated this phenomenon. Nevertheless, there is a significant exception to this pattern: The further into the future we attempt to project our lives, the less the MPFC activates. Essentially, our brain treats our distant future self as someone we barely know and, therefore, someone we do not need to prioritize. This peculiar brain behavior may impede our ability to make choices that benefit both our future selves and society at large. Research reveals that the more our brain regards our future self as a stranger, the less self-control we have in the present, leading to a reduced likelihood of making socially responsible decisions that could benefit the world in the long term. We become less adept at resisting temptations, engage in more procrastination, exercise less, save less for retirement, give in sooner when faced with frustration or temporary discomfort, and show reduced concern about or effort to address long-term challenges such as climate change. This cognitive gap underscores the importance of incorporating our physical selves into the learning process (Hershfield, 2011).

The promise of experiential futures

In contrast to most futures practices and writings, which tend to stay at a high level of abstraction, relying on narratives, diagrams, and descriptions, experiential futures offer something new to the field. Paraphrasing the experiential futurist Dr. Stuart Candy, this approach intentionally juxtaposes "experience" and "future," where immersing oneself in the immediate sensory and mental impressions of our current reality is set against the distant future. The objective here is to effectively leverage this contradiction, tapping into the creative tension it generates and making the absent and abstract future more comprehensible and manageable. An experiential scenario, at its core, is one that is brought to life—a tangible exploration of "what if" scenarios, emphasizing the texture of the experience over textual descriptions. It serves to openly contemplate the future, whether through materialization, performance, or a combination of both (Candy, 2018).

Engaging with experiential futures through speculative artifacts, experiments, simulations, roleplay, and aesthetic learning processes or interactive installations can allow individuals to break free from cognitive biases and embrace a broader range of possibilities. Roleplay cultivates empathy and enhances interpersonal skills by encouraging learners to assume different roles and perspectives. An example comes from Suita, Japan, where citizens participating in "energy-visioning" workshops using future design methodologies, such as roleplay, successfully developed proactive future visions that sometimes imposed costs on the current generation, highlighting the success of participatory futures design in addressing uncertainty and promoting long-term thinking (Uwasu, Kishita, Hara, & Nomaguchi, 2020). Additionally, aesthetic learning processes, such as arts and design-driven experiences, appeal to our senses and emotions, fostering a profound connection with the subject matter. This shift in perspective enables a deeper understanding of the nuances and intricacies of the future, empowering individuals to make more informed and adaptable decisions or engage in deeper reflection. As we move beyond one-dimensional narratives and embrace embodied learning in futures thinking, we perhaps unlock a more profound and expansive understanding of the world that lies ahead, equipping ourselves to navigate uncertainties with greater foresight and wisdom. As we empathize with our future selves and those of others, we may develop a newfound sense of purpose or agency toward a desired future by embodying alternatives.

Embodied learning outcomes: Internalizing knowledge, enhancing memory retention, and developing empathy

Embodied learning not only enhances knowledge internalization but also significantly improves memory retention and active rehearsing by forging stronger neural connections when learners physically engage with the subject matter, leading to better retention of information. For instance, when studying a historical event through roleplay, students actively embody the characters, emotions, and actions of the time, creating vivid memories that are easier to recall later. Unlike learning through solely verbal instruction, learning by doing offers an opportunity for the learner's mind and body to collaborate by simultaneously engaging multiple sensory and cognitive processes. Therefore, learners are able to thoroughly understand and internalize the information provided and, in that way, build knowledge by shaping abstract thinking (Sani, Firstanti Wardany, Herlina, & Vernanda, 2021).

Moreover, our bodies play a vital role in memory retention. Through hands-on, physical experiments and simulations, learners actively rehearse concepts, reinforcing their understanding through repeated practice. This active involvement in the learning process fosters a deeper level of comprehension due to sensory stimulation. Multisensory experiences provide memory cues that facilitate information recall and knowledge application because these memories are tied to physical experiences (Moffitt, 2023). As a result, embodied learning becomes a powerful tool for creating a lasting impact on learning journeys.

Although empathy responses can vary greatly among individuals, one effective way of cultivating empathy is by adopting an embodied approach that allows learners to step into someone else's shoes. Embodied learning has been shown to foster empathy and emotional responses by physically connecting learners to the subject matter, making it personally relevant. By envisioning and being fully immersed in the potential consequences of our actions, we are also compelled to confront their moral implications. Modern technologies like VR also increase the sense of embodiment by immersing individuals in realistic and vivid experiences, enabling them to make decisions with lasting impacts (Hershfield, 2011). In addition, VR and embodied experiences can enhance emotional and social skills by providing a nuanced understanding not only of the situation but also of others' emotions, thereby cultivating empathy and greater sensitivity to the feelings of other people (Bertrand, Guegan, Robieux, McCall, & Zenasni, 2018; Papoutsi, Drigas, & Skianis, 2021).

Embodying future generations

At the Danish National School of Performing Arts, I had the unique opportunity of witnessing the transformative power of embodied learning in action. Over the course of two years, I collaborated closely with young minds on the MFA in performing arts program, exploring how active and dramatic approaches could enrich their academic, affective, and aesthetic learning experiences. Throughout our journey, we delved into the realm of futures thinking, its tools, and its methodologies, pushing the boundaries and reimagining their potential. We encouraged the students to hack and crack conventional norms, allowing this to serve as a wellspring of inspiration for their performances and storytelling about new futures. One particular exercise stood out as a powerful embodiment of futures thinking. Students were divided into groups and tasked with designing future scenarios based on a range of present dilemmas around politics, data, privacy, health, and more. Once the scenarios were crafted, another group was assigned to enact and perform those future worlds, fully immersing themselves as future generations confronted with the limitations or consequences of the past.

This embodied experience proved to be a profound and eye-opening journey for the students. By directly engaging with a *colonized future*, they gained a new level of understanding of the implications of present actions. The exercise instilled in them a sense of empathy and foresight, as they comprehended the far-reaching consequences of decisions made in the present for future generations.

Through this, I witnessed how the integration of the body in the learning process transcends traditional methods, fostering a deeper understanding of both us and the world we inhabit. By utilizing embodied learning techniques, the students at the Danish National School of Performing Arts not only honed their artistic skills, but also developed a heightened awareness of the impact of present choices on our collective futures.

Museums as catalysts for embodied futures

Cultural institutions, such as museums, hold immense potential as catalysts for embodied learning and drivers for democratizing futures processes through increased participation. Traditionally known for preserving the past, telling us about our becoming, and who we were, some of these institutions are now transforming into dynamic spaces that invite visitors to engage with the future in innovative and thought-provoking ways. By offering immersive and embodied experiences, museums can enable visitors to step into potential futures and explore the consequences of present actions. Consider a futures exhibition that invites visitors to step into a future where they can experience and question life in a sustainable and technologically advanced society. Through active participation in such an immersive experience, visitors can gain a tangible sense of what such a future might look and feel like, spurring them to contemplate the actions required to bring it to fruition, simultaneously redefining the museum's role as more than a mere repository of artifacts.

Futures Literacy (UNESCO, n.d.), a key concept embraced by a global network of museums in Futures Oriented Museum Synergies seeks to equip visitors with the ability to critically analyze and understand the unfolding possibilities of tomorrow. One way of achieving this is by engaging with *Futures Literacy Laboratories*, a phase-based collaborative process built on the core principles of a) revealing assumptions, b) reframing the future, and then c) rethinking the present by stretching the imagination, questioning existing paradigms and playing an active role in future imageries, and eventually seeing the present anew.

An example of this concept was seen in Futurium, Berlin, in 2022, where my dear friend and fellow UNESCO Chair, Loes Damhof, and I designed an experiential futures literacy tour through the museum's exhibition on the future of mobility. We engaged in a process similar to that described and time-travelled with visitors to the year 2072 (to be able to keep an open mind and conversation, rather than a conversation of likelihood or possibility). In this future, with the aid of technological advancements, participants had to imagine experiencing and sensing the world through the eyes of a non-human species while observing an installation called the "Urban Jungle" that depicted a future city scenario. Here, they were required to address two things: 1) How they felt in their new body and 2) where they belonged. This journey offered a unique and empathetic perspective, stimulating reflections on their place in a transformed world and the implications of human actions and choice, challenging visitors to rethink their perception of the future from the perspective of human-centered design. As many perhaps realized, humans are just one part of a larger whole, not at the center, and human-centered design should thus be a thing of the past. By embracing the role of engaging with the future, museums are not only redefining their purpose but also playing an instrumental role in nurturing a more thoughtful, responsible, and creative society.

Embodying the change we seek

By recognizing the significance of the physical dimension and engaging in immersive experiences, we can move beyond the confines of traditional education and conventional narratives. Embodied learning allows us to internalize knowledge, enhance memory retention while we explore possibilities, and embrace the complexities of the systems at play in futures thinking. This may be an overlooked way of learning that can help us bridge gaps between presents and unknowns. Through the critical thinking that embodiment allows, we may have a pathway for a new and profound sense of agency. Because, when we put ourselves in someone else's shoes, whether virtually or physically, signs tell us that we may be able to shed prejudice and develop empathy not only for ourselves, but for other species and future generations as well. Empowered with this awareness, learners are better equipped to make informed and responsible decisions that contribute to a more inclusive, sustainable, and visionary future, and embodied learning emerges as a catalyst for fostering a generation of proactive and compassionate global citizens. As we embody futures, we unlock new insights and possibilities, envisioning a world that is equitable, inclusive, and sustainable. Cultural institutions, redefining their roles, offer immersive and thought-provoking experiences that empower learners to actively imagine their own future and challenge the futures that are dominant and widely used.

Through this transformative journey, we discover the power of embodiment in cultivating a society that is creative, compassionate, and foresighted. As we stand at the crossroads of time, we embark on a path of co-creating a future that embodies the change we seek—a future that embraces uncertainty with wonder and forges a path towards imaginative and purposeful possibilities.

Project Futurium

PROJECT DESCRIPTION BY LOES DAMHOF

Imagine entering a museum or any cultural space, where, from the moment you step over the threshold, your current shape and form changes completely. You are no longer human but something new entirely. Before you enter you have no inkling of what the new shape may be, and after leaving the space, you return to your old shape to forget what happened altogether.

Sounds strange and bizarre? This is a reframe scenario: a future that is not supposed to be probable or desirable, but is designed to challenge our anticipatory assumptions: the blind spots we tend to overlook when we plan or prepare for the future (Miller, 2018). In this particular scenario it might raise questions about what you think a cultural space should be. But it might also trigger the importance of remembrance when we learn. It might be interesting to change our shape for a short time, but if we forget it ever happened, what is the point? The assumption here being, of course, that we only learn when we can make sense of it (Damhof, 2022).

*If we forget the experience, does it mean that nothing changed?
Is it worth it?*

Embodied learning in futures, as described so eloquently by my friend Nicklas Larsen, adds several layers to how we experience futures and how we can better understand our actions in the present.
At the same time, it also changes how we relate to change.
In the mentioned example of the Futures Literacy Tour at Futurium in Berlin, we used the museum as a third facilitator. Participants in the tour were asked to use the space while going through a Futures Literacy Lab. Besides exchanging ideas with other visitors and thinking out loud, their bodies were having an experience too. Moving through the space, observing, responding, and seeing novelty not only enhanced their museum experience but also made their futures much more vivid... It was the combination of the collective engagement and the individual

Figures 1 – 4:
Futurium, Berlin
© David von Becker

sensory experience they appreciated most (FORMS book, in manuscript). At the end of the tour, we collected their impressive new questions around the future of mobility which they left on the window overlooking Berlin. But did we capture all that we wanted?

Bodies store experiences, memories, ancestral heritage, and futures, long after we have forgotten all about them. Something changes inside of us when we have an experience, whether we are aware of the change or not. Our bodies learn something, whether we remember it or not. Experiencing futures changes the body, and, besides creating space for empathy and an enhanced imagination, it changes the conditions of change. The body will remember the future when the time is right. And whether our minds know it or not might not be worth remembering.

References

Alford, K., et al. 2024. ***Cultivating futures thinking in museums.*** Manuscript, tba.

Bertrand, P., Guegan, J., Robieux, L., McCall, C. A., & Zenasni, F. 2018. Learning empathy through virtual reality: Multiple strategies for training empathy-related abilities using body ownership illusions in embodied virtual reality. ***Frontiers in Robotics and AI,*** 5(26): 1-18.

Candy, S. 2018. Experiential futures: A brief outline [Blog post]. ***The sceptical futurist,*** October 31. Accessed online https://futuryst.blogspot.com/2018/10/experiential-futures-brief-outline.html. Viewed January 22, 2024.

Clughen, L. 2023. 'Embodiment is the future': What is embodiment and is it the future paradigm for learning and teaching in higher education? ***Innovations in Education and Teaching International.*** Accessed online https://www.tandfonline.com/doi/full/10.1080/14703297.2023.2215226. Viewed January 22, 2024.

Damhof, L. 2021. Sensing and sense-making - Why we need the trickster to truly embrace uncertainty. ***Medium,*** February 20. Accessed online https://loesdamhof.medium.com/sensing-and-sense-making-a12b43ce0762. Viewed January 30, 2024.

Futurium Berlin. n.d. ***Official Website.*** Accessed online https://futurium.de/en. Viewed January 22, 2024.

Hershfield, H. E. 2011. Future self-continuity: How conceptions of the future self-transform intertemporal choice. ***Annals of the New York Academy of Sciences,*** 1235: 30-43.

Miller, R. 2018. ***Transforming the future - Anticipation in the 21st century.*** London: Routledge.

Moffitt, S. 2023. Kinesthetics, physical leaning, embodiment and muscle memory [Blog post]. Grey Swan Guild, March 27. Accessed online https://greyswanguild.medium.com/kinesthetics-physical-learning-embodiment-and-muscle-memory-507ca5d6023a. Viewed September 19, 2023.

Mulgan, G. 2020. The imaginary crisis (and how we might quicken social and public imagination). ***UCL Science, Technology, Engineering and Public Policy Working Paper Series.*** Accessed online https://www.ucl.ac.uk/steapp/sites/steapp/files/2020_04_geoff_mulgan_swp.pdf. Viewed January 22, 2024.

Nguyen, D. J., & Larson, J. B. 2015. Don't forget about the body: Exploring the curricular possibilities of embodied pedagogy. ***Innovative Higher Education,*** 40(4): 331-344. Accessed online https://www.academia.edu/6617799/Dont_Forget_About_the_Body_Exploring_the_Curricular_Possibilities_of_Embodied_Pedagogy. Viewed January 22, 2024.

Paniagua, A., & Istance, D. 2018. Embodied learning. In OECD, ***Teachers as Designers of Learning Environments: The Importance of Innovative Pedagogies:*** 117-127. Accessed online https://read.oecd-ilibrary.org/education/teachers-as-designers-of-learning-environments/embodied-learning_9789264085374-11-en#page2. Viewed January 22, 2024.

Papoutsi, C., Drigas, A., & Skianis, C. 2021. Virtual and augmented reality for developing emotional intelligence skills. ***International Journal of Recent Contributions from Engineering Science & IT,*** 9(3): 35-53.

Sani, Y., Firstanti Wardany, O., Herlina, H., & Vernanda, G. 2021. The implementation of embodied learning: A literature review. ***Edukasi,*** 15(1): 8-18.

UNESCO. n.d. ***Futures Literacy.*** Accessed online https://en.unesco.org/futuresliteracy/. Viewed January 22, 2024.

Uwasu, M., Kishita, Y., Hara, K., & Nomaguchi, Y. 2020. Citizen-Participatory Scenario Design Methodology with Future Design Approach: A Case Study of Visioning of a Low-Carbon Society in Suita City, Japan. ***Sustainability,*** 12(11): 4746.

Photo: Erich Goldmann

STATEMENT

LOES DAMHOF

UNESCO CHAIR ON FUTURES LITERACY
IN HIGHER EDUCATION
GRONINGEN, NETHERLANDS

It is not what we do today that impacts the future; it is how we think about the future that impacts today.

Since 2016, I have been designing and facilitating futures literacy processes around the world that are based on using collective intelligence to create new knowledge. The group process is important: By sharing our images of the future, we acknowledge that there is not one single future, but that there are many. We are diversifying futures. Futures thinking and futures work is not about finding a consensus or working towards a common goal. It is about creating awareness about how our images shape, feed, and change our thinking and being. The images being shared with the collective enhance our perception and imagination, but they can also create a safe space to talk about what matters to us most. By taking participants at least 50 years into the future, they are forced to leave their expertise of the present behind. After all: No one knows what happens 50 years from now. By using a time frame like this, we create an even playing field to explore futures. And since our images mirror data about what we are anticipating now, we are actually talking about the present.

Besides using the collective as fertile ground to challenge our assumptions and to overcome the poverty of imagination, nurturing futures thinking as an individual capability is just as important. We do not always have the time or energy to engage with others and collaborate in futures work. But this does not mean that futures thinking cannot be taken onto the streets. This is a myth; this notion that anticipation is a privilege, applied by the lucky few. It is not.

Everybody anticipates, and everybody can imagine. Connecting to those innate capabilities is continuous work and, to be able to see novelty in the familiar, we need to enhance our own perception as well. By standing still, by being alert, through careful observation, by asking ourselves: what if? Embracing complexity and uncertainty can foster a new sense of agency that, in return, may lead to new futures. And wherever that may lead us, at least it will not be because of a lack of imagination.

Photo: Erich Goldmann

CYNTHIA SELIN

PROFESSOR AND CONSULTANT IN FORESIGHT, SUSTAINABILITY, AND INNOVATION
PORTLAND, UNITED STATES

CULTIVATING CREATIVITY AND FREEING THE IMAGINATION: THE CASE FOR PARTICIPATORY FUTURING

Imagining the future in narratives and numbers

Today's world is defined by profound complexities and daunting uncertainties. The climate crisis, the potentials of artificial intelligence, looming food scarcities, and geopolitical dysfunctions are but a few of the intricate collective challenges we face. These are not just tricky problems, they are "wicked"—complex, multifaceted problems that are difficult to define and solve due to their numerous interdependent variables, inherent uncertainties, and conflicting stakeholder perspectives (Rittel & Webber, 1973). Rather than getting caught in endless cycles of futility, despair, and doomsday scenarios it is vital to pivot towards innovative thought, novel methods of inquiry, and proactive strategies that offer creative ways forward. Creating compelling alternatives and co-imagining desirable futures in inclusive and bold ways are essential efforts to navigate such intricate challenges.

Part of the equation involves reducing the craving for absolute certainty and easy solutions. Instead, let us harness the collective imagination to unleash creative approaches that source unique knowledge from unconventional places. Let us formulate refreshing perspectives that recognize and even celebrate uncertainty, rather than masking it. Convening difficult conversations and grappling with uncertainty ought to be an inclusive, collective effort, striving to amplify voices in a democratic vein. When the goal is explicitly focused on "desirable futures," as in this collection of papers, it must be recognized that one community's desirable future is another's nightmare, thus raising the stakes for care and conscientiousness around authentic and fair participation in such deliberations.

This paper delves into the challenges of grappling with our uncertain futures, emphasizing the limitations of prediction, and, consequently, control and hubris. Embracing uncertainty means acknowledging inherent biases and limited perspectives—accepting gaps in knowledge and the specter of ignorance. While this level of self-awareness is daunting for individuals, organizations, and societies alike, it prepares the ground for transformative thought and makes way for inspired visions and perceiving fresh opportunities.

A promising avenue for such expansive thinking is participatory futuring. This involves collaboratively crafting scenarios, democratizing foresight, and kindling collective imagination. While no silver bullet, these practices can dislodge entrenched habits of mind and bring novel perspectives, illuminating alternative pathways. It is this act of opening up to alternatives—engaging in deliberative discourse, breaking unreflexive behaviors, and challenging institutional and societal norms—that grants the space to envision and act differently and to potentially unravel—or at least make headway on—some of the more sticky, wicked problems. In making the case for and sharing some examples of participatory futuring, this paper then derives strategies and principles helpful in nurturing more diversity, creativity, and reflexivity in the quest to articulate futures worth fighting for. Intertwining artistic ways to open up inquiries by using participatory foresight practices better navigates weighty uncertainties and co-creates desirable futures.

Formidable futures: Challenges to navigating change

The barriers to productive strides in managing uncertainty are numerous. There is a problematic compulsion towards predictive counting and, as we will establish, many biases impeding navigating change that lurk along individual, organizational, and societal lines. After outlining some of the ways in which grappling with unpredictable futures is limited through an over-reliance on quantification, we can then look to some alternative approaches that prioritize creative thought and more holistic inquiries.

Social psychology and cognitive science research informs us how different biases creep in when individuals are confronted with deep uncertainties. Historically, our cognitive systems have been fine-tuned for survival, privileging rapid, heuristic-based decisions over deliberative reasoning when we are faced with ambiguous situations. This predisposition often manifests itself in cognitive biases such as ambiguity aversion, where individuals favor known risks over unknown risks, or confirmation bias, where we selectively seek and interpret information consistent with our own pre-existing beliefs (Schirrmeister, Göhring, & Warnke, 2020). Our brains are also wired for pattern recognition, leading to potential overfitting in uncertain situations where we may perceive patterns or correlations where none exist. Our normal tendency to see the world through our own blinders gets amplified under conditions of uncertainty. These cognitive barriers can impede our capacity to effectively navigate and respond to situations characterized by deep uncertainty, underscoring the necessity for interventions that augment our natural proclivities with more adaptive and creative ways of seeing. Part of the corrective involves injecting greater diversity into foresight and visioning efforts in order to challenge entrenched ways of seeing and enable the productive questioning of assumptions.

Decision-making under conditions of uncertainty is mired by social and cognitive habits that lock people and organizational systems into unhelpful ways of thinking about the future. Organizational cultures that prioritize consensus can inadvertently foster groupthink, a phenomenon wherein the desire for harmony or conformity in the group results in poor decision-making outcomes. Such environments can stifle dissenting opinions, critical questioning, or alternative perspectives, thus reducing the diversity of thought that is crucial for navigating ambiguous landscapes and coming up with fresh solutions. Additionally, organizations with rigid hierarchical structures or deeply ingrained legacy systems might exhibit inertia, resisting change even in the face of compelling evidence that transformation is essential. This resistance can stem from an aversion to the perceived risks associated with change, or from entrenched power dynamics that benefit from the status quo. This phenomenon is linked to what Heffernan characterizes as "willful blindness" (2011). In essence, these organizational barriers can obstruct the seeing of novel solutions, rendering institutions less resilient and less responsive to the multifaceted challenges posed by uncertain environments. Generative imagination is stifled.

These problems of foresight also accumulate on an epistemological level. Hardened ways of knowing create both barriers to and opportunities for seeing anew and usefully grappling with uncertainty. The impulse to imagine alternative futures is a basic human trait, evidenced in tracking the seasons, stargazing, consulting oracles, and other early forms of prediction. Yet the pursuit of the future has largely turned into a numbers game over the past century. Particularly with the 18th-century surge of statistics, an increasing emphasis has been placed on quantifying and calculating probabilities (Selin & Pereira, 2013). This quantitative obsession positions the future as a mere extension of the past—a ledger awaiting entries. Calculating probabilities of the likelihood of different futures tends to over-rely on the extrapolation of historical data, missing too much and creating unhelpful illusions. This approach narrows the field of inquiry to those factors amenable to quantification, at the exclusion of "softer" factors like human values, slower phenomena like environmental change, and harder-to-render systemic interactions that transpire in the crevices between disparate factors. This probabilistic mindset limits the scope of what is imagined to be possible—and tends to hold people in a mindset that seeks to control, ignore, or conceal uncertainty.

The epistemological orientation of plausibility appears more promising than probability. Probability is a narrower vantage point, whereas plausibility frees thinking beyond calculating likelihoods. Widening the aperture of futures affords more learning and more space to weave together disparate forces and knit together diverse perspectives. As the philosopher Stengers lays out, "The probable belongs to a logic of conformity" and we need views that enable the "eruption of other ways of feeling, thinking, acting" (2017, 18).

While quantifying uncertainty and simulating change in stochastic models and through data science leads to great strides in aviation, computing, medicine, and many, many other sectors, yielding greater advancements through accuracy and precision, some of the more formidable societal-level ills are poorly handled by straight-line extrapolations and singular forecasts. There is a time and place for data-driven speculation and the quantitative modeling of uncertainty. However, some problems are obdurate to change in surprising ways, defy extrapolative thinking, or require novel and imaginative thought to make headway.

What is needed instead is more diverse and imaginative imagination. This involves co-creation, surfacing diverse points of view. And it involves more open-ended systems-level analyses, taking into account a broad array of factors and appreciating how factors interact and how they might change in sync to create new dynamics and dilemmas. While it is perhaps wildly comfortable to anticipate and tame futures through precise quantification, when approaching some of the stickier and more intractable problems of the 21st century this mastery and control approach to the future breaks down and becomes a liability. If novelty and unpredictable uncertainty is to be honestly confronted, switching the mindset away from probability is necessary. Part of the solution to envisioning anew is attempting more spacious points of view that bring together an array of different perspectives, data, and ways of imagining.

Foundations for fostering collective imaginations

The upshot of these limitations in creating and sharing desirable futures is that there is a need to open up the collective imagination. There is a need for methods and tools that pry open assumptions about change that are often obscured and limited due to cognitive constraints and hardened societal epistemologies. There is a need for strategic conversations that enable people and organizations to confront taken-for-granted expectations. On a societal level, there is a need for discursive shifts that embrace plausibility over probability, allowing more systems-level analyses over narrow accountings of discrete variables. Responding to these challenges is complicated and requires efforts across many sectors and professions. In this paper, the gaze is focused upon how creative methods and tools of strategic foresight and participatory futuring can play a role in offering correctives and new ways forward.

There are many approaches to strategic foresight and anticipation, with long histories in many different disciplines, different epistemological stances, and different priorities in data collection and analysis. Participatory futuring refers to practices that seek to engage individuals in collective inquiries to explore alternative futures and systemic change. Future studies, foresight, scenario planning, and other approaches to anticipation share many traits that have been well-explored in the literature. Roughly, these approaches are known to take a systems view, focus on plausibility over probability, lean into ambiguity, and aim to use the future to make better sense of the present. By disposition, these approaches mean to support decision-taking and policymaking by adding in a richer account of how historical changes might evolve into the future to create novelties.

Many—but not all—approaches to foresight and anticipation recognize the importance of carefully drawing in a diverse array of people. My colleagues and I have investigated the inclusion of stakeholders in the development and use of scenario planning and have discovered that users, experts, and decision-makers are regularly engaged, but often in circumscribed roles (Andersen et al., 2021). Others argue for increasing participation and promoting reflexivity to cope with the different pluralistic attitudes toward the future (Mangnus, Oomen, Vervoort, & Hajer, 2021). While the immediate goal of engaging more voices is to inject more diverse perspectives, it is also important to recognize that when only few experts or people in positions of power with tight agendas are engaged in foresight, there is a risk of perpetuating bad systems and injustice. It is a question of power and tyranny. Many make the case for decolonizing anticipation that involves freeing the imagination, which, according to Bourgeois, Karuri-Sebina, and Feukeu (2022), can pave the way "to creating new forms, reforming old paradigms, and thinking about and (re)inventing our futures as spaces of possibility (Sen, 1999), or sensing and making sense of novelty (Miller, 2011)." Bisht argues for the role of imaginative storytelling to evoke more culturally inclusive modes of foresight in order to overcome the tendency of images of the future to be "predominantly expert-led and 'colonized' by historically popularized worldviews" (2022, 217). Krishnan also sees the limitations and conformities of probabilistic framings and instead proposes making way for closer examination of "whose futures are privileged and whose are dispossessed in decision-making" (2022, 104), an effort that depends on a broader array of engaged voices and more participatory practices of foresight.

But while the objective and social importance of engaging diverse voices is clear, how exactly we fold in unique and uncommon perspectives and create opportunities for authentic engagement is not clear. There are open questions and debate in the literature about which audiences and users to include, how to ensure a level playing field and ease the unhelpful power dynamics that crop up in deliberation and engagement, and how to invite and celebrate plurality and increase agency without devolving into fragmentation. In addition to addressing some of these outstanding issues, it is also essential to inspire creativity to break through hardened and limiting ways of knowing the future. In order to really harness the power of the imagination to overcome the status quo and look beyond dominant narratives, the tools and methods of participatory futuring need to embrace a systems-level, multi-perspective view and foster a greater sense of agency to empower original thinking. This pursuit of greater spaciousness and creativity in the imagining and rendering of alternative futures might help us to move away from the onslaught and overload of dark futures, and towards more desirable ones.

Creative approaches to participative foresight: The case of *Emerge*

There are scores of approaches that could be considered participatory futuring, yet here we will focus on how a public festival called *Emerge* acts as a stand-in for a methodological approach that blends collective imagination, creativity, and foresight. *Emerge* is an art, science, and technology festival devoted to the creative imagination of alternative futures that I co-founded with colleagues in 2012 (Arizona State University, n.d.; Selin et al., 2015). Each year, faculty directors curate and organize an interactive collection of exhibits and experiences designed to provide members of the public a space to construct, elaborate on, and project plausible futures in imaginative ways. The public is invited to interactively explore futures through performance and play, art and experimentation, designed artifacts, and deliberative experiences. The festival self-consciously strives for diversity in sharing alternative futures by drawing in artists, science-fiction writers, scientists and engineers of all stripes, dancers, futurists, faculty, and students with members of the public. "*Emerge* is thus a temporally and socially diverse space where multiple knowledges work to open up more robust and eclectic forms of anticipation" (Selkirk, Selin, & Felt, 2018). *Emerge* explicitly seeks to harness different types of transdisciplinary knowledge and unleash novel ways of knowing, and, in doing so, trigger new ideas about alternative futures.

The methodologies encapsulated in the festival build on other efforts emanating from scenario planning (Ramirez & Wilkinson, 2016; Selin, 2007), design fiction (Bleecker, 2009; Selin & Boradkar, 2010), experiential futures (Candy & Dunagan, 2017), and work related to the intersection between scenarios and design (Selin, Kimbell, Ramirez, & Bhatti, 2016). These approaches all seek to take foresight and the building of desirable futures out into participatory spaces that can be as ordinary as facilitated workshops and as diverse as a shopping bazaar, emergency response charette, mountaintop, or urban walking tour. While a festival is hard to position as a methodology, *Emerge* can be understood as a particularly charismatic case of participatory futuring that positions, in sharp relief, some key actors that enable more creative and more inclusive inquiry. In its playful, embodied, immersive, and tangible form, the *Emerge* festival lends itself as a good case study for more concretely laying out some methodological guides for participatory futuring. By explaining the strategies deployed to engage diverse audiences, the *Emerge* festivals can be seen as a series of experiments, without precise controls or replicability, but occurring annually and thus enabling lessons about cultivating critical public imaginations.

While there have been years of *Emerge* to sample from, and these have been written about from different vantage points (Davies et al., 2015; Selkirk et al., 2018), the examples below draw from the festival held in 2017. I directed this event with the curatorial support of the philosopher Dehlia Hannah and the art and science studies scholar Hannah Star Rogers. We took our inspiration from Mary Shelley's *Frankenstein* as a modern myth, a 200-year-old science-fiction story that explores themes of human creativity, societal responsibility, and scientific ethics. As with all *Emerge* festivals, we strove to incite the imagination through performances, play, interactive exhibits, art, deliberative games and workshops, and hands-on activities.

Design strategies & principles for engaged practice

Throughout the years of running *Emerge*, several design strategies and guiding principles for engagement have emerged as central to the effort. These are neither pre-meditated strategies nor principles decided up front. Instead, these design strategies and their underpinning principles have been established on the basis of learning what works and what does not and from exploring why and why not. By sharing the intentions of and experiences with *Emerge*, three strategies will be emphasized: supporting access and empathy, allowing for disciplinary or epistemic diversity, and creating opportunities for critical appraisal and agency. From these lessons learned on how to design and host public conversations about the future, four main principles are derived that may be usefully applied in other settings where the goal is to increase creativity and critical imagination in participatory settings.

Support multiple forms of access

A first essential step is to know your audience well and to architect low barriers to their participation. Though obvious, this move is often not well implemented and leads to interventions that are disconnected from the needs, worldviews, and capacities of those who should be engaged. Careful attention to pre-existing judgements, the knowledge base of your audience, and an appreciation of their goals and intentions is paramount. The goal should be to meet people where they are with a clear articulation of the purpose for engagement. For *Emerge*, the audience is a diverse public audience that includes members of the community, families, children, alumni, faculty, and students. This means that the offerings ought to delight and dignify casual visitors but also provide opportunities for greater exploration for those with more sophisticated tastes. Access is first opened up through an alluring hook, often beautiful imagery or exhibitry, intriguing questions, or an easy starting point.

In the case of Ali Schachtschneider's work on *Edible Skin*, audiences are drawn in with horrific fascination to the prospect of fashion as an extension of the body:

> *From growing and consuming second-skins, to grown materials extending and altering the relationship with materials on the body, to swallowable pills that cause cellulose-material to form on the surface of skin, the work uses biotechnology and biomaterials to explore an alternative future where the relation between living and non-living, things and bodies, is expanded and blurred.* (Arizona State University, 2017b)

Audiences see the artist's images, videos, and props that show her clothed in a gooey substance, replacing fashion with biological materials made of cellulose. Some might become entranced by the grotesque prospect of eating "skin," while others can ask the artist her intention. The curious-minded would discover her research on fast fashion and critique of the enormity of waste created. Others could probe further to learn more about the interlinkages between our food systems and shortages wrought by climate change. Here the experience evokes multiple points of entrée, allowing audiences to connect with their own concerns.

When futures are presented in accessible ways that stimulate discourse, they pave the way for novel perspectives and mutual understanding. A single point of intrigue can foster newfound insights in another. By crafting aesthetic and conceptual touchpoints, audiences are ushered into a dialogue, creating a fertile ground for enhanced empathy. Once immersed, multiple narrative pathways emerge, enriching appreciation for diverse futures.

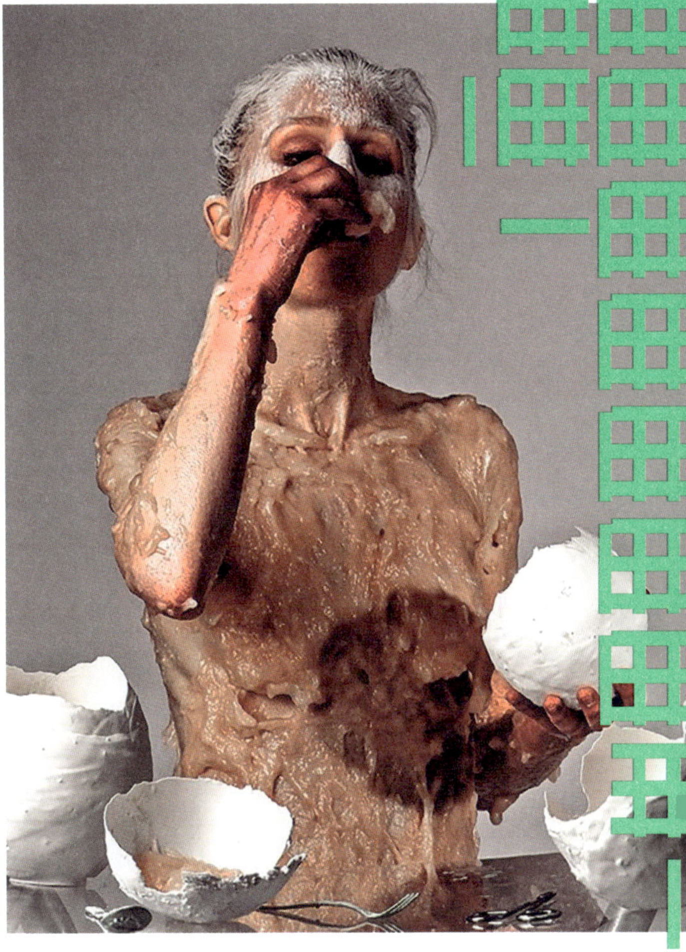

Figure 1:
© Ali Schachtschneider, photographed by Hiu Zhi Wei

Allow for disciplinary or epistemic diversity

Complexity in each of *Emerge*'s offerings has proven vital, with exhibits emphasizing the confluence of diverse factors shaping new realities and new futures. Contemporary challenges demand a multidisciplinary approach, addressing multifaceted issues from varied perspectives. Equally crucial is valuing epistemic diversity, recognizing the myriad ways diverse audiences perceive and interact with the world. Addressing profound uncertainties means acknowledging the spectrum of viewpoints, each offering distinct insights and potential solutions. For truly complex issues, people naturally hold divergent perspectives on the underlying dynamics. As an experience, *Emerge*'s offerings are meant to create scaffolding that is complex enough (but not too complex) to allow for both disciplinary and epistemic diversity, in terms of not only the futures portrayed but also the avenues through which audiences might interpret them.

One installation that underscores the importance of a holistic look at alternative futures is Karolina Sobecka's *Cloud Services* (Arizona State University, 2017a). Sobecka's transmedia installation featured a cloud generated under a glass jar as a symbol of the atmosphere whilst also being a meditation on the metaphor of a cloud as data storage. Her work probes how new forms of data and computation might be used to directly manipulate the environment. The cloud then becomes not only a beautiful whisper of weather, or a storage site for otherwise invisible data, but also a reflection on how we might directly experiment with cloud engineering. With the specter of geo-engineering on the near horizon, what data we encode in clouds and with which repercussions is made visible. Here we have an embodied scenario, a performance of a scientist in the lab creating clouds, as an entry point for audiences to tease apart the amalgamation of numerous trends—in synthetic biology, in climate engineering, in data science.

Figure 2:
© *Karolina Sobecka*

Sobecka's work is a look at how data intermingles with natural phenomena in a visceral and ethereal way and invites audiences to rethink their relationship to microbes, to climate, to information, and to engineering. In drawing in the audience into different framings of ordinary phenomena (a cloud), lateral thinking (Bono, 1992) is activated, sparking enhanced creativity through the juxtaposition of seemingly unrelated things. It encourages people to probe the interstitial places between the disciplines and to try on different ways of knowing. In these cracks and crevices, novel insight, something fresh, comes shining through.

Create opportunities for critical appraisal and agency

Over the years of curating and hosting *Emerge*, a strategy that encourages participants to critically challenge their own deeply held assumptions on their own terms has arisen. Part of the challenge then becomes engineering some interpretive flexibility into the offering, enabling audiences to make up their own mind about what they are seeing and what is to come.

David Bowen's *Fly Blimps* (n.d.) innocently and playfully featured a series of helium-filled balloons floating in a room softly populated by fluffy pillows, ambient lighting, and relaxing music. Audiences were able to come and sit among the floating blimps only to realize that the movement of the blimps is powered by the antics of ordinary house flies. The flies act as the brain of the devices, their collective movements determining how the blimps move about the room and interact with other objects in the space. Each blimp is outfitted with a chamber with food, water, and light for the creatures, and small sensors that detect the changing light patterns produced by the movement of the flies. The data collected dictates the flight paths. Here we have an alluring entry point, a sight to behold, and an offering that invites further exploration. Some may become intrigued about what it means to hybridize nature with artificial intelligence. Others might probe deeper into questions about the boundaries between animal and machine. Beyond the handwringing of the power of algorithms and hyped-up references to the Fourth Industrial Revolution, the piece creates an opening for audiences to ponder what new forms of control and feedback might be possible.

Figure 3: © *David Bowen*

Essential to the creative power of this vision, is how it does not over-determine meaning. It makes no judgment about the morality or desirability of this future, nor does it over-render the new reality, explaining what has happened to lead to this particular device. It leaves much open to the imagination, inviting audiences to fill in the blanks. As we develop finer-tuned ways to invent otherworldly images, from VR-enabled futurescapes to AI-produced stories, the risk of over-rendering futures is high. Such over-rendering can curtail audiences' own imaginations. It is important to build in some interpretative flexibility, enabling users to make their own sense, to tell their own stories, to ignite their own imaginations. Akin to Vygotsky's zone of proximal development from the literature on learning and creativity (1978), the idea is to provide some scaffolding for the imagination so as to enable people to come to their own interpretations. The balance is to get just enough (and not too much) information so that public audiences can do their own worldbuilding.

Guiding principles

Through these strategies, *Emerge* directors and curators have sought to encourage *Emerge* collaborators to create interactive and engaging experiences that invite new ways to see a particular problem, ask new questions, and make new connections. From these strategies and through years of engaging public audiences, four main principles have developed that define how *Emerge* operates. First, we encourage our collaborators to develop experiences that are **inclusive**. Inclusive refers to experiences that are accessible to many, thoughtfully participative, and enable people to interact with the content on their own terms. Second, we seek experiences that are **integrative** of different worldviews and disciplinary perspectives. This integration connects to the need for futures to be explored holistically, drawing in a systems perspective that reveals multiple dimensions of a problem or issue. Third—and essential to the entire undertaking—is **imaginative**. Here we insist that the experiences are designed to evoke fresh perspectives using creative methods. New ideas about the future ought to be shared and grappled with, taking care to not over-determine the audience's interpretation of the possibilities. Lastly, we have an eye on **intrigue**, working with our *Emerge* collaborators to create layers of discovery so as to encourage iterative exploration and offer a way for people to become curious and stay with their curiosity throughout the experience and beyond.

Forays into new futures

Navigating and managing uncertainty are crucial capacities in today's society, and yet narrowly framed probabilistic methods have become the default. This comes at the great expense of imagination. It has become clear that honestly reckoning with change dynamics and developing viable and just pathways through seemingly intractable problems requires methods that inspire creativity and new ways of seeing.

Einstein said that you cannot use the same logic to get out of the problem that you used to get into it. The quest for mastery and control, for prediction and certainty, has driven much industrial, social, and computational progress over the last century—for better and worse—but now is the time for another logic of change that opens up the terrain of the future to more original thinking and more diverse voices. Another quote, controversially attributed to Einstein, reminds us: "Not everything that can be counted counts, and not everything that counts can be counted" (O'Toole, 2010). When we foray into new futures, we need to be vigilant in our understanding that not everything meaningful can be quantified and that an over-reliance on numbers can miss the bigger picture. We can miss big thinking and fresh perspectives with such a calculating stance, losing sight of externalities, of values, of diverse perspectives, and of the surprising ways that discrete variables impact one another to create novel interactions. Instead of just entertaining macro-dynamic forces along a binary of impact and likelihood as probabilistic reasoning might suggest, greater spaciousness is opened through inclusively generated plausibilistic imaginations.

In order to confront and solve some of our grand challenges, breaking free from ingrained thought and default action patterns is paramount. If the past is not a good guide to the future, if yesterday's patterns cannot—or should not—foretell tomorrow's promises, there is a need to experiment with new ways of envisioning change to thwart an over-reliance on historical extrapolation which can inadvertently truncate our vision, skewing us towards reductionist outcomes or repeating past mistakes. While there is undoubtedly solace in predictability, a genuine embrace of the myriad uncertainties impinging upon our most interesting problems demands a shift from probabilistic thinking to a more expansive engagement with plausibilistic thinking. The challenge now is to recognize how and why the limits of this mindset emerge, and to experiment with different ways to think and imagine and address the complex problems that defy extrapolative, easy answers.

As proposed in this paper, one way through these limiting approaches to the future is to work to inspire diverse audiences to engage in their own process of discovery, rather than predetermining which future matters most for them. By letting go of probabilistic assessments and instead opening up a sense of wonderment, radically participative approaches to foresight cultivate a deeper sense of spaciousness and grow agency. This greater space, to entertain even more possibilities for change, provides entry points for more people to connect to and share their own ideas of the future, to question their own assumptions and narrow frames, and to create more viable options for acting anew. Through supporting more creative approaches to the future that are guided by inclusivity, integrating a systems perspective, building up imaginative capacities, and sparking intrigue, it just might be possible to make progress on divining fairer futures. In our effort to create desirable futures, actively seeking out unconventional perspectives that challenge the status quo can foster deeper inquiry, inspiration, and more positive change.

References

Adam, B., & Groves, C. 2007. ***Future matters: Action, knowledge, ethics.*** Leiden: Brill.

Anderson, P. D., Hansen, M. & Selin, C. 2021. Stakeholder inclusion in scenario planning—A review of European projects. ***Technological Forecasting and Social Change,*** 169: 120802.

Arizona State University. (n.d.) ***Emerge: A festival of futures*** [Website]. Accessed online https://emerge.asu.edu/. Viewed September 30, 2023.

Arizona State University. 2017a. ***Cloud Services, emerge2017: Frankenstein.*** Emerge: A Festival of Futures. Arizona State University. Accessed online https://emerge.asu.edu/2017/exhibits/cloud-services/. Viewed September 30, 2023

Arizona State University. 2017b. ***Edible Skin, emerge2017: Frankenstein.*** Emerge: A Festival of Futures. Arizona State University. Accessed online https://emerge.asu.edu/2017/exhibits/edibleskin/. Viewed September 30, 2023.

Arizona State University. 2017c. ***Fly Blimps, emerge 2017: Frankenstein.*** Emerge: A Festival of Futures. Arizona State University. Accessed online https://emerge.asu.edu/2017/exhibits/fly-blimps/. Viewed September 30, 2023.

Bisht, P. 2020. Chapter 14: Decolonizing futures: Finding voice, and making room for non-Western ways of knowing, being, and doing. In R. Slaughter, & A. Hines (eds.), ***The knowledge base of futures studies 2020:*** 216-230. Association of Professional Futurists and Foresight International.

Bleecker, J. 2009. ***Design fiction: A short essay on design, science, fact and fiction.*** Near Future Laboratory 29. Accessed online https://systemsorienteddesign.net/wp-content/uploads/2011/01/DesignFiction_WebEdition.pdf. Viewed February 21, 2024.

Bono, E. de. 1992. ***Serious creativity: Using the power of lateral thinking to create new ideas.*** New York: HarperBusiness.

Bourgeois, R., Karuri-Sebina, G., & Feukeu, E. 2022. The future as a public good: Decolonizing the future through anticipatory action research. ***Foresight.***

Bowen, D. (n.d.). ***Fly Blimps*** [Website Entry]. Accessed online https://www.dwbowen.com/fly-blimps. Viewed September 25, 2023.

Candy, S., & Dunagan, J. 2017. Designing an experiential scenario: The people who vanished. ***Futures,*** 86: 136-153.

Davies, S. R., Selin, C., Rodegher, S., Allende, C. A., Burnam-Fink, M., DiVittorio, C., Glerup, C., Keys, C., Kimball, M., Liao, M., Monfreda, C., & Trinidad, B. 2015. Studying Emerge: Findings from an event ethnography. ***Futures,*** 70: 75-85.

Heffernan, M. 2011. ***Willful blindness: Why we ignore the obvious at our peril.*** New York: Walker & Company/Bloomsbury Publishing.

Krishnan, A. 2022. Unsettling the coloniality of foresight. In J. Engle, J. Agyeman, & T. Chung-Tiam-Fook (eds.), ***Sacred civics: Building seven generation cities***: 93-106. London: Routledge.

Mangnus, A. C., Oomen, J., Vervoort, J. M., & Hajer, M. A. 2021. Futures literacy and the diversity of the futures. ***Futures,*** 132: 102793.

O'Toole, G. 2010. Not everything that counts can be counted. ***QuoteInvestigator. com,*** May 26 (revised September 5, 2011). Accessed online quoteinvestigator. com/2010/05/26/everything-counts-einstein/. Viewed September 27, 2023.

Ramirez, R., & Selin, C. 2014. Plausibility and probability in scenario planning. ***Foresight,*** 16(1): 54-74.

Ramirez, R., & Wilkinson, A. 2016. ***Strategic reframing: The Oxford Scenario Planning Approach.*** Oxford University Press.

Rittel, H. W. J., & Webber, M. M. 1973. Dilemmas in a general theory of planning. ***Policy Sciences,*** 4(2): 155-169.

Schirrmeister, E., Göhring, A., & Warnke, P. 2020. Psychological biases and heuristics in the context of foresight and scenario processes. ***Futures & Foresight Science,*** 2(2): 1-18.

Selin, C. 2007. Professional dreamers: The past in the future of scenario planning. In B. Sharpe, & K. van der Heijden (eds.), ***Scenarios for success: Turning insight into action***: 27-51. London: Wiley.

Selin, C. 2015. Merging art and design in foresight: Making sense of Emerge. ***Futures,*** 70: 24-35.

Selin, C., & Boradkar, P. 2010. Prototyping nanotechnology: A transdisciplinary approach to responsible innovation. ***Journal of Nano Education,*** 2(1-2): 1-12.

Selin, C., & Pereira, A. G. 2013. Pursuing plausibility. ***International Journal of Foresight and Innovation Policy,*** 9(2/3/4): 93-109.

Selin, C., Kimbell, L., Ramirez, R., & Bhatti, Y. 2016. Scenarios and design: Scoping the dialogue space. ***Futures,*** 74: 4-17.

Selkirk, K., Selin, C., & Felt, U. 2018. A festival of futures: Recognizing and reckoning temporal complexity in foresight. In R. Poli (ed.), ***Handbook of anticipation: Theoretical and applied aspects of the use of future in decision making:*** 1-23. Cham: Springer.

Stengers, I. 2017. The insistence of possibility: Towards a speculative pragmatism. ***Parse,*** 6: 13-19.

Vygotsky, L. S. 1978. ***Mind in society: The development of higher psychological processes.*** M. Cole, V. John-Steiner, S. Scribner, & E. Souberman (eds.). Cambridge, MA: Harvard University Press.

Photo: private

ALICE COMI

ASSOCIATE PROFESSOR,
TONGJI UNIVERSITY,
COLLEGE OF DESIGN
AND INNOVATION
SHANGHAI, PR CHINA

FUTURE MAKING, FUTURECASTING, AND MATTER: THE BERLIN-BRANDENBURG INTERNATIONAL AIRPORT CASE STUDY

Introduction

Opening nearly ten years late and three times over budget, Berlin-Brandenburg International (BER) airport is a case study of dystopian future making. I use this case study to argue that future making is fraught with political struggles and to discuss how failure to engage in a co-creation process might turn desired futures into dystopian realities. I then offer guidance on how organizations and their audiences could use "matter" (e.g., bodies, objects, and spaces) to negotiate their clashing interests and co-create futures that are both desirable and realizable. My main questions are: *What can we learn from failed attempts at future making? How can we make sure that future making is successful, despite the clashing interests of the collaborating actors?*

Future making has gained considerable importance in organization and management studies (Wenzel et al., 2020; Wenzel, 2022). Future making is a form of inquiry where actors engage with the matter at hand to imagine and reify a desired future (Comi & Whyte, 2018). In contrast to other perspectives (such as forecasting), future making emphasizes the sensorial dimension of practitioners' orientation towards the future. It places the attention on making a realizable course of action for the future, through practical engagement with the situation, and the bodies, objects, and spaces that constitute our present (Whyte, Comi, & Mosca, 2022).

This concept, future making, resonates with *futurecasting*. The latter is defined as the collaborative process of designing desired futures (Shamiyeh, 2024). Both futurecasting and future making shift the focus away from rationalistic techniques of predicting probable futures, and instead bring into view a concern with crafting desired futures. While futurecasting focuses on imagining, prototyping, and sharing (Shamiyeh, 2024), I mobilize the concept of future making to foreground the shift from imagining to reifying desired futures. Future making emphasizes the role of matter in crafting desired futures, and the practices by which actors *make* a course of realizable action for the future.

Specifically, future making entails iterative practices of imagining, testing, stabilizing, and reifying (Comi & Whyte, 2018). In *imagining*, actors give material form to their abstract vision for the future. In *testing*, they validate imaginings of the future against multiple constraints, tracing what might be a feasible course of action. In *stabilizing*, actors commit to realizing a given course of action for the future, for instance by resisting further adjustments. In *reifying*, they give a more definitive form to their imaginings of the future, using the matter at hand to share their vision and persuade stakeholders of its feasibility (Comi & Whyte, 2018). This work "is partly driven by a preconceived design or strategy for the future, and partly lodged into the habituated actions that practitioners deploy" (Comi & Whyte, 2018: 1076).

Previous research has begun to acknowledge that future making is not without challenges (Thompson & Byrne, 2021). The work of imagining, testing, stabilizing, and reifying futures is inherently complex, which might result in the failure of the project at hand, and even make for dystopian rather than desirable futures. Dystopian futures may result from premature closure of inquiry, reliance on blind hunches, and/or moral disengagement from the futures in the making (Whyte et al., 2022). Although these risks are heightened in contexts where actors lack a sensorial engagement with physical matter (e.g., in online environments), dystopian futures are created in any context, and are unfortunately on the rise.

BER's megaproject (Figure 1) has been of great interest in academia. Scholars have developed various explanations for its failure. Geraldi and Stingl (2016) argued that BER's fiasco can be explained by mobilizing different yet complementary theories of decision making, namely cognitive, political, and contextualist. Taken together,

Figure 1: A rendering of Berlin's planned airport © *Photograph credits: picture alliance/ Andreas Franke, 2012*

these suggest that actors are limited by bounded cognition and influenced by political interests that might clash with the project interests. Actors craft "narratives which will shape processes of attention, prioritization and ultimately decisions," by means of "surfing on waves of meaning, in a highly ambiguous world" (Geraldi & Stingl, 2016: 9-10).

Wagner (2016: 5) used the case study of BER to develop the concept of a "project wave," which explains project failure through the metaphor of compounding waves of ignorance (where actors pretend not to know, are not supposed to say, or are kept in the dark). In the first wave, the project initiators pretend not to know about the actual cost and schedule, and instead paint a rosy picture to lure others into taking up the project. As the first wave mounts, a second wave forms: Experts are hired to work on the project but are required to cover up the unfeasibility of its cost and time projections. At this point, the initiators (pretending not to know) and experts (not supposed to say) work in concert, producing materials—e.g., brochures, press kits, slide decks—to persuade owners, funders, and sponsors. As the latter are kept in the dark about the cover-up, the waves can no longer be stopped; and the project will turn out to be over budget and time.

Fiedler and Wendler (2016) and Landis (2022) provided similar explanations of BER's "epic fail," suggesting that the governments of Berlin and Brandenburg—albeit inexperienced in airport construction—naively thought they could manage the building process by themselves. Wishful thinking, delusional optimism, and overconfidence bias were compounded by major mistakes: The project managers failed to develop control mechanisms to keep cost and delays at bay, to communicate and engage with the project stakeholders, and to leverage best practices in contracting and management. They were overly reliant on public funding and unable to detect early-warning signals of failure.

In what follows, I will expand and complement previous explanations of BER's fiasco, by reading this case study through the lens of future making. I will highlight the political dynamics inherent in future making, and the role of matter in such dynamics.

The case study

A complete fiasco

Berlin-Brandenburg International (BER) airport is a prime example of project failure. It opened in October 2020, with a delay of nine years and costs soaring to €6 billion—more than three times the estimated budget (Connolly, 2020; Nicola, 2020). Yet, BER is not expected to become profitable before 2025, as the COVID-19 pandemic triggered a steady reduction of air traffic (Euronews, 2020). And FBB (Flughafen Berlin-Brandenburg), the state-owned company that operates Berlin airports, has already received substantial public grants, including a €1.7 billion grant from the EU (European Commission, 2022).

BER has become a dystopian and unsustainable reality. Things did not start well: Just before the planned 2012 opening, the regional office in charge of fire safety declined to grant approval, as smoke detectors and fire doors were not functioning properly (Bowlby, 2019). FBB attempted a quick fix—i.e., hiring workers to operate doors manually in case of fire. When this solution failed, scheduled flights were redirected to other airports (DW News, 2020), and the grand opening with the then Chancellor Angela Merkel was cancelled. With the unopened airport coming under the spotlight, BER's head of construction conducted a survey to document all faults and problems.

They found more than half a million to fix: tangled cabling, short escalators, unbuilt rooms (Bowlby, 2019), cracked tiles (Spiegel International, 2013c), incorrectly numbered doors (Berliner Zeitung, 2020), and wrong lighting—including lights that could not be switched off (since the control system was not in place) (Spiegel International, 2013a). As BER remained unfinished, the costs for energy (e.g., air conditioning and lighting), maintenance, and security skyrocketed to €20 million per month (Spiegel International, 2013c). In 2018 alone, 750 monitors for displaying flight information had to be replaced at the cost of €500,000 because they had reached their end of life before the airport could open (Smith, 2019).

When it was first conceived in the aftermath of the Fall of the Wall, BER was imagined as the symbol of a reunified country, and a showpiece of German engineering excellence. How could such a vision turn into dystopia? As BBC's Chris Bowlby (2019) nicely put it, BER's story shows "how a noble ambition ... was slowly suffocated by political wrangling, bungling incompetence, and the world's worst tangle of badly installed cabling."

Various factors entwined to make BER a disaster. First, the lead architect—Meinhard von Gerkan of gmp (Gerkan, Marg and Partners Architects)—believed that airport "passengers have no desire to buy anything," and accordingly designed as few shops as possible (DW News, 2020). But despite Gerkan's contempt for shopping, modern airports largely rely on commercial spaces. It was only at a late stage that FBB realized that Gerkan had kept commercial spaces to a bare minimum. Hence, they requested the addition of an entire floor, while construction was ongoing (DW News, 2020).

Unavoidably, this triggered rework at construction stage. But it was not the only design change: The building concept, in fact, was frequently revised in response to the conflicting requirements of multiple actors. The Mayor of Berlin, for instance, insisted on adding terminal bridges to accommodate the large Airbus A380, although this super-jet was unlikely to be used by carriers at BER (in an irony of fate, Airbus A380 production stopped before BER could open). And further changes became necessary to add gates for low-cost carriers, which in the meantime had become increasingly influential in the airline industry (Bowlby, 2019).

As a result, Gerkan's terminal design was redrawn to double its capacity (while construction was still ongoing). Compounded by ineffective management, "all these changes meant the airport builders simply lost control of what was being done, especially the hugely complicated technical infrastructure" (Bowlby, 2019). BER's construction company went out of business (BBC News, 2020), amidst a high turnover of chairmen, project managers, and technicians (Glucroft, 2020). Notably, BER's CEO Schwarz was dismissed from his position and BER's technical director Grossman was accused of corruption (Grasso Macola, 2021), while BER's lead architect Gerkan was laid off (Glucroft, 2020) and later re-hired.

Political dynamics at BER

The unfinished airport was encountering mounting resistance from public opinion. Not just because BER was overpriced, faulty, and unsustainable; it was also problematic in terms of its ecological and social impact (Sedlin, Beckmann, & Tan, 2020). To start with, the selection of Schönefeld as a building site for BER was highly controversial, as this area was quite close to Berlin and densely inhabited. Many residents were rehoused to make space for the airport terminal, and many others were affected by air and noise pollution from the new airport (DW News, 2020). A new district was built to accommodate displaced residents (at the government's expense), and almost 10% of the airport budget was spent on soundproofing the remaining households (DW News, 2020).

Schönefeld was far from being a suitable location, especially if we consider that another six locations were available and preferable in terms of "(1) environmental impact, (2) profitability, (3) traffic connection, (4) technical airport planning and (5) regional development" (Sedlin et al., 2020: 13). Nevertheless, Schönefeld was chosen for political reasons: A poll revealed that the majority of Berliners preferred an airport close to the city, and the Federal Court of Auditors had indicated that the extension of the existing airport, Schönefeld, was preferable to the buildup of an entirely new one. Furthermore, this closeness of the new airport to Berlin's center was financially preferable for the capital (Sedlin et al., 2020).

Although public consultations were held, they were merely window dressing. According to Sedlin et al. (2020), the decision to locate the new airport in Schönefeld had been made by the relevant governments (i.e., the Federal Administration, the Municipality of Berlin, and the State of Brandenburg) before the start of public consultations. The so-called "Citizens' Dialogue" was used to facilitate the planning process, rather than reach wide consensus. As Sedlin et al. (2020) further explain, the outcomes of the public consultations were not legally binding, while citizens struggled to access the planning materials and to organize for getting their voices heard.

According to Diekmann, Kröger, and Reimann (2013) of *Der Spiegel*, BER is essentially a story of political deception. As the quote below suggests, material artifacts (e.g. architectural renderings) were used not to engage citizens in a collaborative inquiry about their futures, but to seduce and lure them into buying a grand yet unrealizable vision:

> *At the beginning everything looks wonderful: opulent models, lovingly decorated with plastic figures ... The costs seem bearable, politicians present their project euphorically. What a beautiful perspective for the region! And of course, the whole thing shouldn't take too long, just a couple of years.*

The role of matter

The matter mobilized by BER's proponents was not limited to architectural renderings, but comprised a range of visual and material artifacts—e.g., models of the yet-to-be airport, press kits, and media galleries, as well as projections of future income, rising employment, and regional development (Figure 2). Here, I suspect, the matter was mobilized to conceal the fact that BER was far beyond budget.

As Flyvbjerg, Holm, and Buhl (2002: 279) found, the cost estimates of public works projects are "highly and systematically misleading." The best explanation for cost underestimation is not error, but "strategic misrepresentation, that is, lying." Interestingly, this was also suggested by the lead architect of BER, Gerkan. As he declared in an interview with *Spiegel International* (2013b),

> *I could name a dozen projects off the top of my head that consistently began with a lie. The ICC (International Congress Centrum) in Berlin, for example, was planned for 120 million Deutsche Marks and ended up costing 924 million. Do you think everyone believed in the 120 million?*

In his retrospective book, *Blackbox BER*, Gerkan further denounced political pressure to "get things done," despite concerns about the unfeasibility of the project, its rising costs and delays (Glucroft,

Figure 2: At the groundbreaking ceremony in September 2006, managers and politicians dig the soil against the background of a photo-realistic rendering of the yet-to-be "Berlin Brandenburg International" (BBI), originally planned for completion by October 2011. © *Photograph credits: picture-alliance/ dpa/ Patrick Pleul, 2006*

2020). At the same time, Gerkan pointed the finger at the project management, accusing FBB of concealing issues and falsifying reports intended for the Supervisory Board (Glucroft, 2020). FBB, for its part, was extremely critical of Gerkan's design of the main terminal. They even considered an alternative plan, where the main terminal was discontinued and replaced by an industrial prefabricate, more functional and easier to operate (Traufetter & Wasserman, 2017).

The stalling project gave way to a spiral of corruption: According to an inquiry by DW, construction workers were stealing materials from the building site, while airport officials and managers were caught taking bribes (DW News, 2020). Four people were incriminated as part of an investigation into a construction company in charge of the fire and smoke detection system (BBC News, 2016). And a whistleblower who had reported cases of corruption was poisoned with a deadly substance in his coffee, which caused him several months of sickness and led to an investigation into the causing of bodily harm (BBC News, 2016).

While corruption was escalating, the project came to a point at which dismantling the unfinished airport and rebuilding it from scratch would have been more cost effective than trying to fix all the problems (Rooks, 2018). Still, the project leaders decided not to do so, falling victim to the "sunk-cost fallacy," where actors "avoid cutting their losses because they are emotionally attached to the time and resources they have already spent on a project" (Kingsland, 2019).*

* For further details, see Deutsche Welle's documentary "Berlin's 'new' BER Airport: A story of incompetence and corruption," available at: https://tinyurl.com/yhpebb8d (viewed May 16, 2024)

Discussion and lessons for future making

Why did a grand vision such as BER turn into a dystopian and unsustainable reality? My short answer: In the case of BER, future making (i.e., the process of imagining and making a course of action for the future) was fraught with political dynamics. Specifically, it was the failure to engage in a co-creation process (see Shamiyeh, 2024) that turned a desired future into a dystopian reality. The project actors, in fact, failed to engage in collaborative practices of future making, and instead entered into competition, seeking to realize their different, and inconsistent, imaginings of the future.

First, the politicians pursued a dream of grandeur, but failed to detect early-warning signals in the airline industry, while also remaining unresponsive to the needs of local residents and the natural environment. Second, local residents attempted to defend the future of their town (and rightly so) but failed to organize and negotiate with other actors, who desired a future airport in the vicinity of the city center.

Third, gmp architects envisioned an aesthetically pleasant, yet self-centered design concept: For instance, they kept the number of commercial spaces to a minimum, neglecting the design requirements of their client (FBB). They even failed to effectively communicate their concept design, given the late stage at which FBB realized that the airport was too small and the shops were too few.

Fourth, FBB attempted to force their imaginings of the future onto citizens, instead of negotiating a common imagining of the future with citizens. They also failed to imagine and materialize alternative forms of governance that would have been more suitable for dealing with a complex future. They probably underestimated the complexity of the future in the making, trusting in their past successes and in the myth of "German efficiency."

Overall, this speaks of a failure, on the part of the various actors, to appreciate their interdependencies, and to negotiate among different imaginings of the future. Instead of making their common future together, actors pursued solipsistic and clashing imaginings of the future. They pitted desired futures against one another, failing to see their systemic nature. Although they did not engage in a turf war, their inability to deal with conflicting imaginings derailed the future of the project.

Not just human, but also non-human actors became enmeshed in the political dynamics of BER. I suspect that matter (e.g., building models) was used not as aids to work out contentious issues, but as allies to lure others into buying a grand yet unfeasible vision. Artifacts materialized imaginings of the future, which, however, were not adequately tested against the design requirements of the various stakeholders. This prevented actors from becoming aware of the unfeasibility of their imaginings, and from calibrating them vis-à-vis present and future constraints.

The design concept kept changing, but many such changes were unnecessary. For instance, it was unnecessary, and even detrimental, to add bridges for the Airbus A380. This suggests that project actors failed to stabilize their imaginings of the future. As a result, the design concept fluctuated continuously without a strong sense of direction: It was left at the mercy of powerful actors—their ebbing and flowing desires and even caprices. Unavoidably, this resulted in further delays and a waste of public funds.

Finally, the dystopian reality of the unfinished airport escalated to a point at which taking down the main terminal would have been more cost effective. I argue that the decision to fix rather than rebuild the main terminal reveals not just a sunk-cost bias (Kingsland, 2019), but also a failure to recognize the unsustainability of the future in the making.

What future making lessons can be learned from this case study?

Although future making is inherently challenging, I believe the following insights from the case study are especially useful in contexts such as project-based work where future making is fraught with political dynamics that arise from the clashing interests of various actors (see also Comi & Vaara, 2022). In these contexts, I suggest that matter (e.g., bodies, objects, and spaces) should be used to: (1) initiate collaborative rather than competitive practices of future making; (2) test and stabilize common imaginings of the future; (3) appreciate rather than downplay the uncertainty of the future in the making; (4) recognize and dismiss imaginings of the future that have become unsustainable; and (5) give voice to under-represented human and non-human actors. Specifically,

1. **Initiate collaborative rather than competitive practices of future making.** Matter such as bodies, objects, and spaces should be mobilized to co-create imaginings and courses of action for the future. In the case of BER, matter was used to push forward desired yet unilateral imaginings of the future, rather than build a shared and realizable course of action for the future.

2. **Test and stabilize common imaginings of the future.** Visual and material artifacts such as drawings, sketches, and images are instrumental to not just create and share imaginings of the future, but also to test their feasibility against multiple constraints (e.g., environmental standards, planning regulations, ...) and stabilize such imaginings of the future in the face of changing requirements (see Comi & Whyte, 2018). This, I believe, would have been especially useful in BER's case, since the project was derailed by design re-work, which was carried out at the

construction stage. Here, design re-works and delays compounded in a negative spiral: This could have been mitigated (at least to some extent) by using various artifacts (e.g., computer models and simulations, project management tools, ...) to test assumptions and courses of action, and to stabilize (or freeze, see Whyte, Ewenstein, Hales, & Tidd, 2007) desired imaginings of the future.

3. **Appreciate rather than downplay the uncertainty of the future in the making.** Scholars of future making place the emphasis not on anticipating what the future might look like, but on making desirable and realizable courses of action for the future. This is predicated on appreciating that the future is, to a large extent, unknown and unknowable (Wenzel et al., 2020) and that making desired and realizable futures is fraught with challenges (Thompson & Byrne, 2021; Whyte et al., 2022). In the case of BER, on the contrary, managers and politicians alike seemed to assume a stable future, which they could colonize with their desires and plans.

4. **Recognize and dismiss imaginings of the future that have become unsustainable.** Future making involves recognizing and dismissing imaginings that are desired, but not (or no longer) sustainable and realizable. The problem of escalating commitment to desired imaginings of the future is evident in the case of BER, where actors completed plans that were no longer reasonable (e.g., designing to accommodate a large aircraft when its use was already declining).

5. **Give voice to under-represented human and non-human actors.** Future makers, I suggest, should be concerned with giving voice to under-represented human actors (e.g., marginalized communities) as well as non-human actors such as animals, the land, and the landscape. This is important to making futures that are genuinely shared and more sustainable. In the case of BER, however, this concern was not adequately taken into consideration, with entire communities being dislocated to make space for the new airport.

These five lessons will hopefully prove helpful to managers who are facing complex challenges and dealing with contentious issues about the futures they are making; and inspire further research on future making, its politics and matter.

References

BBC News. 2016. Berlin Brandenburg airport corruption 'whistleblower poisoned.' ***BBC News,*** May 2. Accessed online https://tinyurl.com/4u3r4u35. Viewed February 7, 2024.

BBC News. 2020. Germany's new Berlin airport set for take off, nine years late. ***BBC News,*** April 29. Accessed online https://tinyurl.com/3v8xu7jb. Viewed February 7, 2024.

Berliner Zeitung. 2020. These are BER's seven most embarrassing fails. ***Berliner Zeitung,*** October 23. Assessed online *https://tinyurl.com/yvtcs6d8*. Viewed February 7, 2024.

Bowlby, C. 2019. Berlin Brandenburg: The airport with half a million faults. ***BBC News,*** June 29. Accessed online https://tinyurl.com/4tu5k3kx. Viewed February 7, 2024.

Comi, A., & Vaara, E. 2022. Political dynamics in knowledge work: Using visual artifacts to deal with pragmatic boundaries. ***Organization Science,*** 33(5): 1837-1860.

Comi, A., & Whyte, J. 2018. Future making and visual artefacts: An ethnographic study of a design project. ***Organization studies,*** 39(8): 1055-1083.

Connolly, K. 2020. We were a laughing stock: Berlin airport finally finished as Covid bites. ***The Guardian,*** October 7. Accessed online https://tinyurl.com/mr424wzh. Viewed February 7, 2024.

Diekmann, F. Kröger, M., & Reimann A. 2013. Wie die Politik die Bürger täuscht. ***Der Spiegel,*** January 9. Accessed online https://tinyurl.com/2zpt2k8n. Viewed February 7, 2024.

DW News. 2020. Berlin's 'new' BER Airport: A story of incompetence and corruption. ***DW News,*** October 30. Accessed online https://tinyurl.com/yhpebb8d. Viewed February 7, 2024.

Euronews. 2020. Berlin airport opens 10 years late and three times over budget. ***Euronews,*** October 31. Accessed online https://tinyurl.com/4xsaeam8. Viewed February 7, 2024.

European Commission. 2022. ***State aid: Commission approves €1.7 billion German measure to recapitalise Flughafen Berlin Brandenburg in the context of the coronavirus pandemic.*** Press release, February 1. Accessed online https://tinyurl.com/2uthmvvk. Viewed February 7, 2024.

Fiedler, J., & Wendler, A. 2016. Berlin Brandenburg Airport. In G. Kostka & J. Fiedler (eds.), ***Large infrastructure projects in Germany: Between ambition and realities:*** 87-146. Cham: Palgrave Macmillan.

Flyvbjerg, B., Holm, M. S., & Buhl, S. 2002. Underestimating costs in public works projects: Error or lie? ***Journal of the American Planning Association,*** 68(3): 279-295.

Geraldi, J., & Stingl, V. 2016. From visions of grandeur to grand failure: Alternative schools of descriptive decision theories to explain the Berlin Brandenburg Airport Fiasco. In ***Proceedings of EURAM 2016:*** Article 2298. Academy of Management.

Glucroft W. N. 2020. Berlin's new airport: A story of failure and embarrassment. ***DW,*** October 31. Accessed online https://tinyurl.com/3e3hxmvk. Viewed February 7, 2024.

Grasso Macola, I. 2021. Berlin Brandenburg Airport: a construction timeline. ***Airport Technology,*** February 9. Accessed online https://tinyurl.com/mrypkv2y. Viewed February 7, 2024.

Kingsland, P. 2019. Breaking the curse: will Berlin Brandenburg Airport finally open in 2020? ***Airport Technology,*** July 30. Accessed online https://tinyurl.com/mrxas9hf. Viewed February 7, 2024.

Landis, J. D. 2022. Epic fail and cautious success - Berlin Brandenburg Airport and New York LaGuardia Terminal B. In J. D. Landis (ed.), ***Megaprojects for megacities - A comparative casebook:*** 348-381. Edward Elgar Publishing.

Nicola, S. 2020. Berlin $7 billion airport finally opens in the depths of a crisis. ***Bloomberg,*** October 30. Accessed online https://tinyurl.com/yc46pmmp. Viewed February 7, 2024.

Rooks, T. 2018. Tear down Berlin's unfinished airport and start over! ***DW,*** January 3. Accessed online https://tinyurl.com/mrwef52w. Viewed February 7, 2024.

Sedlin, T., Beckmann, V., & Tan, R. 2020. Public participation and airport development: The case of the site selection for Berlin Brandenburg airport (BER) in Germany. ***Sustainability,*** 12(24): 10535.

Shamiyeh, M. (ed.). 2024. ***Practices of futurecasting: Ways of sharing imagined tomorrows.*** Basel: Birkhäuser.

Smith O. 2019. When will Berlin's disastrous ghost airport finally open? ***Telegraph,*** April 17. Accessed online https://tinyurl.com/5n85h83k. Viewed February 7, 2024.
Spiegel International. 2013a. Berlin airport can't turn lights off. ***Spiegel***

International, February 28. Accessed online https://tinyurl.com/3wrf2r9r. Viewed February 7, 2024.

Spiegel International. 2013b. The men behind Germany's building debacles. ***Spiegel International,*** June 14. Accessed online https://tinyurl.com/2dew5wma. Viewed February 7, 2024.

Spiegel International. 2013c. Unfinished airport costs 20 million Euros a month. ***Spiegel International,*** May 27. Accessed online https://tinyurl.com/57rhkrcn. Viewed February 7, 2024.

Thompson, N. A., & Byrne, O. 2021. Imagining futures: Theorizing the practical knowledge of future-making. ***Organization Studies,*** 43(2): 247-268.

Traufetter G., & Wassermann A. 2017. An end to Berlin's neverending airport fiasco? ***Spiegel International,*** December 11. Accessed online https://tinyurl.com/yjx6tyts. Viewed February 7, 2024.

Wagner, D. N. 2016. Breakin' the project wave: Understanding and avoiding failure in project management. ***PM World Journal,*** 1(1): 1-21.

Wenzel, M. 2022. Taking the future more seriously: From corporate foresight to "future-making". ***Academy of Management Perspectives,*** 36(2): 845-850.

Wenzel, M., Krämer, H., Koch, J., & Reckwitz, A. 2020. Future and organization studies: On the rediscovery of a problematic temporal category in organizations. ***Organization Studies,*** 41(10): 1441-1455.

Whyte, J., Comi, A., & Mosca, L. 2022. Making futures that matter: Future making, online working and organizing remotely. ***Organization Theory,*** 3(1): 1-20.

Whyte, J., Ewenstein, B., Hales, M., & Tidd, J. 2007. Visual practices and the objects used in design. ***Building research and information,*** 35(1): 18-27.

SARAH DAVANZO

CHIEF DATA OFFICER,
PIERRE FABRE
NEW YORK, UNITED STATES

Photo: Erich Goldmann

THE DILEMMAS & DELIGHTS OF CORPORATE TOMORROWING

Large corporations are some of the most influential forces on earth. They literally shape our local and global futures through their operations, investments, research, lobbying, and impact on culture. Their actions, priorities, and ambitions drive so much of our collective behavior and who we become as human beings. The corporate world exploits the "self-fulfilling prophecy," where their predictions come true because of their belief or expectation that their predictions would come true, and because of the wheels they set in motion that enable their predictions to come true.

The power and tremendous resources coming from large corporations can (and, I would argue, should) be ethically harnessed to lead the way in foresight and *futurecasting*. In this paper, we will discuss how tools like biomimicry, social experiments, data and AI diversity, and guerilla tactics can all be used in corporate settings to both predict and usher in the future. We will also cover the ethical responsibilities of corporations to use their power wisely.

For example, ingredients featured in major products become must-haves for our physical and mental health, even though we have previously never heard of them or found them relevant. Acai berries, turmeric, coconut oil, and probiotics come to mind in recent years. Though some of us may learn about these health-conscious ingredients through our doctors, most of us discover them through food or beauty marketing. The idea of walking 10,000 steps a day originally came from a Japanese marketing company in 1965 to sell pedometers. This is an example of how business influences culture, ergo the future.

It is not well-known that many large companies have staff dedicated to futurism and foresight, who are paid to predict what consumers will want and need in the coming years. According to the University of Houston's Foresight Department, more than 25% of Fortune 1000 companies have an internal resource that is dedicated to futurism and foresight. Large multinational businesses are placing increasing value on future preparedness, future-proofing operations, and creating products and services that anticipate future needs. There is even a trendy new C-suite role called the "Chief Futures Officer" or "Chief Futurist Officer," who is responsible for future-proofing the organization by mitigating risks, preparing for future eventualities, and seizing budding opportunities while they are nascent (and cheaper to acquire!).

Their predictions, calculations, and speculations have a trickle-down impact, influencing society and life on Earth. Their jobs are profoundly powerful. But what informs them how to do these jobs well, and responsibly? There is yet to be an industry-wide certification standard ensuring methodological rigor. This should concern us. Fields like law, medicine, and engineering have a single source of methodological truth. Not so the field of futures. These professionals acquire competencies from a hodge-podge of private courses, university programs, professional associations, and think-tank certifications with varying degrees of qualitative and quantitative rigor. Accreditation entities tend to be academic and professional networks that excel at theory but can be unimaginative and fall flat in practice.

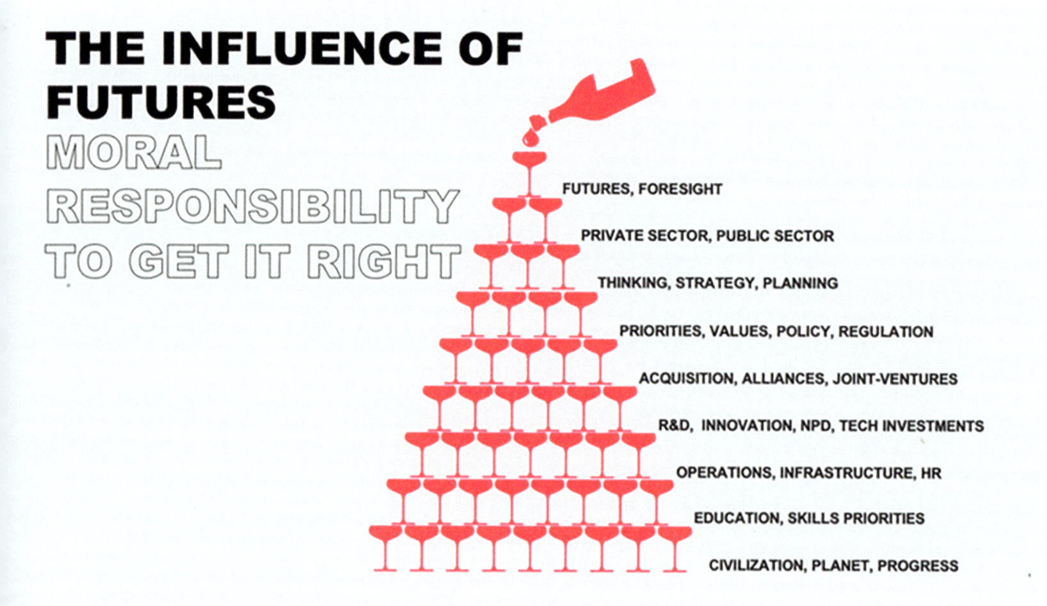

Figure 1: Corporate foresight has a trickle-down influence on society and the world at large. © *DaVanzo*

Corporate foresight leaders often land their position indirectly, starting their careers in anything from strategy and business development to M&As, issues monitoring, or sustainability. A current trend is to evolve a business's "Insights" function, which is responsible for market and consumer research and seeking cultural insights as well as foresight. Consumer and market insights (CMI) functions are expanding their deliverables to provide "consumer foresight" and "cultural foresight." Since culture is constantly shifting, it needs constant monitoring; CMI teams are installing permanently active "Cultural Intelligence Systems" comprised of people, digital toolstacks, and processes dedicated to tracking and measuring cultural shifts. This is a first step towards setting up a company function dedicated to the future.

The world of the enterprise futurist

What challenges do these corporate futurists face?

- Answering to shareholders and boards of directors who demand to know the value of the futures work, showing how it directly drives business growth through key performance indicators (KPIs).
- Pressure to be data-driven, quantitative, methodologically agnostic, and rigorous. Accuracy and objectivity are paramount because companies make major investments and decisions based on the work.
- The expectation that their work will unlock competitive advantage and lead to pragmatic business applications for corporate strategy, M&A, R&D/innovation, ERM, CSR/impact, technology/IT/data/digital, marketing, issues management (corporate communications), operations, and other functions of a business.
- Straddling the worlds of futurism, which refers to what futures are imaginable or possible, and foresight, which refers to futures that are expected to be plausible based on data analysis.
- The requirement to comply with diversity, equity, inclusion, & access (DEI&A) standards and the ability to withstand DEI&A scrutiny.
- Steering the company towards both preferable and plausible futures while also delivering the business objectives. Enterprise futures professionals constantly balance "good for business" and "good for people and planet."
- Communicating the future and delivering storytelling in modalities that work globally, multilingually, and cross-culturally.

Corporate future departments and roles tend to be open and experimental, tapping global experts and leveraging a wide range of vendors, which results in diverse methods and outputs. Enterprise-level organizations can afford ambitious, expensive, high-quality future experiences, speculative fiction artifacts, and precious research publications. It is not uncommon for a corporation to build an entire room dedicated to mocked-up future products and prototype technologies, with furniture and objects that look like they came straight out of a sci-fi movie. These "rooms of the future" become spaces where employees empathize with future consumers and work on new products for a future context. They make the future so irresistible that it becomes inevitable.

Corporations are patrons of futuristic artists, game designers, “design fiction” designers, and science fiction writers. Futurists are responsible for bringing the future to life and communicating it in memorable ways. They keep futurist creators on speed dial to tap for storytelling and communication. The field of “speculative design” is growing because the future is abstract, and people have difficulty imagining future scenarios.

Enterprise futurists are also pioneering quantitative foresight methods and artificial intelligence (AI) for predictive modeling, which can be too costly for small businesses or non-profit organizations. Due to an increasing need for accurate, unbiased, and data-informed foresight, the day-to-day work of corporate futurists is becoming less art and more science. Algorithms help data scientists identify patterns and measure trends. Corporations with robust foresight capabilities have large “social listening” and “search listening” teams focused on analyzing social media chatter and Google search trends.

The shareholders and boards of directors of publicly listed companies want hard data to support any futures speculation. They are not going to make investments based on a futurist’s *feeling* or on a bunch of conversations that a futurist has with a dozen experts. There is too much at stake. As a result, old-school qualitative futurists are being replaced by quantitative futurists who work with big data, open data, AI, algorithms, and technology platforms. Some futurists in the world’s largest companies are becoming specialists in a new field called “Alternative Data” or “Exotic Data.”

In my career, I have had the privilege of working with some of the world’s largest multinational corporations, toiling and playing in the world of foresight and futurism. I am familiar with the challenges presented by such a niche corporate function as well as the almost more challenging task of earning buy-in from corporate leadership.

Corporate persuasion with biomimicry

One of the biggest challenges an enterprise futurist faces is persuading their audience to believe that fantastic change is imminent and that the unimaginable is not only possible, but likely. Famously, futurists in the early 1900s who read the signals predicted handheld personal communication devices (i.e., cellphones). They were ridiculed. It seemed like an impossible prospect. Showing that the impossible is possible and, in fact, inevitable is the most challenging job of an enterprise futurist. How do we show the unknowable?

One effective way enterprise futurists tell and sell the future is through biomimicry.

Figure 2: Octopus as an analogy for the future of skin, illustrating how biomimicry helps with communicating plausibility © *DaVanzo*

When I was leading strategic foresight and futurism for one of the world's largest beauty companies, I was responsible for a data-driven point of view on the Future of Skincare 2030. This project was designed to inform long-term strategy, M&A, R&D, and the giant leaps that technology was expected to make more than ten years in the future (moonshots). Billions of dollars were riding on the accuracy of the foresight and its potential to change the game of the beauty industry. The goal was to leapfrog the competition, disrupt, and move into new business territories.

We launched a six-month foresight methodology combining quantitative and qualitative foresight techniques, leveraging several different futures consultancies and a dozen international futurists. Ultimately, we had a solid, data-informed point of view of what was possible and plausible in skincare a decade into the future. The process was designed to be inclusive and equitable, with contributions from cultures all over the globe. From this work, we identified a dozen characteristics of the future of skin, such as texture transformation, color shifting, color correcting, emotional expression, self-healing properties, regeneration, and more.

We were confident in our quantitative foresight. We had so much corroborating data that clearly showed inevitable future technological and scientific advancements. On the other hand, the futurism—the imaginative possibilities—of applying technological and scientific achievements to day-to-day life was hard to imagine. Most people found the future vision too unfamiliar, outlandish, and disruptive: "Color-shifting and self-healing skin? That's crazy!" Our challenge was to communicate and convince corporate leadership that some wild possibilities could be realities in skincare.

We toyed with communication methods such as staging an immersive experience in a futuristic bathroom or producing a graphic novel depicting "Skincare 2030." But these techniques did not address the lack of believability of our vision of the future of skin. The future still seemed like science fiction.

We turned to biomimicry to help us make the future plausible and believable. We set out to identify a plant, animal, or organism that possessed future skin properties, such as color-shifting and self-healing membranes. We scoured biomimicry databases like asknature.org and biomimicry.net for life forms that portrayed the features of our future vision. Our logic: If it exists in nature, it can exist in the future.

Bearing in mind the dozen characteristics of the future of skin mentioned above, we set out to find an organism with all these characteristics. We found a unique and rare breed of octopus with all of the features we were looking for, proving that the characteristics of the future of skin are already evident in the animal kingdom. What was difficult to comprehend or imagine in theory was brought into reality with a present-day example from nature. Our audience could now visualize that the unbelievable future we were forecasting was possible, plausible, and powerful.

Co-creating the future with social experiments

When I was leading strategic foresight and futurism for one of the world's largest beverage companies, I was responsible for a data-driven point of view on the Future of Beverages 2030, again to inform strategy, M&A, product, and portfolio development. The goal was to identify new ways in which the company could branch out from its core business and attract new, younger consumers. Our challenge was this: What will the children and teens of the future want to drink?

While we conducted extensive research into beverage trends, especially among influencers and early adopters, we knew there was so much about the future that was not yet trending. We would have to invent future beverages, exploring the edges and corners of our imagination to conceptualize what did not yet exist. It was an exercise in forecasting what the year 2030 would be like—what events would be taking place, how would people socialize and consume food, what cultural shifts may occur, and how might daily life be different? But yet again—how could we communicate this to the leadership of a multi-billion-dollar company?

Our solution was to invite the future into our laboratory and *show* it to our audience instead of trying to tell it. We created a maker space in the form of a beverage lab. After analyzing patents and research papers and scouring for emerging technologies and flavor sciences, we stocked this lab with the "ingredients of the future." Then the games began.

The players in our future lab were Gen Z tweens chaperoned by their parents. We played in a synesthesia wonderland of future flavors and experimental technologies to tantalize one's sense of sound, touch, taste, and sight. Flowers were infused with flavors and flash freeze-dried, crunching in the mouth. Flavor mixtures were vaporized

Figure 3: Maker Lab social experiment to co-create the future of beverages with tomorrow's consumers © *Bruce King-Shey*

and ingested by inhalation. Through role-playing, experimentation, and trial and error, we co-created an array of future beverages with kids.

If we had invented them ourselves, they would have seemed unusual and unrealistic, feeding the skepticism of our corporate leadership audience. But in this social experiment, we showed these leaders an army of future consumers consuming the outlandish beverages they invented.

Growing demand for data & AI diversity

Throughout my career as an enterprise futurist and foresight consultancy leader, I have discovered that the most surefire way to communicate the plausibility of futures is through abundant and diverse data sets. The more different the types of data, the more robust and believable the scenario. Data diversity is critical to communicating the future in different ways; just as there are at least a dozen different "learning styles" (e.g., visual, aural, kinetic, etc.), there are at least a dozen different communication modalities.

The surest way to achieve data diversity is with:

- Diverse team members on the project (representing the full spectrum of human diversity in age, gender, culture, ethnicity, socio-economics, personality, neurodiversity, etc.)
- Diverse partners and vendors (including diversity of leadership, ownership, and employees)
- Diverse methodologies (quantitative, qualitative, online, offline, primary, secondary, mixed, etc.)
- Diverse AI platforms (yes, you read that right!)

In the age of AI, we can fall into the trap of relying on a handful of AI platforms in our foresight work, mistakenly thinking that they are more or less the same. But the modern Chief Futures Officer *must* diversify AI platforms to combat the cultural skews of the AI's programmers and training materials. In DEI&A conversations, we typically address diversity as it relates to human beings. What we do not discuss enough is the need for AI diversity, a lack of which can result in false futures.

Beauty 2030 Methodology

Diverse data inputs & processes

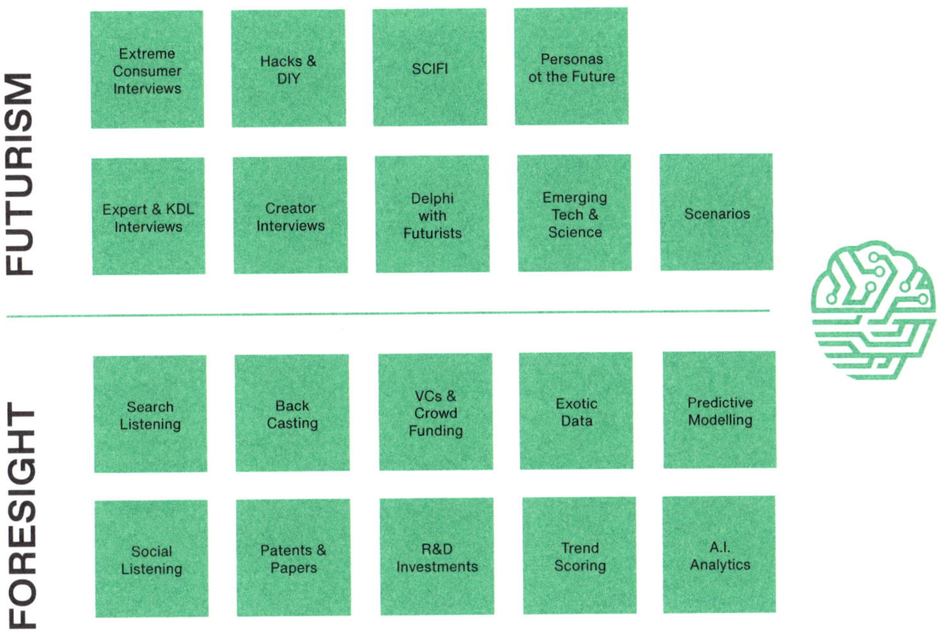

Figure 4: Methodology including diverse inputs and processes to maximize data diversity © *DaVanzo*

I conducted an experiment to illustrate this point by comparing the envisioned futures of two AI platforms: one built in the US with American/Western training material and one built in China with Chinese training material. I fed both the same prompt—how will robots help society in the future? I gave the prompt in their natural, local languages. The difference in results could not be starker.

The Chinese-created AI forecasted that robots would educate and upskill elderly Chinese in rural China, a critical social problem growing today. The American-created AI predicted robot use in commercial settings, such as warehouses, to improve human efficiency and productivity. The differences in these two plausible future scenarios reflect cultural priorities, highlighting the need to use multiple AI platforms for diverse futures.

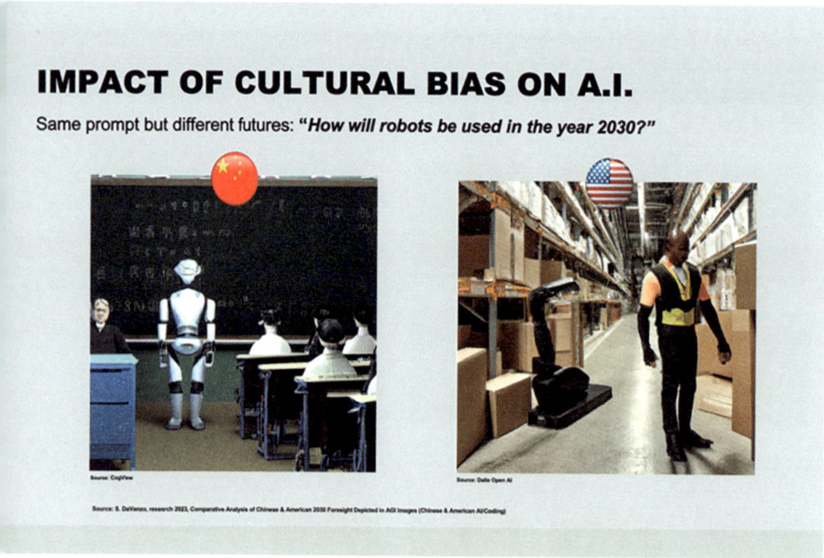

Figure 5: Chinese vs. American AI platforms imagine different futures from the same prompt, illustrating the need for AI diversity. © *DaVanzo*

New corporate approaches: Futures activism & guerilla foresight

An "art activist" uses creative media such as performance art, public installations, or other artistic expressions, to bring about social, cultural, or political change. A "futures activist" uses similar creative experiential tactics combined with strategic foresight and futurism to build and co-create better futures.* *Tomorrowing* can be spontaneous. Serendipitous art, games, happenings, research, and social experiments can engage people and inspire positive change to help build better futures.

Foresight and futurism are too often formal activities with rigorous methodologies and multiple steps and stakeholders. Enterprise futurists can tend to work in a silo, serving the C-suite and not the entire organization. But it does not need to be this way. What if we approached futures as "interventions"? What if *tomorrowing* happened in unexpected places in the corporate world, such as in the cafeteria, in the restroom, near the photocopiers, or beside the coffee maker? What if we modeled futures on movements? What if the corporate world used games and play activities to stimulate *tomorrowing* today?

In one of my corporate "Chief Futurist Officer" roles, I was

---

* https://futuresactivist.com/ (Viewed March 28, 2024)

responsible for managing short, medium, and long-term foresight and futurism to inform innovation (to generate concepts to drive new product development). One "futures activism" method that was highly effective and efficient, saving time and money, was through a hacked Monopoly game. We skinned the Monopoly board and replaced real estate properties with emerging technologies and scientific advancements. The cards were replaced with prompts to think about the conversion of trends and consumer needs in the future (which had been validated by extensive data analytics). Players purchased innovation spaces that they thought would be most valuable in the future. Through this game, the organization was able to align on innovation priorities and where to direct its leadership energy. This creative down-and-dirty game is an example of *guerrilla foresight*.

Figure 6: MONOPOLY 2030 game, where players bid on the future instead of real estate to align on innovation priorities © *DaVanzo*

When a corporate foresight leader takes on the persona of a "futures activist," that individual is focused on elevating curiosity about the future, companywide. When the enterprise futurist wears the futures activist hat, that person stimulates futures-thinking and action. Passion for futuristic topics spreads like contagion. Businesses that adopt an activist approach to foresight and the future are simultaneously creating a corporate culture of change and curiosity.

Jolting business associates out of their everyday tasks and into futures thinking ignites fresh curiosity and a corporate culture steeped in a futures mindset.

Using *tomorrowing* for transformation

The acting Chief Futures Officer within an enterprise should be a change agent. When a business decides that it needs to transform radically, a foresight leader is the ideal person to contextualize the transformation and present a view of what can work.

The future is a sexy topic. Who does not want to participate in a project that starts with "The future of..."? *Tomorrowing* can be a way to get all functions of an enterprise, from the junior to senior staff and across all departments and businesses, to come together to focus on what is universally relevant: our shared future. Therefore, insightful CEOs and transforming corporations can drive change and modernization through foresight and futurism activities, events, and workstreams that co-create the future with employees.

Figure 7: A draft of a Futurist's Code of Ethics © *DaVanzo*

FUTURIST'S CODE OF ETHICS

FUTURISTS BEAR THE RESPONSIBILITY OF DATA-DIVERSITY, HUMAN DIVERSITY & AI DIVERSITY FOR DEBIASED RIGOROUS ANALYTICS WITH TRANSPARENT AND TRUSTWORTHY METHODS THAT ARE INCLUSIVE AND EQUITABLE TO ENSURE THAT FORESIGHT IS ACCURATE, GENERATIVE AND NOT SELF-SERVING.

The weight on the futurist's shoulders is heavy. Their work steers the business, which in turn steers society. Businesses' decisions impact their employees, constituents, customers, community, stakeholders, suppliers, business partners, politicians, and more. What the Chief Futures Officer whispers into the ear of the CEO can influence so much more than just the business—it can be the seed of a self-fulfilling prophecy that makes the predicted future come to fruition.

The ethical futurist

As such, the Chief Futures Officer is responsible for "getting it right." This means ensuring that the data and AI are diverse, that methods are rigorous and trustworthy, and that approaches are ethical and equitable. While there may not be one governing accreditation body for the futures profession, I believe we should work toward a code of ethics or to an overarching principle that we can cling to. Physicians take the Hippocratic Oath to "do no harm" and bankers swear: "I will keep confidential that which has been entrusted to me; I will not abuse my knowledge; I will act openly and accountably, and I know my responsibility to society..." There ought to be some universal standards of practice in the futures world to maximize accuracy, equity, responsibility, and possibility.

Enterprising futurists also bear the responsibility of making futures preferable and principled. Otherwise, the futures games that corporations play will result in all players losing. The enterprise futurist has the money and means to rigorously divine the future and bring it to life in exciting and creative ways. But this individual also has pressures that accompany the pleasures, such as accountability to the enterprise, its employees, stakeholders, and society at large.

The power of corporate *tomorrowing* to shape *all* our tomorrows, for good or bad, is a force that must not be underestimated or underused.

Photo: Erich Goldmann

USING THE POWER OF GAMEWORLDS

Introduction

You pick up a token and move it off the board, finally eradicating the last fossil fuel energy plant in the EU. Your team was able to replace fossil fuels with sustainable energy systems and innovative batteries that no longer use chemicals but, rather, are powered by great wells of water and gravity. Your team worked tirelessly and shared the labor. It took negotiation, inventiveness, and leverage to get there, but success is yours, and the planet's as well!

This imaginary game scenario on energy is one that you might have designed for your organization. Games are fantastic tools for imagining the future. As their own special breed of art form, games model challenges, present risks, and set up rewards for players. They can also reveal possibilities that were unimagined before playing.

People wanting to design games for futurecasting have chosen a powerful way to model possible worlds. Using games to speculate about the future, we can craft games that reflect revolutionary new social rules and environmental conditions. A game could model something incredibly local or vastly global; scale is part of the interesting flexibility of games as a medium for thought experiments and even persuasion. Games can be shared among makers, distributed among institutions, and even sold to players out in the world.

In this paper, I will discuss two key challenges for game designers: how to think about abstracting the system in which you are engaging, and how to approach difficult, prosocial topics and themes without losing player interest. For over 20 years I have led the game research laboratory Tiltfactor, designing and testing online games, sports, tabletop, and VR games that address societal issues. Our team has included designers, artists, and social psychologists invested in building better futures through play. We use play and the structure of games for transformation, and to measure success, and we have conducted many experiments using these games to understand how particular design strategies impact players.

Abstracting the system

Games are created from actions (called "mechanics" in game-speak), themes, and components (music, images, models, and animations in video games; dice, boards, cards, and pieces in tabletop games). The trick to creating a good game that really models a system or phenomenon is to decide what to leave out and what is crucial to include. If you are building a nuclear energy simulator to get players to understand nuclear energy, you might have to go into some scientific detail when you decide what players are doing and where the human decisions come in. But if you are making a nuclear power grid and your aim is for players to understand the network, it would not be necessary to model the science. The same goes for any system you are looking at: Do you want to make new laws for AI in your game or do you want to model how an AI learns? The right level of detail to include in the game depends on the end focus that you want your players to work on. Often those new to game design err by adding too much detail, and therefore not removing enough complexity so that they actually create a simulation that is overly complicated and impossible to play. Or the opposite can happen and players can use a simple existing game (such as *Snakes and Ladders*) and modify it to try to model a topic that does not quite fit into that game model well. The "fit" of what the players are doing related to the larger concept is a key aspect that requires practice to get it right.

Keeping player interest

As game designers, we understand that we construct imagined worlds in which players make meaningful decisions to accomplish a goal. Players will not play unless they find a game "fun"—that elusive term I prefer to think about as "immersed" or "engaged." A game can become an experiential future—players can live it, sense it, experience it. Therefore, the first thing to decide is what immersive experience you will make and what format it will take. Board games, sports, and role-playing games are the most affordable to prototype and produce and might serve your purpose better than an expensive digital game. It depends on your situation, but developing digital games without an experienced team and a grand budget rarely works out well.

And what about your topic? What if it is not "fun" at all? No worries. Games are made about all kinds of phenomena. Energy grids, train systems, making tea, even packing and unpacking one's belongings. My team has made games on more difficult or emotional subjects ranging from poor public health and racism and sexism, to sexual assault and non-sustainable and polluting habits. In this work, we have uncovered techniques to approach difficult topics, keep player interest, and treat the subject with respect. These techniques will be useful to your own situations when you think about using a game in your work.

There is infinitely more to be said on how to playtest and develop games, but I have limited space in this volume. I refer you to *Game Design Workshop* by Tracy Fullerton for further practice.

Reaching around reactance

At the Tiltfactor lab, we developed the "Embedded Design" approach that offers novel, evidence-based strategies for including persuasive content in a game. Embedding persuasive content or interactions in a game circumvents players' psychological defenses, and fosters a more receptive mindset for internalizing a game's intended message (Kaufman, Flanagan, & Seidman 2015; Kaufman, Flanagan, Seidman, & Wien, 2015). We found that Embedded Design can be used without sacrificing players' enjoyment or a game's replayability. The approach promises to revolutionize the ways game makers can take on serious issues in games.

Embedded Design is necessary because theories in psychology show us that presenting difficult themes or subjects in what some call "serious games" is quite tricky. If designers directly follow logical and well-intentioned assumptions on how to confront an issue head-on, they may assume that players will shift their beliefs once informed. But time and time again that assumption has been proven false. In light of what we know from contemporary psychology, it is often not effective, and even potentially harmful, to tackle difficult subjects directly. There is a large body of social psychological research on persuasion and attitude change, and this research has repeatedly demonstrated that people resist persuasive communications if these are perceived as manipulative or directive, or if their own identity or freedom is somehow challenged (Brehm, 1966; Brehm & Brehm, 1981). Surprisingly, this resistance reaction happens even when a person's own beliefs are in agreement with the message (Worchel & Brehm, 1970).

A persuasive game could easily fail to interest players, let alone foster some kind of transformative experience, due to player reactance. It seems obvious to say, but to do their magic, games must engage players. A second challenge in designing games for social impact lies in the format of a game itself: to the player, a game must feel fair, offer agency, and allow the player to experience a sense of freedom (Huizinga, 1938). Thus, the very fabric of what makes a game a game must be maintained. Serious game designers face a seemingly intractable problem, as "message-driven" experiences will likely trigger reactance. Our team has worked on this thorny contradiction for years, and we have discovered techniques to solve the clash between messaging and the freedom of play. Of the many options the Embedded Design suite offers, here are three "embedding" strategies. The first is called "Intermixing": balancing "on-message" and "off-message" content to render the former less overt or threatening. The second we call "Obfuscating," or using framing devices or genres that divert expectations or focus away from the game's persuasive intent. A third approach is "Distancing," or involving fiction and metaphor to increase the psychological gap between players' identities and beliefs and the game's characters and persuasive content (Flanagan & Kaufman, 2016). In the examples in this paper, I will show how Embedded Design strategies are employed in different ways to create effective game interventions.

Distancing through theme

Fiction's power to influence people's thinking and its role in personal transformation have long been studied. Stories are not just entertainment or powerful sales tools—fiction helps to position the imagination to enact different desired outcomes.

Before the global pandemic, a non-profit group approached our team to see if it would be possible to create a game involving vaccination. They had tried video commercials and print media as well, but they had doubts whether any of their promotional materials could shift someone's mindset about the polemic beliefs around vaccination in the United States. We developed *POX* as a board game and as an app that demonstrated the systems thinking behind disease spread and vaccination. We set out to create a cooperative experience that models the logic of how a disease spreads, starting with two "patient zero" spots on the grid board.

Each turn, a direction card is drawn, and currently infected spots on the board infect the next spot in the direction shown. The board contains several spots where vulnerable populations cannot be vaccinated and are at higher risk of dying from infections. On other turns, players can vaccinate three people in the community (i.e., three spots) or treat and cure one person who is already infected. This meaningful choice between player actions is key to the persuasive element and ultimate meaning of the game. Not vaccinating, and choosing instead to cure infected people in the community, is more costly and also does not scale well as disease vectors spread.

Instead of attempting to persuade with facts, we made an experience that *uses* the facts to create its rules and structures. The theme was about an outbreak of "disease" in your neighborhood, and the visuals abstractly represent your neighbors. We created a board game, and then a digital version of that game. Then, we created an additional version of the game that used a fantastic visual element to see which of the games might be the most effective—the regular *POX* board game, the digital app, or the new *ZOMBIEPOX* board game (the zombie outbreak was also situated narratively in the neighborhood). Then we examined how the games played out in a randomized control study.

Figure 1: The three versions of the *POX* game © *Flanagan*

In the study, we paired off players playing one of three conditions—the base game, the digital version of that game, and the outlandish zombie-themed version. Each game was set up to offer the same options to the players (i.e., the digital and non-digital decks were "stacked" to be identical) and they were each played when seated at tables, the players facing each other across the board. Players played and we tracked conversations, their decisions, and whether they lost or won the game. We found that among all three versions, the analog, zombie version was the most effective at getting players to value vaccination and favor increasing funding for public health. The least effective at changing mindsets was the digital version. Players of the digital game, in the same setting, played shorter games, spoke to each other less, and were less likely to consider the ramifications of their decisions (Kaufman & Flanagan, 2013, 2016).

The game works well to impart the value of vaccination, in part through its good abstract model of the mechanics of disease spread, and in part through the Embedded Design approach of "distancing." Psychological Reactance Theory is an important framework that can help us understand people's responses to persuasion and the power of engaging fantastic, fictionalized worlds when framing belief or behavior change. In the *POX* study, the fanciful theme—not the more plausible theme—helped get around psychological reactance about vaccination in general. The imagined space of the storyworld creates a distance far from our daily experience, so players can feel safe and autonomous in making decisions without threatening their own sense of freedom or identity (Brehm & Brehm, 1981; Brehm, Stires, Sensenig, & Shaban, 1966). People who perceive their freedom to be threatened become irritated and resistant to messages; in effect, they shut down. The feeling of control, or agency, is an integral part of the efficacy of a highly fictionalized game setting—psychological reactance happens among players as they work to assert control.

By creating a compelling fictional situation, game interactions can feel apart from everyday life, and by distancing players from the present, these interactions bypass difficult barriers and have an important impact on players. Imagine the impact such a game can have on your constituencies to inform policymaking. Imagine that impact in commercial products and public services that influence hundreds, thousands, tens of thousands of players.

You're racist? Obfuscating the message

Some particularly thorny social issues can seem intractable to fight against—fake news, rising extremism, stereotypes, and gender bias are a few examples. One may think that phenomena like gender bias and racism are unchangeable social phenomena, or only impacted by policy, formal education reforms, or improved societal conditions. Yet for most individuals on the "bell curve" of bias, theories that counter-stereotypical examples can shift biases have persisted (Finnegan, Oakhill, & Garnham, 2015; Gregg, Seibt, & Banaji, 2006).

There are techniques my team has learned through prototypes, rigorous testing, and commercial release; we spent years creating a series of games that can shift biases.

Figure 2: *Buffalo* game cards © *Flanagan*

I will describe one example, *Buffalo: The Name-Dropping Game*, a card game intended to reduce knee-jerk biases that lead to racism, sexism, and other discrimination. The game is simple: the orange deck contains adjectives, such as descriptors of age, ethnicity, personality, or physical characteristics. The blue cards contain nouns including professions or social roles and group affiliations such as environmentalist. To play the game, players collectively reveal one card from each deck simultaneously, and the first person to name a real or fictional character, living or deceased, who matches the pair receives the cards as points. Players win by having the most cards as points. When players are stumped by the combination, they must leave the vexing combination on the table and draw two more cards. Occasionally a wild card, the *Buffalo* card, appears and allows players to sweep all of the cards from the table, gaining many more points than a typical round. Buffalo creates a surprising array of social categories and unexpected roles. In some cases, these are directly counter-stereotypical combinations.

It is important to note what we did not do: We did not tell players that the aim of the game was to reduce prejudice and bias. That approach, we found through other psychological studies, would only backfire. Very few people think they are as biased as they truly are. In the game's development, we thought through theming the game around brain health, but that has a "useful" type of tinge to it that might not bring most players to experience the benefits of the game. So, we just decided to present the game as a party game, like some of the games you might find available in retail shops. Not explicitly stating the goal of the game invited people to open up and play.

In a randomized experimental study, players were put into either a group to play the game before completing a questionnaire or a no-game control condition in which participants completed the measures prior to gameplay. The card pairings used in each condition were identical. We measured "social identity complexity," which is the breadth and the inclusiveness of the way a person understands their social identity. This measure is a reliable way to assess inter-group tolerance, such as gender, ethnicity, religion, etc. We also used the universal orientation scale, a measure of non-prejudice.

The results show that even a single session was enough to trigger a higher degree of change and intergroup perceptions and judgments about others. Playing this game for just a 20-minute session reduced biases, measured by two different social psychology tools that detect stereotyping and discrimination. By creating fun, unexpected combinations of nouns and adjectives, we were able to generate change. From the Embedded Design toolbox, we used "Obfuscating," or framing devices or genres that divert expectations or focus away from a game's persuasive intent. This way, we were able to reveal blind spots and make new unconscious connections in the minds of players.

Clearly no one expects a fun party game to be filled with social messages! By varying the content to include fun and even outlandish themes, we can insert pro-social messaging into the design without overtly *telling* players what to think.

Games are effective interventions in part because they are often played again and again, and studies show that reducing automatic stereotypes is most effective if multiple counter-stereotypical encounters are experienced over time (Lenton, Sedikides, & Bruder, 2009). This work reminds us that our biases are malleable: learning about them can give you the self-insight you need to shift them.

Mix it up

Our team worked with climate scientists to increase sustainable thinking to combat climate change within the general population, and to promote sustainable behaviors. Behavior change via an intervention is notoriously difficult to measure, but our study set up ideal conditions. We decided to hack a popular party card game with subtle climate content and study real-world recycling behaviors.

Figure 3: The *Cops Arrest Manatees* card game © *Flanagan*

We developed two versions of *Cops Arrest Manatees*: The climate change-related version includes some cards with climate change themes in a raucous style. For example, a card with the situation "A sad polar bear on a melting iceberg," might be drawn to match with other cards to create a cause-and-effect combination. We created a third of the cards with climate-related content (35%). In our neutral condition set, none of the cards were climate-related.

In a field experiment, nearly 200 adults played one of two versions of the game, and their recycling and donation behaviors were monitored to see if they would recycle. In the study, players were given plastic drink cups from which to drink water. Each cup, however, was secretly labeled with invisible ink so that we could track players' recycling behavior and which condition of the game they had played—versions of the game with or without the climate content. At the end of the study, we went through the trash to find out who had recycled! The bad news is that only 10% of participants recycled in the control group (those who played without climate content). But after playing our edited version of the game, 31% of players recycled their cups.

Again, no one knew we were studying sustainable behaviors—the players did not detect the game's message at all. But they unconsciously associated climate challenges with the experience, and it triggered significant recycling behaviors as compared to the condition without any climate material in the game.

These results show that games are a vital tool for imagining desired futures. Games have the capacity to nudge us towards a more equitable and just future. Many of them are also low-tech, which makes them physical, haptic, softer, and local, increasing agency in immersive and enacted experiences with other people.

Get moving

Can we change hearts and minds among insurance companies, politicians, and policymakers about the state of the healthcare system in the United States? Our team developed a game in collaboration with the Dartmouth Center for Health Care Delivery Science and the Rippel Foundation. Our team created a novel "role-playing sport" that was based on a complex data-driven computational simulation of healthcare systems in the real world. The game, called *RePlay Health*, places players in an immersive fictional world in which they take on the role of individual characters who each have specific personal risk factors and privileges. The game models the impact of healthcare systems and policies on individual people and how they can seek care in the contemporary US healthcare system.

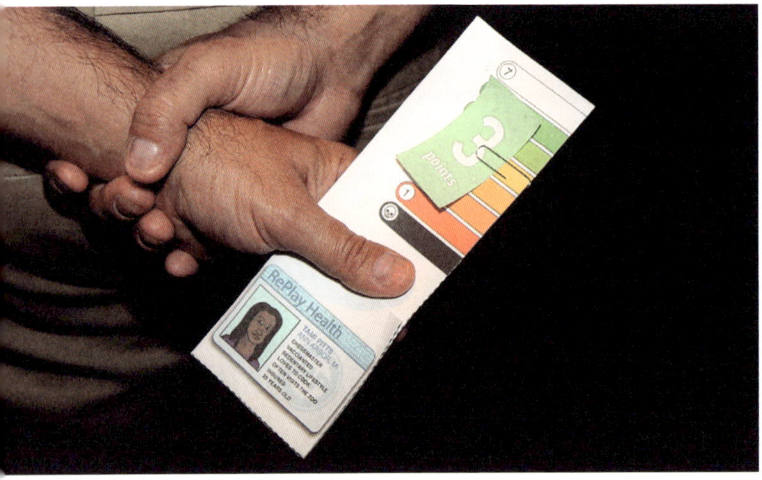

Figure 4: *RePlay Health* player identity wallet © *Flanagan*

To start the game, each player is given a wallet with an identity that shows specific health factors and financial means. The wallet also contains a chart where players can keep track of their character's personal health. Players must balance performing physical activities to score points with trying to monitor and improve their character's health. During the game, it is likely that players' characters experience health challenges and players must decide whether they should take time off from work and lose the opportunity to score points to recover now or push their luck and hope for the best.

Players learn that the system is flawed and, in between rounds, they can get together to vote to change the system. *RePlay Health* provides an abstract model of a healthcare system that sets the context for larger decisions to be made regarding healthcare policy. Players can experiment with the model to see how health productivity and costs relate to each other.

An experiment was used to evaluate *RePlay Health* and whether it inspires shifts in thinking about public health and healthcare policy or not. In the study, we compare the impact of actively playing the game as opposed to merely being a spectator. Pretest and posttest measures showed that active players developed a deeper concern and understanding of healthcare policies and how they relate to overall health. The healthcare policies modeled in the game, such as improving post-discharge care and increasing access to healthy food, were prioritized higher by active players. Players rather than spectators were significantly more likely to identify environmental or systemic factors in healthcare. Significant results emerged in the week between the actual game being played and the posttest measurement, and this shows that playing a game that is embodied can have a strong and lasting impact on attitudes and demonstrates the effectiveness of experiential actions in role-playing games (Kaufman, Flanagan, Seidman, & Wien, 2015).

Figure 5: *RePlay Health* players, mid-game © *Flanagan*

This study was a precursor to emerging research that shows that the use of objects and haptic sense improves learning (Novak & Schwan, 2021).

This final point about embodiment is one often overlooked in the digital age: Games and play scenarios bring forth an interdependent world that, through embodied action, leads us to "enacted cognition" and the embodiment of futures (Varela, Thompson, & Rosch, 2017). Enacting is key to play, simulations, and games, and what we are doing with our bodies and minds aids learning, understanding, and processing (Fugate, Macrine, & Cipriano, 2019). Research shows that children learn and retain more from embodied, active learning (Goldstein, Thompson, & Kanumuru, 2022). I have linked games, play, and embodied cognition because games—be they board games, card games, video games, sports, or role playing games—are sites where people gather and act out their own agency based on rules. Clearly, in a role-playing sport, there is a high degree of embodiment, but even board games and digital games trigger the sense of embodiment. It could be because games allow players to feel that they are the force that moves a game forward, that their agency controlling a character, decision, and even embodied identities can be felt.

Play is inherently embodied, and games create imagined worlds. In fact, researchers at the mindCORE Institute at the University of Pennsylvania found two subnetworks in the brain in the "default mode network" or DMN, which is a suspected "seat of the imagination" and the area we use to daydream too. One part of the DMN envisions future events, and the other determines whether the event will be good, or bad (Lee, Parthasarathi, & Kable, 2021). In games, we are actively creating what we imagine. We enact and embody ideas and, simply put, they matter more. They open up blind spots and persuade us with the emergent common sense that players develop to navigate the game's rules.

Conclusion

I have presented useful techniques in game design that, from a psychological perspective, open up the play experience while also focusing on pro-social content. There are further techniques that we do not have space to explore here, including creating surprise "aha" realizations to shift mindsets about gender roles (Freedman, Green, Seidman, & Flanagan, 2021), delaying the revelation of information so players can "bond" with characters (Flanagan & Kaufman, 2016), and more. There are endless possibilities for using games for futurecasting.

Acknowledgements

I would like to thank the Tiltfactor team: Post-docs, staff, students and all of our collaborators, who made this research possible, as well as the National Science Foundation (US), the National Institute of Justice, and Dartmouth College. Special thanks go out to Dr. Melanie Green, Dr. Geoff Kaufman, Dr. Gili Freedman, Max Seidman, Sukdith Punjasthitkul, and Danielle Taylor.

References

Brehm, J. W. 1966. ***A theory of psychological reactance.*** New York: Academic Press.

Brehm, J. W., Stires, L. K., Sensenig, J., & Shaban, J. 1966. The attractiveness of an eliminated choice alternative. ***Journal of Experimental Social Psychology,*** 2: 301-313.

Brehm, S. S., & Brehm, J. W. 1981. ***Psychological reactance: A theory of freedom and control.*** New York: Academic Press.

Finnegan, E., Oakhill, J., & Garnham, A. 2015. Counter-stereotypical pictures as a strategy for overcoming spontaneous gender stereotypes. ***Frontiers in Psychology,*** 6: 1-15.

Flanagan, M., & Kaufman, G. 2016. Shifting implicit biases with games using psychology: The embedded design approach. In Y. Kafai, G. Coleman, & B. Tynes (eds.), ***Diversifying Barbie and Mortal Kombat: Intersectional perspectives & inclusive designs in gaming:*** 219-233. Pittsburgh: CMU/ETC.

Freedman G., Green M. C., Seidman M., & Flanagan, M. 2021. The Effect of Embodying a Woman Scientist in Virtual Reality on Men's Gender Biases. ***Technology, Mind, and Behavior,*** 2(4): 1-11.

Fugate, J. M. B., Macrine, S. L., & Cipriano, C. 2019. The role of embodied cognition for transforming learning. ***International Journal of School & Educational Psychology,*** 7(4): 274-288.

Fullerton, Tracy. 2018. ***Game design workshop: A playcentric approach to creating innovative games.*** 4th edition. Boca Raton: CRC Press.

Goldstein, T. R., Thompson, B. N., & Kanumuru P. 2022. Do embodiment and fictionality affect young children's learning? ***Journal of Experimental Child Psychology,*** 213:105275.

Gregg, A. P., Seibt, B., & Banaji, M. A. 2006. Easier said than done: Asymmetry in the malleability of automatic preferences. ***Journal of Personality and Social Psychology***, 90: 1-20.

Huizinga, J. 1971 (1938). ***Homo Ludens: A study of the play element in culture.*** New York: Beacon Press.

Kaufman, G., & Flanagan, M. 2013. Lost in translation: Comparing the impact of an analog and digital version of a public health game on players' perceptions, attitudes, and cognitions. ***International Journal of Games & Computer Mediated Simulations***, 5(3): 1-9.

Kaufman, G., & Flanagan, M. 2015. A psychologically "embedded" approach to designing games for prosocial causes. ***Cyberpsychology: Journal of Psychosocial Research on Cyberspace***, Special Issue on Videogames, 9(3): 5.

Kaufman, G., Flanagan, M., & Seidman, M. 2015. Creating stealth game interventions for attitude and behavior change: An 'embedded design' model. ***DiGRA '15 - Proceedings of the 2015 DiGRA International Conference***, Digital Games Research Association, 12.

Kaufman, G., Flanagan, M., Seidman, M., & Wien, S. 2015. "RePlay Health": An experiential role-playing sport for modeling health care decisions, policies, and outcomes. ***Games for Health Journal***, 4(4): 295-304.

Kaufman, G., & Flanagan, M. 2016. Playing the system: Comparing the efficacy and impact of digital and non-digital versions of a collaborative strategy game. **DiGRA/FDG '16 - Proceedings of the First International Joint Conference of DiGRA and FDG,** Dundee, Scotland: Digital Games Research Association and Society for the Advancement of the Science of Digital Games, 1(13). Accessed online http://www.digra.org/digital-library/publications/playing-the-system-comparing-the-efficacy-and-impact-of-digital-and-non-digital-versions-of-a-collaborative-strategy-game/. Viewed January 23, 2024.

Lee, S., Parthasarathi, T., & Kable, J. W. 2021. The ventral and dorsal default mode networks are dissociably modulated by the vividness and valence of imagined events. ***Journal of Neuroscience***, 41(24): 5243-5250.

Lenton, A. P., Sedikides, C., & Bruder, M. 2009. A latent semantic analysis of gender stereotype-consistency and narrowness in American English. ***Sex Roles: A Journal of Research***, 60(3-4): 269-278.

Novak, M., & Schwan, S. 2021. Does touching real objects affect learning? ***Educational Psychology Review***, 33: 637-665.

Varela, F. J., Thompson, E., & Rosch, E. 2017. Enaction: Embodied cognition. In Varela, F. J., Rosch, E., & Thompson, E., ***The embodied mind: Cognitive science and human experience***, revised edition: 147-184. Cambridge, MA: MIT Press.

Worchel, S., & Brehm, J. W. 1970. Effect of threats to attitudinal freedom as a function of agreement with the communicator. ***Journal of Personality and Social Psychology***, 14(1): 18-22.

LAURENT BONTOUX

SENIOR FORESIGHT FOR POLICY EXPERT
AT THE EUROPEAN COMMISSION'S
JOINT RESEARCH CENTER
BRUSSELS, BELGIUM

HOW TO MAKE FUTURES PLAUSIBLE? PERSONAL EXPERIENCES FROM EU POLICYMAKING

Introduction: Including strategic foresight in evidence-informed policymaking

The way most people engage with the future is through forecasting, i.e., by extrapolating current conditions (as measured by data) into the future. This fits well with "evidence-informed policymaking," which is now considered best practice at the European Commission and elsewhere and a source of credibility. However, we know that to prepare well for the future it is also necessary to engage in strategic foresight, or futurecasting. Foresight makes it possible, mostly through qualitative approaches, to prepare for the new and unexpected in a future that does not exist yet. How is it possible to reconcile these apparently contradictory approaches? This paper describes how the European Commission, in its current efforts both to push for evidence-informed policymaking and to develop the use of strategic foresight, reconciles them. Foresight helps to "think the unthinkable," to prepare for the future by generating future narratives with the plausibility required to influence policymaking. Indeed, plausibility is what connects the future to the current reality and to evidence that people recognize and accept.

A brief history of foresight at the European Commission

Foresight started to be used for policy at the European Commission in 1989, with the creation by President Jacques Delors of the Forward Studies Unit (Cellule de Prospective), directly attached to his cabinet, and the simultaneous creation of the Institute for Prospective Technological Studies (IPTS) at the Joint Research Centre (JRC) in Ispra, Italy.

Since then, and while the Forward Studies Unit disappeared after President Delors' departure and the IPTS moved to Seville (Spain), foresight has continued to be used at the European Commission. The IPTS continued its foresight practice for a number of years, the Directorate General for Research and Innovation funded foresight projects through various programs, and the use of foresight for policy continued to grow steadily. By 2015, the JRC had moved its foresight activities to Brussels and, in 2017, it created the Competence Centre on Foresight within the EU Policy Lab to consolidate and strengthen its foresight for policy offers. In 2019, President von der Leyen introduced strategic foresight in the mission letter of Vice-President Maroš Šefčovič, "*putting foresight at the heart of better policymaking.*"

This relatively long institutional history, spanning more than three decades, bears witness to the capacity of foresight to provide useful insights for policymaking and to generate indications of confidence from the highest decision-making level.

Foresight is part of "evidence-informed policymaking"

This political impetus has increased attention on foresight at a time when the European Commission is also putting a strong emphasis on "evidence-informed policymaking" and on professionalizing policymaking practice further. As a result, in parallel with the promotion of foresight for policy, the European Commission has taken two significant steps. Firstly, it has developed a competence progression model for policymaking (*Competence Framework for "Innovative Policymaking"*) containing seven competence clusters, one of which is "*Be futures literate*" (European Commission, 2022). This framework describes all the skills that any policymaking team needs to master to achieve a high level of excellence in making and implementing policies.

Secondly, it included strategic foresight as *Tool #20* in the Better Regulation toolbox, the document that provides guidance to the European Commission on how to prepare an as-good-as-possible legislative proposal using various Better Regulation instruments (European Commission, 2021). The Better Regulation toolbox provides guidance on how best to perform steps in the policymaking cycle such as impact assessment, stakeholder consultation, evaluation, and many others. This is part of the work that the EU institutions have been doing to ensure that policy decisions are informed by the best possible evidence and that citizens and stakeholders are listened to. These are still early days, but *Tool #20* is starting to penetrate EU policymaking practice. Figure 1 illustrates where foresight already contributes to EU policymaking.

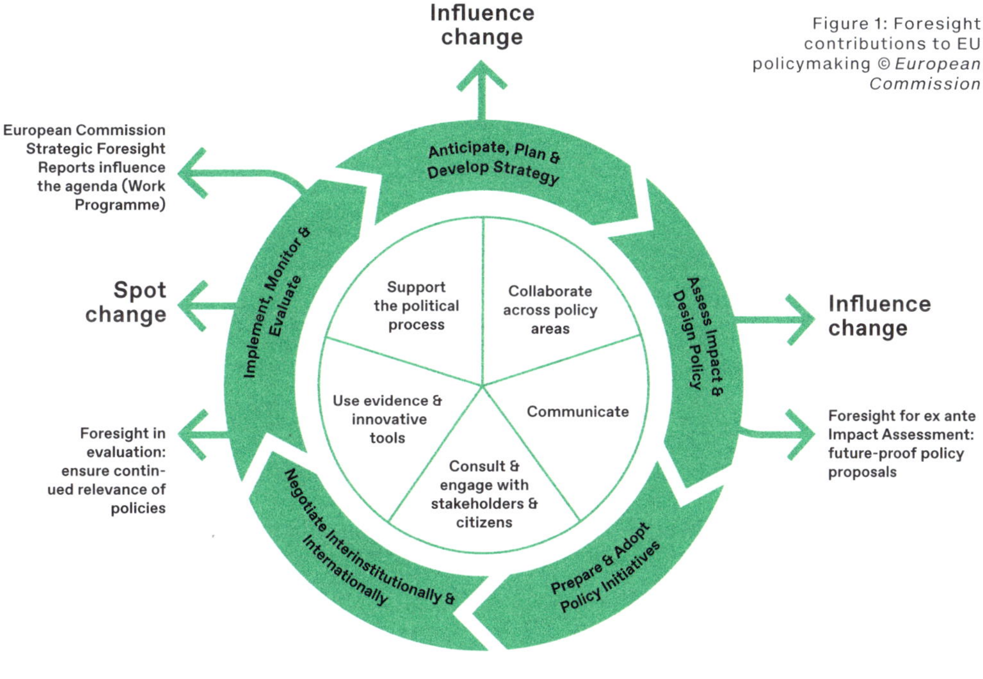

Figure 1: Foresight contributions to EU policymaking © *European Commission*

Applying foresight to make policies robust for the future

The foresight tool in the EU Better Regulation toolbox can be used to broaden and deepen the reflection on the robustness of policies over the long term. A first approach, requiring little time and resources, consists of confronting the policy problem with a *set of megatrends* as a systemic challenge to understand how it could evolve in a holistic perspective. Megatrends are long-term global driving forces that are observable in the present and are likely to continue to have a significant influence for a few decades. This approach can be carried out in a three-hour workshop bringing together a small but diverse group of policymakers from relevant domains. The diversity of perspectives and expertise is essential to obtain sufficiently robust results from this method, which can be seen as a screening exercise. The European Commission monitors 14 *Global Megatrends* relevant for the future of the world, with a focus on the EU, to provide a capacity to apply this approach (European Commission, 2020a; see Figure 2).

Figure 2: Using the megatrends cards
© *Bontoux*

A second approach, based on full-fledged foresight scenarios, provides a much deeper way to "stress-test" proposed policy initiatives. The scenarios offer a reasonably comprehensive and realistic set of possible alternative future conditions with which policy options can be confronted. This allows the exploration of key uncertainties and the discovery of possible long-term implications related to the policy issue at stake. This approach is well suited to policies intended for application in volatile and uncertain environments, or with possibilities of diverse outcomes. The rich contexts created by foresight scenarios help shed light on how the policy issue might evolve, its drivers, and how the various stakeholders might change over the long term. To reduce the time and resources needed to carry out this approach, the JRC has developed a set of Reference Foresight Scenarios on the "global standing of the EU in 2040" that can be applied repeatedly to a broad range of policy issues (Vesnic Alujevic, Muench, & Stoermer, 2023).

A third approach consists in confronting existing policy proposals with a set of possible "wild cards." Wild cards are high-impact low-probability events. The advantage of this approach is that it, too, can be performed quickly. A downside is that its quality depends on the type and number of (arbitrarily selected) wild cards used in the exercise. A prototype and an application case have been developed at the European Parliament.

So, a lot can be done, and is being done, to apply foresight concretely to policymaking. In such a positive context, it is important to understand how to make futures, as created by strategic foresight processes, plausible.

The challenges of applying foresight in real (policymaking) life

This steady improvement of the policymaking process, combined with the increasing demands put on the EU institutions, creates a culture of efficiency at the European Commission with a focus on a capacity to deliver on time, according to the demands from the top leadership, and to the highest possible quality standard. By the nature of the EU treaties, strong emphasis is also given to economic impacts connected to a quantitative culture, where processes are tightly controlled, validated in standardized ways, and monitored. Efficiency is also strongly associated with widely held assumptions supporting a broad range of modeling exercises and extrapolations.

All this is geared towards enabling policymaking to build a perceived desired future as efficiently as possible. This tends to happen either by solving issues encountered when implementing existing policies (on the basis of the results from implementation reports), by reacting to current events (e.g., as illustrated by the COVID-19 pandemic and Russia's invasion of Ukraine), or by preparing to address clearly identified emerging threats (e.g., through the EU Green Deal). This last example has been put in place to address the challenges created by climate breakdown and environmental degradation, aiming at "*transforming the EU into a modern, resource-efficient and competitive economy, ensuring no net emissions of greenhouse gases by 2050 and economic growth decoupled from resource use*" (European Commission, 2019). These approaches anchor policymaking clearly to objective elements. They create a path dependency that channels imagination into a frame of extrapolation from the past and of continuity of trends.

While solving implementation difficulties and addressing identified forthcoming issues are necessary and conventional acts of policymaking, acting in reaction to unforeseen events creates unique challenges. This is especially the case in our current time, recognized broadly as the so-called "*VUCA world,*" characterized by volatility, uncertainty, complexity, and ambiguity, in which many people now also talk of "*polycrisis*" (Whiting, 2023) and "*permacrisis*" (Spicer, 2022).

This sense of crisis is a major issue for policymaking for two main reasons. The first is that a perceived crisis creates an unnerving sense of uncertainty and fear, pushing people to look for "safe ground." Psychologists have shown that when people feel that they are under threat from a crisis, they become more rigid and hang on more tightly to their beliefs (Staw, Sandelands, & Dutton, 1981). Researchers have also discovered that creativity tends to decrease in periods of crisis (Simonton, 1990).

The second reason is that reacting to unforeseen adverse events forces fast decision making, with little time available to consult, ponder options, and reflect on long-term consequences, all necessary to good policymaking practice. While this is all very understandable, these periods of fast decision making most often have consequences for the long term. At that moment, being able to reassess assumptions and having a long-term vision can be a source of resilience and help overcome the crises successfully. Indeed, a lack of long-term vision favors a focus on the past and on familiar solutions, a direct result of the lack of creativity mentioned above.

Calling on foresight

As is already well known, *"the role of public policy is to create a desirable future. However, policymaking often suffers from presentism bias, i.e. it focuses on today's issues and ignores future challenges and opportunities. While the future is uncertain and cannot be predicted, foresight offers a well-established toolbox to help deal with it, in all its uncertainty and complexity"* (Störmer, Bontoux, Krzysztofowicz, Florescu, Bock, & Scapolo, 2020). In view of the above, when engaging in the application of foresight to policymaking, an essential question emerges: What is realistic and achievable in terms of foresight processes considering real-life circumstances? How can that be applied to the creation of a truly desirable future?

To build a desired future, it is necessary to imagine it first. Then, for this image of the future to drive policymaking successfully, it has to feel realistic and achievable, even if challenging, in addition to being desirable. Research is providing some elements in support of the usefulness of being able to imagine specific futures to drive decision making. Imagined future scenarios seem to be better preserved in long-term memory when they are integrated with people's pre-existing autobiographical knowledge, and potentially drive behavior (Jeunehomme & D'Argembeau, 2021).

However, a major challenge to getting people to accept a future vision is to first help them to discard the images that they already have of the future.

This happens by making them realize that these images might correspond to a "used future" (Inayatullah, 2008). A "used future" is an image of the future that is either borrowed from a place with other circumstances or inherited from a past that no longer corresponds to the current reality. As such, it no longer provides the right context to build a positive future, or to address the right challenges.

Reaching this point requires overcoming three main hurdles. First, it is necessary to overcome the organizational culture and the risk of group-think stemming from established practice. It is also necessary to overcome the crisis of imagination stemming from the fear of the unknown (Yates, 2021), the feeling of *"permacrisis,"* and other factors more specific to our generation (see above).

Second, especially when using scenarios describing possible future worlds with a broad brush, one must be able to help the target audience understand why and how these scenarios are relevant to their specific topic of interest. This is especially the case for scenarios offering alternative futures for large systems such as, for example, the world (Arup, 2019) or the EU in 2050 (Matti, Jensen, Bontoux, Goran, Pistocchi, & Salvi, 2023). In cases when even some participants in scenario-building exercises have difficulty believing some scenarios, a backcasting exercise can help people realize how these scenarios could come about, even if people feel that the probability is very low.

Third, the foresight scenarios must offer enough meaningful novelty to the users and help them consider elements that they would not have considered otherwise while remaining firmly believable for them. This is a key challenge, especially considering what people sometimes refer to as "reality overtaking fiction." Here, what a particular set of people might consider as the limit of the possible could still remain well within what could actually happen, but their imagination is not able to reach that far. The challenge for the foresight professionals is then to help this group enter as far as possible into the intellectual challenge zone, without reaching what the group would cease to consider as believable.

So how can foresight address this challenge and help improve policymaking? By being sufficiently robust, relevant, and savvy.

Plausibility of scenarios in real (policymaking) life

JRC foresight practice tries to address these issues systematically. Here are five examples of best practice applied successfully at the JRC that are relevant for making scenarios "plausible." They address different aspects of "plausibility." They are presented below without any order of importance.

First, it is necessary to use trusted processes to build scenarios. Fortunately, the toolbox for building foresight scenarios is rich enough to be able to rely on tried and tested approaches when developing new scenarios, and to adapt these processes optimally to each project and set of circumstances. Using reputable methods, also applied and validated widely outside of the European Commission, helps instill confidence in the participants and/or users of the scenarios. They also ensure a high enough level of quality of the output to match expectations.

Second, ensuring that the foresight output will serve the defined purpose requires involving the client or future user from the start. This is essential as it allows us to understand and manage expectations best and allows the project team to grasp the parameters that will make the foresight product optimally usable. The plausibility and believability of the output for the client are key characteristics in this respect.

Third, the JRC has tools to help users understand what (often general) scenarios mean for their specific topic of interest. The Scenario Exploration System is a case in point (European Commission, 2020b). It is a tool that allows diverse "explorers" to discover future scenarios to simulate possible responses connected to any issue of interest to the participants (see Figure 3). While the safe space that it provides is a vast oversimplification of reality, it still provides enough complexity to challenge participants in a way that is usually perceived as realistic (Bontoux et al., 2020). The FuturGov game is another such tool, offering realistic experiences about the future to the users (European Commission, 2020c).

Figure 3: The Scenario Exploration System in use at the European Forum Alpbach 2023 © *Bontoux*

Fourth, the JRC sometimes uses future personas as a powerful way to stimulate people's imagination while strengthening a sense of realism and proximity. The work on farmers of the future is an excellent case in point, helping to ground the strategic reflection on the future evolution of the European Common Agricultural Policy (Krzysztofowicz, Rudkin, Winthagen, & Bock, 2020). The realism brought into the personas has been convincing enough for the results of this work to bear the passage of time and retain strategic value several years after its publication.

Finally, and in an approach akin to the development of personas, speculative design opens doors on tangible experiences of possible futures. The physical prototypes that this approach delivers offer a very rich material experience. They help mobilize various senses to generate a deeper understanding of diverse innovations that could be perceived as being very futuristic as well as of the promise that these innovations hold. This call upon multiple senses generates a deeper perception and understanding than a classic approach using discussion, text, and pictures.

More generally, a long experience in co-creation processes for policymaking has led to the formulation of five key principles that need to be respected to ensure high-quality processes such as foresight for policy (Matti et al., 2022). These principles are:

- Principle 1 – Clarity of scope and purpose;
- Principle 2 – Focus on outcome and transparency;
- Principle 3 – Inclusiveness and representativeness;
- Principle 4 – High-quality tailored process;
- Principle 5 – Systemic perspective.

The respect of these principles contributes to the plausibility and credibility of the whole process and its outcomes.

Concluding remarks

Plausibility in its various aspects is essential for strategic foresight to have an impact on policy. The realism of the future images generated by foresight exercises is likely to make a significant difference in the impact to be expected from such work. This paper offers a personal understanding of how this takes shape in a European policymaking context and shares experiences of and insights into what is done currently to reach the highest professional standards and obtain the best possible impact. While a lot is known about what should be the ideal circumstances for good strategic foresight, actual conditions do not always allow them to happen. However, a few basic elements help maintain a high level of credibility and plausibility in foresight work. They range from the application of robust processes and the establishment of a good mutual understanding between foresight professionals and their clients, to the availability of applied tools to help users "live" through scenarios. This can happen either by taking roles in them, seeing "personas" live in them, or experiencing related speculative design outputs. Further work is needed to strengthen the capacity to evaluate the impacts of foresight for policymaking.

References

Arup. 2019. ***2050 scenarios – Four plausible futures.*** London: Arup. Accessed online https://www.arup.com/perspectives/publications/research/section/2050-scenarios-four-plausible-futures. Viewed January 29, 2024.

Bontoux, L., Sweeney, J. A., Rosa, A. B., Bauer, A., Bengtsson, D., Bock, A.-K., Caspar, B., Charter, M., Christophilopoulos, E., Kupper, F., Macharis, C., Matti, C., Matrisciano, M., Schuijer, J., Szczepanikova, A., Criekinge, T. van, & Watson, R. 2020. A game for all seasons: Lessons and learnings from the JRC's Scenario Exploration System. ***World Futures Review,*** 12(1): 81-103.

European Commission. 2019. ***Communication from the Commission: The European Green Deal.*** Accessible online https://eur-lex.europa.eu/legal-content/EN/TXT/HTML/?uri=CELEX:52019DC0640. Viewed February 5, 2024.

European Commission. 2020a. ***Competence Centre on Foresight: The Megatrends Hub.*** Accessible online https://knowledge4policy.ec.europa.eu/foresight/tool/megatrends-hub_en. Viewed February 5, 2024.

European Commission. 2020b. ***Competence Centre on Foresight: The Scenario Exploration System (SES).*** Accessible online https://knowledge4policy.ec.europa.eu/foresight/tool/scenario-exploration-system-ses_en. Viewed February 5, 2024.

European Commission. 2020c. ***Competence Centre on Foresight: FuturGov Game.*** Accessible online https://knowledge4policy.ec.europa.eu/foresight/topic/futurgov-game_en. Viewed February 5, 2024.

European Commission. 2021. ***Better regulation: guidelines and toolbox.*** Accessible online https://commission.europa.eu/law/law-making-process/planning-and-proposing-law/better-regulation/better-regulation-guidelines-and-toolbox_en. Viewed February 5, 2024.

European Commission. 2022. ***Visualisation: Competence framework for "innovative policymaking".*** Accessible online https://knowledge4policy.ec.europa.eu/visualisation/competence-framework-innovative-policymaking_en. Viewed February 5, 2024.

Inayatullah, S. 2008. Six pillars: futures thinking for transforming. ***Foresight,*** 10(1): 4-21.

Jeunehomme, O., & D'Argembeau, A. 2021. The role of self-reference and personal goals in the formation of memories of the future. ***Memory & Cognition,*** 49: 1119-1135.

Krzysztofowicz, M., Rudkin, J., Winthagen, V., & Bock, A. 2020. ***Farmers of the future, EUR 30464 EN.*** Luxembourg: Publications Office of the European Union. JRC122308.

Matti, C., Rissola, G., Martinez, P., Bontoux, L., Joval, J., Spalazzi, A., & Fernandez, D. 2022. ***Co-creation for policy: Participatory methodologies to structure multi-stakeholder policymaking processes, EUR 31056 EN.*** Luxembourg: Publications Office of the European Union.

Matti, C., Jensen, K., Bontoux, L., Goran, P., Pistocchi, A., & Salvi, M. 2023. ***Towards a fair and sustainable Europe 2050: Social and economic choices in sustainability transitions.*** Luxembourg: Publications Office of the European Union.

Simonton, D. K. 1990. Political pathology and societal creativity. ***Creativity Research Journal,*** 3(2): 85-99.

Spicer, A. 2022. If "permacrisis" is the word of 2022, what does 2023 have in store for our mental health? ***The Guardian,*** December 30. Accessible online https://www.theguardian.com/commentisfree/2022/dec/30/permacrisis-word-of-2022-2023-mental-health. Viewed February 5, 2024.

Staw, B. M., Sandelands, L. E., & Dutton, J. E. 1981. Threat rigidity effects in organizational behavior: A multilevel analysis. ***Administrative Science Quarterly,*** 26(4): 501-524.

Störmer, E., Bontoux, L., Krzysztofowicz, M., Florescu, E., Bock, A., Scapolo, F. 2020. Chapter 12: Foresight – Using science and evidence to anticipate and shape the future. In V. Šucha, & M. Sienkiewicz (eds.), ***Science for Policy Handbook:*** 128-142. Elsevier.

Vesnic Alujevic, L., Muench, S., & Stoermer, E. 2023. ***Reference foresight scenarios: Scenarios on the global standing of the EU in 2040.*** Luxembourg: Publications Office of the European Union. JRC132943.

Whiting, K. 2023. This is why "polycrisis" is a useful way of looking at the world right now. ***World Economic Forum,*** March 7. Accessible online https://www.weforum.org/agenda/2023/03/polycrisis-adam-tooze-historian-explains/. Viewed February 5, 2024.

Yates, V. 2021. An imagination crisis? ***The Rights Studio,*** August 27. Accessible online https://www.rights-studio.org/journal/an-imagination-crisis. Viewed February 5, 2024.

Photo: Erich Goldmann

STEFANOS PAVLAKIS

CO-OWNER AND CREATIVE PRODUCER OF STORY DEALER BERLIN-HEIDELBERG WITH HANS GEISSLINGER AND HANS RUDI FISCHER
BERLIN, GERMANY

LEANING INTO THE UNKNOWN:

Insights into an immersive method of co-creation. Making futures tangible when working with companies, collectives, and communities.

In place of an introduction

The fear of the unknown is much more present today than it was forty or fifty years ago. Centuries of collective efforts aimed at rationalizing existence and making the future calculable have, ironically, led to an uncertainty in most domains of life. It would seem as though the atmosphere, the biosphere, and the technosphere have taken on a life of their own. If we believe the scientific data, it is clear we are on the brink of an era of radical transformations on a planetary scale (Davies, 2016; Haff, 2013; Latour, 2018; Scherer, 2022).

Due to the powerful transformative momentum, anticipating potential futures has become even more difficult today. We therefore need ways to expand our sense of what is possible and to train ourselves to thrive under conditions of change. Storydealing is an empirical method using group enactments as a way of creating collective, transformational experiences. Those participating in storydealing enactments are faced with unexpected, surprising challenges. To work out solutions they need to take ownership of a staged story by actively choosing how it unfolds in their own unique way. Experiencing *group enactments* of this kind has empowering and transformative effects on a team.

Brokers of awe: The origins of storydealing

During the 1980s, the State Senate of Berlin decided to offer children's camps to support low-income families. Among those who followed the call to plan and hold these camps was the Berlin-based group of educators, artists, and sociologists that later formed "Story Dealer AG." They held three fourteen-day holiday camps per year, each with fifteen to fifty children, all roughly the same age. The campsites were located outside Berlin, usually in forests in Bavaria.[1] The children did not necessarily know each other beforehand. After meeting at the campgrounds, the kids had to work out a new pecking order. The process came at a high price. New friendships and "gangs" were formed on the basis of exclusion, with some kids even being bullied.

In an attempt to defuse this antagonistic behavior, the storydealing camp counselors introduced an evening ritual. Before bedtime, they would enact stories of magic and adventure around a bonfire. The stories had a captivating effect on the children. Shaking in expectation, and in slight fear of the unusual surroundings, the kids would huddle together, and listen in awe. The counselors noticed that some kids spent much of the next day enthusiastically impersonating characters from the bonfire tales.

The joy with which the kids picked up and expanded on the stories the next day inspired the counselors to search for ways in which they could build on their unexpected success. Was it possible to develop a single story that could continue to unfold for the duration of the holiday camp, rather than having to come up with new ones every night? And could the storydealing counselors provide a framework to help the kids be able to fully immerse themselves in these stories?

---

1 At the time, West Berlin was surrounded by a wall. It was impossible to have camp sites near it because the surrounding area was literally on "enemy territory."

On the wings of joy: Where magic transforms reality

It took Story Dealer AG two years to create its first immersive story. By 1983, the group was ready. *Saurierjagd* (in English: Dino Hunt) was not to be narrated around a bonfire, but rather unfold in real life. Co-created by thirty-six children and six storydealing camp counselors, the enactment started the way any activity-based holiday camp would.[2] A group of children arrived at the campgrounds and was introduced to their counselors and familiarized with their surroundings. Next, the activity that would go on to form the core of their activity-based holiday was introduced. In this case, it was a circus program. The children would train for it and later present it to the people in the surrounding villages.[3]

What followed was the total derailment of anything one could expect of a holiday camp. On day three, with rehearsals for the circus in full swing, a group of children heard a mysterious sound coming from the nearby woods. The counselors dismissed the reports as fantasies.[4] Nevertheless, more and more kids reported hearing suspiciously loud and unidentifiable noises. During dinner time, a police car stopped by. The officer asked to speak with the Head Counselor. When the counselor returned, everyone wanted to know why the police were there. Instead of an answer, the kids were sent to bed. No one slept that night. Gossip filled the dormitories. It was now self-evident, the children whispered to one another, that the mysterious sounds in the woods were the reason why the police were there.

The following day, the kids took part rather unenthusiastically in the daily program, and on day five a mutiny broke out. After military helicopters flew over the campsite, the children refused to continue with their training. They demanded to be told the truth about the sounds in the wood. It was then reluctantly explained to them that the police had spotted oversized footprints in the nearby woodlands. The counselors had been instructed to stay away from the forests and be ready to evacuate if needed. It was unclear what kind of animal had made its way into the woods. Nevertheless, a police consultation with the Archaeological Institute of Munich revealed extravagant potential scenarios, all involving a dinosaur. One of the theories was that a dinosaur egg that had been safely tucked away under protective layers of soil

---

2 Holiday camps followed an experiential education program.

3 Note that the "official" activity on offer was already quite exciting.

4 A popular way of making something staged appear real is to deny its existence from a position of power.

for millions of years had hatched due to the remarkable summer heat.[5]

The possibility of an egg hatching under such circumstances seemed entirely plausible to the children. Panic and enthusiasm ensued. Should they evacuate the site? After all, dinosaurs are dangerous. But the counselors argued that the police would be in charge of the evacuation, if necessary. Until then, everyone could continue enjoying the camp... But none of the kids wanted to continue with their circus training. A plenary was held around a bonfire. With much effort, the children convinced the hesitant counselors to change the camp's course.

The next morning, the camp was transformed into a site of feverish activities, all aimed at addressing the emergent danger. Work groups and a daily plenary session were introduced. The counselors held a first aid workshop and the children attended a "Dinosaurs for Dummies" course, given by those who knew the most about them. When did dinosaurs exist, what species were there, and why did they become extinct? On day six, the children set up a chemical lab to develop a special dinosaur-shrinking serum. The next day, they created a dino-tracking and forensic team. They trained in the areas adjacent to the woods. Later, a construction group took on the task of building a gigantic dinosaur trap. Unconvinced by the technical and scientific approaches of their peers, some of the children formed a spin-off group and set up a wizard's academy in the attic of the main camp house. They practiced telepathy, magic spells, and communicating with extinct species.

Adults from the surrounding area, who were drawn into the feverish activities,[6] watched on, suspended between awe and disbelief. Enacting a story as a *real event* had a profound effect on the children. With a stunning decisiveness and a sense of urgency, they interpreted everything happening around them as proof that a dinosaur had actually come to life. Thus, in the summer of 1983, a group of thirty-six children, together with their storydealing counselors, went out in the woods at night in search of the dinosaur. A small group on the front lines attempted to shrink the dinosaur with the shrinking serum. In the pitch dark, the volunteer hunters set off to the site where the cage had been built, armed with spears dipped in the serum. At the same time, the rest of the group herded the dinosaur towards the hunters, using torches and drums. The group chanted and shouted and ran. After attacking, all groups dispersed in panic. Luckily everyone was still alive, when they met back at the campsite.

The following morning, the forensic team assessed the situation and found a huge, burnt, cow-sized carcass trapped in the cage. Hot ashes, bones, and several dozen burnt spears were also found at the site. It would appear as though an overdosage of the serum had set the dinosaur aflame. The young animal had been hit with too many spears and had perished. The group had mixed feelings upon hearing the findings. Everyone visited the site. They wanted to see the carcass

---

5 Indeed, the summer of 1983 was referred to in Germany as the hottest summer of the century.

6 Where else could the group source the material needed to construct a giant trap, if not from a nearby village?

with their own eyes...The last days of the camp were spent performing mourning rituals, including a burial, and organizing a grand party to celebrate their survival.

Over the next decade, Story Dealer AG held twenty-eight holiday camps with even bolder variations of the same idea, each time creating excursions that combined reality and tale. All of the *Travels of Awe*,[7] as they were called, were co-created worlds enacted *as real events* in the public realm.[8] During each camp, the world as it was known was suspended and something new was collectively put into action.

Predicting the future was not at the core of these experiments. Instead, the intense explorations of co-creation laid the foundation for a method of training groups how to perform near-impossible tasks within the frame of unimaginable events. In situations of radical change, the foundations of what we think we know are shaken. What we believe as impossible moves into the realm of the possible. By having participants experience transformation firsthand and unexpectedly, storydealing radically impacts the ways in which change is internalized.

Figure 1: Light Painting from the intervention "Chasing Shadows". Group work.

7 *Phantastische Reisen*, the German name used by Story Dealer AG for their enactments with children, literally translates as *Fantastic Journeys*. I feel that *Travels of Awe* best captures the spirit of these immersive experiences and will use this name in the text.

8 For an extensive account of many of Story Dealer AG's *Phantastische Reisen*, please refer to Hans Geißlinger's *Die Imagination der Wirklichkeit* and *Überfälle auf die Wirklichkeit*.

Game changer: Storydealing with high-performance teams

Changes in corporate culture typically take place in three to five-year cycles. Whereas Story Dealer AG worked predominantly with children, STORY DEALER, a second-generation grouping, offers modular training programs for organizational transformation. In high-performance organizations, it is difficult to do without an entire team for two weeks in a row. As a result, the new types of storydealing enactments are usually limited to a maximum of two and a half days. Reducing the time dedicated to the immersive experience does not necessarily mean that concessions need to be made regarding the scale or complexity of the enactments, nor does it impact their team-empowering character. To counterbalance the time constraints in business environments, STORY DEALER introduced group consultations in advance, with the aim of producing the best possible co-creational experience for all participants. A notion of constructing reality remains relevant but is not the focus. What is important is creating situations in which teams can bond and experience transformation, rather than talk about it.

In business contexts, we speak of storydealing interventions. These entail up to three enactments over a three to five-year period, framed by interviews, consultations, and feedback sessions. Naturally, not all clients will follow the entire program. Having a modular architecture enables STORY DEALER to have "pit stops," pauses, and exit points at all stages. Interventions may include:

- *An orientation session* (to find out about the organizational structure, company history, current situation, team, requirements, and the goals of the intervention, steps already taken, failures, achievements, etc.)
- *Narrative interviews* with specific team members (hearing their perspectives, involving them in the planning process)
- Management consultations, i.e., steering sessions throughout the intervention
- Identifying and working with a *Core Crew* (enactments are developed in close collaboration with this group)
- Designing and presenting a concept, plot, and story (including location scouts, feasibility checks, materials tests, and identifying external specialists, if needed)

- The staged enactment(s)
- Feedback and reflection sessions
- Consultation on how to embed gains on an operational level
- Fine-tuning through workshops, if needed

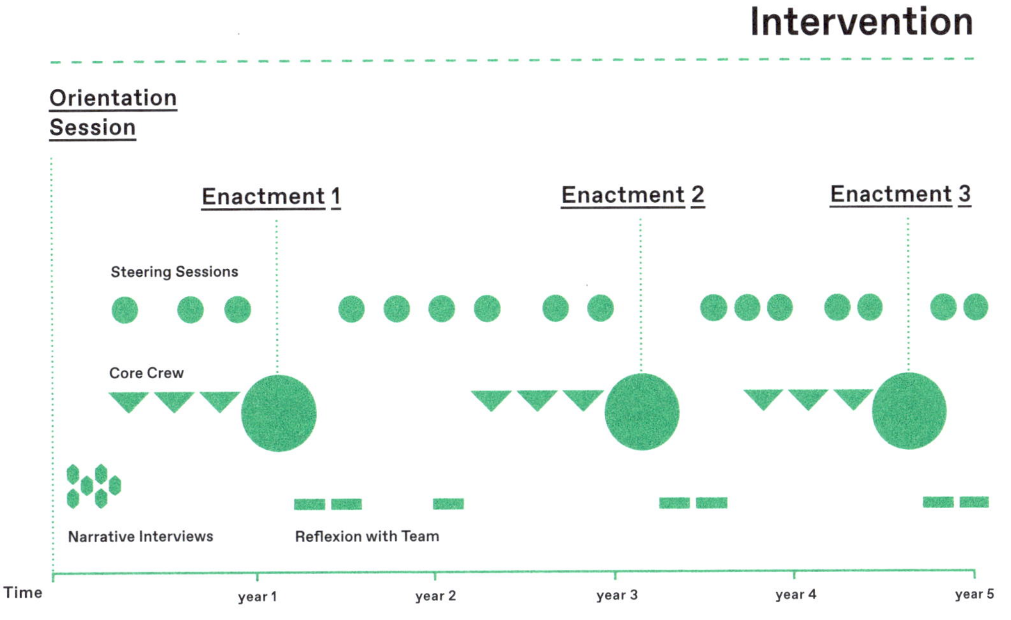

Figure 2: The architecture of an intervention on a timeline. For a full account of the architecture of an intervention, please refer to *Der Fluss informeller Erzählung*
@ Geißlinger & Pavlakis, 2023

Chasing shadows: A case study

Client: Reinsurance company, software development department

Participants: The entire department (72 employees)

Duration of the enactment: 48 hours

Aim: Creating an empowering experience as part of a change management project. Giving participants the opportunity to test out new behavioral patterns without being monitored.

STORY DEALER was approached by the head of the software development department of a Swiss reinsurance enterprise to create a group enactment. An organizational development initiative was already underway; however, it had not been well received. The core issue, as STORY DEALER was told, was a pervasive feeling of loss of face amongst the staff, most of whom were highly specialized engineers. They had been increasingly asked to use existing code in new products and to find workarounds for their clients' needs. The engineers felt that this stripped them of much of their autonomy (and authority). STORY DEALER was therefore asked to create an immersive enactment that would revitalize the team and provide an experience of how it might feel to work on a pre-developed product, adjust it, and pass it on to another team.

The head of the department had already announced a two-day meeting to evaluate the ongoing change process. STORY DEALER proposed to fully redesign the two-day session in co-authorship with a few employees from within the department (the Core Crew), and in consultation with the management. Preparations in the run-up to the meeting were held in secret. The employees, however, received an official but rather cryptic invitation. A date, a time, and a location were announced and participants were requested to bring walking boots, winter clothing, and a flashlight. The invitation became the talk of the coffee breaks.

Buses were arranged for the travel. During the trip from Zurich to Lake Constance, the employees were played a pre-recorded audio message, announcing a transformation was underway. They were asked to imagine themselves as renowned photographers, and were invited to participate in the Fourth International Biennial of *Light Painting*. Naturally, this required the engineers to immediately transform themselves into artists. They therefore had to come up with a convincing new biography for themselves, such as their field of practice, where they come from, and why there was no information about them online. Participants needed to adopt identities they could enact with ease. They were then asked to practice introducing themselves with their new identities to their fellow co-workers during the bus ride and be ready to face the local press upon arriving at Lake Constance.

STORY DEALER had, in fact, publicly announced a biennial art event at Lake Constance. A website had been designed and a press conference was held a day before the artists arrived. On arrival, the local press was waiting for the group. After a round of short interviews, the artists attended a plenary session held behind closed doors. During the session, there was a prevailing feeling of both surprise and stress. Although most were enjoying their ephemeral transformations into "exotic artists," some were also seriously doubting whether they could cope with the assignment. Many had next to no skills in photography. Some were asking themselves why the entire exercise had been made into such a big deal. Why a fake biennial? Why the press? Why all the hassle? ... and, incidentally, what is light painting anyway?

After the artists had been briefed on the technical aspects and some of the aesthetic possibilities of painting with light, they were asked to retire to their rooms in small task groups and practice. Sixteen groups had to make space for darkrooms[9] in the hotel, without the hotel staff noticing. Since they had to learn new skills in a very short time, the groups decided to share the knowledge acquired in the darkrooms with each other. There were image-sharing groups as well as ambassadors sharing practical tips.

In a second secret plenary, the artists were briefed for the main event. Four times throughout the night, the groups would walk to the city and work with light painting. The assignment was to capture the department's expected behavioral norms within an image. Which of these norms were helpful, which could be changed, and which ones could be done without? Each group was given two hours for each image.[10] For the first excursion, the groups were able to choose what they wanted to work on, and how. For the remaining three sessions, they were asked to work on a picture from another group, developing it in such a way that a continuity, but also a transformation, was clearly visible.

Under heavy snowfall, five bonfires were lit and two food and beverage stations were installed in the hotel's back garden to keep the artists warm and provide them with a secluded space to exchange their ideas. The light-painting excursions were kicked off at 7:30 pm. Sixteen groups of artists combed the city's dark corners in search of

---

9 Light painting involves the use of a camera with an open shutter, preferably in absolute darkness.

10 Teams could make as many trials as needed and return with the picture they felt best captured the issue at stake.

architectural elements that could serve their ideas. Upon returning and behind closed doors, each group presented their results to their peers. They described their intentions, aesthetic aspirations, and the techniques used, and also shared the problems they encountered. At the same time, the final images were shown to the public on large-scale projections at the hotel's entrance. One ambassador per group offered warm drinks to curious visitors and chatted with them at the projection site. Meanwhile, sixteen groups took part in feverish talks on behavioral patterns within the department, and on how to depict them. Which image would each group select to develop further?

Each of the groups created four images, all looking to change and improve upon the aesthetic concepts and abstract ideas of the previous group. At 6:45 am, seventy-two tired, cold, and blissfully happy artists entered the hotel's breakfast hall. They had succeeded in achieving their task and were proud of their work. Not wanting to split up into small groups, they managed to convince the restaurant staff to quickly re-position the furniture so all seventy-two artists could sit at one long table. The rearrangement perfectly captured the mood of the moment; everyone was united in a cause, ready to take on new challenges, and feeling blissful after having mastered something complex and inspiringly different.

Figure 3 and 4: Light painting from the intervention "Chasing Shadows". Group work.

Conclusion

In situations of radical change, the foundations of what we think we know are shaken. What we believe to be impossible suddenly becomes probable. In such situations, experiencing change, rather than talking about it, can be incredibly empowering. Working with transformational experiences fosters embodied learning by inspiring and bonding groups and communities. The storydealing method works by giving groups near-impossible quests in staged situations unfolding in the public realm. To rise to the surprising challenge, participants in storydealing enactments form tight-knit work groups and toil towards an aspired goal. They become agents of the story through which they actively initiate and perform change to achieve their goal. Storydealing is a tried and tested method that has been developed over forty years of working with groups. It is suitable for situations in which transformation is anticipated, yet met with reluctance, as well as for all kinds of anticipatory processes and transformative learning environments.

References

Davies, J. 2016. ***The birth of the Anthropocene.*** Oakland: University of California Press.

Dewey, J. 2005. ***Art as experience.*** London: Penguin Publishing Group.

Figgis, M. (Dir.) 2001. ***The Battle of Orgreave.*** Accessed online https://www.youtube.com/watch?v=3ncrWxnxLjg&list=PLr_alA4xBuk0FnZGm1_Hai6wHv9b0suru&index=16. Viewed September 20, 2023.

Geißlinger, H. 1992. ***Die Imagination der Wirklichkeit. Experimente zum radikalen Konstruktivismus.*** Frankfurt & New York: Campus.

Geißlinger, H. (ed.) 1999. ***Überfälle auf die Wirklichkeit.*** Heidelberg: Carl-Auer-Systeme Verlag.

Geißlinger, H., & Pavlakis, S. 2023. Der Fluss informeller Erzählung. ***OrganisationsEntwicklung,*** April 2023: 16-25.

Haff, P. K. 2013. Technology as a geological phenomenon: implications for human well-being. ***Geological Society, London, Special Publications,*** 395(1): 301-309. Accessed online https://pne.people.si.umich.edu/PDF/Haff%20 2013%20Technology%20as%20a%20Geological%20Phenomenon.pdf. Viewed August 15, 2023.

Latour, B. 2018. ***Das terrestrische Manifest.*** Berlin: Suhrkamp.

Pavlakis, S. 2012. ***Towards the production of an aesthetics of relation.*** PhD dissertation. Dundee: Department of Fine Arts, University of Dundee.

Scherer, B. 2022. ***Der Angriff der Zeichen.*** Berlin: Matthes & Seitz.

AFTERTHOUGHTS

KARLHEINZ SCHWUCHOW
TEACHER & TRENDSCOUT,
ACADEMIC & AUTHOR
BREMEN, GERMANY
Photo: Erich Goldmann

BEYOND THE OBVIOUS: RE-IMAGINING CORPORATE STRATEGY

The future can no longer be seen as an extrapolation of the past—perhaps it never could, even in the heydays of strategic planning. As making predictions about the future has become increasingly impossible, a new approach to corporate strategy is needed that breaks away from outdated ways of thinking. In order to make a future plausible that does not exist yet, businesses need to act as imagination machines, shaping and not just trying to predict the future. At the intersection of analysis and imagination, futurecasting can be a potential solution.

Lessons learned

- Outside the Manager's Microcosm:
  Scenarios Modify Mental Models
- The End of Competitive Advantage:
  Developing Transient Advantages in New Arenas
- Towards an Ambidextrous Organization:
  Balancing Exploitation and Exploration
- Strategic Intuition as a Game Changer:
  Combining Rational Thinking and Creative Imagination
- Less Artificial, More Intelligent:
  The Future of AI Spotting New Realities

Living in a non-linear world: From forecasting to scenarios

The historical development of corporate strategy has been shaped by a strong reliance on historical trends and current data. In the early 1920s, Harvard Business School developed the Harvard Policy Model, one of the first strategic planning methodologies for private businesses. This model defines "strategy" as a pattern of purposes, and implies that organizational strategies should be geared toward finding a fit between the organization and its environment (Andrews, 1980).

The rise of information technology and the use of computers for commercial business applications in the 1950s led to an ever-increasing spread of data analytics to improve managerial decision-making. Planning systems were expected to produce the best strategies.

When strategic planning arrived on the scene in the mid-1960s, corporate leaders embraced it as "the one best way" to devise and implement strategies that would enhance the competitiveness of each business unit. Strategic planning, as it has been practiced, has really been strategic programming, the articulation and elaboration of strategies, or visions, that already exist (Mintzberg, 1994).

As one of the pioneers in this field, Royal Dutch Shell set up a planning department, called Group Planning, in 1959. The first planning exercises, designed to determine the company's strategic positioning, were initially based on forecasting methods that evaluated the future using simple extrapolations of past trends. They looked at how the future might unfold and the impact this could have on the company.

In 1965, the company started a new activity called Long Range Studies. The aim was to rethink long-term planning in the context of an uncertain future. This was based on the scenario method developed by Herman Khan, a former RAND Corporation analyst and founder of the Hudson Institute (Cabanes, Roger, & Doganova, 2023).

In 1967, the company began to develop the first long-term studies highlighting alternative futures. It introduced a computerized forecasting tool called the Unified Planning Machinery (UPM). Based on a wide range of variables (raw materials, geopolitical issues, international politics, cultural values), the aim was to develop alternative scenarios for the future up to the year 2000, in particular to test the viability of the idea of "eternal growth."

This work considerably improved the understanding of the company's geopolitical and competitive environment. By this time, the oil industry was already beginning to question forecasts that implied constant expansion and infinite growth. The presentation of the first results of the Meadows Report in 1971 on the limits to growth, together with a BP study that forecasted a supply constraint linked to voluntary action by OPEC member countries, highlighted new risks and new areas of uncertainty (Cabanes et al., 2023).

At Shell, the fear was that this would suppress discussion rather than encourage debate on different perspectives. In addition, the reliability of the forecast results was becoming less and less satisfactory.

For Pierre Wack, Shell's scenario planning theorist, the objective has never been to predict the future. The aim of a scenario is to modify the mental model of decision-makers faced with an uncertain future. A manager or decision-maker always acts rationally on the basis of their mental model, i.e., their view of the world, their habits, their experience, and their perception of their environment. Wack calls a decision-maker's mental model the "microcosm." When a manager makes a decision, they evaluate a set of alternatives within their own analytical framework. A manager decides rationally according to their own "microcosm" (Cabanes et al., 2023).

The aim of a scenario is therefore to question, challenge, or influence the decision-maker's "microcosm." This is why scenarios are less concerned with predicting outcomes than with understanding the forces that would lead to those outcomes. Scenario design is first and foremost a learning process, designed to provide a better understanding of a company's internal and external environment. The use of several imaginative stories about the future helps managers better understand their decisions in the present, question their own mental models, and modify them if necessary. They thus enable managers to renew their perception of the environment, to perceive contingency factors, and to develop new analytical skills.

Scenarios enable a common vision of the future to be expressed, and a shared understanding of new realities to be developed throughout an organization. However, these scenarios will only be accepted and effective when they have truly transformed the decision-maker's initial mental models. To achieve this, it is important to avoid studies that include several scenarios describing alternative outcomes along a single dimension (Cabanes et al., 2023).

The value of scenarios lies in the way they enable us to modify, amend, and transform our visions of a world in the making. The key to the success of scenario planning is not the identification of a future event, but its ability to elicit action in response to a new perception of the future. This success, however, depends on the integration of scenarios into organizational processes and routines such as strategy development, risk management, innovation, and public affairs (Royal Dutch Shell, 2012).

By 1973, the pioneering team of economists, engineers, and scientists had shared these early scenarios with Shell's management, daring them to think the unthinkable: What if the world faced an oil crisis?

When the Yom Kippur War broke out in October of that year, the West's support for Israel angered Arab states, who consequently imposed an oil embargo on Western governments—a response to US support for Israel. Within weeks, the price of crude oil soared from around

$2.50 a barrel to $11. The high price restricted economic activities in the West, causing a slump in the stock market and a rise in unemployment.

But Shell's decision-makers were mentally prepared for the worst because they had already imagined it. These disciplined imaginings of the early scenarios team included choices Shell could make to cushion the blow from an oil crisis. Thus, the company was able to recover more quickly than its competitors (Royal Dutch Shell, 2012).

The company has produced Shell Scenarios ever since. These have helped anticipate and adapt to momentous events like the collapse of communist Europe in 1989, the surge in world energy demand, and the threat of climate change.

Arie de Geus, former Corporate Planning Director, has played a key role in linking scenario planning to strategic practices throughout Shell's global group of companies. In 1988, he published an article in the Harvard Business Review entitled "Planning as Learning." This argued that the ability to continually rethink one's purpose and methods is not just a valuable add-on to corporate practices, but the single factor most responsible for competitive advantage.

It allows companies to live in harmony with the business environment, to switch from a survival mode when times are turbulent to a self-development mode when the pace of change is slow. A pattern that is also evident in Shell's history as it switches from expansion to self-preservation and back again to growth (Geus, 1988).

This process is based on institutional learning—management teams changing the shared mental models of their company, their markets, and their competitors. For this reason, we can see planning as a learning process and corporate planning as institutional learning (Geus, 1988).

Trapped in old conventions: The limits of analytics

The traditional approach for developing business strategies has been based on analytical techniques, breaking down a goal or set of intentions into steps, formalizing those steps so that they can be implemented almost automatically, and articulating the anticipated consequences or results of each step (Mintzberg, 1994).

Until today, the pioneering work by Michael Porter of Harvard Business School in the 1980s—in particular his books "*Competitive Strategy: Techniques for Analyzing Industries and Competitors*" (1980) and "*Competitive Advantage: Creating and Sustaining Superior Performance*" (1985)—still impacts management education and business practices. His views have shaped the way organizations analyze their competitive environment and make strategic decisions.

Porter emphasizes that companies must strive for a sustainable competitive advantage—a unique and lasting difference that gives them an edge over rivals and can be maintained over time. It involves creating value for customers in a way that is difficult to imitate. This can be achieved by offering distinctive products or services, providing comparable value at a lower cost, or a combination of both. Sustaining this advantage requires ongoing innovation, adaptability, and strategic choices that are difficult for competitors to replicate.

When it comes to understanding industry dynamics and assessing strategic opportunities, Michael Porter's Five Forces Framework has become a cornerstone in the field of business strategy. It provides a systematic way to evaluate the attractiveness and competitive intensity of an industry. By examining the five key forces, businesses can gain valuable insights into the potential threats and opportunities they face (Porter, 1979).

The strong and coherent analytical methodological framework Porter developed led to a one-size-fits-all model for strategy and execution: analyze, plan, execute.

Today, however, it must be stated that these concepts are no longer the gold standard, as they focus too much on the economic conditions of their era of origin, long before the rise of the Internet. The emphasis on competitors, suppliers, and buyers, the assumption of a relatively stable and predictable business environment and strong entry barriers, as well as the inability to account for external factors that may disrupt or transform an industry, represent substantial drawbacks. As a consequence, companies can no longer rely on the idea of a sustainable competitive advantage but need to explore and exploit a portfolio of transient advantages, shifting from pure analysis to imagination and design (McGrath, 2013).

Interactions and feedback loops among competitive forces are not taken into account, nor are the diversity and complexity of competitor behavior or unprecedented levels of uncertainty, volatility, and rapid technological advancements. Thus, a more dynamic and adaptive approach to strategy is needed to navigate these complex landscapes, including a stronger emphasis on external stakeholders. The shift is from internal optimization to external interaction. Organizations need to maximize short-term growth and develop a long-term perspective at the same time—exploit existing markets and explore new business opportunities, incorporating stability and change in an ambidextrous manner.

Porter's value chain, the linear model of suppliers and distributors based on the process view of organizations, is largely outdated in today's era of platform-based business models. It was created in 1985, a time when size and scale were regarded as being crucial for competitive advantage and profitability. Today, organizations have become business ecosystems where the focus is on co-opetition, not competition. Competitors become complementors that offer their products or services on the platform seeking to maximize the total value of an expanding ecosystem—there is no longer a need to own unique, inimitable resources. Resource control is being replaced by resource orchestration. The emphasis is on interactions that yield network effects and provide growth and sustainability—not protecting market niches or erecting industry barriers. Competition is multi-layered and does not just rely on product differentiation or lower costs. (Parker, Alstyne, & Choudary, 2016).

Technology disruption and strategic alliances can significantly impact a company's success, often beyond industry boundaries. These can be altered—rather than sticking to fixed categories. Thus, the notion of competition is changing and industries—other organizations doing the same—are being replaced by competitive arenas—solutions that fulfill particular customer needs (McGrath, 2013).

The emphasis Michael Porter puts on competition and industry structure overlooks the impact of collaboration and non-market factors. Relatively little importance is attached to the role of innovation and creativity in strategy, and the significance of non-business factors. This narrow focus may prevent organizations from exploring new opportunities and redefining industry boundaries. Companies can make existing competition irrelevant by value innovation, leading to a "Blue Ocean," a new and uncontested market (Kim & Mauborgne, 2005).

Today, strategy needs to be viewed as a roadmap to future growth in dynamic markets and with a high degree of uncertainty. Thus, the goal of strategy is directional, not predictive. It is about where to compete and how to win—an integrated set of choices that fit together and reinforce one another. With industry boundaries changing and entry-barriers disappearing, a new approach to strategy is needed (McGrath, 2013).

This requires a shift away from pure analytics and the strategy models that dominated the past towards developing an integrative perspective. Data analytics is about finding lots of something that has already happened as data and—by definition—can only be from the past. Data analytics looks for prevailing patterns: the patterns that are prevalent in the period leading up to the present. Thus, any sample drawn from the past is utterly unrepresentative of the universe that includes the future—unless one assumes that the future will be identical to the past. For the part of the world where things can be other than they are, imagination and intuitive thinking are needed (Martin, 2022).

From formal planning to strategic thinking: The role of intuition and creativity

As highlighted above, the traditional approach to corporate strategy has been a structured and systematic process of developing actionable plans to achieve specific objectives, dominated by data analytics rather than creative thinking. It is about breaking down an objective into steps, designing how these steps may be implemented, and estimating the anticipated consequences of each step.

Strategic thinking, in contrast, is about synthesis, an intuitive process identified with the brain's right hemisphere that explores creative ideas about what needs to be done. It involves judgment and intuition to formulate an integrated perspective, a vision of where the organization should be heading. Strategic planning has not only never amounted to strategic thinking but has, in fact, often impeded it (Mintzberg, 1994).

Formal planning, by its very analytical nature, has been and always will be dependent on the preservation and rearrangement of established categories—levels of strategy, organizational structure, product categories. But real strategic change requires not merely rearranging the established order, but inventing a new one. The outcome of strategic thinking is an integrated perspective of the enterprise, a not-too-precisely articulated vision of direction. Once managers understand this, they can avoid other costly misadventures caused by applying formal techniques, without judgment and intuition, to problem solving (Mintzberg, 1994).

Strategy-making needs to encourage the informal learning that produces new perspectives and new combinations. The failure of planning to transcend existing structures explains why it has discouraged serious organizational change and, rather, promoted strategies that were extrapolated from the past or copied from others. In this context, scenarios fail and new principles to guide strategic choices are needed.

In order to develop new perspectives, companies need to correctly match their strategy-making processes to their competitive circumstances, advance beyond analysis, and systematically anticipate challenges and harness imagination. The classic approach, focusing on planning and optimizing efficiency, works best in a predictable and stable environment in which today's most attractive positions and most rewarded capabilities will, in all likelihood, remain the same tomorrow. An adaptive strategy, on the other hand, is more flexible and experimental in order to fit environments that are persistently unpredictable, implying experimentation and visionary creation as companies in this situation need to constantly refine goals and tactics and shift, acquire, or divest resources (Reeves, Haanaes, & Sinha, 2015).

The challenge is to free the mind of all expectations and let the brain make its own connections. This requires moving beyond ordinary intuition: a vague feeling, gut instinct (fast judgments based on previous experience), expert intuition. When one recognizes a new situation and turns off the expert intuition, this leads to a powerful combination of rational thinking and creative imagination: strategic intuition. An important aspect is the ability to develop the so-called "beginner's mind" by deliberately pushing aside what one knows from previous experience and opening up to new insights. While existing paradigms offer efficient solutions to common problems, they can restrict the willingness to see new and different solutions (Duggan, 2007).

Cultivating new mental models: Leaving the past behind

While strategic planning processes are goal-driven, strategic intuition offers a way to answer the question "What is a good goal?" It builds on a selective projection of past elements into the future in a new combination. To succeed in this search process, preconceived notions of what the problem is—or what a solution might be—need to be abandoned. This opens up new opportunities and different directions (Duggan, 2007).

This approach is regularly opposed by the mental models of successful organizations—deeply rooted assumptions and generalizations, based on experiences, beliefs, and knowledge—which have become uniform as a by-product of organizational alignment. As cognitive frameworks that developed over time to comprehend and navigate reality, they cement the way things are done (Reeves & Fuller, 2021; Jones, Ross, Lynam, Perez, & Leitch, 2011).

Mental models, which provide the mechanism through which new information is filtered and stored, can be hard to identify and shift because they are usually unconscious and deeply embedded, driven by organizational structures and the prevailing culture.

To open up for a different future and explore new opportunities, existing mental models—e.g., how particular processes operate or how value is created—need to be reimagined and redefined. The capability to think counterfactually, to envision what is not but what could be, enables the conception and realization of new unprecedented ideas, opening up portals to alternative futures. Quoting Albert Einstein: "Imagination is more important than knowledge. Knowledge is limited, imagination encircles the world." Martin Reeves and Jack Fuller (2021) highlight innovation and growth as a result of imagination.

This requires the capability to see prevailing mental models as choices, to manipulate and evolve them and cultivate multiple alternative mental models—thus overcoming the dominant mental model of a business or industry. To accomplish this, it is necessary to preserve and encourage the creative capacity of an organization to reimagine the future rather than focusing on planning and executing current issues (Reeves & Fuller, 2021).

Moving beyond artificial intelligence: The future is human

In the recent past we have experienced a hype regarding artificial intelligence (AI), triggered in particular by ChatGPT. When assessing its future impact, it is necessary to realize that the technology behind AI is a set of algorithms that takes data and makes decisions, predictions, and classifications in ways that previously required human intelligence.

To succeed, AI builds on a continuous supply of high-quality data that it needs for training the algorithm. It can then support decisions at an unprecedented speed. But AI algorithms are only as good as the data they have been trained on. Organizations, however, have to cope with biased, incomplete, or inconsistent data. Besides the lack of data quality, they often do not have the necessary quantitative database. Organizations can have the most advanced machine-learning model, but if they are not asking the right questions or providing the right data, the utility of that model is severely limited. They need effective data platforms and processes to enable effective machine-learning platforms and processes (Kiron & Schrage, 2019).

Furthermore, an extrapolation of past scenarios might not or might only inadequately reflect future challenges, particularly in business environments characterized by high volatility. While they lead to seemingly evidence-based future scenarios, they process data from the past and cement the status quo. Consequently, AI is best suited for handling repetitive, data-driven tasks and making data-driven decisions. Thus, the essence of the AI paradigm shift is the transformation of all business processes within an organization—whether related to breakthrough innovation, everyday customer service, or personal productivity (Daugherty & Wilson, 2018).

Rapidly developing self-learning algorithms develop into a black box by processing data in a way that is no longer comprehensible, making it hard to understand how decisions are made. The limitations in interpreting qualitative data are still significant. Flexibility and judgment are qualities that algorithms do not (yet) possess. AI also falls short in understanding human emotions, cultural norms, and social cues. While it excels at specific tasks (narrow AI), it lacks the ability to transfer knowledge from one domain to another, a hallmark of human intelligence. This represents a substantial drawback and challenges human capabilities, like creativity and imagination, to leverage AI and uncover new paths to growth and previously unimaginable futures, outside the constraints of what is currently possible.

The technical staff with the experience and training needed represents another bottleneck.

As strategic decisions have significant consequences, a key consideration is AI transparency, in the sense of understanding why it is making a certain prediction and what extrapolations it is making from which information. A strategy for AI matters less than clearly articulating the strategic aspirations, goals, and outcomes that leaders wish to optimize. If this is the case, AI can enhance the formulation and execution of strategy (Kiron & Schrage, 2019).

Undoubtedly, AI will play an increasingly important role in business and society—though one of the strongest limitations is its inability to tackle "unknown unknowns," the questions and scenarios we have not even considered yet. AI tools excel at providing answers when the questions are clear, but they are far less effective at posing new questions or exploring uncharted territories that could lead to breakthroughs or better decision making. AI cannot answer questions that we do not even know we should ask. It cannot fill in knowledge gaps if we are unaware they exist. These limitations underscore an irreplaceable need for human curiosity and critical thinking.

The human ability to ask questions—especially the ones we have not yet thought of—creates a unique advantage in leveraging AI tools to their fullest potential. The marriage of human intuition and AI analytics can be harmonious, but it requires a human driver at the wheel, steering through the vast landscape of possibilities. As AI is likely to become less artificial and more intelligent over time, it will eventually be leveraged as an "imagination machine" to boost creativity and develop new products and services to tackle unaddressed challenges (Reeves & Fuller, 2021).

Creating desired futures: Imagination and analysis

If we are aiming for a disciplined and systematic approach to identifying where to play and how to win in the future, and how to ensure organizational resiliency in the face of unforeseen disruption, then we need strategic foresight—the powerful dual ability to see the future beyond the immediacy of day-to-day operations and to develop and execute the right strategy that takes us from adaptation to creation (Webb, 2024).

As there are multiple plausible futures, companies need to reimagine corporate strategy: maximize short-term growth and develop long-term optionality and the ability to quickly exercise options. They must execute on their current business models while exploring many others—exploit existing advantages in current markets while working toward multiple unknown and non-existent potential future states (Reeves, Moldoveanu, & Job, 2023).

This implies departing from relying on empirical data about the present and venturing into the domain of imagination. By imagining what could be possible, the seeming inevitability of the status quo and the limitations of a mere analytical extrapolation from the present will be overcome. Such prospective hindsight offers means to reflect backwards from an imagined future.

To articulate desirable futures and how they might become reality, methodological strategies need to be developed which enable the exploration of alternatives that already exist at the fringes of the mainstream, and imagined alternatives that do not (yet) exist (Gümüsay & Reinecke, 2022).

References

Andrews, K. 1980. ***The concept of corporate strategy.*** Homewood, IL: Irwin.

Cabanes, B., Roger, O., & Doganova, L. 2023. Case study: How Shell anticipated the 1973 oil crisis, Paris. ***Polytechnique Insights – A Review by Institut Polytechnique de Paris,*** November 2. Accessed online https://www.polytechnique-insights.com/en/columns/society/case-study-how-shell-anticipated-the-1973-oil-crisis/. Viewed January 24, 2024.

Daugherty, P., & Wilson, H. 2018. ***Human + machine: Reimagining work in the age of AI.*** Boston: Harvard Business Review Press.

Duggan, W. 2007. ***Strategic intuition: The creative spark in human achievement.*** New York: Columbia Business School Publishing.

Geus, A. de. 1988. Planning as learning. ***Harvard Business Review,*** March-April: 70-74.

Gümüsay, A., & Reinecke, J. 2022. Researching for desirable futures: From real utopias to imagining alternatives. ***Journal of Management Studies,*** 59(1): 236-242.

Jones, N. A., Ross, H., Lynam, T., Perez, P., & Leitch, A. 2011. Mental models: an interdisciplinary synthesis of theory and methods. ***Ecology and Society,*** 16(1): 46. Accessed online https://www.ecologyandsociety.org/vol16/iss1/art46/. Viewed January 24, 2024.

Kim, Ch., & Mauborgne, R. 2005. ***Blue ocean strategy - How to create uncontested market space and make the competition irrelevant***. Boston: Harvard Business School Press.

Kiron, D., & Schrage, M. 2019. Strategy for and with AI. ***MIT Sloan Management Review,*** Summer. Accessed online https://sloanreview.mit.edu/article/strategy-for-and-with-ai/. Viewed January 24, 2024.

Martin, R. 2022. ***A new way to think. Your guide to superior management effectiveness***. Boston: Harvard Business Review Press.

McGrath, R. 2013. ***The end of competitive advantage: How to keep your strategy moving as fast as your business.*** Boston: Harvard Business Review Press.

Mintzberg, H. 1994. The rise and fall of strategic planning. ***Harvard Business Review,*** January-February: 107-114.

Parker, G., Alstyne, M. van, & Choudary, S., 2016. ***Platform revolution: How networked markets are transforming the economy - and how to make them work for you.*** New York: W.W. Norton & Company.

Porter, M. 1979. How competitive forces shape strategy. ***Harvard Business Review,*** March-April: 137-145.

Reeves, M., Moldoveanu, M., & Job, A. 2023. Radical optionality. ***Harvard Business Review,*** May-June: 113-121.

Reeves, M., & Fuller, J. 2021. ***The imagination machine - How to spark new ideas and create your company's future***. Boston: Harvard Business Review Press.

Reeves, M., Haanaes, K., & Sinha, J. 2015. ***Your strategy needs a strategy: How to choose and execute the right approach***. Boston: Harvard Business Review Press.

Royal Dutch Shell. 2012. ***40 years of Shell scenarios***. The Hague: Shell. Accessed online https://www.shell.com/news-and-insights/scenarios/what-are-shell-scenarios.html. Viewed April 20, 2024

Webb, A, 2024. Bringing true strategic foresight back to business. ***Harvard Business Review,*** January 12. Accessed online https://hbr.org/2024/01/bringing-true-strategic-foresight-back-to-business. Viewed January 24, 2024.

BOLKO VON OETINGER

VICE CHAIRMAN OF THE BOARD OF THE BMW FOUNDATION HERBERT QUANDT
MUNICH, GERMANY

WHAT DID I TAKE AWAY AS A PRACTITIONER?

Management is constantly grappling with the question of where a company should develop, where its future is, and how to make it tangible. Numerous strategy approaches (e.g., what if, if only, Darpa Hard Tests, three horizons, retropolation, scenarios, etc.) lead to important insights, especially about the driving forces that determine future developments. In these studies, the strategist regularly comes up against a fault line at which a particular sentence is often uttered: "Of course, we don't have a crystal ball."

As was to be expected, the crystal ball did not appear at the "Shared Desired Futures" conference either. However, what was not to be expected was the fact that two core components of the conventional strategy and innovation processes also fell by the wayside; neither customers nor competitors had their proper place. This sent a strong message about breaking away from the status quo and from existing processes in order to take a completely new look at possible futures.

While listening to the conference, I asked myself how one could use the various ideas of futurecasting in the conventional corporate strategy process.

My observations draw on approaches and concepts that were presented and discussed at the conference, without identifying the authors in detail. Where unique terms or metaphors were introduced, I have referred to the author. One particularly rich source on "Worldbuilding" was a series of interviews with Alex McDowell, who also gave the keynote speech.

Thinking optimistically about futurecasting

The speeches, panels, and presentations were stimulating and made the idea of an unknown future enjoyable, tangible, and communicable. Futurecasting is extremely inspiring, and the outlook and approaches were very optimistic. Dystopias were nowhere to be seen. Obama's mantra "yes we can" was in the room.

We know from practical experience that existing business models only represent a small section of a much larger opportunity space. As practitioners, we spend most of our time adapting the successful models that generate our profits in line with changing conditions. We rarely give up today's successful models in order to look around for alternative possibilities. And when we do try, we struggle with the legacy of the established business. The well-known personal decision by Immanuel Kant—Kant fired his long-time valet (Martin Lampe)—and its unforeseen negative consequence—Kant could not stop comparing Lampe with his successor—led to the philosopher's famous written note: "The name Lampe must be completely forgotten." In addition to the amusing observation that Kant had to remind himself in writing to forget something, the story testifies to the enormous energy required to detach oneself from the past: Forgetting is hard work (Oetinger, 2006).

To make the break, it is helpful to envisage long periods of time, 20-30 years. Surprising results should be conceivable. The Futurecasting conference opened up numerous access points to future spaces of possibility. The paths are not easy, but they are accessible. There is no silver bullet, no dominant method, but the breadth of approaches, the holistic view, and the role of detailed analyses from the various branches of science and fields of research provide many approaches that can support practitioners.

The future is being created

The innovation-driven future is not a condition that already exists years in advance and moves towards us with unbridled power. On the contrary, the future is an active development process created by those who are investing in the future now. For this reason, we already have opportunities today to discover weak indications of the developments of tomorrow.

The seedlings of technical developments that have the potential to shape our reality decades later can already be discovered today. Yet, it is equally likely they will have no major influence on future developments.

The multitude of approaches and of their potential combinations means that it is extremely speculative to closely circumscribe future reality. Therefore, our modus operandi should be to play with different possibilities rather than sketch a precise picture.

Science fiction is too utopian

In order to catapult oneself mentally from the present into a future of some kind, it would be obvious to use science fiction as an aid. With a creative leap, classic science fiction takes us into a radically different, highly speculative world, albeit a utopian one, i.e., a purely imaginary world in which significant changes to the current situation do not (yet) seem possible. Despite the attractiveness that a utopian concept may have, it lacks the decisive quality of a reference point that defines what needs to be worked on in the future and to which the company can fundamentally orient itself. This is why science fiction leaves the strategist more or less clueless.

If science fiction no longer originated from the realm of fantasy but, rather, drew on realizable approaches, the distance between science fiction and science facts (Merchant, 2018, quoting Josh Wolfe) would be reduced and the utopian would fade. Under this condition, science fiction could play a role in corporate strategy.

Scenarios are too specific

Scenarios are a valuable tool in strategy because they illustrate the sensitivities of emerging problems. They are developed for possible changes to the existing business model and can lead to disruption, in which existing technology suddenly opens up to customer groups that have never had access to it before (e.g., personal computers, smartphones, etc.). But even in the event of disruption one is still surrounded by traditional products, technologies, customers, and competitors. This is the business world we are familiar with, and its rich development potential. Scenarios develop very specific futures and are therefore naturally helpful. But this is not sufficient. Companies need to evaluate alternative futures that are much more fundamental and comprehensive. They require a further qualitative step.

"Worldbuilding": Creating alternative "worlds"

The future of companies is usually associated with the future of their products, services, and business models. The future in future-casting goes far beyond this: It is the future of a large space, which Alex McDowell refers to as a "world" and exemplified as a creative director on Steven Spielberg's 2002 film *Minority Report*. The movie conceives a reality in the year 2054 based on technologies that were already to be found as "seeds" in laboratories in the late 1990s. Meanwhile, some of these technologies have become reality today. Spielberg worked with a kind of "ad hoc think tank" (Wired Staff, 2012), a small group of scientists and technology experts who scoured leading industrial companies, universities, and research organizations for these "seeds," acting like "techno-truffle pigs," who, together with the film people, conceived the future world of the year 2054.

This approach offers a major advantage: Alex McDowell's fictitious worlds have a high "first level of believability" (Underkoffler in Wired Staff, 2012) because no new technologies have to be invented for them due to the fact that technologies that already exist but are at a very early stage are translated into possible products or services.

These comprehensive spaces of alternative "worlds" and the things that could take place in them in detail can be described in the form of stories. As expressed by Angela Wilkinson at the conference: "Future is a story, not a forecast."

Thus, the development of alternative "worlds" goes one important step beyond scenarios and leads from the familiar business world into radically unfamiliar spaces, which, in contrast to science fiction, have access to reality and thus the potential to be realized.

The exemplary success of *Minority Report* should not obscure the fact that "Worldbuilding" is quite a challenge, because you are actually trying to look very far into the future and, in addition, in great detail. Not to be overlooked is a critical question from psychology, which surprisingly did not play a role in the conference. This is what Daniel Gilbert calls the "illusion of foresight" (Nagel, 2023), which states that we usually believe what we see (deficiencies are easily ignored), that our thoughts are strongly influenced by present experiences, and, finally, that we rationalize past decisions after the fact. We might only be at the beginning of "Worldbuilding" as a major tool for corporate strategy. Therefore, it is worth looking deeper into the details of process.

"Worldbuilding" has some remarkable features:

1. **Close to reality.** In laboratories, we can already find early-stage cutting edge technologies that have the potential to shape the future. It is therefore a matter of investigating universities, research-intensive companies, startups, inventors, and investors as we search for developments and ideas that could revolutionize the world that we are investigating (e.g., transport, health, housing, military...). In this case, we would use early elements of the factual world to shape the fictitious one (Reeves & Fuller, 2021).

   We know from innovation research that this approach has the advantage that we do not concentrate on developments about which we know nothing but, rather, on those about which we know at least enough to speculate (Stanford Business, 2022).[1] This creates connections to reality that are not found in the purely fantasy-based approach of science fiction.

2. **Life in a fictitious world.** In the imagined world, people should be able to move as they would in today's world. For example, you should be able to put your children or grandparents in this fictitious world, read a current magazine from it, or think about what you will have for breakfast—in 30 years' time! The imagined world must be so detailed that people can easily spend time in it. The stay is of a playful nature so that the imagined world can be experienced even more vividly through role-playing games.

   To produce such a comprehensive fictitious world you have to create sufficient material in terms of breadth (what kind of technological changes can be expected) and depth (what will technologies achieve). The result is not static stage sets of the future, but new interpersonal behavioral processes that are set against the background of the fictitious world.

   Ideally, the futurecasting practitioner should be able to occupy several fictitious worlds at the same time. Just as archaeologists try to develop theses about possible connections from a wide variety of unrelated excavation pieces that only reveal partial information, futurecasting practitioners can get their ideas from several different futures in order to speculate about an overall picture. Playing with different possibilities and not defining a precise picture of the future increases the power of the imagination (Reeves & Fuller, 2021).

3. **Level of detail.** Imagined life in the fictitious world can only be developed if a relatively high level of detail is achieved. Alex McDowell uses the metaphor of the "street corner." The street corner is a small unit of analysis that is symptomatic of the macro world because it is

1 Kuang Xu, "Don't focus on what you don't know. Focus on the fact that you know a little" (Stanford Business, 2022).

important for the bigger picture. It points to the need to work on the detail of the future. Behind every detail of the new world in Spielberg's *Minority Report* there are numerous in-depth back-up analyses. This is not only necessary in order to describe "life," but also helpful for a completely different reason: Neuroscientists have pointed out that, firstly, the more distant the future we imagine, the less creative our brain becomes, but that, secondly, creativity increases again with the level of detail.[2] The more detailed the imagined world, the more we will discover, including developments that we had not even expected.

In order to keep an inhabited fictitious world alive you have to speculate continuously about future developments. Thus the "Worldbuilding" process incorporates the basic idea of evolution, a constant change brought about by the life of the inhabitants of the fictitious world. We still know little about this, but it is possible that "Worldbuilding" will always remain a kind of work in progress.

4. **Prototypes on a narrative level.** Technological developments that are in their infancy do not necessarily have to prevail. It may be too early to commit oneself, especially if one only sees the first seedlings today. In addition to prototypes that are derived from the fictitious world, the reverse approach can also be taken: That is to say, the future technology is placed in a selected fictitious world and used there as an experiment, e.g., as a medical robot in a doctor's office of the future. Kirby calls these "diegetic prototypes." The fictitious world represents the testing ground for whether and how the robot is accepted by the patient, and whether and which political, economic, and social conclusions can be drawn from the resulting technology. Although the technology serves as a "carrier bag" (Kirby) for the story, this is not its dominant feature. More important are the conclusions drawn from the technology for its environment. These influence the design process of the prototype.

5. **Plausibility.** The imagined world should be plausible, i.e., comprehensible. Its consequences must be accepted, whether they suit you or not. It does not have to be probable or desirable; it is a mere possibility. In other words, we have access to the future, but we cannot predict it. We can, however, examine the possibilities that arise from the detailed work. Plausibility has a dialectical relationship: The less plausible an idea is, the stronger the learning effect; the more plausible it is, the less we learn. What you perceive as plausible depends on whether you can understand the new properties from your own experience ("corroboration," Keane), whether the new properties are not too complex (highly complex properties are less plausible than simpler ones), and whether you can make friends with them despite the lack of evidence and without simply making something up ("conjecture," Keane).

2 Matter of discussion of Panel No 1 of "Futurecasting and Sensemaking" (Liu, Kable, Byrne, Miller)

Ideas with a high degree of plausibility ("plausibilistic imaginations," Selin) lead to narratives. This is where their creative value lies; on the other hand, approaches that seek what is likely to happen ("probabilistic reasoning," Selin) lead to quantitative assessments, which are naturally based on a more precise and therefore often restrictive definition of developments.

Communicate with stories—evoke emotions

There was quite a broad consensus that future fictitious worlds can best be communicated by good stories. But what is a story? The conference provided some valuable insights.

Purely functional descriptions of fictitious worlds are informative, but do not emotionally touch the listener. This is not decisive in a purely analytical environment but in business practice it is crucial. Organizations only change when their employees change. This is largely a question of emotions. We all remember the extraordinary power of fairy tales: Just think of Hansel and Gretel, or Cinderella, in which we experience how people behave under the most difficult, often life-threatening conditions. Stories are about people, not about abstract descriptions.

Where stories were told at the conference, e.g. about life in the year 2054 (*Minority Report*), about a patient in a doctor's office interacting with a care robot, about the development of the self-driving car, or about provocations for Times Square, the viewer could briefly feel like a visitor to this fictitious world or a participant in the development process.

If you want to communicate the fictitious world you should do so in the form of stories about interpersonal and, therefore, emotional processes. Details like putting your grandchildren in the new world in 30 years' time can lead to your emotional acceptance or rejection of the whole picture of the future. The future remains pale as an abstract structure, but becomes colorful as a social construct. Films or anecdotal/biographical representations convey social emotionality well. You have to experience now how people will live in the future. "Words may inspire but only action creates change" (Simon Sinek, quoted by Wei Liu). These "actions"—in 30 years' time—must be seen today in order to prepare for change. Role-playing games can help, because they present the story of the fictitious world as a theater play, similar to the "wargaming" approaches of the military. Playful interactions will lead to new conclusions. Strong stories have valuable exploratory side effects.

The supporting role of data

Despite the current huge importance of big data, especially in artificial intelligence, the role of data in the development of future worlds was seen not as central but as having a supporting function. The reason is obvious: We have no data about the future, which exists today exclusively in our imagination. But the stories that describe future worlds tell us what data (signals) we should be looking for.

Data can also help us model and, thus, better understand plausible futures. It is therefore worth looking for valuable data. Since development and innovation processes take place in networks, data are particularly valuable if they can be networked. Therefore, we need to collect data in order to scan future worlds for their signals and extract value from networking. We should not leave this process to the big US technology companies, who collect data without any restraint in order to search for clues about the future.

Diversity leads to richer alternatives

In the futurecasting process, one must constantly make subjective decisions about what to look for, which technological developments could have a transformative character, and which should be dropped. Many speakers and panel participants pointed out the usefulness of having a high level of diversity among the people involved in this process. The more participants with different perspectives (personality, culture, fields of activity, quality of expertise, positions, functions, age ...) are involved, the richer the alternatives will be. Researchers, strategists, entrepreneurs, visionaries, technologists, and many others will contribute to a holistic, broad picture and increase the quality of decisions on which paths to take.

Conclusion

The most valuable message that a practitioner could take away from the conference on futurecasting was the importance of the leap from conventional strategy concepts to the "Worldbuilding" idea. This is my personal view. I was encouraged to draw this conclusion by the observation that "Worldbuilding" might develop into a game-changer in the conventional strategy process. And this is not surprising, as it was not developed by business people or business professors, but by movie people, people from the, so to speak, periphery of the strategy field. The center did not envision it.

"Worldbuilding" changes the perspective in strategic analysis. The process of futurecasting is deliberately not aimed at a company's customers, but at alternative worlds into which customers are placed at a later time. To better understand this leap, it is worth recalling traditional film production, in which the script is written first and the creative director's world, in which the plot takes place, only follows later. In *Minority Report,* the process was reversed: the fictitious new world was created first, and the plot was only designed in the second step on the basis of key elements of the new world. This reverse order created a radically new story, but with the necessary basic believability. Applied to classic strategy, this means that one should start by developing the "world" of the future and only consider future customers, products, and business models in the second step. The results will be richer than those produced by the traditional strategy process.

References

Merchant, B. 2018. Nike and Boeing Are Paying Sci-Fi Writers to Predict Their Futures. Welcome to the Sci-Fi industrial complex. ***OneZero***, November 28. Accessed online https://onezero.medium.com/nike-and-boeing-are-paying-sci-fi-writers-to-predict-their-futures-fdc4b6165fa4. Viewed January 24, 2024.

Nagel, C. 2023. ***Leading with Depth: The Impact of Emotions and Relationships on Leadership.*** Bicester, UK: Phoenix Publishing House Ltd.

Oetinger, B. von. 2006. Vergessen: Immanuel Kant und die Erinnerung an das Vergessen. B. von Oetinger, ***Hänsel und Gretel und die Kuba-Krise. 13 Wege Strategie neu zu denken,*** 77-88. Munich/ Vienna: Carl Hanser.

Reeves, M., & Fuller, J. 2021. ***The imagination machine - How to Spark New Ideas and Create Your Company's Future.*** Boston: Harvard Business Review Press 2021.

Stanford Business. 2022. Voices: Kuang Xu, associate professor of O.I.T. Fall: 58-59.

Wired Staff. 2012. Inside Minority Report's 'Idea Summit,' Visionaries Saw the Future. ***Wired,*** June 21. Accessed online https://www.wired.com/2012/06/minority-report-idea-summit/. Viewed January 24, 2024.

BIOGRAPHIES

Balcom Raleigh, Nicolas

UNESCO Co-Chair of Learning for Transformation and Planetary Futures

Nicolas Balcom Raleigh helps innovators who are addressing the climate emergency to develop and benefit from the capability to vary their modes and purposes for imagining futures (aka futures literacy). His approach emphasizes co-inquiry, informed by an appreciation for complexity, unknowability, emergent novelty, and insightful value-creation for participants. He is UNESCO Co-Chair of Learning for Transformation and Planetary Futures
and a Doctoral Researcher in Futures Studies at the University of Turku, and the President of Foresight Europe Network for 2023-2024. Page 166

Bassett, Caroline

Professor, Fellow of Corpus Christi College Cambridge, and Director of Cambridge Digital Humanities

Caroline Bassett is a Professor of Digital Humanities, a Fellow of Corpus Christi College, and Director of Cambridge Digital Humanities. Her research explores digital technologies and cultural change, with a focus on gender and technology, critical theories of technology, speculative fiction, and utopian futures. Her recent books include Furious and Anti-Computing and her current research projects are investigating AI and the automation of writing and asking how we may re-think creativity. Page 224

Bayer, Carmen

Sociologist at the Robert Jungk Library for Future Studies

Carmen Bayer is a sociologist at the Robert Jungk Library for Future Studies. Her work focuses on the implementation of Zukunftswerkstätten (Futures Workshops) and the training course Zukunftswerkstätten gekonnt anleiten (Masterfully Leading Futures Workshops). In addition, she is working on the development of the Jungk Library's digital program and responsible for projects related to the climate and energy strategy of the Province of Salzburg and the series of JBZ working papers on migration and integration. She has been a Project Collaborator for the JBZ since 2020. Page 255

Bleecker, Julian

Designer, Entrepreneur, and Researcher

Julian Bleecker is a leading researcher, designer, and entrepreneur in the fields of technology and innovation. He founded Near Future Laboratory and OMATA, and is the originator of the concept of Design Fiction. Bleecker has published extensively on design, technology, and the future, and his book The Manual of Design Fiction is widely recognized as a pioneering work on the subject. Recognized with numerous awards and accolades, he and his work are known for a uniquely innovative and forward-thinking approach to shaping the future through design. Page 102

Bontoux, Laurent

Senior Foresight for Policy Expert at the European Commission's Joint Research Center

Dr. Bontoux's foresight work brings future-oriented systemic thinking into EU policymaking using participative approaches involving all relevant stakeholders. This inclusiveness is essential to building the best collective intelligence for effective policymaking.

Dr. Bontoux has spent most of his career working at the science/policy interface. Beyond sustainable development, his portfolios have focused on health and environmental risk assessment. This has enabled him to gain hands-on experience on how to use various types of scientific evidence in policy and on the reality of engaging with diverse stakeholders. Page 408

Brueckner, Sophia

Futurist Artist, Designer, and Engineer

Sophia Brueckner is a futurist artist/designer/engineer who researches how technology shapes us. Inseparable from computers since the age of two, she believes she is a cyborg. Creating new ways to apply science fiction to the design process, Sophia Brueckner prototypes alternatives to the tech industry's limited visions for how we live with technology. As an Associate Professor at the Stamps School of Art & Design and Co-Director of the Center for Ethics, Society, and Computing (ESC) at the University of Michigan, she invites others to embody an attitude of "critical optimism" and imagine what technological futures they might prefer for themselves. Page 242

Buchinger, Eva

Sociologist at the Austrian Institute of Technology (AIT)

Eva Buchinger is a sociologist working at the Austrian Institute of Technology (AIT). She specializes in social systems theory and innovation policy. She is presently working on the "ethics of emerging technologies" and "demand-driven innovation policy." Her long-term experience includes research management (research field "Societal Futures" at AIT), academic teaching (Vienna University of Technology, Vienna University of Economics and Business), scientific community engagement (President of RC51 Sociocybernetics of the International Sociological Association ISA, Board Member of the Austrian Sociological Association ÖGS and Viennese Sociological Association WGS, Editorial Board Member of journals such as ÖZS, W&U, and SYSTEMA), and, last but not least, policy consulting (Austrian government and EU institutions). Page 182

Byrne, Ruth

Professor of Cognitive Science at Trinity College Dublin, University of Dublin, Ireland

Ruth Byrne is the Professor of Cognitive Science at Trinity College Dublin, University of Dublin, Ireland. Her research focuses on human thinking, including experimental and computational investigations of reasoning and imaginative thought. She has published over 100 scientific articles and her books include The Rational Imagination: How People Create Alternatives to Reality (2005, MIT press), Deduction, co-authored with Phil Johnson-Laird (1991, Erlbaum), and, most recently, Thinking, Reasoning, and Decision-making in Autism, co-edited with Kinga Morsanyi (2019, Routledge). Page 92

Carson, Gail

Director of Network Development at ISARIC & Chair of GOARN

Dr. Carson graduated from Edinburgh Medical School (1994), completed her infectious disease training in Manchester (2008), and moved from Public Health England in 2012 to help set up the International Severe Acute Respiratory & Emerging Infection Consortium (ISARIC). Over the past 20+ years, she has worked with the WHO at country level and sat on multiple WHO committees and working groups. In 2016, she was elected to the Steering Committee of the WHO-hosted Global Outbreak Alert & Response Network (GOARN). She was elected Deputy Chair in 2018 and became Chair in 2022.

In 2018, she was awarded a Distinction in the Diploma of Organizational Leadership at Saïd Business School, University of Oxford, of which she is an Associate Fellow.

All of the above was recognized in the King's Honors List in 2023 by the award to Dr. Carson of the OBE for her contribution to global health. Page 53

Comi, Alice

Associate Professor, Tongji University, College of Design and Innovation

Alice Comi, PhD, is an Associate Professor at Tongji University, College of Design and Innovation. She explores the creative intersections between designing and organizing, with particular attention to practices of future making and the role of visual artifacts. Her work has been published in international peer-reviewed journals in design and organization studies.
Page 366

Damhof, Loes

UNESCO Chair on Futures Literacy in Higher Education

Loes Damhof was elected Lecturer of the Year amongst all higher education institutions in The Netherlands in 2016 and used the accompanying prestigious Comenius Award to develop Futures Literacy pilots. In 2018, she was appointed as a UNESCO Chair on Futures Literacy in Higher Education for her research into the impact of Futures Literacy and the design principles of Futures Literacy interventions. In addition to her research and teaching practice, she consults and trains the staff of global organizations such as FutureWomenX, UNESCO, UNFCCC, ClimateKIC, FORMS, the UN, the Copenhagen Institute for Futures Studies, and Oxfam in multidisciplinary projects. As a Futures Literacy expert, she designs, develops, and facilitates so-called Futures Literacy Labs: collective intelligence knowledge creation processes across the globe that challenge and raise fundamental questions on leadership, migration, climate change, and technology. She is a Future Fellow at Hawkwood College and a Steering Committee Member of Futures Oriented Museum Synergies and co founder of Emergence Academy. Page 348

DaVanzo, Sarah

Chief Data Officer, Pierre Fabre

Sarah DaVanzo is Chief Data Officer of Pierre Fabre, a multinational life sciences company, leading intelligence & strategic foresight. Prior to this, Sarah was Chief Strategy Officer of the cultural intelligence and futures agency, Sparks & Honey, before joining the L'Oréal Group as VP of Insight & Foresight. She entered foresight and futurism in the 1990s when she was leading post-apartheid strategy and "tomorrowing" for the South African gold industry. She leans heavily on "exotic data" and quantitative foresight, and is a pioneer in the use of AI in foresight.

Her career spans 22 countries at the intersection of innovation, marketing, trends and culture, insights, and foresight. She acquired methodological rigor from her training and education from a dozen futures institutions (e.g., University of Houston, DARPA, NASA, MIT, WFSF, Singularity University, UNESCO Futures Literacy). Sarah's foresight and futurism has impacted nearly one hundred Fortune 500 companies and government agencies. Her personal foresight projects are: https://futuresactivist.com and https://curious-futures.com Page 380

Doctorow, Cory

Science Fiction Author, Activist, Journalist, and Blogger

Cory Doctorow (craphound.com) is a science fiction author, activist, journalist, and blogger, the co-editor of Boing Boing (boingboing.net) and the author of young adult novels like Pirate Cinema and Little Brother and novels for adults like Rapture of the Nerds and Makers. He is the former European Director of the Electronic Frontier Foundation and co-founded the UK Open Rights Group. Born in Toronto, Canada, he now lives in London. Page 222

Flanagan, Mary

Transdisciplinary Artist and Researcher

Mary Flanagan is an innovator focused on how people create and use technology, and the biases inherent within technology. Her groundbreaking explorations have been supported by numerous foundations and international organizations. Her books, essays, and artworks explore game design for social change and offer critical takes on technological systems. Mary Flanagan has lectured widely, including at the 2018 World Economic Forum at Davos. She is the Sherman Fairchild Distinguished Professor of Digital Humanities at Dartmouth College and leads the laboratory Tiltfactor.org. Page 394

Hargrave, Josef

Director and Global Foresight Leader at Arup

Josef Hargrave leads a global, multi-disciplinary team of designers and consultants who specialize in research, design, strategy, innovation, thought leadership, and vision-making for the future of the built environment. He is also an Associate Lecturer on the MA Innovation Management course at Central Saint Martins and a member of the World Cities Summit, Science of Cities Knowledge Council, and International Panel of Experts at Singapore's Urban Redevelopment Authority. Page 144

Inayatullah, Sohail

UNESCO Chair in Futures Studies

Professor Sohail Inayatullah is the UNESCO Chair in Futures Studies at the Sejahtera Centre for Sustainability and Humanity, IIUM, Malaysia. Since 2000, he has been Professor of Futures Studies at Tamkang University, Taiwan. He teaches online through the Metafuture School and is a Researcher with Metafuture. His recent books include CLA 3.0: Thirty Years of Transformative Research and The End of the Cow: And Other Emerging Issues. Page 152

Keane, Mark T.

Chair of Computer Science at University College Dublin

Mark Keane has been Chair of Computer Science at University College Dublin since 1998 and was Director of ICT (2004-2006) and Director General (2006-2007) at Science Foundation Ireland (SFI). He has published over 200 articles and 20 books, (including Cognitive Psychology: A Student's Handbook, Taylor & Francis, 2020, which was co-authored with Michael Eysenck, has been published in six languages, and is now entering its 8th edition). His work in Cognitive Science is concerned with how people generate new ideas from old knowledge (using analogy, concept combination, metaphor) and how they deal with things they do not know or expect (surprise, unexpectedness). In the area of artificial intelligence, he works on case-based reasoning, machine learning, and explainable AI. Page 270

Kirby, David A.

Professor of Science, Technology, & Society

David A. Kirby is Professor and Chair of the Department of Interdisciplinary Studies and Director of the Science, Technology, & Society Program at Cal Poly University in San Luis Obispo. His research examines how movies, television, and computer games serve as vehicles for the communication of science and technology. He is the author of the books Lab Coats in Hollywood: Science, Scientists, and Cinema and the forthcoming Indecent Science: Religion, Science, and Movie Censorship. Page 256

Lang, Trudi

Co-Director, Oxford-Hyundai Motor Group Foresight Centre

Trudi Lang is Titular Associate Professor in Management Practice and Co-Director of the Oxford-Hyundai Motor Group Foresight Centre at the University of Oxford's Said Business School. Focusing on a discrete set of high-impact themes, the Centre seeks to contribute significant research to the scholarly understanding of how foresight is conducted to inform business strategy, while also producing impactful outputs for practitioners. Prior to joining the Oxford faculty, Trudi Lang served as Director of Strategic Foresight at the World Economic Forum. Page 50

Larsen, Nicklas

Senior Advisor and Head of Arts and Culture at the Copenhagen Institute for Futures Studies (CIFS)

Nicklas Larsen works to empower learners and leaders and to cultivate cultures of anticipation, using futures as a catalyst for renewed agency. Taking a multifaceted approach in diverse creative, educational, and cultural environments, he extends his efforts to critical domains such as the policy, civic, and philanthropic sectors, and multilateral institutions.

Holding a UNESCO Co-Chair position in Anticipatory Leadership & Futures Capabilities, he serves as the Senior Advisor of Arts and Culture and as a Board Member at the pioneering non-profit think tank the Copenhagen Institute for Futures Studies. Moreover, he is a Member of Faculty at Parsons School of Design in Paris, leads Teach the Future in Denmark, belongs to Future Oriented Museum Synergies, and is involved with the Network of Institutions for Future Generations. Page 334

Liu, Wei

Associate Professor, Faculty of Psychology, Beijing Normal University

Dr. Wei Liu is Associate Professor at the Faculty of Psychology, Beijing Normal University. He serves as a Board Member of the International Chinese Association for Computer Human Interaction, a Judge in the China-US Youth Maker Competition, and the Director of the Design Psychology Research Center at the Beijing Design Society. He has been engaged in teaching and research in applied psychology, user experience design, and innovation and entrepreneurship education for over 20 years. Amongst his honors he has been a Fulbright Research Scholar and Cyrus Tang Young Scholar. Page 200

Livne, Shahar

Conceptual Material Designer

Shahar Livne (Israel, 1989) is an award-winning conceptual material designer based in Eindhoven, The Netherlands. Her body of work focuses on conceptual material research in a multi-leveled methodology, bringing to life unique stories through objects and installations centered around materials as carriers of narratives. Some of Shahar Livne's projects deal with obscure materials such as blood, man-made fossils, crystallization, and more. The starting points of her projects are often stories about places, cultures, and relations with resources in the past, present, and future. In 2020, she was crowned Dezeen Awards Emerging Designer of The Year. She is currently presenting her work internationally and creating new research projects with various companies and institutes as an autonomous designer, curator, educator, and collaborator. Page 328

Luebkeman, Chris

Leader, Strategic Foresight Hub, ETH Zurich

Dr. Chris Luebkeman founded and leads the Strategic Foresight Hub in the Office of the President at ETH Zurich. He is also the CEO and Founder of [y]our 2040, a community-based think-do-tank shaping positive futures around the world. Dr. Luebkeman is a Member of the Nominating Committee for the prestigious Lee Kuan Yew World City Prize, the External Advisory Board of the Urban Redevelopment Authority of Singapore, the Advisory Board of the Strategic Foresight Community of WEF, and the Brain Trust of the Climate Music Project. Prior to ETH Zurich he was a corporate intrapreneur at the global engineering consultancy Arup, which he joined as the Director of Research and Development and where he later founded the Foresight, Innovation, and Incubation Team. Dr. Luebkeman taught design studios and courses on technology at MIT, the Chinese University of Hong Kong, and the University of Oregon. He has spoken broadly including at TED conferences and the Aspen Ideas Festival, and hosted conversations for WEF. He holds a Doctorate in Architecture from ETH Zurich, a Master's Degree in Civil Engineering from Cornell University, and a Bachelor of Engineering and a Bachelor of Science from Vanderbilt University. Page 180

Mankowsky, Alexander

Futures Studies and Ideation, formerly at Mercedes-Benz

The title "futurist" was assigned to me by others—some labeled me a "philosopher"—and a now defunct AI program offered "pipe smoker" and "social scientist." The latter is true. I learned the importance of maintaining a sense of time to foster agency and achieve a positive perspective for everyone. My years in industry taught me that avant-garde thinking and acting do not need a label at all. Creativity for the common good can be found everywhere. Page 60

McDowell, Alex

Creative Director, Production Designer, Professor, Worldbuilder

Alex McDowell, RDI, is a creative director, production designer, professor, and worldbuilder. British, and living in the US since 1986, he has been a designer across multiple media since 1975 and in film for 30 years, working with Steven Spielberg, Tim Burton, and David Fincher amongst many directors. He is Co-Founder and Creative Director of the Experimental Design Studio, Director of the World Building Institute and World Building Media Lab, and Professor at USC School of Cinematic Arts. A Royal Designer for Industry, he is the originator of worldbuilding, a narrative design system for media, education, corporations, and institutions. His practice is designed for platforms that do not yet exist. Page 292

Miller, Riel

Author on the theory and practice of using the future to change what people see and do

Recognized as an innovative and globally experienced project initiator, designer, and manager, Riel Miller is widely published in academic journals and other media on a range of topics, from the future of the Internet to transforming strategic processes. He is an accomplished keynote speaker and facilitator. From mid-2012 to early 2022, Riel Miller served as Head of Foresight and Futures Literacy at UNESCO. Currently he is: Senior Fellow, J. Herbert Smith Centre for Technology Management and Entrepreneurship, Deep Change Initiative, Faculty of Engineering, University of New Brunswick (Canada); Senior Fellow, Ecole des Ponts Business School, Ecole des Ponts, Paris (France); Senior Advisor, University of Stavanger/NIFU (Norway). Page 124

Montgomery, Elliott P.

Senior Strategic Foresight Specialist, Autodesk

Elliott P. Montgomery is a design researcher, strategist, and educator whose work focuses on speculative inquiries at the confluence of social, technological, and environmental impact. He is currently Senior Strategic Foresight Specialist at Autodesk. He is also the Co-Founder of The Extrapolation Factory, an award-winning design-futures research studio based in Brooklyn. He was previously a Design Research Resident at the US Department of Energy's Advanced Research Projects Agency and has received the Graham Foundation's Individual Grant. Page 308

Oetinger, Bolko von

Vice Chairman of the Board of the BMW Foundation Herbert Quandt

Bolko von Oetinger is a retired executive of the Boston Consulting Group and Honorary Professor for Strategic Management at WHU in Koblenz/Vallendar (Germany). As Vice Chairman of the Board of the BMW Foundation Herbert Quandt and a Board Member of the Wittenberg Center for Global Ethics, he is an advocate for sustainability in management. He pursues his interests in innovation as a Member of the Advisory Board of the Center for Future Design in Linz. Bolko von Oetinger holds a Doctorate in Foreign Affairs from the Free University of Berlin and an MBA from Stanford Graduate School of Business. Page 446

Offenhuber, Dietmar

Professor of Design / Public Policy and Urban Affairs

Dietmar Offenhuber is Professor at Northeastern University in the areas of Information Design and Urban Affairs. He holds a PhD in Urban Planning from MIT. His research focuses on the relationship between design, technology, and urban governance. Dietmar Offenhuber is the author of the award-winning monograph Waste is Information (MIT Press) and has published books on urban data and accountability technologies.
His upcoming book Autographic Design considers material forms of visualization and evidence construction. Page 190

Papadimitriou, Irini

Creative Director and Curator

Irini Papadimitriou is a digital culture curator, and currently Director of Exhibitions at Diriyah Art Futures. She was previously the Creative Director at FutureEverything, Artistic Director at Sea Art Festival, Busan Biennale, Digital Programs Manager at The Victoria & Albert Museum (V&A), and Head of New Media Arts Development at Watermans. Irini Papadimitriou is a Co-Founder of Maker Assembly, a critical gathering about maker cultures. Recent exhibitions include Artificially Intelligent, V&A London; You and AI: Through the Algorithmic Lens; Plásmata: Bodies, Dreams, and Data, Onassis Foundation, Athens; Money, Ruins, and the Sea, NeMe, Cyprus; Trustworthy AI: Imagining Better Machine Decision Making, Mozilla Festival, London. Page 232

Pavlakis, Stefanos

Co-Owner and Creative Producer of STORY DEALER BERLIN-HEIDELBERG with Hans Geisslinger and Hans Rudi Fischer

Stefanos Pavlakis (PhD, MFA, BA) is a practicing visual artist, a systemic coach, and one of three partners of STORY DEALER, Berlin-Heidelberg. Since 2009, he has co-authored and co-produced more than 40 storydealing enactments in Europe, South America, and China and frequently gives presentations, workshops, and talks on the storydealing method. Stefanos Pavlakis coaches individuals during their personal journeys of transformation, and groups/teams on issues relating to culture change, awareness, and identity. As a visual artist and a director of audiowalks and experimental films, he has presented works in numerous national and international exhibitions and film festivals. Page 420

Pfeiffer, Christin

Senior Consultant at UNESCO SHS and Coordinator of the UN Strategic Foresight Community of Practice

Dr. Christin Pfeiffer was the Head of Futures Literacy and Foresight at UNESCO/SHS in Paris until September 2023, where she designed and managed futures-related projects with global, regional, and national stakeholders. She dealt with a broad portfolio of initiatives in Africa, the Arab States, and Asia Pacific, coordinated the HLCP Foresight Network, and represented UNESCO in the UN Futures Lab. With its 37 Chairs in Futures Studies and Anticipation, UNESCO works towards strengthening the capacity of member states to create knowledge on transformative policies for inclusive and resilient futures. Page 130

Popper, Ari

Founder and CEO, SciFutures

Ari Popper is the Founder and CEO of SciFutures, an award-winning foresight and innovation agency that uses sci-fi prototyping to help its clients create meaningful change. SciFutures has a network of over 300 sci-fi writers around the world and works in a wide variety of industries with organizations like Visa, Hershey's, Honda, NATO, JPMorgan Chase, and Coca-Cola. SciFutures' work has been featured by the BBC, Fast Company, Boston Globe, Wired Japan, CNBC, New Yorker, and CNET Magazine. Page 286

Reeves, Martin

Chair, BCG Henderson Institute

Martin Reeves is a Senior Partner and Managing Director in the San Francisco office of Boston Consulting Group and Chair of the BCG Henderson Institute, BCG's think tank for exploring ideas from beyond business, which have implications for strategy, management, and leadership. He is a regular contributor to HBR, MIT SMR, and Fortune. Martin Reeves is the Co-Author of The Imagination Machine and Your Strategy Needs a Strategy, and Editor of the book series Inspiring the Next Game. Page 82

Reinprecht, Claudia

Austrian Foreign Ministry

Claudia Reinprecht has served in the Austrian Foreign Ministry since March 2004. After diplomatic postings in Vienna, Brussels, Amman, Hong Kong & Macao, and Paris (UNESCO), she has served as Head of Department for Transport, Telecommunications, and Innovation Diplomacy. She is also Austria's focal point for the European Digital Diplomacy Network and Austria's coordinator for the EU's connectivity initiative Global Gateway.

Having studied in Salzburg/Austria and Salamanca/Spain, Ambassador Claudia Reinprecht acquired a Master's Degree and a PhD in law. Prior to her entry into the Austrian diplomatic service, she specialized in international public law, international criminal law, and refugee law. In addition, she acquired a General Executive MBA post-graduate degree from the Austrian Business School LIMAK in Linz in 2013. Page 142

Revell, Tobias

Design Futures Lead, Arup

The Design Futures Lead at Arup University's Foresight Faculty, Tobias Revell leads innovative and critical design processes and outcomes in research and client work; he is a driver of and advocate for design across the organization. He has a 47.6% share in the research and curatorial project Haunted Machines, is a member of the technological research outfit Supra Systems Studio, and teaches at several design schools. In his practice, he lectures and exhibits internationally on design, technology, imagination, and speculation. He is completing a PhD examining the role of design in the social construction of AI at Goldsmiths, University of London. He previously held several leadership roles in design at University Arts London and was Founding Director of the design research studio Strange Telemetry. Page 105

Ringler, Marie

Member of the Global Leadership Group Ashoka

Marie Ringler is one of the most sought-after thought leaders and speakers in the Ashoka community. Her bold and creative thinking on systems change, social entrepreneurship, philanthropy, rethinking democracy, and new leadership has made her a frequent speaker at international events and conferences including the Global Peter Drucker Forum, St. Gallen Symposium, Académie Européenne de Philanthropie Stratégique, ConSozial Nürnberg, REHA:NEXT, European Forum Alpbach, TEDxSalzburg, Zukunft Personal, numerous events of Ashoka's corporate partners, and Ashoka's own global events. Page 66

Roth, Susann

Advisor, Department of Communication and Knowledge Management, Asian Development Bank (ADB)

Susann Roth leads the Asian Development Bank's Knowledge and Innovation Management Program and the team that set up ADB's innovation hub, which supports futures thinking and foresight, design thinking, decision making in complex contexts, institutional change management, and innovation and knowledge ecosystem development in developing member countries. She regularly authors blogs, articles, and books and speaks on TV talk shows and at global events such as the Global Future Forum, the Global Knowledge Management World Conference, and the Global Leaders' Forum. Page 78

Schwartz, Guido

Strategy & Innovation Lead, Airbus

Guido Schwartz teamed up to build the Innovation Department in Airbus DS from 2015-2019. He was Co-Lead of the department for three years and Department Leader for one year. He initiated an internal incubation program and started and maintained external and cross-divisional collaborations such as with BizLab and the Protospace. Guido Schwartz was a Co-Founder of the #Africa4Future initiative and mentored and coached external startups and internal intrapreneurs on three continents. He implemented the #BlueBox system throughout Europe with the team and was involved in various internal innovation initiatives like #DreamBig or the Innovation Factory. Now in the Netherlands, he engages in research to support the sustainable transition towards carbon-neutral aviation. Page 70

Schwuchow, Karlheinz

Teacher & Trendscout, Academic & Author

Professor Dr. Karlheinz Schwuchow has been a Professor of Global Management at Bremen University of Applied Sciences since 1999, where he heads the CIMS Center for International Management Studies. After studying business administration in Germany and graduating with an MBA in the USA, he worked at USW The German Management Institute from 1985 to 1991 and obtained a Doctorate in Business. He then worked in management and strategy consulting and was the Founding Managing Director of the Center for Financial Studies in Frankfurt/Main. From 2001 to 2004, Professor Schwuchow was Managing Director of the GISMA Business School in Hannover, and in 2010/2011 he was Academic Director of the LIMAK Austrian Business School at the Johannes Kepler University Linz. He also teaches and conducts research as a visiting professor in Brazil, China, India, and South Africa.

His current work focuses on international leadership development, innovative methods of management learning, and strategy and organizational development. He is the author or editor of more than 200 publications in the fields of human resources and corporate management. Page 434

Selin, Cynthia

Professor and Consultant in Foresight, Sustainability, and Innovation

Dr. Cynthia Selin is a future-oriented scholar and consultant focused on sustainability and the governance of emerging technologies. By creating new methods, concepts, and platforms for confronting uncertainties, her work—as a social scientist and scenario planner—stimulates improved strategic capacities and imaginations. Dr. Selin leads Scenaric, a firm specialized in strategic foresight, and is an Associate Fellow at Said Business School, University of Oxford where she has taught in the award-winning Oxford Scenarios Programme for over a decade. Page 350

Shamiyeh, Michael

UNESCO Chairholder, Professor, and Advisory Board Member

Michael Shamiyeh works with organizations to create a new and meaningful future (rather than fix the problems of the past). He combines the client's unique business experience, analytical rigor, and the output of creative collisions (the clash of multiple perspectives to reframe habitual thinking) to transform insight into impact. Michael Shamiyeh holds a UNESCO Chair for Anticipatory Techniques and Future Design, is a partner of the International Board Foundation (IBF), and was a Visiting Professor at the Department of Mechanical Engineering (CDR) at Stanford University, USA, from 2017-2020. Together with both institutions, he founded the Center for Future Design (CFD) in Linz. Since 2020, he has also been an Advisory Board Member of voestalpine. Page 12

Time's Up

Laboratory for the Construction of Experimental and Experiential Situations

Time's Up investigates the possibilities of haptic interactive human-scale immersive environments. As a laboratory for the composition of experimental situations, we create narrative spaces, especially in the context of constructing experiential models of possible futures and building physical narratives that explore contemporary and emerging sociopolitical issues. Our process applies tools from arts and design, sociology, mathematics, cultural studies, science, and technology.

Time's Up has worked from its base in Linz, Austria, since 1996 and has exhibited and collaborated with a large number of inspiring partners throughout Europe, Asia, Africa, North America, and Australia. Page 318

Wally, Stefan

Participatory Futurism, CEO of the Robert Jungk Library for Future Studies

Stefan Wally, Salzburg, Austria: CEO of the Robert Jungk Library for Future Studies and formerly a Head of Office to Members of Salzburg's Provincial Government. Besides lecturing on comparative political science, European politics, and economics at various colleges, Stefan Wally produces publications in the field of political science and scenario studies. His academic background is in political science and general management. Born on October 19, 1970, he is the father of two children, aged 16 and 19. Page 252

Wilkinson, Angela

Secretary General and CEO of the World Energy Council

Dr. Angela Wilkinson is the 6th Secretary General and CEO of the World Energy Council, a diverse community network of over 3,000 member organizations that has been instrumental in promoting better energy developments in over 100 countries for nearly 100 years.

Dr. Wilkinson has led the Council since 2019 as it defines, enables, and accelerates successful energy transitions through its unique network, practical insights, and leadership dialogues. She has over 35 years' experience of leading national and international multi-stakeholder transformation initiatives on a wide range of global energy, climate, and sustainable development-related challenges. Her previous roles have included board-level and senior executive responsibilities in the public, private, academic, and civic sectors. She is also a published author. Page 210

Wolf, Stefan

Corporate Foresight and Future Research, Volkswagen

Working for VW since 2002, Dr. phil. Stefan Wolf was part of the team that founded the corporate university VW AutoUni Wolfsburg. In 2007, he trained young leaders of VW Germany in business management.
He switched to Light Commercial Vehicles (LCV) as Head of Corporate Foresight in 2012 and was part of a transformation task force in 2019. He also teaches corporate foresight and futures research at various universities of applied sciences, including Braunschweig (2007-2015), Hannover (2015-2020), Bremen, and Kempten. Before joining VW, he worked in Switzerland for the consultancy Prognos AG and at EXPO 2000 GmbH in Hannover (theme park/communications). Dr. Wolf studied Philosophy and Social Sciences in Bamberg and Montpellier (PhD in 1994). Page 112

ACKNOWLEDGEMENTS

Listing the names of all the authors, interview partners, colleagues, and members of organizations who have shared their insights with me over the years would go far beyond the scope of these acknowledgments. They have been and continue to be an incredibly valuable reservoir of new knowledge.

One person who deserves special thanks and to whom I dedicate this book in gratitude for his commitment to my work is Professor Steven Floyd (1950–2022). He was highly respected in his many professional roles within the strategy and management community worldwide and as an editor and leader of various professional teams.

I met Steve for the first time in Switzerland when he held the Chair of Strategic Management at the University of St. Gallen. Our contact resulted from an article I had published in 2007,* in which I had dealt with the different cognitive approaches to imagining the future in architectural design and strategic management. To my astonishment, he, who came from a completely different world than I, had read the article, which resulted in e-mail correspondence and, later, in personal meetings. With extraordinary foresight, he built the bridge between the two very different worlds, introduced me to the management community, and, over the following years, supervised my doctoral thesis in this field. With more than 20 years of professional experience in architectural design and completed studies in London, Vienna, and Harvard, I was not only a latecomer, but also an absolute exotic at the business school. His unwavering support, friendship, and mentoring in later years made my career possible. Thank you very much, Steve!

Heartfelt thanks also go to UNESCO for their trust in my activities and for awarding me a UNESCO Chair in 2021. Deep thanks go as well to all the participants and sponsors of the Desired Futures Conference series and the alumni/ae of the Center for Future Design in Linz, Austria. Without their insights, contributions, and suggestions, a book on this topic would not have been possible. The Austrian Federal Government, the province of Upper Austria, the city of Linz, and the University of Arts Linz —the location where I am based and do most of my work—have always supported my activities, for which I am equally grateful.

Finally, I would like to recognize all those in the background whose great commitment made this volume possible: Agnes Buchberger, assistant at the Center for Future Design, who carefully coordinated this book's production; Walter Stromberger and his dedicated design team, who never tired of coming up with new and impressive designs; Jeff Crowder, my valued proofreader for many years and also of this publication. I am also appreciative of David Marold from Birkhäuser and especially of Ulrike Ruh, the Birkhäuser Verlag Editorial Director, to whom I have entrusted the publication of most of my futures-related books over the past fifteen years.

We hope this book will make a significant contribution to the field and move futures scholarship and practice forward.

MIchael Shamiyeh

---

* Shamiyeh, M. 2007. Design New Futures! ***Archis Volume Magazine,*** 14(4): 14-19.